Contents

Part 1 Body in action   1

  1   THE HUMAN BODY   2

  2   FOOD AND DIET   37

  3   PHYSICAL FITNESS   53

  4   MEASURING PHYSICAL PERFORMANCE   70

  5   SPORT AND INJURY   85

  6   DRUGS AND SPORT   104

  7   SUCCESS IN SPORT   118

Part 2 Sport in society   135

  8   THE HISTORY OF SPORT   136

  9   AMATEUR AND PROFESSIONAL   147

10   ORGANISATION OF SPORT IN BRITAIN AT NATIONAL LEVEL   160

11   ORGANISATION OF SPORT IN BRITAIN AT LOCAL LEVEL   170

12   SPONSORSHIP IN SPORT   179

13   LEISURE AND SPORT   192

14   SPORT AS A CAREER   209

15   WOMEN AND SPORT   217

16   INTERNATIONAL SPORT AND POLITICS   228

APPENDIX   243

INDEX   251

Introduction

There is no doubt that the impact of sport on society today is immense. From the family out jogging to the highly tuned athlete in the Olympic final all levels of ability and commitment find an expression in sport. The media constantly send images of sport into every home, with an abundance of analysis, comment and speculation. Sport is also big business involving large sums of money in the production of goods and the promotion of sporting events of all kinds.

It was only when we came to revise the first edition of Sport Examined that we realised the great increase in information relevant to sport in the last few years. We have updated some chapters and completely rewritten others to keep pace with these developments.

A textbook of this type would be impossible to write without the help, advice and encouragement of a large number of people. In particular we would wish to express our thanks to:

Dr. Craig Sharp, Dr. W. van Mechelen, Dr. Colin Boreham, Reg Simmonds, Jenny Filby, Janet Kendrick, pupils of the Deanes School, and most importantly of all, our wives, Liz and Marilyn.

We have enjoyed revising this edition and hope that it will be not only useful for a variety of examination, and National Curriculum, courses but will be a good read for all those interested in sport.

SPORT
EXAMINED

SECOND EDITION

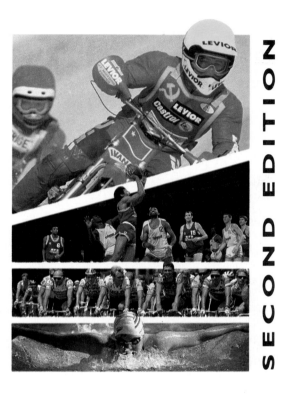

Paul Beashel
John Taylor

Nelson

Thomas Nelson and Sons Ltd
Nelson House Mayfield Road
Walton-on-Thames Surrey
KT12 5PL UK

51 York Place
Edinburgh
EH1 3JD UK

Thomas Nelson (Hong Kong) Ltd
Toppan Building 10/F
22a Westlands Road
Quarry Bay Hong Kong

Thomas Nelson Australia
102 Dodds Street
South Melbourne
Victoria 3205 Australia

Nelson Canada
1120 Birchmount Road
Scarborough Ontario
M1K 5G4 Canada

First published by Macmillan Education Ltd 1986

Second edition published by
Thomas Nelson and Sons Ltd 1992

ISBN 0-17-438452-1
NPN 9 8 7 6 5 4 3

Printed in Spain

Body in action

Part
Part 1

1 THE HUMAN BODY

Aims

To gain knowledge and understanding of:

◆ the systems of the human body including:
  the skeletal system
  the muscular system
  the circulatory system
  the respiratory system
  the nervous system
  the hormonal system
  the digestive system

To develop the skills of:

◆ comprehension
◆ oral and written communication
◆ data collection and interpretation
◆ presentation of data

For each of us our single most precious possession is our body. Yet it is surprising how much we take it for granted and are quite satisfied to know little or nothing about it. Our body demands little from us other than food, clothing and shelter. It carries out most of its important jobs such as breathing and digesting without any conscious effort from us at all. It is usually only when we are ill or have injured our body in some way that we suddenly appreciate just how important it is to us. In fact we realise it is us!

In this chapter we are going to look at the structure and functions of the human body because a sound understanding of how we work is essential if we are to gain a real understanding of how the body is involved during physical activities.

THE BODY SYSTEMS

To live we have to be able to breathe, move and be aware of what is going on around us. We need to get supplies of energy into the body, convert it so that it can be used by the various body parts and also get rid of any waste products.

The body has developed special systems within it in order that these and other life-preserving activities can be carried out.

Although we will look at a number of these body systems separately it is important to remember that they all co-operate together to keep the body working effectively.

THE HUMAN SKELETON

What Does the Skeleton Do?

The human skeleton has four main functions:

1 Protection The skeleton has been designed to protect the delicate parts of the body. The brain is completely surrounded by the skull and the ribs form an expandable cage around the heart and lungs.

2 Support Without a skeleton the body would be flabby and shapeless. The arrangement of the bones gives shape to the body as a whole. The bones are also used to suspend some of the vital organs, keeping them in a constant position.

3 Movement Our skeleton is jointed to allow us a wide range of movement. There are different kinds of joints in the body to allow movement of various kinds. Ligaments hold the bones together at the joints and all movement is caused by the contraction of muscles acting on the bones.

4 Blood production Red blood cells and some white cells are formed in the marrow cavities of larger bones.

The body systems

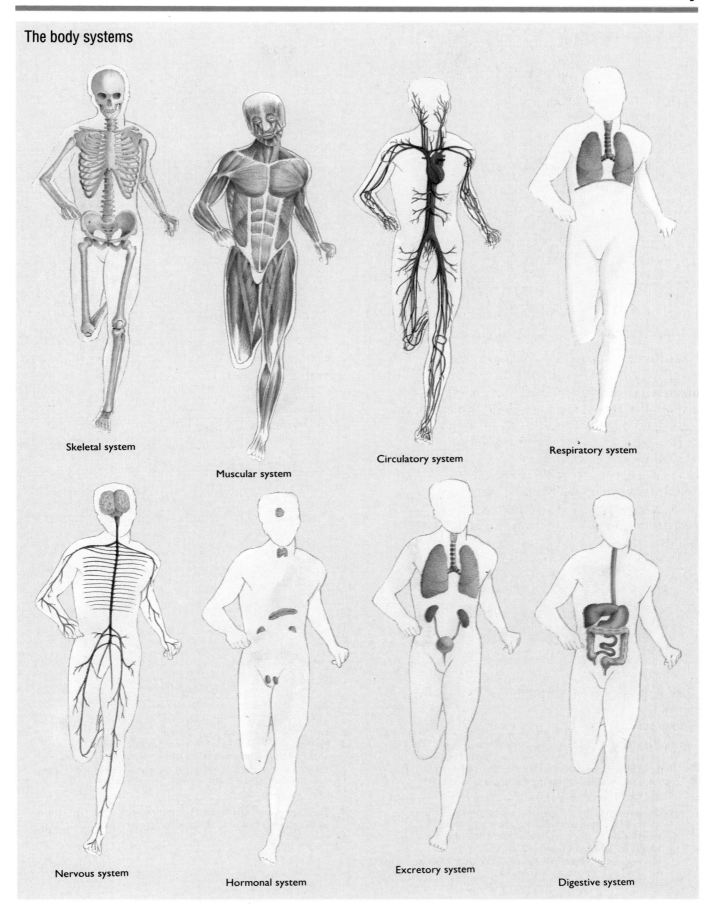

Skeletal system

Muscular system

Circulatory system

Respiratory system

Nervous system

Hormonal system

Excretory system

Digestive system

The human skeleton

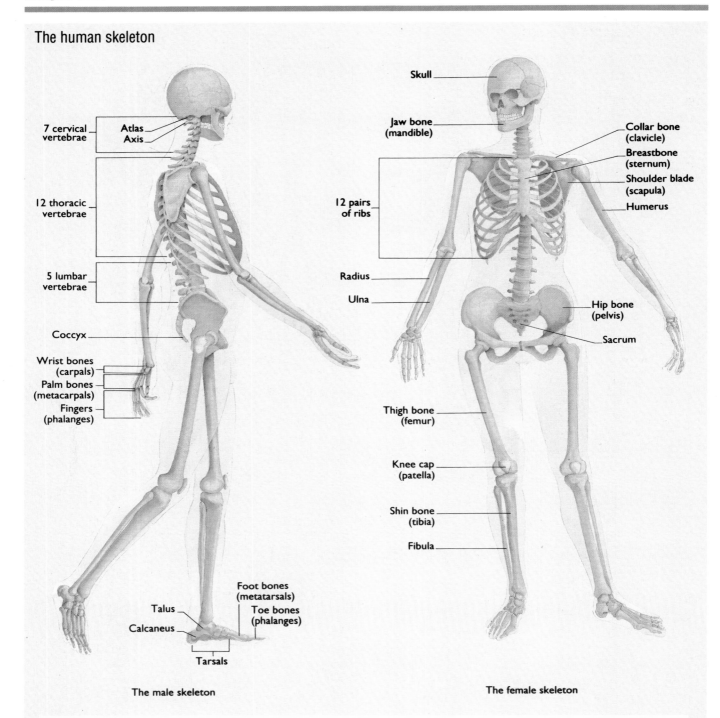

7 cervical vertebrae
Atlas
Axis
12 thoracic vertebrae
5 lumbar vertebrae
Coccyx
Wrist bones (carpals)
Palm bones (metacarpals)
Fingers (phalanges)

Talus
Calcaneus
Tarsals
Foot bones (metatarsals)
Toe bones (phalanges)

The male skeleton

Skull
Jaw bone (mandible)
12 pairs of ribs
Radius
Ulna
Collar bone (clavicle)
Breastbone (sternum)
Shoulder blade (scapula)
Humerus
Hip bone (pelvis)
Sacrum
Thigh bone (femur)
Knee cap (patella)
Shin bone (tibia)
Fibula

The female skeleton

Functions

1 **Protection** The skeleton protects the delicate parts of the body. The brain is completely protected by the skull, the vertebral column protects the spinal cord and the ribs form an expandable cage around the heart and lungs.

2 **Support** Without a skeleton the body would be flabby and shapeless. The arrangement of the bones gives shape to the body as a whole. The bones are also used to suspend some of the vital organs, keeping them in a constant position inside the body.

3 **Movement** The skeleton is jointed to allow us a wide range of movement of various kinds. Ligaments hold the bones together at the joints and all movement is caused by the contraction of muscles acting on the bones.

4 **Blood production** Red blood cells and some white blood cells are formed in the marrow cavities of larger bones.

What Is the Skeleton Made of?

The skeleton is made up mainly of bone.

Mature bone is a hard, rigid non-elastic tissue. The hardness is caused by large amounts of calcium salts; mainly calcium phosphate and calcium carbonate. Collagen fibres which are both tough and stringy make the bone exceptionally strong yet very light.

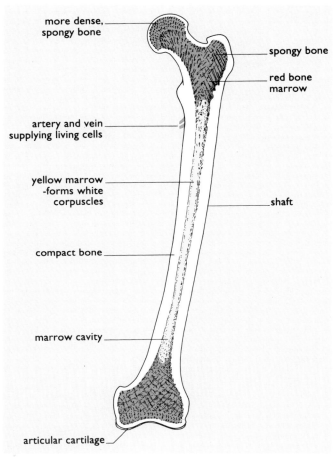

Cross section of a mature bone

There are four basic types of bones in the human body. Their sizes and composition are related to their different jobs.

1 Long tubular bones (the limbs)
2 Shorter bones of fibrous tissue (the wrist and ankle)
3 Flat, plate like bones (the skull and scapula)
4 Irregular bones (the vertebrae and the face)

The femur (thigh bone) is the longest bone in the human body. It is stronger, weight for weight, than steel and is able to withstand forces of up to two tons per square inch (300 kg/cm2) when the body takes part in physical activity.

How a Broken Bone Heals Itself

Bone is brittle. This means that it can easily break or fracture, particularly as a result of a blow or fall. It has the ability to repair itself even if normal bone growth may have stopped many years before.

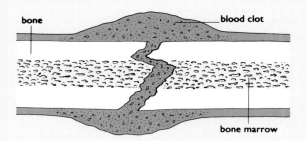

1 Blood oozes out of the blood vessels which have broken as a result of the bone injury. It forms a clot or haematoma around the jagged ends of the bones and quickly hardens.

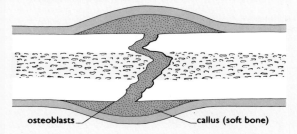

2 In a few days minerals from the sharp ends of the broken bone have been reabsorbed into the bloodstream leaving the ends soft and rubbery. At the same time connective tissue forms a callus (soft bone) to hold the broken ends together. Within this 'glue' special cells called osteoblasts (bone matter) appear to strengthen the bone ends, depositing collagen, calcium salts and other materials.

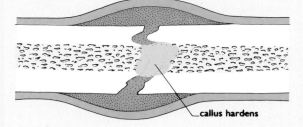

3 After a few weeks new soft bone starts to take the place of the repair tissues bridging the gap between the bone ends. When this soft bone (callus) hardens the mended bone can be fully used once more. The material around the damaged area is gradually reabsorbed and replaced by still newer bone so that eventually the site of an injury cannot be detected, even by X ray.

The Parts of the Skeleton

The skeleton is divided into two main parts: the *axial* skeleton and the *appendicular* skeleton.

The axial skeleton

The axial skeleton consists of the skull, vertebral column, ribs and sternum and it forms the support of the body.

The skull

The skull is made up of 28 bones; 8 of them form the cranium. The cranium of a new born child is separated by 6 gaps called fontanelles, each protected by a membrane. These give the skull flexibility at birth and also allow for growth. The bones become fused together to form an immovable joint (suture) by the time the child is about two. Another 14 bones are known as the facial bones while 6 others make up the auditory ossicles (the small bones in the ears).

The skull's function is to protect the brain, the eyes and the ears.

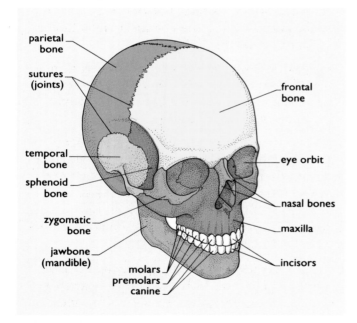

The rib cage

Humans have 12 pairs of ribs which are joined at the back to the vertebral spinal column (thoracic vertebrae). The upper seven pairs of ribs are joined at the front to the breast bone (sternum). The next three pairs are attached to the seventh rib and are called false ribs. The last two are unattached and are called the floating ribs.

The ribs, sternum and vertebrae together form a cage which protects the lungs and heart.

The vertebral column

The vertebrae interlock to form a strong hollow column through which the spinal cord travels and is well protected. As well as being strong the spine is also very flexible. It is shaped like a shallow 'S' and allows movement in all directions.

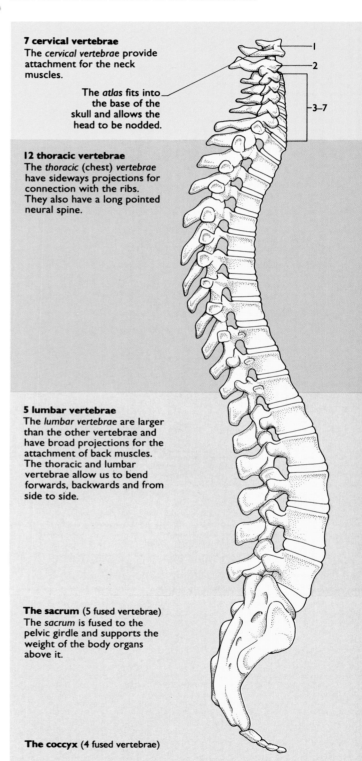

7 cervical vertebrae
The *cervical vertebrae* provide attachment for the neck muscles.

The *atlas* fits into the base of the skull and allows the head to be nodded.

12 thoracic vertebrae
The *thoracic* (chest) *vertebrae* have sideways projections for connection with the ribs. They also have a long pointed neural spine.

5 lumbar vertebrae
The *lumbar vertebrae* are larger than the other vertebrae and have broad projections for the attachment of back muscles. The thoracic and lumbar vertebrae allow us to bend forwards, backwards and from side to side.

The sacrum (5 fused vertebrae)
The *sacrum* is fused to the pelvic girdle and supports the weight of the body organs above it.

The coccyx (4 fused vertebrae)

The appendicular skeleton

The appendicular skeleton consists of the arms and shoulder girdle and the legs and hip girdle.
The functions of the limb girdles are:
1 To provide a more or less rigid connection between the axial skeleton and the limbs.

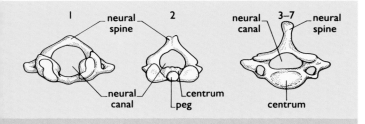

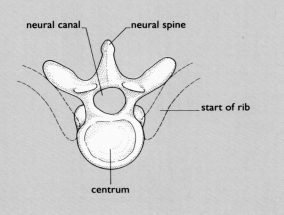

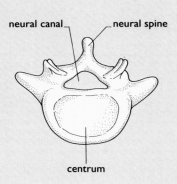

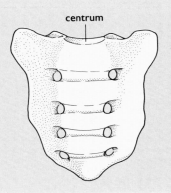

2 To provide suitable surfaces for the attachment of the muscles that move the limbs.
3 To provide stability by separating the joints.

The limbs

The basic bone pattern of the arms and legs is very similar.

The humerus is the long bone of the upper arm and the radius and ulna form the forearm. There are eight small carpal bones in the wrist, and five metacarpal bones which form the palm of the hand. There are fourteen phalanges - two in the thumb and three in each of the four fingers.

The femur is the long thigh bone. The tibia and fibula form the lower leg. The patella (knee cap) overlaps the femur and tibia. Seven tarsal bones form the ankle, five metatarsal bones the arch of the foot and fourteen phalanges the toes.

How do we move?

The human skeleton is jointed in order that the muscles may lever the bones about one another and so create movement. There are over 100 different joints in the body but they can best be described according to the amount of mobility or movement which they allow.

Immovable joints are fixed joints in which no movement is possible between the bones. Examples include the joints between the flat bones of the skull in adults.

Slightly movable joints have joint surfaces which are separated by some substance which is less hard than bone so that slight movement is possible. Examples are the joints of the spine which have discs of cartilage between the vertebrae (see page 6), and the joints between the ribs and the sternum.

Freely movable (synovial) joints all have a layer of tough but smooth and slippery cartilage called hyaline covering the heads of the bones which form the joint. This, together with a liquid called synovial fluid which is formed within the joint, allows friction-free movement. The bones forming the joints are held together by sheets of rounded bands of tough fibrous tissues called ligaments. These ligaments vary in size and shape. They keep the two bone ends together and prevent the bones from dislocating during movement. Surrounding the joint is a capsule of membranous material whose inner lining, the synovial membrane, produces the synovial fluid.

The appendicular skeleton

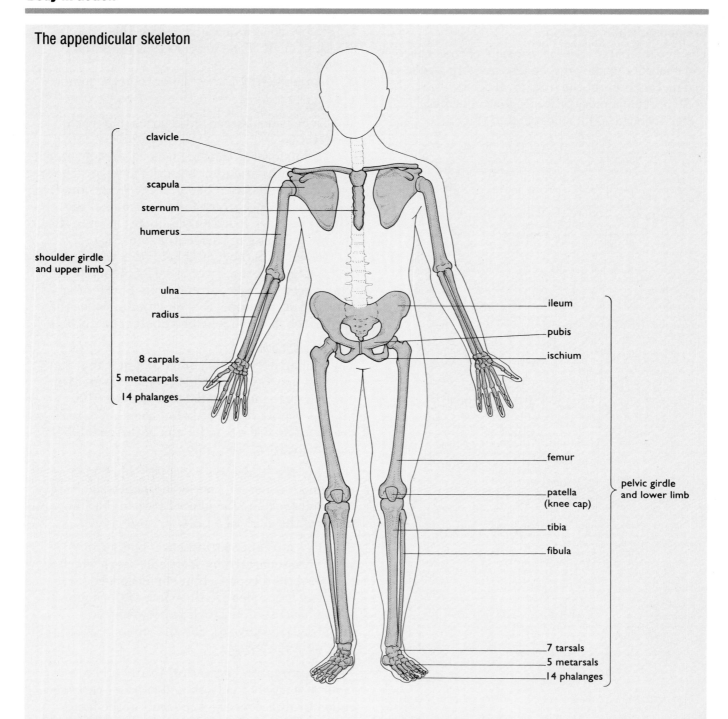

clavicle

scapula

sternum

humerus

shoulder girdle
and upper limb

ulna

radius

8 carpals

5 metacarpals

14 phalanges

ileum

pubis

ischium

femur

patella
(knee cap)

tibia

fibula

pelvic girdle
and lower limb

7 tarsals

5 metarsals

14 phalanges

The shoulder girdle

The shoulder girdle consists of two clavicles (collar bones)
and two scapulae (shoulder blades). The clavicles are joined
at one end to the sternum by cartilage. The scapulae are
bound only by muscles to the back of the thorax and not
fused to the spine. This arrangement allows a great deal of
mobility in the arms and the shoulders but is not as effective
as that of the pelvic girdle in transmitting force to the body.

The hip girdle

The hip (pelvic) girdle which transmits the weight of the
trunk to the legs, is a much heavier structure than the
shoulder girdle. It consists of two halves fused firmly
together and to the backbone. Each half consists of three
bones, the ileum, the ischium and the pubis. The pelvic girdle
supports the lower abdomen and provides a base for each of
the large thigh bones (femurs) to fit into. The fusion of the
pelvic girdle to the spine is very effective in transmitting
force from the legs to the body as the spine is the central
support of the whole body. The pelvis of the female is wider
but shallower than the pelvis of the male. This is to make
childbearing easier.

Different synovial joints found in the body

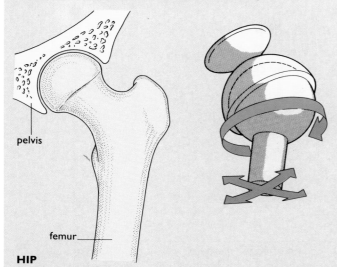

HIP

Ball and socket joint

The almost hemispherical surface of one bone fits into a cup like depression of the other. Movement is free in every direction.

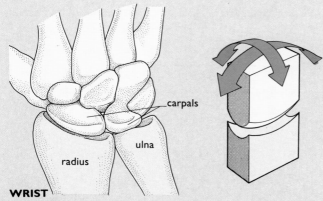

WRIST

Condyloid joint

Movement in two planes is possible because the dome shaped surface of one bone fits into the hollow formed by one or more other bones forming the joint. Rotation is prevented by the attachment of ligaments.

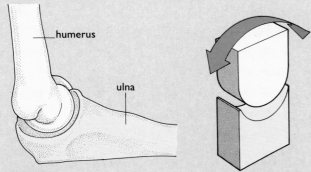

ELBOW

Hinge joint

Movement is allowed in one plane only due to the shape of the bones as well as the strong ligaments which prevent side to side movement.

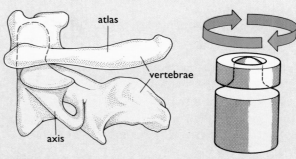

NECK

Pivot joint

The ring-like atlas vertebra fits over a peg on the axis vertebra allowing the head to rotate

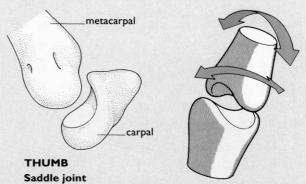

THUMB

Saddle joint

Convex and concave bone surfaces are placed against each other. This allows movement in two planes at right angles to each other. The joint at the base of the thumb allows movement in two directions.

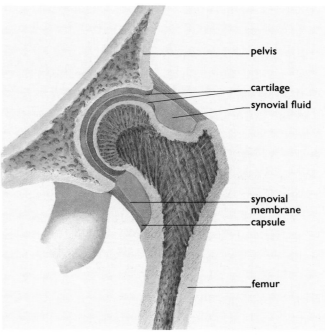

The hip joint is a typical synovial joint

THINGS TO DO 1

Complete the following five sentences by selecting the appropriate phrases:

1 An important function of the skeleton is to
 A produce hormones
 B support the body
 C carry nerves
 D make the blood flow quickly

2 The heart is protected by the bones of the
 A skull   B pelvic girdle
 C shoulder girdle   D thoracic cage

3 An example of a hinge joint is found in the
 A elbow   B hip
 C shoulder   D wrist

4 In a synovial joint, the synovial membrane
 A binds the bones together
 B increases mobility
 C produces synovial fluid
 D acts as a shock absorber

5 A vertebra is an example of
 A a short bone   B a long bone
 C a flat bone   D an irregular bone

6 Complete the following sentences:

  (i) The marrow cavities of large bones produce ....

  (ii) The purpose of ligaments around bones is to prevent the bones from ....

  (iii) The .... synovial joint allows movement in all directions.

7 Explain the functions of the human skeleton.

8 Complete the following table:

Position of bone in the body	Anatomical name of bone	Type of bone
Upper arm	Humerus	Long
Spine		
Thigh		
	Metatarsal	
Knee		
	Scapula	

9 Skeleton search

The twenty two words connected with the skeleton have all been hidden in the diagram. They have been printed across (backwards or forwards), up or down, or diagonally, but always in a straight line without letters being missed. You can use the letters in the diagram more than once, but you do not have to use them all.

When you have finished you should have 14 letters left over. Use 12 to find another word connected with the theme of the puzzle.

1 Atlas	9 Humerus	17 Scapula
2 Axis	10 Lumber	18 Spine
3 Bone	11 Metatarsals	19 Sternum
4 Cervical	12 Ossicles	20 Tarsals
5 Clavicle	13 Patella	21 Tibia
6 Coccyx	14 Phalanges	22 Ulna
7 Fibula	15 Ribs	
8 Fontanelles	16 Sacrum	

```
A  F  I  B  U  L  A  I  B  I  T
F  O  N  T  A  N  E  L  L  E  S
A  S  C  A  P  U  L  A  P  E  L
N  S  U  R  E  M  U  H  L  C  A
L  A  C  I  V  R  E  C  L  M  S
U  B  O  N  E  P  I  A  U  E  R
M  U  C  C  I  S  V  R  D  N  A
B  R  C  L  S  I  C  A  R  C  T
E  I  Y  O  C  A  T  L  A  S  A
R  B  X  L  S  L  A  S  R  A  T
D  S  E  G  N  A  L  A  H  P  E
E  N  I  P  S  T  E  R  N  U  M
S  I  X  A  P  A  T  E  L  L  A
```

MUSCLES AND MOVEMENT

Almost every single movement of the human body, both internal and external, happens as a result of the shortening (contracting) and lengthening (extending) of muscles. Muscles are not just concerned with movement. They assist in the circulation of blood, and protect and keep in place the abdominal organs. They also give us our own individual shape. Many of our muscles are under our control and we make use of them when we walk, take part in sport etc. These are called *skeletal* or *voluntary muscles*. Other muscles are not under our voluntary control but work automatically without needing any conscious orders from us. These are called *smooth* or *involuntary muscles* and they operate such things as the movements of the bowel, the uterus and the bladder. Involuntary muscles are also found in the walls of the blood vessels.

The heart is a very specialised type of involuntary muscle (called cardiac muscle) because its fibres contract on their own constantly and tirelessly. The rate and extent of contraction is controlled by a complex system of both nervous and chemical factors and is out of our voluntary control.

The Skeletal Muscles of the Body

There are over 600 voluntary muscles in the body and over 150 of them are in the head and neck alone. Some of the major muscles and their actions are shown below.

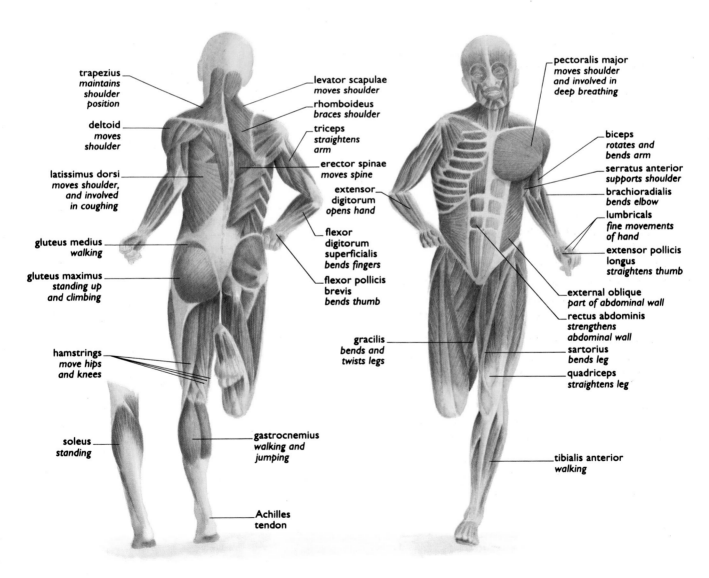

trapezius
maintains
shoulder
position

deltoid
moves
shoulder

latissimus dorsi
moves shoulder,
and involved
in coughing

gluteus medius
walking

gluteus maximus
standing up
and climbing

hamstrings
move hips
and knees

soleus
standing

levator scapulae
moves shoulder

rhomboideus
braces shoulder

triceps
straightens
arm

erector spinae
moves spine

extensor
digitorum
opens hand

flexor
digitorum
superficialis
bends fingers

flexor pollicis
brevis
bends thumb

gastrocnemius
walking and
jumping

Achilles
tendon

pectoralis major
moves shoulder
and involved in
deep breathing

biceps
rotates and
bends arm

serratus anterior
supports shoulder

brachioradialis
bends elbow

lumbricals
fine movements
of hand

extensor pollicis
longus
straightens thumb

external oblique
part of abdominal wall

rectus abdominis
strengthens
abdominal wall

sartorius
bends leg

quadriceps
straightens leg

gracilis
bends and
twists legs

tibialis anterior
walking

The Structure of Skeletal Muscle

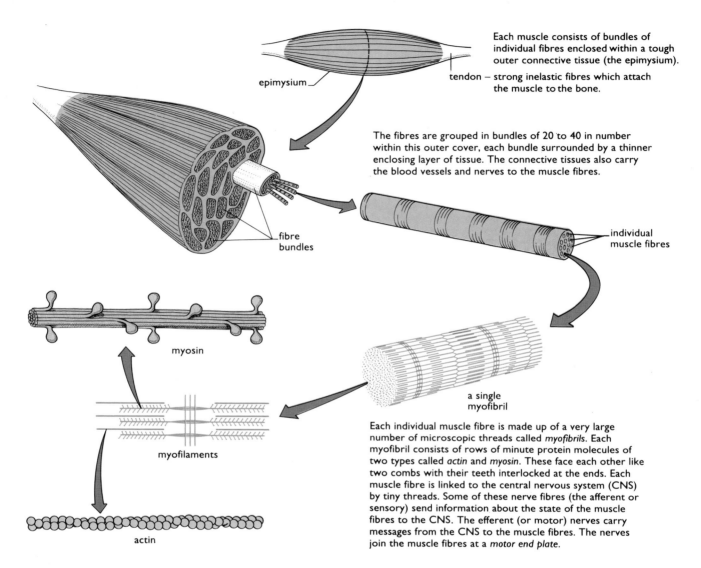

Each muscle consists of bundles of individual fibres enclosed within a tough outer connective tissue (the epimysium).

tendon – strong inelastic fibres which attach the muscle to the bone.

The fibres are grouped in bundles of 20 to 40 in number within this outer cover, each bundle surrounded by a thinner enclosing layer of tissue. The connective tissues also carry the blood vessels and nerves to the muscle fibres.

epimysium

fibre bundles

individual muscle fibres

myosin

myofilaments

a single myofibril

actin

Each individual muscle fibre is made up of a very large number of microscopic threads called *myofibrils*. Each myofibril consists of rows of minute protein molecules of two types called *actin* and *myosin*. These face each other like two combs with their teeth interlocked at the ends. Each muscle fibre is linked to the central nervous system (CNS) by tiny threads. Some of these nerve fibres (the afferent or sensory) send information about the state of the muscle fibres to the CNS. The efferent (or motor) nerves carry messages from the CNS to the muscle fibres. The nerves join the muscle fibres at a *motor end plate*.

The voluntary muscles in our body make up the bulk of our flesh and account for up to 40% of our body weight. Each muscle is made up of thousands of long, narrow muscle cells or fibres containing elements which can contract. The muscle fibres are enclosed within a tough outer connective tissue called the *epimysium*.

The fibres are grouped in bundles (*fasciculi*) of 20 to 40 in number, each bundle being enclosed by a thin surrounding layer of tissue.

Each individual muscle fibre is made up of a very large number of microscopic threads called *myofibrils*. Each myofibril consists of rows of minute protein molecules of two types called *actin* and *myosin*. These face each other like two combs with their teeth interlocked at the ends.

Each muscle fibre is linked to the central nervous system (CNS) by tiny nerve fibres. Nerves enter muscles at the neuromuscular hilus. Some of these nerve fibres (the afferent or sensory) send information about the state of the muscle fibres to the CNS. The efferent (or motor) nerves carry messages from the CNS to the muscle fibres. The nerves join the muscle fibres at the *motor end plate*. The connective tissue carries the blood vessels and nerves to the muscle fibres.

If all the bundles of muscle fibres are arranged parallel to each other (such as in the sartorious muscles of the upper leg) then contraction will occur over a greater distance than if the bundles are arranged in a fanlike shape such as in the deltoid muscles of the shoulder. The lesser contraction length is compensated for by a much stronger muscle.

How Muscles Work

Muscles contract or shorten when stimulated to do so by the Central Nervous System (CNS). Messages are sent via motor nerves to a motor neuron. This motor neuron will then split into 5 - 2000 branches, each branch being linked to an individual muscle fibre at a motor end plate.

Stimulation of a motor nerve will bring about a release of chemicals from the linked motor end plates. These chemicals then become involved in a complex series of chemical reactions which result in the actin and myosin molecules sliding past each another and shortening the muscle fibre.

When a motor neuron is stimulated then all the connected muscle cells will contract simultaneously. How a muscle responds depends upon the number of muscle fibres in each motor unit and the number of motor units stimulated. It is therefore possible to carry out fine accurate movements as well as rapid large movements.

Motor units in large muscles such as the hamstrings will service over 1000 muscle fibres each. Motor units servicing smaller, more sensitive muscles, such as those controlling the movements of the eyes, will only have 5 - 20 muscle fibres under their control.

There are thousands of mitochondria present in muscle cells. These are tiny structures which receive oxygen coming to the muscles. It is within the mitochondria that the oxygen is released to help keep the muscles working. The oxygen is transported to the mitochondria by myoglobin, a protein in the muscle cells which extracts oxygen from the haemoglobin of the blood. This exchange of oxygen and waste products takes place in the capillaries (the smallest blood vessels) which surround every single muscle cell.

Muscle Contractions Need Energy

Energy is required for muscular contraction. This is supplied by a substance called *adenosine triphosphate* (ATP) which is made and used in all cells. When a muscle fibre is stimulated to contract, it is the myosin molecules acting on the ATP which results in the muscle contracting. The ATP is broken down to *adenosine diphosphate* (ADP) by this reaction. As the supplies of ATP in the muscles are very small it has to be reformed if further muscular contraction is to follow. ATP is reformed in one of three ways, depending on the severity and length of the contractions.

1 The creatine phosphate system

The ATP broken down by the contraction of muscle can be continuously reformed by the breakdown of another high energy substance, also stored in the muscles, called *creatine phosphate* (CP). As long as the supplies of creatine phosphate last, muscular contractions can take place even in the absence of oxygen.

This anaerobic (without oxygen) system of obtaining energy for muscular contraction is used by sprinters and throwers. It is used by all sportsmen and sportswomen involved in events where an all out effort is required for a short period of time. The stores of CP are used up within 30 to 60 seconds. Therefore an alternative source of energy must be found if muscular contractions are to continue.

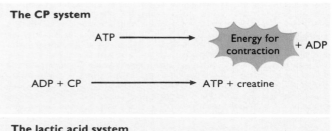

The CP system

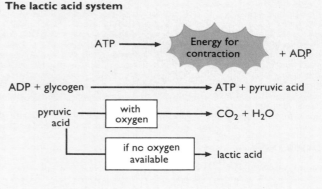

The lactic acid system

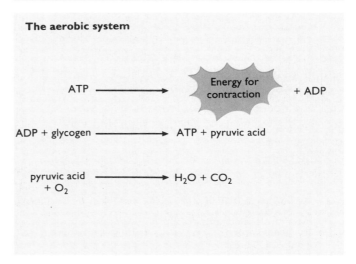

The aerobic system

2 The lactic acid system

ATP can be formed by the breakdown of *glucose*. Glucose which has been formed through the digestion of food, is stored in the muscles and liver as glycogen. When glycogen is broken down in the chemical reaction to produce ATP, a substance called *pyruvic acid* is formed. If oxygen is also available then this pyruvic acid is changed to carbon dioxide and water which are removed through the lungs. If there is insufficient oxygen available then the pyruvic acid is converted into *lactic acid* which builds up in the working muscles as well as overflowing into the bloodstream. Lactic acid makes muscular contractions difficult and causes tiredness. If there is sufficient build-up of lactic acid then the affected muscles will become painful. They may even stop working altogether.

Lactic acid will be converted back, eventually, into pyruvic acid. This will in turn be converted to carbon dioxide and water when sufficient oxygen becomes available.

A weight lifter uses the anaerobic CP system of obtaining energy for an all out effort

Rowers use the lactic acid system to obtain energy to work flat out for a short period

Oxygen debt

If you are exercising using the CP system or the lactic acid system of providing energy then you are working with an insufficient supply of oxygen! Your body copes by causing you to breathe more deeply and rapidly in order to get more oxygen to the working muscles. A shortage of oxygen is called an oxygen debt. This debt has to be repaid as soon as possible. This is why you continue to breathe deeply and rapidly even after you stop exercising vigorously. You are repaying your oxygen debt.

The body's second method of producing ATP (and therefore energy) is limited in three ways.

(i) by the amount of glycogen available,
(ii) by the level of lactic acid,
(iii) by the amount of oxygen debt with which the body can cope.

After 12 miles the energy requirements of a marathon runner are being supplied by the aerobic system

The lactic acid system is used by sportsmen and sportswomen who work flat-out for periods of up to two minutes. An 800 metre runner must train his body over a number of years in order to cope with the high levels of lactic acid and the high oxygen debt which build up in his event.

3 The aerobic system

The body's third source of ATP depends on a sufficient amount of oxygen being breathed in during exercise and is therefore an aerobic system. In this type of exercise the effort must be less intense than in the other two systems. If sufficient oxygen is available the activity can be carried on almost indefinitely. The pyruvic acid produced by breaking down the glycogen is changed to carbon dioxide and water which is then removed through the lungs. Consequently there is no oxygen debt to be repaid at the end of the activity. When the body is working at a level at which there is no oxygen debt build up then a steady state exists. This aerobic system is important during lengthy activity below maximal effort, for example when jogging.

Although some sportsmen and sportswomen use one system more than another, many sports require two or more of the systems to be used. A hockey player for instance may be working using the CP system in a rapid dribble for goal, using the lactic acid system whilst running from one end of the pitch to another, and working aerobically during a quiet part of the game.

Muscle Speed

Whether standing still or playing squash, our muscles are working together in a variety of ways. Some work slowly and maintain contraction for long periods of time. Others make powerful fast contraction to cause movement. To meet these different demands we have at least two distinct types of muscle fibres. These are the *slow twitch* and the *fast twitch fibres*.

Slow twitch fibres have a very good oxygen supply. They contain much greater levels of myoglobin and mitochondria. These fibres get much of their energy by using oxygen. Their contractions are relatively slow but capable of being prolonged or repeated many times. Slow twitch fibres are therefore the muscle cells used for endurance activities. They are dark red in colour.

Fast twitch fibres contract very quickly (about twice the speed of the slow twitch fibres) but they also tire very quickly. They are capable of a rapid release of energy and are the muscle cells used when speed is required. They are white in colour. There appear to be two distinct types of fast twitch fibres: fast oxidative glycolytic fibres (FOG) and fast glycolytic fibres (FG). The FOG fibres are fast contracting but they also possess good endurance properties. It is the FOG fibres which are used for fast powerful contractions but can also be trained to improve performance in endurance activities.

Muscles tend to be composed of both types of fibres, although the amounts may vary considerably from muscle to muscle and from one person to another. All the muscle fibres in a motor unit are of the same type however. The nervous system activates slow twitch muscle fibres when a person is walking or jogging but both fast and slow twitch muscle fibres are brought into use when rapid or explosive activities are undertaken.

Many athletes have now been fibre typed. This procedure involves taking a small sample of muscle tissues from the athlete, usually from the thigh or calf muscle. The muscle sample is then sliced, stained and put under the microscope for analysis.

Recent research has shown that long-distance runners, cyclists, rowers and cross-country skiers have relatively more slow twitch fibres in vastus lateralis, gastrocnemius or deltoid muscles. Top international endurance athletes can have up to 80% of their skeletal muscles composed of slow twitch fibres. The sprinters, jumpers and general-power athletes have a greater proportion of fast twitch fibres in the vastus lateralis muscles.

A number of researchers are trying to discover whether individuals are born with a particular proportion of slow and fast fibres or whether it is possible to change the basic proportion of each through the appropriate type of training. Although there is no conclusive evidence to date, it is clear that the muscle profiles shown by Olympic athletes are a result of both genetic and training factors.

Types of Muscle Action

Muscles can pull by contraction but they cannot push. If one muscle acts across a joint to bring the two bones closer together, then another muscle is needed to pull them apart.

This means that all joints must have at least two opposing (antagonistic) muscles crossing it. Most joints of the body have many more than two, so allowing many different types of movement.

Almost every movement of the human body happens as a result of contracting and extending muscles

Tendons

It is tendons which attach muscles to bone. Tendons vary in size and shape according to their position on the body. The tendons working the muscles of the fingers and hand are like cords whilst the tendons working for some of the back muscles are like broad flat sheets. Normally one end of a muscle is attached by one or more tendons to a fixed point (*the origin*). The other end is attached to the part of the body which moves when the muscle is contracted (*the insertion*). When muscles contract it is usually the insertion which will move towards the origin, although the reverse can take place.

Recent research has shown that tendons are springy. The Achilles tendon stretches by as much as 8% during running. They stretch and recoil like a spring and so store and then release kinetic energy generated by the active muscles. Up to 93% of the energy generated by the gastrocnemius muscle is saved by the rebound action of the Achilles tendon. The tendons on the soles of the feet can also act to store and then release kinetic energy. The net effect of this is that up to 50% of the energy generated by the muscles used for running is not lost and can be used for the next stride. Some of this stored energy is lost if the runner is wearing shoes and shoe manufacturers are now attempting to develop material which will have the same energy storing properties as our tendons.

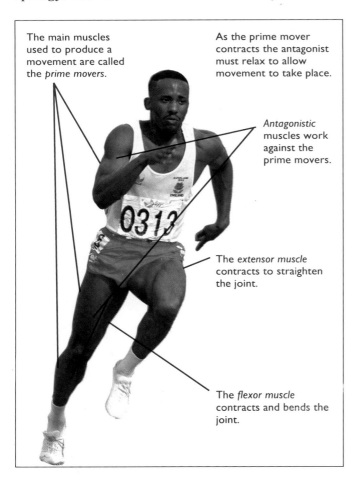

The main muscles used to produce a movement are called the *prime movers*.

As the prime mover contracts the antagonist must relax to allow movement to take place.

Antagonistic muscles work against the prime movers.

The *extensor muscle* contracts to straighten the joint.

The *flexor muscle* contracts and bends the joint.

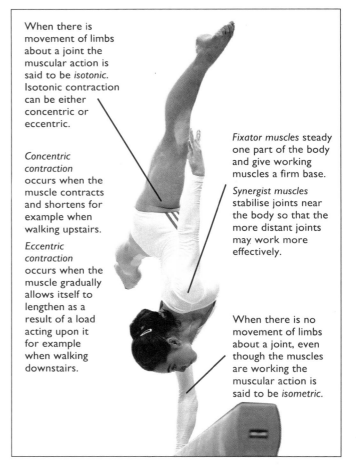

When there is movement of limbs about a joint the muscular action is said to be *isotonic*. Isotonic contraction can be either concentric or eccentric.

Concentric contraction occurs when the muscle contracts and shortens for example when walking upstairs.

Eccentric contraction occurs when the muscle gradually allows itself to lengthen as a result of a load acting upon it for example when walking downstairs.

Fixator muscles steady one part of the body and give working muscles a firm base.

Synergist muscles stabilise joints near the body so that the more distant joints may work more effectively.

When there is no movement of limbs about a joint, even though the muscles are working the muscular action is said to be *isometric*.

Muscles and Leverage

Movement takes place when the skeletal muscles pull hard enough on the bones to make them move. They use the bones as levers.

All levers are rigid structures which are hinged at one point (the pivotal point) and which have forces applied to them at two other points. One of the forces is a weight or object to be moved whilst the other force is the effort or energy which will cause the movement. There are three different types of lever systems, the body having examples of all three.

First order levers

In this lever system the fulcrum (the pivotal point) lies between the resistance (the weight) and the point of effort. Everyday examples of first order levers include a crowbar and a pair of scissors.

First order leverage is used to keep the skull upright as well as to extend both the arms and legs.

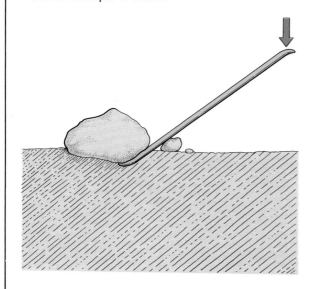

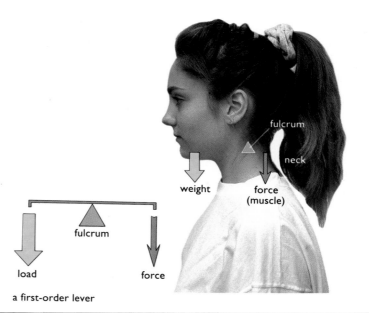

a first-order lever

Second order levers

In this lever system the resistance (weight) lies between the fulcrum (the pivotal point) and the point of effort. Everyday examples include lifting a wheelbarrow as well as standing on your toes.

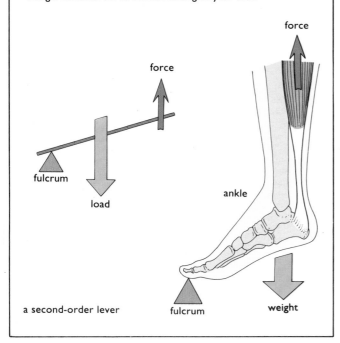

a second-order lever

Third order levers

In third order levers the point of effort lies between the pivotal point and the resistance. Most of the levers of the body act as third order levers because muscle (force) is attached between the joint (fulcrum) and the load (weight of the body). Although this may be mechanically inefficient it does mean that the muscles need to contract only a short distance in order to make the far ends of the limb move a long way.

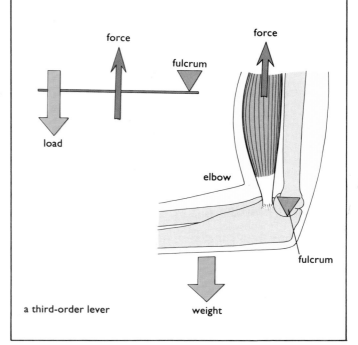

a third-order lever

Things to remember

- Whatever position you are in always ensure that all unsupported body parts are balanced.

- When picking up objects bend your knees and crouch down so that your back stays upright.

- Keep your back hollow - do not allow your body to fold up.

- When sitting on a chair ensure that there is support under the thighs as well as for the lumbar region.

- When lifting weights keep the weight as close as possible to the centre of gravity of the body.

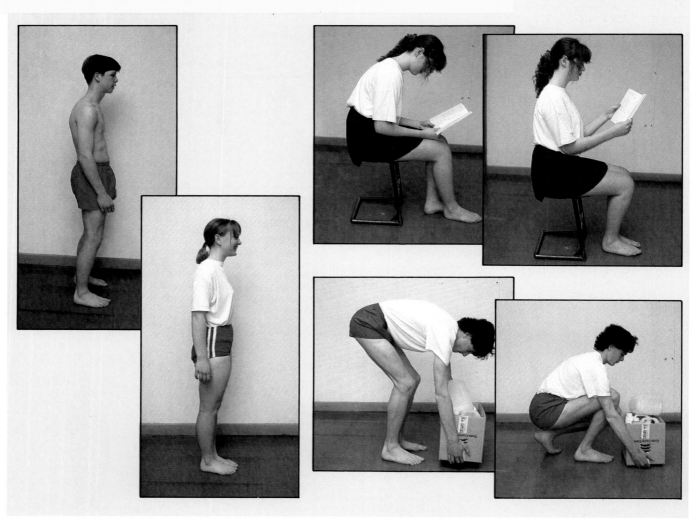

Examples of good and poor posture

The Co-ordinated Action of Muscles

Skilful movement is the result of many sets of muscles working smoothly together. Fortunately, although we decide which activities we attempt, we do not decide which muscles to use. Such decisions are made by the CNS and are normally out of our control. There are many stretch receptors (proprioceptors) which help the CNS send messages to the spinal cord when the muscle is being stretched. The proprioceptors send information to the brain about the position of the limbs. They help the brain to work out a pattern of muscular contractions which will produce skilled movement.

Muscle Relaxation

Muscles contract quickly but relax less swiftly. Therefore the speed of limb movement depends on the speed at which you can relax muscles so that they do not act as brakes on your movement. The more relaxed the antagonistic muscles, the faster and more powerfully the prime movers can contract. A relaxed muscle can be stretched further than a tense one. Tendons act as buffers and protect the limbs from the sudden and violent strain which muscles could inflict directly on the bones. Tendons also add a catapult effect to muscular contractions if the muscle is well stretched before the contraction.

It is therefore most important to warm up fully before taking part in vigorous exercise. The antagonist muscles get torn most often because they are at the mercy of the contracting muscles.

For example, sprinters using their powerful quadriceps (prime movers) may tear the hamstrings (antagonists).

Tearing a hamstring is very painful

THINGS TO DO 2

1   Complete the following sentences using the appropriate word:
    (i)   When performing pull-ups on a bar, the biceps
       A extend   B adduct
       C contract   D rotate

    (ii) The hamstrings are a group of muscles found in the
       A chest   B upper leg
       C lower leg   D arm

    (iii) Muscles which straighten a limb at a joint are called
       A fixators   B extensors
       C abductors   D flexors

2   Complete the following sentences using your own words:
    (i)   Muscles which are under our control are called .... muscles whilst those which work automatically are known as .... muscles.

    (ii) Each muscle fibre is made up of a very large number of tiny threads called ....

    (iii) Muscles contain stores of .... which supplies the energy for muscular contraction.

    (iv) Muscles are attached to bones by means of ....

3   With the aid of diagrams explain the structure of muscle and how muscles contract.

4   Most bodily movements involve third class levers. Give a sporting example and explain how the system works.

5   'There is no need to worry about our posture. Our body maintains good posture naturally.' Argue against this point of view.

6   Explain why some sportspeople attempt to develop slow twitch fibres whilst others attempt to develop fast twitch muscle fibres.

7   Complete the following table:

Position in body	Name of muscle
Upper leg	
	Trapezius
Chest	
	Gastrocnemius
Shoulder	

8 Name the main muscles
   contracting to produce the
   movements in the
   diagrams.

   (i)   ....

   (ii) ....

   (iii) ....

   (iv) ....

   (v)   ....

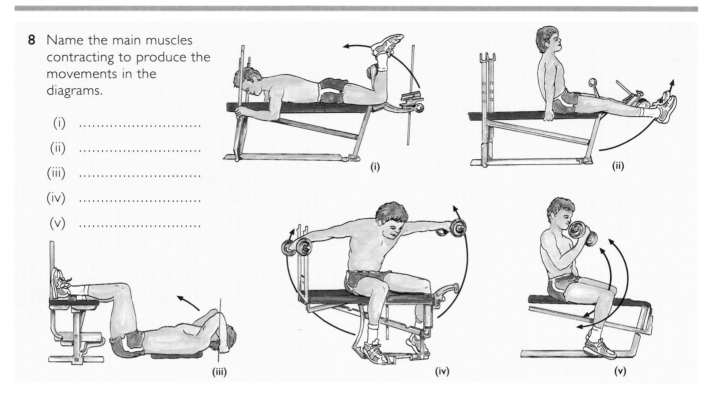

THE CIRCULATORY SYSTEM

We have seen that the muscle cells which contract to cause movement require energy in order to work effectively. Energy supplies in the muscles are quickly used up unless oxygen is available to reoxidise some of the by-products. This oxygen is carried to the muscles in the bloodstream. Waste products must also be removed from the cells and are carried away in the bloodstream. The circulatory or cardiovascular system of the body can be seen as a delivery service as well as a waste disposal system. Blood is the major means of transport in the body.

Pumped by the heart, the blood travels around the body in a continuous network of blood vessels. These vary in size from about 1 cm to 0.001 mm in diameter. Blood performs a large number of vital activities including delivering food and oxygen to the cells. It carries away the waste products and the excess heat generated by some of the internal organs. It also distributes the hormones which keep the body working efficiently. The special agents which fight disease as well as those which help to rebuild tissues are also delivered where needed.

Vital to this system is the heart which is a hollow muscular organ about the size of a closed fist. It lies in the thorax between the lungs and above the diaphragm. Its function is to keep the blood flowing continuously around the body.

The heart is made up of two linked muscular pumps which are separated by a solid wall of muscle called the septum. Each of the two pumps has two chambers, a thin walled atrium (auricle) above and a thick walled ventricle below, connected by a valve which allows the blood to flow in one direction only. The atria are the chambers which receive the blood. The ventricles are the chambers which pump the blood out of the heart.

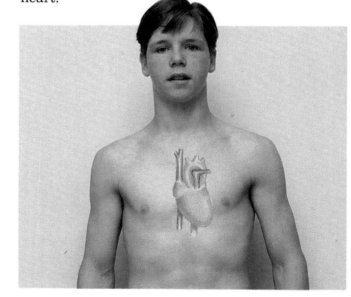

The structure of the heart

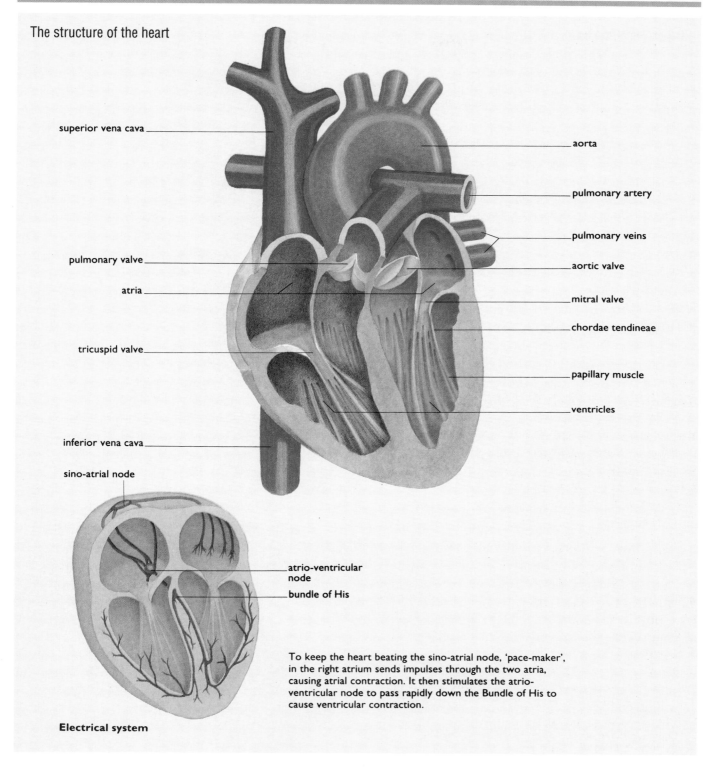

superior vena cava

aorta

pulmonary artery

pulmonary veins

pulmonary valve

aortic valve

atria

mitral valve

chordae tendineae

tricuspid valve

papillary muscle

ventricles

inferior vena cava

sino-atrial node

atrio-ventricular node

bundle of His

To keep the heart beating the sino-atrial node, 'pace-maker', in the right atrium sends impulses through the two atria, causing atrial contraction. It then stimulates the atrio-ventricular node to pass rapidly down the Bundle of His to cause ventricular contraction.

Electrical system

The Action of the Heart

When the body is at rest the heart beats between 50 and 80 times a minute, pumping the 4.7 litres (10 pints) or so of blood around the body. At rest the blood will take about 20 seconds to circulate once around the system. The heart has the ability to respond immediately when any extra demand is placed upon it. During hard physical labour or stressful situations the heart rate can increase up to 180 or 220 beats per minute. The heart of a trained athlete could be pumping up to 45 litres of blood a minute.

The action of the heart

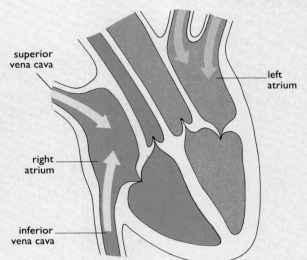

Deoxygenated blood enters the *right atrium* via the *vena cava*. In its journey around the body the blood has been relieved of much of its oxygen but has picked up a number of waste products, including carbon dioxide. It is a dull red colour.

The newly oxygenated blood enters the *left atrium*. At this point the heart is between beats and the atrium is relaxed.

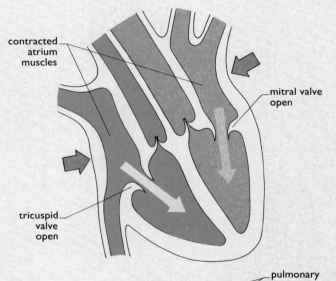

The atrium muscles contract to pump the blood through the *tricuspid valve* and into the *right ventricle*.

The atrium muscles contract and the blood is pushed into the *left ventricle*.

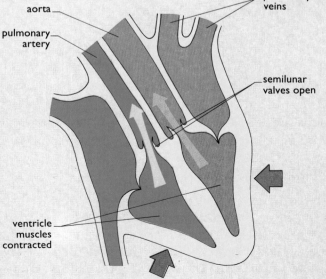

The ventricle muscles contract and the blood is pumped out of the heart via the *semilunar valves*, along the *pulmonary artery* leading to the lungs. In the lungs the blood releases its carbon dioxide and is supplied with fresh oxygen. The blood, now scarlet in colour, returns to the heart along the pulmonary vein.

The ventricle muscles contract and the blood is pumped out of the heart and into the largest artery, the *aorta*. It then goes on another journey around the body.

The circulatory system

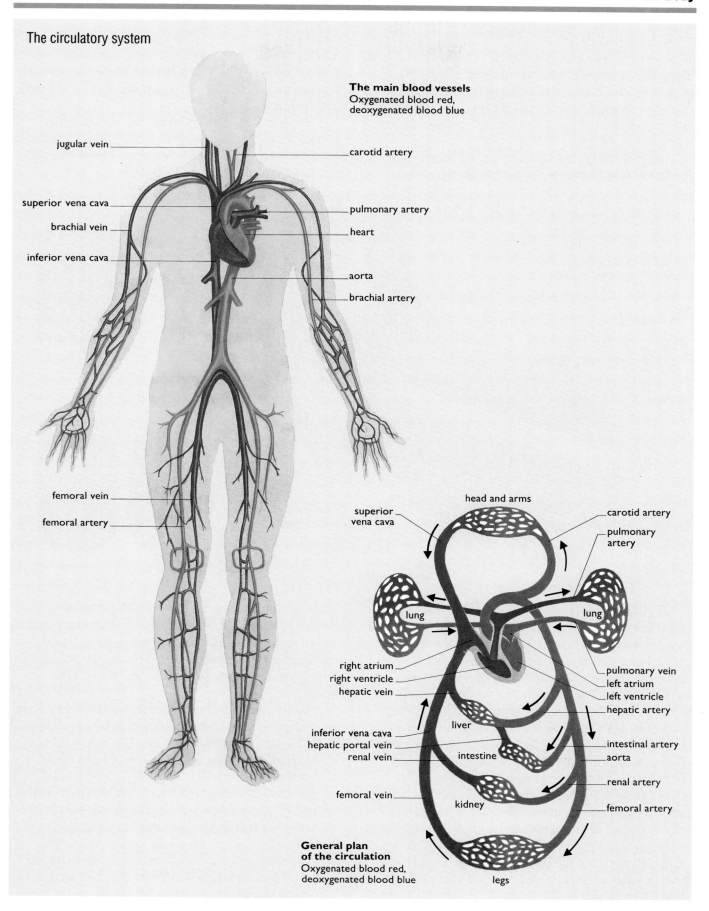

The main blood vessels
Oxygenated blood red,
deoxygenated blood blue

jugular vein

carotid artery

superior vena cava

pulmonary artery

brachial vein

heart

inferior vena cava

aorta

brachial artery

femoral vein

head and arms

superior
vena cava

carotid artery

pulmonary
artery

femoral artery

lung

lung

right atrium
right ventricle
hepatic vein

pulmonary vein
left atrium
left ventricle
hepatic artery

inferior vena cava
hepatic portal vein
renal vein

liver

intestine

intestinal artery
aorta

femoral vein

kidney

renal artery

femoral artery

**General plan
of the circulation**
Oxygenated blood red,
deoxygenated blood blue

legs

Structure of the Blood Vessels

The aorta curves up from the heart and then down along the backbone into the abdomen. From it other arteries branch off to go to the head, the digestive system, the arms and the legs. The main arteries of the body are shown in the diagram on page 23.

Arteries carry freshly oxygenated blood from the heart and convey it to the capillary system.

Most arteries lie deep in the body, but some are nearer to the surface and it is in these places that a pulse can be felt. If an artery is cut a lot of blood will be lost.

By branching and rebranching the arteries become smaller and smaller, finally reaching the smallest arteries called arterioles. These join the smallest vessels, called capillaries.

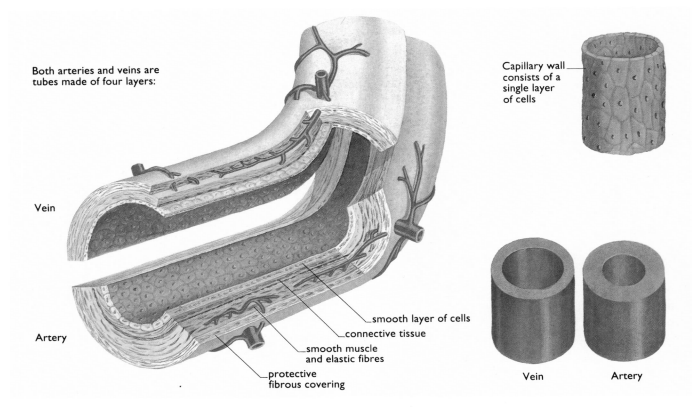

Both arteries and veins are tubes made of four layers:

Vein

Artery

Capillary wall consists of a single layer of cells

smooth layer of cells
connective tissue
smooth muscle and elastic fibres
protective fibrous covering

Vein   Artery

Capillaries are tiny vessels with walls only one cell thick. Oxygen passes through these thin walls into the tissues. Carbon dioxide, dissolved food and other products are exchanged for the oxygen and pass from the tissues into the capillaries. The capillaries are very narrow, so narrow in fact that some of the blood cells are squeezed flat as they pass between them. This slows the flow of the blood down considerably and allows the exchange of the various substances to be made efficiently. The capillary bed is enormous; its capacity far exceeds the 4.7 litres of blood which is pumped around the average male. This helps to explain why it is that, although blood pumps through an artery, it merely oozes in the capillaries. The capillary network is finer and denser in active tissues such as muscle and brain and less dense in less active tissue.

In giving up oxygen and taking on waste products the blood colour turns from scarlet to dull red (deoxygenated blood). It moves from the capillaries into the tiniest of veins called venules which join together to form larger and larger veins.

Since blood is at low pressure in the veins, they are supplied with valves at short intervals along their length. These valves keep the blood flowing in one direction only and it is not able to flow backwards.

A smooth flow of blood back to the heart is also helped by the pumping action of the skeletal muscles squeezing the veins as they contract. Even at this distance from the heart there will still be some arterial blood pressure. The suction action of the atrium will also assist the blood in its return to the heart.

Veins are often near the surface of the body so that excess heat generated within the working muscles can be lost more readily. The main veins of the body are shown on the diagram. The largest is called the vena cava and enters the right atrium of the heart.

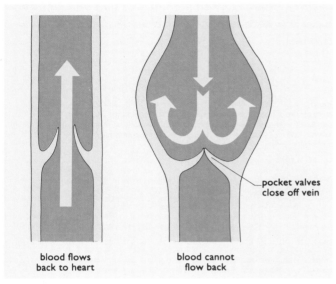

blood flows
back to heart

blood cannot
flow back

pocket valves
close off vein

Veins have valves to prevent blood flowing backwards

Blood Pressure and Heart Disease

Blood is pumped out of the heart under pressure. This pressure is calculated by measuring the pressure needed to stop the flow of blood through an artery. Two readings are normally taken. The *systolic pressure* is the maximum reading as the heart contracts. The *diastolic pressure* is the minimum reading as the heart is relaxed.

Blood pressure is always much lower in children than in adults. This is because as we age our arteries lose some of their elasticity and there is less give in the artery walls. Blood pressure also varies according to our activities. It is normally taken when you are relaxed and resting and therefore at its lowest.

Stressful situations cause the blood pressure to rise. Extremely high readings are recorded for individuals such as pilots as they are landing a plane and people sitting examinations.

There is no such thing as 'normal' blood pressure and doctors only become concerned if both systolic and diastolic readings remain high over an extended period of time. High blood pressure or hypertension is very common and has become associated with a number of serious cardiovascular diseases. It seems to result from the blocking of the smaller blood vessels making

the heart work harder to force the blood around the body. The heart responds to this extra, non-productive work by enlarging. The greater pressure exerted by the heart puts even more strain on the now less springy artery walls. If they rupture in the brain a stroke will occur.

High blood pressure can affect the efficiency of the heart. Coronary heart disease is the biggest single killer in this country accounting for one quarter of all deaths. It kills more than 35000 men before retiring age each year. Thus high blood pressure is of serious concern. Heart disease occurs in the arteries which take blood to the heart muscles. They are the first arteries which branch off the aorta and they are responsible for satisfying the heart's heavy demand for oxygen.

The problem appears to start in early adolescence when fat is deposited on the artery walls. Over the years this will reduce the size of the channels though which the blood can flow. The heart may suddenly require an extra amount of oxygen, perhaps because the person runs to catch a bus. The blood may not be able to get to the heart in a sufficient quantity and the heart will be temporarily starved of oxygen. The result will be a sharp pain in the chest called *angina*. In very severe cases a *heart attack* occurs. Although a great deal of research is being undertaken around the world, there is not much evidence so far that the thickening of the arteries can be reversed. The main factors associated with the development of heart disease include high blood cholesterol levels, cigarette smoking, high blood pressure, diabetes, overweight, family history of coronary disease and strokes, lack of exercise and stress. We will be considering a number of these factors in later chapters.

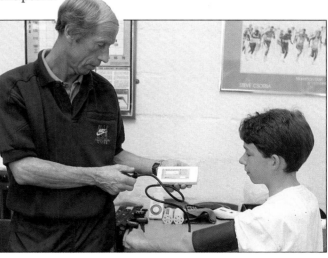

Taking blood pressure

The Blood

The blood is a fluid tissue which provides an essential link between all the other tissues and organs of the body. It consists of plasma and cells (corpuscles). There are two types of cells, *red cells* (erythrocytes) and *white cells* (leucocytes). *Blood platelets* (thrombocytes) are other structures found in the blood. They are not cells but fragments of cytoplasm, and are specially concerned with blood clotting.

The transport of oxygen

Red blood cells contain haemoglobin which is a compound of protein and iron. It gives blood its red colour. Haemoglobin combines readily with oxygen to form a compound called oxyhaemoglobin. Haemoglobin will combine with oxygen where oxygen is plentiful and yet readily loses it where oxygen is scarce, as in the body tissues.

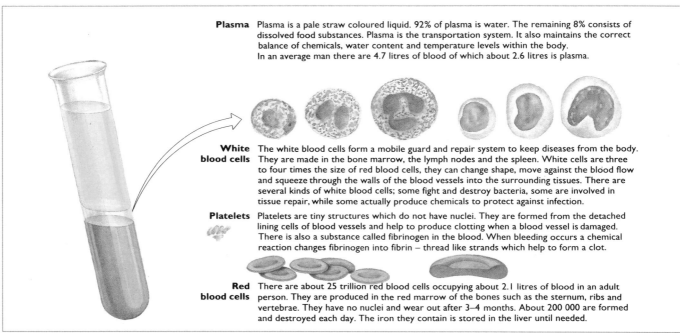

Plasma Plasma is a pale straw coloured liquid. 92% of plasma is water. The remaining 8% consists of dissolved food substances. Plasma is the transportation system. It also maintains the correct balance of chemicals, water content and temperature levels within the body.
In an average man there are 4.7 litres of blood of which about 2.6 litres is plasma.

White blood cells The white blood cells form a mobile guard and repair system to keep diseases from the body. They are made in the bone marrow, the lymph nodes and the spleen. White cells are three to four times the size of red blood cells, they can change shape, move against the blood flow and squeeze through the walls of the blood vessels into the surrounding tissues. There are several kinds of white blood cells; some fight and destroy bacteria, some are involved in tissue repair, while some actually produce chemicals to protect against infection.

Platelets Platelets are tiny structures which do not have nuclei. They are formed from the detached lining cells of blood vessels and help to produce clotting when a blood vessel is damaged. There is also a substance called fibrinogen in the blood. When bleeding occurs a chemical reaction changes fibrinogen into fibrin – thread like strands which help to form a clot.

Red blood cells There are about 25 trillion red blood cells occupying about 2.1 litres of blood in an adult person. They are produced in the red marrow of the bones such as the sternum, ribs and vertebrae. They have no nuclei and wear out after 3–4 months. About 200 000 are formed and destroyed each day. The iron they contain is stored in the liver until needed.

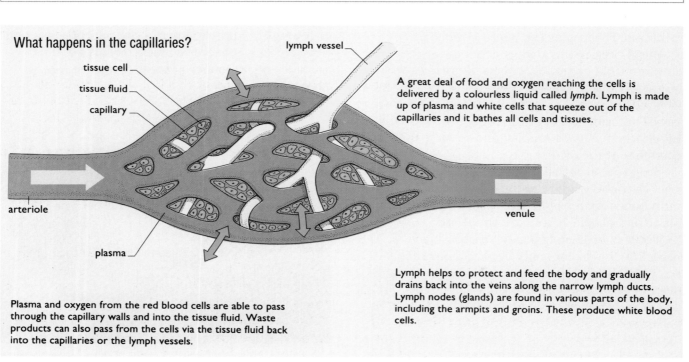

What happens in the capillaries?

tissue cell
tissue fluid
capillary
arteriole
plasma
lymph vessel
venule

A great deal of food and oxygen reaching the cells is delivered by a colourless liquid called *lymph*. Lymph is made up of plasma and white cells that squeeze out of the capillaries and it bathes all cells and tissues.

Plasma and oxygen from the red blood cells are able to pass through the capillary walls and into the tissue fluid. Waste products can also pass from the cells via the tissue fluid back into the capillaries or the lymph vessels.

Lymph helps to protect and feed the body and gradually drains back into the veins along the narrow lymph ducts. Lymph nodes (glands) are found in various parts of the body, including the armpits and groins. These produce white blood cells.

The Human Body

THE RESPIRATORY SYSTEM

The body is made up of millions of cells, all of which require oxygen. The cells need oxygen so that they can break down the sugars from food and free the energy required to carry out their work effectively. Oxygen is taken from the air via the lungs. It is then carried to the cells of the body via the circulatory system. Waste carbon dioxide is collected from the cells and expelled by the body through the lungs. The whole process of freeing energy from our food is called respiration.

What happens when we breathe?

Air enters the body through the *nose* and *mouth*.

Nasal cavity – large dust particles are removed by the coarse nasal hairs. Cilia (tiny hair like structures) trap dust and bacteria in the air and propel them down the throat to be swallowed.

Palate – separates the nasal cavity from the mouth so that food can be chewed at the same time as breathing.

Epiglottis – flap at the back of the throat. It closes when we swallow to prevent food particles from entering the trachea.

Trachea – (windpipe) with hoops of cartilage to prevent collapsing.

The *windpipe* divides into two *bronchial tubes* behind the breastbone. These then branch out again into smaller *bronchi* which in turn become tiny bronchioles.

The *bronchioles* subdivide into alveoli, a vast army of tiny thin walled air sacs.

The *alveoli* make up the bulk of the lung tissues. There are an estimated 300–400 million alveoli in the lungs of an average size man. When the lungs expand or contract it is these tiny air sacs which are actually filling or emptying.

A pulmonary artery carries blood directly from the heart into each of the lungs. This artery divides and subdivides again and again until a network of capillaries surrounds each cluster of alveoli. There is direct contact between the walls of the alveoli and the capillaries. The haemoglobin in the blood of the capillaries takes up oxygen from the alveoli. At the same time carbon dioxide is passed out of the bloodstream and into the lungs. The carbon dioxide is then breathed out into the air. Not all the carbon dioxide is removed. Its presence in the bloodstream is checked by the brain and is used to control our rate of breathing.

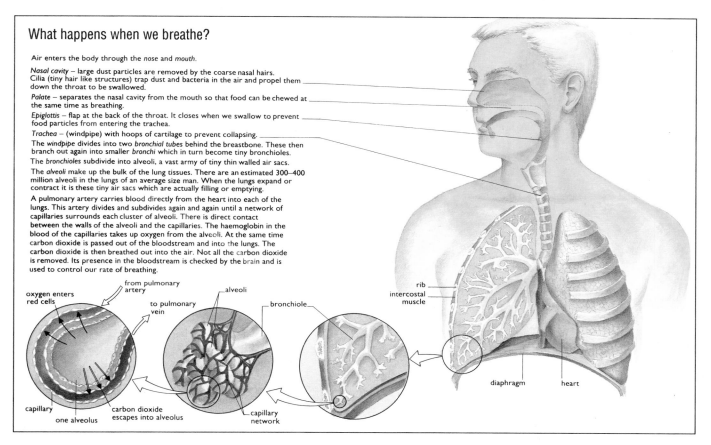

oxygen enters red cells
from pulmonary artery
to pulmonary vein
alveoli
bronchiole
rib
intercostal muscle
capillary
one alveolus
carbon dioxide escapes into alveolus
capillary network
diaphragm
heart

How We Breathe

The lungs are two, thin-walled elastic sacs lying in the thorax. This is an airtight cavity enclosed by the ribs at the side and the diaphragm below. Any change in the volume of the thorax affects the volume of the lungs.

When breathing in (inspiration), muscles across the ribs contract and pull the ribs upwards. At the same time the muscles of the diaphragm contract and flatten out the floor of the rib cage. The lungs increase in size and so suck in air through the nose and mouth.

Breathing out (expiration) occurs when the muscles of the diaphragm and the ribs relax. The diaphragm is pushed back into a domed position by the organs beneath it under pressure from the muscular abdominal walls. The ribs move down under their own weight. The space the lungs occupy is now smaller and so air is forced out again. When the body is at rest the movements of the diaphragm alone are sufficient to fill and empty the lungs.

When at rest we breathe in and out about sixteen times a minute. We take in about 0.5 litres of air with each breath. If there is a rise in the amount of carbon dioxide in the blood, the rate and depth of breathing is increased. This carbon dioxide concentration will rise whenever the body is engaged in physical activity. The rate of breathing can increase up to fifty times a minute. The amount of air taken in with each breath can be up to 2.5 litres. The age as well as the level of fitness of the individual will decide exactly how well the respiratory system can cope with the increased demand made by the muscles.

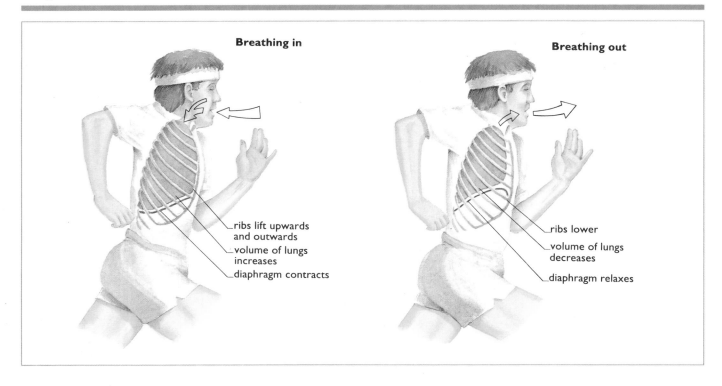

Breathing in

ribs lift upwards and outwards
volume of lungs increases
diaphragm contracts

Breathing out

ribs lower
volume of lungs decreases
diaphragm relaxes

THINGS TO DO 3

1   Complete the following sentences by choosing the appropriate word or words:

(i)   Blood travels from the heart to the lungs in the

    A   pulmonary vein   B   pulmonary artery
    C   aorta   D   vena cava

(ii) In the lungs, oxygen from the air is exchanged for

    A   nitrogen   B   hydrogen
    C   carbon dioxide   D   carbon monoxide

(iii) Oxygen is carried in the blood

    A   combined with haemoglobin
    B   attached to the platelets
    C   inside the white corpuscles
    D   dissolved in water

2   (i)   In the heart the chambers which receive the blood are called the .... and the chambers which pump the blood out of the heart are called the ....

(ii) Blood is carried back to the heart by means of .... and away from the heart in .... The smallest blood vessels are called ....

(iii) Most of the blood is made up of a clear liquid called .... in which there are several types of cell. The three main ones are
    ....,......................., and ....

3   List the functions of blood.

4   Explain how breathing in and breathing out takes place.

5   Describe how the oxygen in the air is transferred to the blood in the lungs.

6   'Heart disease is on the increase in Britain.' Explain why this is true and describe the factors which contribute to the problem.

7   Complete the following table showing the differences between veins and arteries.

	Veins	Arteries
Takes blood from		
Takes blood to		
Blood pressure		
Construction of walls		

THE DIGESTIVE SYSTEM

The body needs a constant supply of food as fuel if it is to remain healthy and active. The digestive system makes the food soluble and breaks it down into molecules small enough to pass into the bloodstream and the lymph system. It also reduces food into the basic nutrients which the body needs for building new tissues, repairing damaged ones and for energy.

The end products of digestion

End product	Where taken	Uses
Amino acids	Taken in the bloodstream to the body tissues.	Building new cells. Repairing worn out tissues.
Simple sugars	Taken in the bloodstream first to the liver and then to the muscle cells.	Energy.
Fatty acids and glycerol	Carried in the lymph vessels to the venous systems.	Energy store. Heat insulation.

How is food digested?

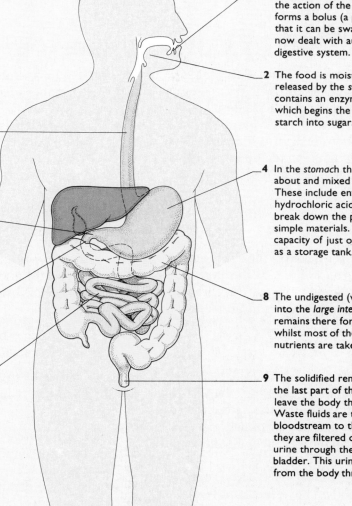

1 Digestion starts in the mouth where food is first ground up and mixed by the action of the *teeth*. The food forms a bolus (a pellet of food) so that it can be swallowed easily. It is now dealt with automatically by the digestive system.

2 The food is moistened by saliva released by the *salivary glands*. Saliva contains an enzyme called ptyalin which begins the process of turning starch into sugar.

3 Food is pushed down the *gullet* (oesophagus) by a wave like muscular movement called *peristalsis*.

4 In the *stomach* the food is churned about and mixed with gastric juices. These include enzymes and dilute hydrochloric acid. They begin to break down the protein to form simple materials. The stomach has a capacity of just over a litre and acts as a storage tank.

5 Food is released in small amounts by the relaxation of the *pyloric sphincter* (gatekeeper muscle) and it moves into the first part of the small intestine, the duodenum. Food spends about 4–6 hours in the small intestine.

6 In the duodenum the food is further digested through the action of a large number of alkaline enzymes. They break down the food into a mixture of simple amino acids, fatty acids and glycerol.

7 Digestion is completed in the small intestine and the usable nutrients are absorbed into the blood and lymph systems through the intestine wall.

8 The undigested (waste) food passes into the *large intestine* (colon). It remains there for about 12 hours whilst most of the water and more nutrients are taken from it.

9 The solidified remains pass through the last part of the system and leave the body through the *anus*. Waste fluids are taken by the bloodstream to the kidneys. Here they are filtered off and pass as urine through the ureters to the bladder. This urine is then expelled from the body through the urethra.

THINGS TO DO 4

I Complete the following sentences by choosing the appropriate word:
  (i) Food is mixed with gastric juices in the
    A oesophagus   B colon
    C stomach   D intestine

  (ii) Waste fluids are taken by the bloodstream to the
    A stomach   B pancreas
    C liver   D kidneys

  (iii) In the digestive system, food is broken down by the action of
    A neurones   B enzymes
    C corpuscles   D vitamins

2 Complete the following sentences:
  (i) Peristalsis is a wave-like muscular movement pushing food down the ....

  (ii) Ptyalin is an enzyme found in ....

  (iii) The colon deals with .... food, removing most of the ....from it.

  (iv) Solid matter leaves the body through the .... and liquids through the ....

3 Explain the purpose of the digestive system.

4 List in order all the digestive organs that food passes through, starting with the mouth. Explain briefly what happens at each stage.

THE NERVOUS SYSTEM

We need to be constantly aware of all that is going on around us, outside of our body. We need to be able to see, hear, feel, smell and taste if we are to survive and thrive. It is the nervous system which has overall control of these vital functions.

The nervous system is made up of the brain, spinal cord, peripheral nerves and the sense organs.

The Brain

The brain is the control centre for every activity of the body, conscious as well as involuntary activities. It is suspended in clear (cerebrospinal) fluid and surrounded by the cranium for its protection.

The Spinal Cord

The spinal cord is about 1 cm wide when it leaves the base of the brain through the opening in the base of the skull. It is made up of nerve cells with nerve fibres and it extends nearly all the way down the spinal canal.

Nerve fibres carry messages to and from nearly every part of the body. They enter and leave the spinal cord in bundles through gaps between the vertebrae.

Nerves

A nerve looks like a white thread and consists of a large number of *neurones* bounded by an outer coat.

Sensory nerves carry information from receptors to the CNS.

Effector or motor nerves carry information to the effector organs from the CNS. Effector organs are the muscles and glands which only work when they receive information from the CNS.

Spinal nerves are mixed nerves carrying information in both directions.

All nerves link the effector and receptor organs to the central nervous system. Receptors or sense organs are of three types depending on where they are found.

1 *Exteroceptors* receive information from outside the body (for example from the eyes and ears).

2 *Interoceptors* receive information from organs inside the body including the lungs and digestive system.

3 *Proprioceptors* are found mainly in the muscles, tendons and joints. They respond to the degree of stretching in their particular body part and so give information about the relative positions of different parts of the body. Proprioceptors enable us to move our limbs with great accuracy and speed without the need for us to actually watch them.

The nervous system

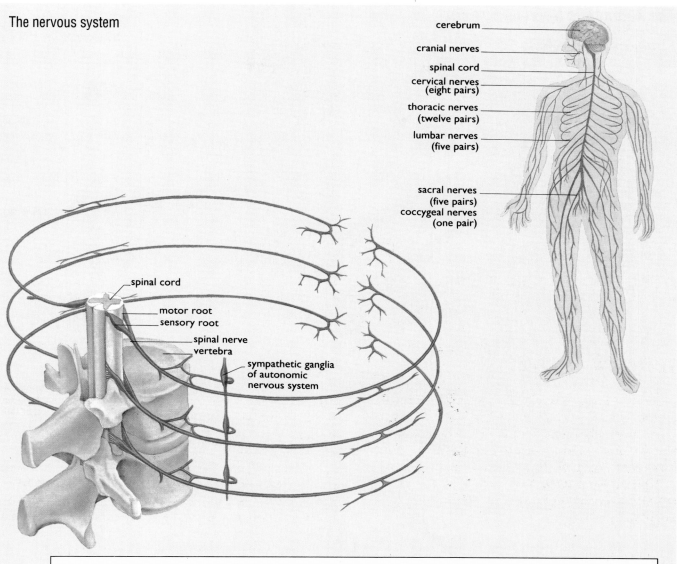

cerebrum

cranial nerves

spinal cord

cervical nerves
(eight pairs)

thoracic nerves
(twelve pairs)

lumbar nerves
(five pairs)

sacral nerves
(five pairs)
coccygeal nerves
(one pair)

spinal cord

motor root
sensory root

spinal nerve
vertebra

sympathetic ganglia
of autonomic
nervous system

The brain

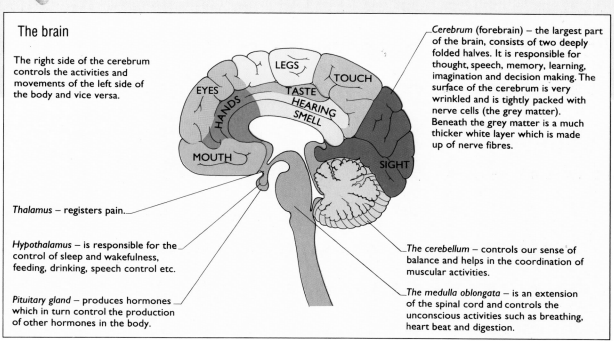

The right side of the cerebrum controls the activities and movements of the left side of the body and vice versa.

Cerebrum (forebrain) – the largest part of the brain, consists of two deeply folded halves. It is responsible for thought, speech, memory, learning, imagination and decision making. The surface of the cerebrum is very wrinkled and is tightly packed with nerve cells (the grey matter). Beneath the grey matter is a much thicker white layer which is made up of nerve fibres.

LEGS
TOUCH
EYES
TASTE
HANDS
HEARING
SMELL
MOUTH
SIGHT

Thalamus – registers pain.

Hypothalamus – is responsible for the control of sleep and wakefulness, feeding, drinking, speech control etc.

Pituitary gland – produces hormones which in turn control the production of other hormones in the body.

The cerebellum – controls our sense of balance and helps in the coordination of muscular activities.

The medulla oblongata – is an extension of the spinal cord and controls the unconscious activities such as breathing, heart beat and digestion.

The Autonomic Nervous System

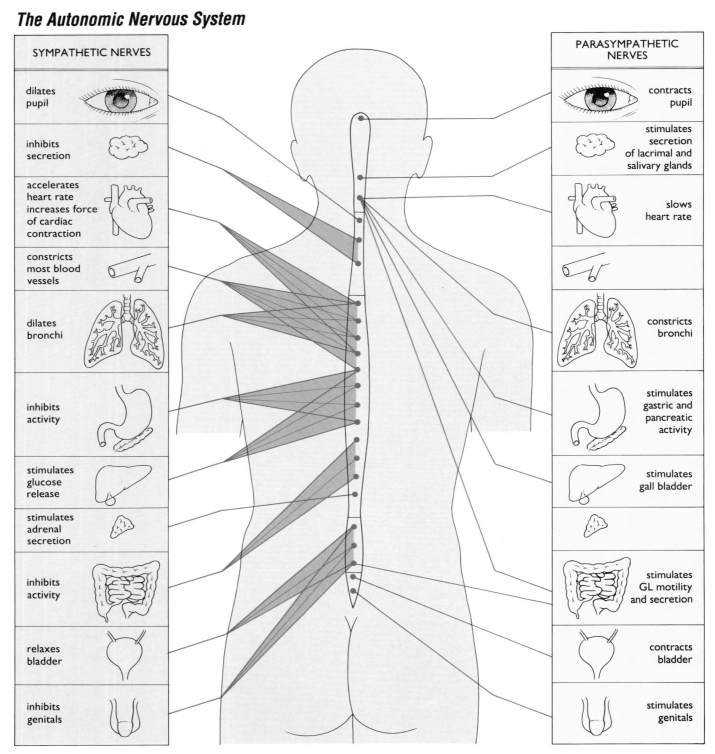

SYMPATHETIC NERVES		PARASYMPATHETIC NERVES	
dilates pupil		contracts pupil	
inhibits secretion		stimulates secretion of lacrimal and salivary glands	
accelerates heart rate increases force of cardiac contraction		slows heart rate	
constricts most blood vessels			
dilates bronchi		constricts bronchi	
inhibits activity		stimulates gastric and pancreatic activity	
stimulates glucose release		stimulates gall bladder	
stimulates adrenal secretion			
inhibits activity		stimulates GL motility and secretion	
relaxes bladder		contracts bladder	
inhibits genitals		stimulates genitals	

Some of our body activities are completely automatic and are controlled by the autonomic nervous system. The autonomic nervous system is responsible for the working of our involuntary muscles. It controls our breathing, our heartbeat and our digestive system as well as a number of other bodily functions. Each of the organs controlled by this system is connected to the sympathetic and parasympathetic neurons which work in opposing ways. The sympathetic neurons accelerate such activity as the heart rate, by the release of adrenalin into the bloodstream. The parasympathetic neuron slows activity down by the release of acetylcholine. All this occurs in the absence of our conscious knowledge or control.

Reflex Actions

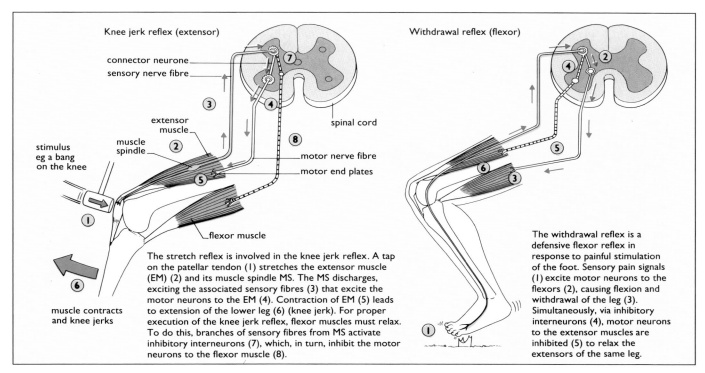

Knee jerk reflex (extensor)

Withdrawal reflex (flexor)

connector neurone
sensory nerve fibre

spinal cord

extensor muscle
muscle spindle
stimulus eg a bang on the knee

motor nerve fibre
motor end plates

flexor muscle

muscle contracts and knee jerks

The stretch reflex is involved in the knee jerk reflex. A tap on the patellar tendon (1) stretches the extensor muscle (EM) (2) and its muscle spindle MS. The MS discharges, exciting the associated sensory fibres (3) that excite the motor neurons to the EM (4). Contraction of EM (5) leads to extension of the lower leg (6) (knee jerk). For proper execution of the knee jerk reflex, flexor muscles must relax. To do this, branches of sensory fibres from MS activate inhibitory interneurons (7), which, in turn, inhibit the motor neurons to the flexor muscle (8).

The withdrawal reflex is a defensive flexor reflex in response to painful stimulation of the foot. Sensory pain signals (1) excite motor neurons to the flexors (2), causing flexion and withdrawal of the leg (3). Simultaneously, via inhibitory interneurons (4), motor neurons to the extensor muscles are inhibited (5) to relax the extensors of the same leg.

Reflex actions are rapid responses to a stimulus by one or more organs. The brain is often aware of the response but is unable to do anything about it. Reflex actions enable the body to protect itself from dangerous or harmful situations. Examples include blinking as a response to a foreign object touching the outside of the eye, and sneezing when a foreign object is in the nose, etc. Reflex actions can also prepare the body for food. For example, the sight of a delicious meal can set our salivary glands working.

Conditioned reflexes

We learn many complex skills during our lifetime. When we first learn to ride a bike we have to give all of our attention and we consciously have to think how to keep our balance, travel in the desired direction, keep pedalling and many other things. As we gain in skill and confidence, many of our movements become almost automatic. We have developed a large number of conditioned reflexes and don't have to consciously think of turning the handlebars, ringing the bell or pedalling.

Conditioned reflexes are reflexes which happen after a pattern of behaviour has been learned and it is set in motion by a stimulus not directly connected with the response. Conditioned reflexes can cause problems if you are trying to change a sporting technique which has become ingrained. Golfers trying to change their swing for instance often find that when they don't concentrate, their old poor swing returns. The conditioned reflex needs to be broken down and a new one established.

The Nervous System in Action

If we wish to perform a particular movement or activity, then the action is said to be voluntary. The cerebral cortex is involved in co-ordinating the many muscles needed to perform the activity. When we are learning a new skill we have to give a great deal of our conscious effort to it. All the parts of our nervous system are involved. As we become more skilful, however, we need to give less conscious attention to it and the skill becomes almost automatic.

The monitoring of the skill is left to our proprioceptors leaving our exteroceptors to take note of other things. This helps to explain how a skilful tennis player can concentrate on exactly where to play his shot (taking into account the position of his opponent, the speed of the ball, the type of playing surface, etc.) and not have to worry about how to play his shot.

THINGS TO DO 5

1 Complete the following sentences by choosing the appropriate word:
   (i) Messages are sent from the brain to the muscle by means of
      A sympathetic nerves
      B autonomic nerves
      C sensory nerves
      D motor nerves

   (ii) The sense organs which give information about the relative positions of different parts of the body are called
      A proprioceptors
      B exteroceptors
      C interoceptors
      D ceptroceptors

   (iii) The part of the brain controlling unconscious activities such as heart rate is the
      A medulla oblongata
      B cerebrum
      C cerebellum
      D thalamus

2 Complete the following sentences:
   (i) Actions over which we exercise control are called .... Body activities which are completely automatic are controlled by the .... nervous system.

   (ii) Information from outside the body is gathered by sense organs and sent to the brain via .... nerves.

   (iii) The .... controls our sense of balance and helps in co-ordination of muscular activities.

3 Explain what is meant by a reflex arc.

4 A hockey player moves to hit a ball.
   (i) Explain how sensory nerves, the spinal cord, brain and motor nerves interact to make the action successful.

   (ii) By referring to conditioned reflexes, explain how the skilful players deal with the situation.

THE ENDOCRINE SYSTEM

Not all co-ordination of our body systems is controlled by the nervous system. Some involves the release of chemicals produced by the endocrine system. The endocrine system is made up of a number of glands which produce hormones. These hormones are released directly into the bloodstream when they are required. Each gland produces its own hormone which can affect particular organs of the body. Hormones are the chemical messengers of the body.

Pituitary gland - lies under the base of the skull. Secretes eight hormones, some of which are responsible for controlling the other endocrine glands of the body. For example, it is a hormone from the pituitary gland which stimulates the thyroid gland to secrete thyroxine. Another pituitary hormone stimulates the gonads (the ovaries and testes) to secrete sex hormones.

Thyroid - produces thyroxine which controls the speed at which oxygen and food products are burned up to produce energy.

Ovaries in female - control the development of secondary sexual characteristics and play an important part during pregnancy.

Pancreas - secretes digestive juices. Also secretes insulin which regulates the amount of sugar in the blood.

Adrenal glands - lie just above and in front of each kidney. The centre of each adrenal gland produces adrenalin and noradrenalin at times of stress. As soon as adrenalin is secreted into the

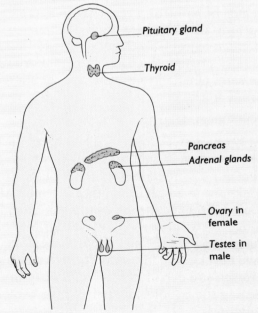

The endocrine glands and their functions

Pituitary gland
Thyroid
Pancreas
Adrenal glands
Ovary in female
Testes in male

bloodstream the cells respond by using up more oxygen and releasing more energy. The heart rate is increased and blood is diverted away from areas such as the digestive system and towards the muscles. The body is prepared for instant action.

Testes in male - control the development of secondary sexual characteristics.

THINGS TO DO 6
Assignments

1 Practical Work - Bones
   In threes, take on the role of the skeleton, examinee and judge. The examinee is asked by the judge to point out the bones shown in the box on the skeleton:

   One mark for each correctly identified bone. Keep your scores!

> scapula, humerus, femur, metacarpals, clavicle, radius, sternum, tarsals, patella, phalanges, fibula, cervical vertebrae, ulna, pelvic girdle, tibia, carpals, metatarsals.

2 Practical Work - Joints
   Examine the joints of your body for:

   Flexion   - angle at the joint becomes smaller.
   Extension - angle at the joint becomes greater.
   Rotation - circular movement of the joint.

   Then complete and extend this table and decide to which type of synovial joint each belongs. (**Reminder**: ball and socket, hinge, saddle, condyloid, pivot.)

Joint	Flexion	Extension	Rotation	Type of joint
Finger				
Thumb				
Wrist				
Elbow				
Shoulder				

3 Practical Work - Muscles

   In pairs, check contraction of major muscles in particular situations by observation and feel. Complete and extend this table.

PARTNER		YOU	
Starting position	Action	Action	Observation
1 Horizontal straight arm	Arm bends at elbow	Resist by holding wrist	Upper arm muscle becomes hard (biceps)
2 Straight arm by side	Raise arm	Resist by holding wrist	
3 Standing upright	Rise on toes		
4 Standing upright	Raise straight leg forward		
5 Lying on floor	Raise legs together 15 cm from the floor and hold		

4 Positioning Body Parts
Trace four copies of the body outline. Mark in the correct places the sets of information shown here:

A **Organs**	B **Bones**	C **Muscles**	D **Joints**
Lungs	Radius	Deltoid	Ball & Socket
Liver	Femur	Quadriceps	Hinge
Heart	Scapula	Soleus	Condyloid
Brain	Patella	Trapezius	Saddle
Stomach	Humerus	Hamstrings	Pivot
Bladder	Sternum	Biceps	
Pancreas	Carpals	Triceps	

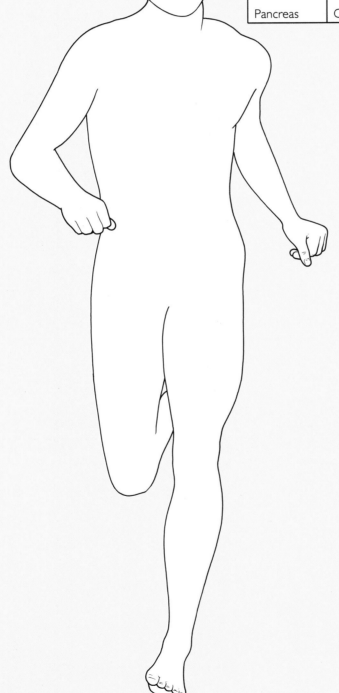

2 FOOD AND DIET

Aims

To gain knowledge and understanding of:
- foods for healthy living
- foods for energy
- energy requirements of activities
- diet and exercise

To develop the skills of:
- planning diets
- analysis
- communication
- data collection and interpretation

The body needs fuel to provide energy for all of its activities as well as to assist in the building and replacing of body tissues. An adult body needs 46 nutrients to remain fit and healthy. A nutrient is a substance essential for the well-being of the human body. Fortunately for us, all 46 nutrients are found in the seven components of a normal diet: carbohydrates, proteins, fats, vitamins, minerals, water and roughage.

CARBOHYDRATES

Carbohydrates are composed of carbon, hydrogen and oxygen and they provide energy for physical activity, transmitting impulses(through the nerves) and for allowing new compounds into the body.

The basic unit of a carbohydrate is a monosaccharide (single sugar) such as glucose, galactose and fructose. Many monosaccharides combine together in food to form larger compounds as shown below.

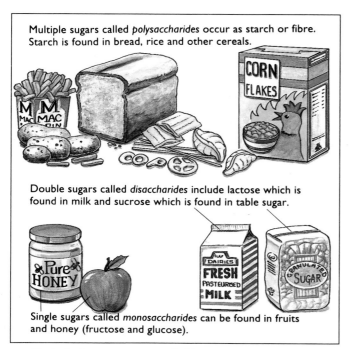

Multiple sugars called *polysaccharides* occur as starch or fibre. Starch is found in bread, rice and other cereals.

Double sugars called *disaccharides* include lactose which is found in milk and sucrose which is found in table sugar.

Single sugars called *monosaccharides* can be found in fruits and honey (fructose and glucose).

Carbohydrates are sugars held together in different ways

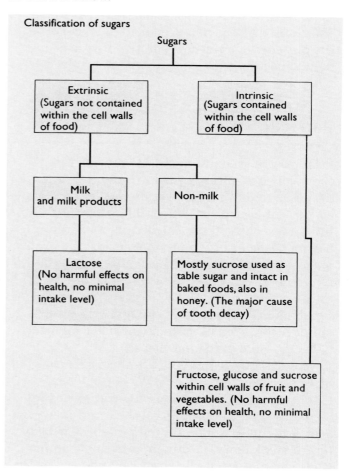

Classification of sugars

Sugars

Extrinsic (Sugars not contained within the cell walls of food)

Intrinsic (Sugars contained within the cell walls of food)

Milk and milk products

Non-milk

Lactose (No harmful effects on health, no minimal intake level)

Mostly sucrose used as table sugar and intact in baked foods, also in honey. (The major cause of tooth decay)

Fructose, glucose and sucrose within cell walls of fruit and vegetables. (No harmful effects on health, no minimal intake level)

Classification of sugars

The process of digestion breaks the disaccharides and polysaccharides into monosaccharides which can be absorbed into the body.

Carbohydrates taken in the form of starch are more beneficial to us than the foods which contain large amounts of simple or refined sugars. This is because the starchy foods contain many vitamins and minerals as well as fibre. Sugary foods contain little in the way of vitamins or fibre but rather a lot of fat.

We should aim to take 80% of our carbohydrates in the form of starchy foods such as bread, rice and other cereals. We currently take up to 18% of our sugar in the form of non-milk extrinsic or refined sugars. This should be reduced to 10% at the most.

Carbohydrates give us energy as they provide the sugar needed for muscular contraction. Muscles can obtain energy from the breakdown of either sugar or fat. Sugar is the more efficient fuel of the two as it needs less oxygen to work. It is of particular importance when the body is working very hard and there is a shortage of oxygen. As the intensity of activity lessens then less sugar will be used as the muscles begin to burn fat in the presence of oxygen. When the body is at rest then almost no muscle sugar will be involved.

PROTEINS

Proteins are used in the body to provide the chemical substances needed to build cells and tissues. Proteins themselves are made from amino acids. Amino acids are the building blocks of all the tissues of the body. The body of an adult person needs 21 different amino acids. It can only make 12 of them itself. It has to extract the other nine from the food we eat. These nine are called the essential amino acids.

Animal protein contains all nine essential amino acids. Animal proteins include lean meat, fish, egg white, milk and cheese.

Most vegetable proteins are short of one or more essential amino acids. We normally eat several types of vegetable proteins at any one meal so it is easy to obtain all the essential amino acids even if we eat no animal protein. The body has to break down all protein into single amino acids before they can be absorbed and used by the body. It therefore makes no difference whether the

protein has come originally from lamb, fish or peanuts.

Protein is never the provider of immediate energy. There is little point in eating extra protein because you are training for sport. Protein is the hardest foodstuff for the body to process and any excess cannot be stored but is either deaminated, forming urea, in the liver or converted into extra body fat.

Some examples of proteins

FATS

Dietary fats are complex, organic substances which are not soluble in water. There are two basic types of fat, visible and invisible.

1 **Visible or saturated fats** are those which are solid or hard at room temperature. Foods very high in saturated fats include butter, suet and lard. Meat, meat products, cheese and cream also contain a high percentage of saturated fats.

2 **Invisible or polyunsaturated fats** are those which are very soft or even liquid at room temperature. They are found naturally in nuts, fish and many types of seeds.

Two of these unsaturated fats, linoleic and linolenic, must be eaten in the diet and are called essential fatty acids.

Some examples of visible or saturated fats

Some examples of invisible or polyunsaturated fats

Fat is the main muscle fuel when resting or asleep. It does not have to be produced directly from dietary fat however. Excess carbohydrates entering the body are converted into fat and stored for future use. This fat can be converted back into muscle fuel if needed.

Saturated fats are known to raise blood cholesterol levels. Cholesterol is a type of fat found mainly in animal produce (for example egg yolks). The body produces its own cholesterol and any excess gained through diet is liable to settle on the walls of blood vessels and impair circulation.

Some nutritionists argue that polyunsaturated fats actually help to lower the levels of cholesterol in the blood. Most nutritionists agree that we all eat too much fat.

VITAMINS

Vitamins are organic compounds which help to regulate the many chemical reactions that are continuously taking place in the human body. Although only minute quantities of these compounds are needed, the body is unable to produce its own supply and so they have to be obtained from the food we eat.

When saturated, they are dissolved in water or fat and go directly into the bloodstream from the intestine.

Vitamins combine with other chemicals in the body to form enzymes. These enzymes act as catalysts. This means that they often cause or help reactions to take place although they themselves are not chemically involved in the reactions. Vitamins are protective substances. Lack of them in the body can result in deficiency diseases.

Although over 50 vitamins have now been 'discovered' it is agreed that 12 of these are essential for the human diet. We need small but regular doses of all of them. A well balanced diet will provide all 12 essential vitamins.

There is no point in taking excess quantities of vitamins. Water soluble vitamins (B and C) cannot be stored in the body and so it is essential that they are included frequently in our diet. Any excess will be simply passed out of the body in the urine.

The fat-soluble vitamins (A,D,E and K) however can be stored in large amounts in the body tissues and any short term lack of them in our diet would probably not cause problems. The liver, kidneys and heart can all be damaged through an excessive intake of fat soluble vitamins.

MINERALS

Minerals are basic elements which are found in the soil and in the air. They are essential for life. They are absorbed by plants as they grow.We get our minerals by eating plants as well as the animals which have also eaten plants. When swallowed they go directly into the bloodstream through the walls of the intestines. We need seven minerals (called macrominerals) in quite large amounts. We need another 14 in minute quantities. We call these *trace minerals*. Some of the most important ones are shown in the chart on page 41.

Sources and functions of vitamins

Vitamin	Foods rich in it	Necessary for	7-10 yrs RNI*	19-50 yrs RNI*	
				Male	Female
A (Retinol)	Milk, butter, eggs, oily fish, cod or halibut liver oil, spinach, carrots	Keeps skin and bones healthy; prevents infection of nose and throat; helps good vision	500 ug/d**	700 ug/d	600 ug/d
B₁ (Thiamin)	Liver, pork, green vegetables, wholemeal cereals	Energy production in all cells	0.7 mg/d***	1.0 mg/d	0.8 mg/d
B₂ (Riboflavin)	Milk, eggs, cheese, green vegetables, liver, kidney	Helps break down food to provide energy; helps good growth	1.0 mg/d	1.3 mg/d	1.1 mg/d
B₃ (Niacin)	Wholewheat cereals, meat, fish	Helps break down food to provide energy; keeps skin healthy	12 mg/d	17 mg/d	13 mg/d
B₆ (Pyridoxine)	Most foods	Helps break down food to provide energy	1.0 mg/d	1.4 mg/d	1.2 mg/d
B₁₂ (Cobalamin)	All animal products, especially liver	Helps to make new red blood cells; keeps nerves healthy, helps growth	1.0 ug/d	1.5 ug/d	1.5 ug/d
Folic acid (one of the Vitamin B complex)	Liver, fresh vegetables	Helps to produce red blood cells	150 ug/d	200 ug/d	200 ug/d
C (Ascorbic acid)	Fresh vegetables and fruit, particularly citrus fruit	Helps heal wounds; keeps gums and teeth healthy; protects against colds	30 mg/d	40 mg/d	40 mg/d
D (Calciferol)	Oily fish and fish oils, eggs, butter, (sunlight)	Builds up bones and teeth	After the age of 3 most people can manufacture sufficient vitamin D from sunlight		
E (Tocopheral)	Most foods but particularly wheat-germ and dark-green leafy vegetables	Helps to protect cells from damage and degeneration	Depends upon the amount of polyunsaturated fat in the body as it acts as an antioxidant		
K (Phytomenadione)	Fresh green vegetables and liver	Essential for the proper clotting of blood	Little research carried out on this but safe level appears to be 1 ug/kg body weight/day		

*   Reference Nutrient Intake (RNI) is the amount of nutrient which is enough for at least 97% of the population
**   ug = microgram or one-millionth of 1 gram
*** mg = milligram or one-thousandth of 1 gram

Sources and functions of minerals

Mineral	Sources	Importance	7-10 yrs RNI*	19-50 yrs RNI*	
				Male	Female
Calcium	Milk and milk products, salmon, sardines, beans, brocolli, green vegetables	Hardening of bones and teeth; muscle contraction; clotting of the blood	13.8 mmol/d**	17.5 mmol/d	17.5 mmol/d
Phosphorus	Milk, cheese, meat, fish, poultry, eggs, peanuts, oatmeal	Bone and tooth formation; energy production	13.8 mmol/d	17.5 mmol/d	17.5 mmol/d
Magnesium	Green vegetables, nuts, whole grains, shellfish	Function of nerves; muscle contraction; storage and release of energy	8.0 mmol/d	12.3 mmol/d	10.0 mmol/d
Sodium	Sodium chloride (salt), cheese, milk, bread, cereals, spices	Contraction of muscles; transmission of nerve impulses; maintenance of body fluid balance	50 mmol/d	70 mmol/d	70 mmol/d
Potassium	Milk, bananas, oranges, vegetables, meat	Function of nerves; muscle contraction	50 mmol/d	90 mmol/d	90 mmol/d
Chloride		Balancing sodium and potassium in cells	50 mmol/d	70 mmol/d	70 mmol/d
Iron	Liver, meat, egg yolk, whole grain or enriched breads and cereals, green vegetables	Production of haemoglobin in red blood cells; delivering oxygen to body tissues to provide energy	160 umol/d***	160 umol/d	260 umol/d (supplemented if high menstrual loss)
Zinc	Seafood, meats, nuts, eggs	Growth; healthy skin; wound healing	110 umol/d	145 umol/d	140 umol/d
Copper	Liver, shellfish, nuts, whole grain cereals	Production of haemoglobin in red blood cells; bone structure	11 umol/d	19 umol/d	19 umol/d
Selenium	Seafood, meat, wheat cereals	Protecting cells from damage	0.4 umol/d	0.9 umol/d	0.8 umol/d
Iodine	Dairy products, seafood, drinking water	Health of thyroid gland which makes hormones	0.9 umol/d	1.0 umol/d	1.1 umol/d
Fluorine	Tea, coffee, soya-beans, sodium fluoride (added to some water supplies)	Bone and teeth formation	Although not essential for human function, it is put into water supplies at 1 part/million in order to reduce tooth decay		

*   Reference Nutrient Intake (RNI) is the amount of mineral which is enough for at least 97% of the population
**   mmol (millimole) = the amount of an element equal to the atomic weight or molecular weight in gram $\times$ 10⁻³
*** umol (micromole) = one thousandth of a millimole

DIETARY FIBRE (NON-STARCH POLYSACCHARIDES)

The bulk of most fruits and vegetables is made up of fibre or cellulose. It is the non digestible carbohydrate material that forms the skeleton of plants and is also found on the outside of seeds, peas, beans and vegetables. It provides a bulky mass for the muscles of the intestines to work on. This makes it easier for the food to be kept moving and finally expelled from the system. This reduces pressure in the intestines and lessens the risk of constipation. It is now also known that many of the substances which make up the dietary fibre can be digested and absorbed into the intestines. These substances lessen the risk of intestinal disorders and related illness. We should all eat more dietary fibre. High fibre food usually contains fewer calories but more bulk. It also needs more chewing. This makes you feel fuller, and reduces your appetite. It also reduces the energy you absorb from food. This will help you slim.

The fibre content of a variety of foods

Food	% fibre
Wheat bran	44.0
Coconut (fresh)	13.6
Cornflakes	11.0
Peanuts	8.0
Muesli	7.4
Sweet corn (canned)	5.7
Brown rice	5.5
Brown bread	5.1
Spring greens (boiled)	3.8
Bananas	3.4
White flour	3.0
Oranges	2.0
Lettuce	1.5
Porridge (cooked)	0.8

WATER

Water is the most essential nutrient. About 80% of the weight of a new born child is made up of water. Even in adulthood it accounts for approximately two thirds of our weight. We could all survive for a number of weeks without food, but four to five days without water would kill any human. Water is the main component of cells and blood. The body needs a constant supply of it. Approximately 50% of our fluid intake comes from our food. Chicken for example is composed of about 68% water and green vegetables are more than 90% water.

It is still necessary to drink plenty of fluids. An inactive person needs to drink about six glasses of fluid a day. A sportsman or sportswoman in training would need to drink much more, as up to 20 pints of water can be lost in a single day. If you lose too much water from the body and it is not replaced, then the building of body tissues, temperature regulation and food production are all affected. A loss of only 2-3% can seriously affect sporting performance whilst the loss of 10% can result in severe dehydration.

Water provides no energy (kilojoules or calories) but it is bulky. There appears to be no danger in drinking too much water.

THE ENERGY PROVIDERS

Carbohydrate, protein and fat all provide the body with potential chemical energy. As food is eaten, digested and absorbed this potential energy is converted into energy which the body can use to keep itself warm, to provide movement, to ensure effective internal communication and many other vital functions. This conversion of energy takes place in the mitochondria of every cell. The end products of carbohydrate, protein and fat are burned up in the presence of oxygen and adenosine diphosphate (ADP) in a process called oxidation. Oxidation enables the release of energy as well as the production of water and carbon dioxide. Some of the energy released is trapped in the high energy bonds of a substance called adenosine triphosphate (ATP) which is the energy currency of the body. The remaining energy is given off as heat.

How are nutrients broken down in the body?

The liver controls more than 500 reactions which activate our metabolism.

A small number of its functions are:

1 Stores glucose in the form of glycogen. The glucose is released and sent to the muscles as a potential fuel when there is a demand.

2 Breaks down excess protein in the form of amino acids. It changes them into nitrogen and organic acids. The nitrogen is changed into ammonia and expelled by the kidneys in the urine as urea. (This process is called deamination.)

Amino acids can also be synthesised back into proteins for body building purposes. Finally they may also be released into the bloodstream for use by other body tissues.

3 Stores minerals such as iron and copper. It also stores and releases a number of vitamins.

4 Produces bile which is necessary for the breakdown of fats in the duodenum.

When food reaches the duodenum the *pancreas* releases an alkaline juice which neutralises any stomach acids and also helps to break down the food. Protein is broken down even further to amino acids by trypsin and chymotrypsin. Carbohydrates are broken down into small sugar molecules. Fats are turned into small units by the action of bile and are then split by the enzyme to form fatty acids and glycerol.

In the *mouth* the enzyme ptyalin present in saliva converts starch to maltose.

The *gall bladder* stores and concentrates bile. Bile is released into the intestine when food arrives.

In the *stomach* protein is broken down into smaller units called polypeptides by the action of the enzyme pepsin. Very little fat is broken down by stomach juices. Carbohydrate is not digested in the stomach.

The *small intestine* is involved in both digestion and absorption. Digestion is completed in the small intestine and the digested food is absorbed into the bloodstream through the millions of villi which line the intestinal walls.

The *colon* absorbs water and electrolytes from the food remains.

Carbohydrates may be: burned up as fuel in the liver; stored in the liver as glycogen; transported as glucose in the blood to other tissues immediately to be used as an energy supply or converted into glycogen to be used later; converted into fat to serve as an energy store.

The Measurement of Energy

All energy transfer produces heat. Nutritionists have developed ways of accurately measuring this heat and therefore the amount of energy being produced. In calorimetry (the measurement of energy expenditure) a calorie is defined as the heat required to raise one gram of water by one degree centigrade. Measurements are calculated in kilocalories (one kcal = 1000 cals) as the calorie unit is so small.

Most current research uses the more accurate energy unit called a joule. A joule is the energy expended when one kilogram is moved one metre by a force of one newton.

1000 joules	=	1 kilojoule (kJ)
1000 kJ	=	1 megajoule (MJ)
1 kcal	=	4.18 kJ

During the most vigorous of physical activities, 75 - 80% of the energy being used is released as heat because people are relatively inefficient as machines. Indeed an old fashioned steam engine is more efficient.

By measuring heat production it is possible to assess energy expenditure. It is a complicated and

time consuming process however and so researchers have looked for more practical ways of assessing energy expenditure. Oxygen is needed for the oxidation process and there is a direct relationship between oxygen consumption and heat production. Carbon dioxide is always given off as a by-product. So by measuring the body's consumption of oxygen and generation of carbon dioxide it is possible to get a very accurate measurement of the various fuels that are being burned off by the tissues as well as to measure the rate of energy expenditure.

How much energy do we need?

A certain amount of energy is needed just to keep the body alive and healthy. This is called the basal metabolic rate (BMR) and can be estimated from body weight for different age and sex groups. For a 65 kg man, BMR will be about 7560 kJ/day, whilst for a 55 kg woman, BMR will be about 5980 kJ/day.

A person's total energy needs are determined by his BMR and his physical activity level (PAL). The chart below shows the energy expenditure of a wide variety of activities. Many of these activities can only be continued for a limited period of time however and an individual's PAL is likely to be much less than any particular PAR.

Energy expenditure of various activities of moderate duration* grouped according to physical activity ratio (PAR)

PAR 1.2	(1.0 to 1.4)	
	Lying at rest:	reading
	Sitting at rest:	watching TV; reading; writing; calculating; playing cards; listening to radio; eating;
PAR 1.6	(1.5 to 1.8)	
	Sitting:	sewing, knitting; playing piano, driving.
	Standing:	preparing vegetables; washing dishes; ironing; general office and laboratory work.
	Standing at rest:	
PAR 2.1	(1.9 to 2.4)	
	Standing:	mixed household chores (dusting and cleaning); washing small clothes; cooking activities; hairdressing; playing snooker, bowling.
PAR 2.8	(2.5 to 3.3)	
	Standing:	dressing and undressing; showering; 'hoovering'; making beds;
	Walking:	3.4 km/hour; playing cricket;
	Industrial:	tailoring; shoemaking; electrical; machine tool; painting and decorating.
PAR 3.7	(3.4 to 4.4)	
	Standing:	mopping floor; gardening; cleaning windows; playing table tennis; sailing;
	Walking:	4.6km/hour, golf;
	Industrial:	motor vehicle repairs; carpentry; chemical; joinery; bricklaying.
PAR 4.8	(4.5 to 5.9)	
	Standing:	polishing furniture; chopping wood; heavy gardening; volleyball;
	Exercise:	dancing; moderate swimming; gentle cycling; slow jogging;
	Occupational:	labouring; hoeing; road construction; digging and shovelling; felling trees.
PAR 6.9	(6.0 to 7.9)	
	Walking:	uphill with load or cross-country; climbing stairs;
	Exercise:	average jogging; cycling;
	Sports:	football; more energetic swimming ; tennis; skiing.

Activities continuous for period of 30 to 60 minutes.
Source: COMA Report

Using the data collected from a large number of individuals the average energy requirements have been estimated for the population at large.

Estimated average requirements for energy (EARs)

Age	EARs MJ/day (Kcal/day)	
	Males	**Females**
0–3 months	2.28 (545)	2.16 (515)
10–12 months	3.85 (920)	3.61 (865)
1–3 years	5.15 (1230)	4.86 (1165)
4–6 years	7.16 (1715)	6.46 (1545)
7–10 years	8.24 (1970)	7.28 (1740)
11–14 years	9.27 (2220)	7.91 (1845)
15–18 years	11.51 (2755)	8.83 (2110)
19–50 years	10.60 (2550)	8.10 (1940)
51–59 years	10.60 (2550)	8.00 (1900)
60–64 years	9.93 (2380)	7.99 (1900)
65–74 years	9.71 (2330)	7.96 (1900)
75+ years	8.77 (2100)	7.61 (1810)

Source: COMA Report

The Energy Equation

As long as the number of kilojoules consumed equals the number of kilojoules we burn, then the individual will remain the same weight. Any excess kilojoules in the form of nutrients are converted into body fat. This is stored just below the surface of the skin as well as around the inner body organs.

If your body needs more energy than your diet is producing, then energy is taken from the stored body fats and you lose weight. One pound of body fat is equivalent to approximately 14650kJ.

Body fatness can be calculated by using the following formula in order to produce a Body Mass Index.

$$\text{Body Mass Index (BMI)} = \frac{\text{Weight in kilograms}}{(\text{Height in metres})^2}$$

For example, a person who is 1.79 metres tall and weighs 75 kg would have a BMI of $75/1.79^2$ = 23.41.

A person with BMI between 20 -25 can be said to be within the normal range. A person with BMI between 25 and 30 can be described as overweight whilst one with BMI greater than 30 can be said to be obese. In Great Britain between 1980 and 1987 the proportion of adults with BMI in excess of 25 increased from 35 to 40% and of those with BMI in excess of 30 from 7 to 10%.

Fat accumulates slowly in the body and also takes some time to be removed. It is relatively easy to put on weight but more difficult to lose it. Being even mildly overweight, 10% or more, can increase the risk of heart, circulation and other health problems.

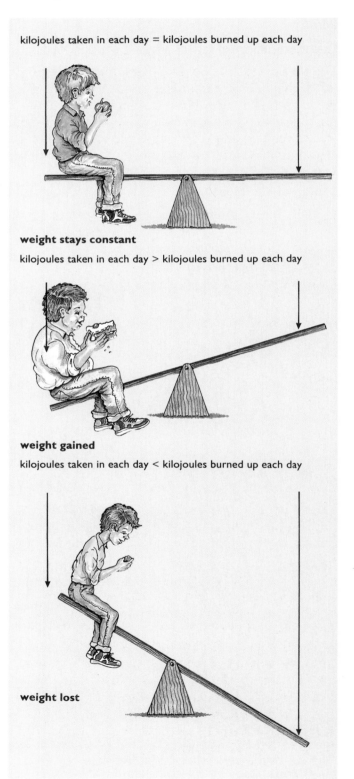

kilojoules taken in each day = kilojoules burned up each day

weight stays constant

kilojoules taken in each day > kilojoules burned up each day

weight gained

kilojoules taken in each day < kilojoules burned up each day

weight lost

The Energy in Food

Nutrients vary in the amount of energy that they provide.

1 gram of carbohydrate	contains 17.1 kJ
1 gram of protein	contains 18.2kJ
1 gram of fat	contains 38.9 kJ

Most of the food which we eat is not pure fat or pure carbohydrate or pure protein. It is usually a mixture of all the nutrients. The amount of energy or kilojoules food contains depends upon how much of the energy giving nutrients it contains. This is shown in the chart below. It is possible to get the same energy from either a tablespoon of butter or two heads of lettuce.

The energy in food

Food	kJ/gram
Margarine	32.2
Butter	31.2
Peanuts (roasted)	24.5
Chocolate (milk)	24.2
Cake (plain)	18.0
Sugar (white)	16.5
Sausages (pork)	15.5
Cornflakes	15.3
Rice	15.0
Bread (white)	10.6
Chips	9.9
Chicken (roast)	7.7
Eggs (fresh)	6.6
Potatoes (boiled)	3.3
Milk	2.7
Apple	1.9
Beer (bottled)	1.2
Cabbage (boiled)	0.34

The three energy giving nutrients differ not only in the amount of energy they provide. They also vary in the cost of processing them in the body. The body can turn dietary fat into body fat so easily that only 6% of the kilojoules you eat in food are used up in the process compared with 15% for carbohydrates and 25% for proteins. Using this information we can see that carbohydrates provide the highest bulk for the fewest kilojoules. Protein provides the next highest bulk and fat the least.

A HEALTHY DIET

The 1991 Department of Health's report by the Committee on Medical Aspects of Food policy (The COMA Report) was the most comprehensive study of nutrition to date. It highlighted many of the problems relating to poor dietary intake as well as giving detailed advice on levels of 33 nutrients according to age, sex and activity level.

The COMA report recommends the following for a healthy diet:

Carbohydrates 50%	of which at least 39% should be in the form of intrinsic and milk sugars and starch; Extrinsic sugars (sugars not naturally incorporated into the cellular structure of food, eg. sucrose) should not exceed about 60 grammes a day or 10% of total dietary energy.
Protein 10 - 15%	Care should be taken to avoid excessive consumption of animal proteins because of the high saturated fat content. We should try to obtain a greater proportion of our protein from vegetable sources.
Fat 35%	This compares with our current level of 38 - 40% Saturated fat should be cut from the current level of 16% to no more than 11% of our daily intake.
Dietary fibre	intake should be increased to 18 grammes a day from the present average of 13 grammes.
Salt	(Sodium chloride) intake should be decreased from the current 3.2 grammes per day to a maximum of 1.6 grammes.
Vitamin C	intake should be increased by one third from the present 30mg a day to 40mg.
Calcium	intake should be increased from the present 500mg a day to 700mg a day.

Many studies of present eating habits show that this balanced diet is not being followed to any great extent in developed countries. It is also clear that there are links between our diet and a number of serious health disorders. For example, high sugar intake and tooth decay; low fibre diet and cancer of the bowel, high fat intake and heart disease.

Why do some people find it particularly hard to lose weight?

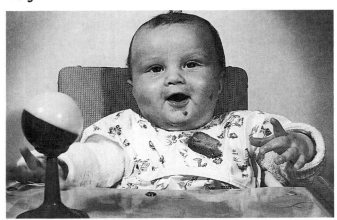

Research shows that we get our basic shape from our parents. If both parents are overweight then there is an 80% chance that any children will also be overweight. If only one parent is overweight then the chance will go down to 40%. It is not clear whether this is mainly a genetic effect or a result of learning eating habits from parents.

When we gain weight the fat cells in our body become larger but they do not increase in number. The actual number of fat cells in the body differs from person to person. They are formed during infancy and early childhood. The number which are formed appears to depend on our eating and activity patterns during these times. If the formation of fat cells can be kept down during these critical times then weight control is less of a problem in later life.

DIET AND EXERCISE

To lose weight permanently it is important not only to consume less calories but also to take more exercise. There are a number of very sound reasons for this:

1 When you diet, up to 25% of your weight loss can be due to the atrophy, that is the wastage of muscle tissue. If you then return to your old eating habits and put on weight again you will put it on as fat. This means that you will have a poorer muscle to fat ratio than before your diet. This muscle loss will apply to inner body muscles including the heart as well as to skeletal muscles.

2 Muscle weighs more than fat but takes up less space. Slimmers who are involved in an exercise programme may well find that their total weight loss is small. They will also find that they will be slimmer than before.

3 Regular exercise helps to maintain muscle tone. This also uses up calories and aids weight loss. The body also continues to burn up calories for several hours after exercising has finished. Regular exercise increases your basal metabolism.

4 Exercise is also an appetite suppressant. When you work your body hard for more than a few minutes then fat is pumped into the bloodstream. The muscles use this fat rather than the sugar in the bloodstream. This means that the blood sugar levels are not reduced and you do not feel as hungry as you otherwise might.

5 Regular exercise also appears to increase the efficiency of the digestive system. Food is processed more quickly and efficiently than in inactive people.

NUTRITION DURING TRAINING AND COMPETITION

The main purpose of fitness training is to put the body under controlled stress so that it gradually adapts to the stress and is therefore able to function better during competition. The body needs energy to function at any level. The more stress it is put under, in the form of exercise, then the more energy it requires. The muscles being used during exercise get much of their energy from the glycogen stores within the muscles and the liver.

In fact when the body is worked very hard the only energy that can be made immediately available is from glycogen. The body's stores of carbohydrates (and therefore glycogen) are limited however. If it were only able to use glycogen obtained from carbohydrate then it would use up all supplies after 70-80 minutes of marathon running.

When the body is being worked at a lower level then it is also possible to obtain energy from the free fatty acids which are released from the fat deposits stored beneath the skin. At lower level activity the body burns a mixture of carbohydrates and fats. The value of this alternative supply of energy becomes clear when the cost of producing energy by the different means is calculated.

When the muscles work anaerobically then only 2 units of ATP are generated for every unit of glycogen. When glucose is used in the process (obtained either directly from the muscles or provided by the liver) then 36 - 38 units of ATP are generated for every unit of glycogen. When the body is able to make use of the free fatty acids then between 80 - 200 units of ATP are generated for every unit of fatty acids.

Endurance training teaches the body to use proportionately more fat during exercise. It must be realised that whatever the level of exercise being performed some carbohydrate is used.

Every time you train you lower the stores of glycogen within the body. It can take up to 48 hours for resting levels to be restored. Heavy training sessions can delay the recovery of glycogen stores to a considerable extent. It can take marathon runners up to a week to get back to their resting levels of glycogen.

The levels of glycogen can be restored more quickly following training if certain simple steps are followed:

1 Aim for a carbohydrate rich diet. This will mean that 50 - 60 % of your total intake should be in the form of carbohydrate. Although it is true that both simple and complex carbohydrates will restore glycogen levels, by eating more of the starchy foods, rich in unrefined complex carbohydrates, you will ensure that you get a diet high in fibre, vitamins and minerals and low in fat.

2 Vary the type of training that you do. If you intersperse hard training days with lighter training sessions then you will ensure that your glycogen reserves are not exhausted. Also ensure that you have rest days. It is better to have a rest day after every three days of training rather than to restrict yourself to one day a week.

3 Muscle glycogen supplies are replenished most rapidly if carbohydrates are taken in the first hour after training. Attempt to have something to eat even if you do not feel particularly hungry.

There is no doubt that a good diet may make its greatest impact on your performance by helping you to recover more effectively between training sessions.

You must ensure that you cut down on your training some days before you intend to take part in any competition. This is to ensure that your glycogen stores are at the highest possible level.

Carbohydrate Loading and Endurance Events

Some endurance athletes, particularly marathon runners, adapt their eating pattern for the week or so before an important event. They follow their last hard training session with a diet which is low in carbohydrate. This diet is maintained for two or three days. They then eat a diet which is very high in carbohydrates for a few days leading up to the competition.

Some endurance athletes adapt their eating patterns for a week or so before a race

There is some evidence to show that the body makes up for the initial lack of glycogen available to it during the low carbohydrate period by absorbing much greater amounts of carbohydrate during the high carbohydrate period. The body appears to overcompensate and therefore has a more than normal supply of glycogen available for use during the actual competition. This would have the effect of allowing the athlete to use glycogen as an energy source for a longer period of time.

As endurance training enables the athlete to get more of his energy from the free fatty acids and thus save his glycogen stores, it would seem that carbohydrate loading would prove more beneficial to the less well trained athlete.

The latest research indicates that it is not necessary to go through the low carbohydrate stage of this cycle. As long as you cut down on the intensity of training which you normally do as the competition approaches and continue with a high carbohydrate diet then your supplies of glycogen will be at a higher level than normal. The last really hard training session should be at least seven days before competition. The intensity of training should then be steadily tapered so that the last two days become rest days.

Start increasing the level of carbohydrate in your diet at least five days before the event. If you already have a diet rich in unrefined, starchy, carbohydrates then just increase the amount that you are eating and cut down on any fat.

Fluid and the Athlete

The body uses a variety of radiation, convection and conduction mechanisms to ensure that it maintains its most effective working temperature (between 37 - 38 degrees C). These mechanism are put under particular stress when hard physical activity is continued for any length of time. Up to 80% of the energy available for use is given up as heat and so the internal body temperature would rise very rapidly if the process of sweating was not started.

Sweat is a dilute version of blood and it is secreted onto the skin surface and allowed to evaporate. Up to two litres of sweat can be lost during strenuous activity in a hot environment. For every one litre of sweat that is evaporated, some 2500 kJ of heat energy is released from the body. Heat is only lost if the sweat actually evaporates on the skin surface. If it just drops off the person then it has not helped the body to lose heat.

If the fluid lost through sweating is not replaced and yet activity is continued then the body loses its ability to control its temperature.

As more fluid is lost as sweating continues, the blood loses a proportion of water and therefore its overall volume. The amount of blood pumped by the heart is reduced as a result. The heart beats faster in order to compensate and the blood flow to the skin is further reduced as the working muscles demand more.

Sweating is reduced and therefore the body temperature rises to a dangerous level. The athlete can suffer from heat exhaustion.

To ensure that you do not suffer from heat exhaustion you should take the following simple steps:

• Get your body used to taking plenty of fluid before, during and after exercise. Follow the same pattern when you are involved in competition.

• Wear suitable clothing and be sure to acclimatize properly if you are competing in unusual climatic conditions.

Although large amounts of water are emptied more readily from the intestines it is wiser to drink water little and often. There is less chance of feeling uncomfortably full. Colder solutions empty from the stomach more rapidly than warm ones.

It is very important to take plenty of fluid before, during and after the competition

Although little water is likely to be absorbed if you are working near your maximum level, you should still take fluid throughout a competition or training session.

Research indicates that there is no significant loss of electrolytes (salts absorbed in the body's fluids) during hard exercise, in fact their concentration level is likely to increase. There is therefore no need to replace lost electrolytes and salt tablets should not be taken. It is probably wiser to stick to pure water when taking on extra fluid. Although commercial products can give you additional readily absorbed carbohydrate they can also induce a feeling of nausea and stomach discomfort.

Summary

Whether you are a high level competitor or just someone who enjoys sport at a modest level, to remain healthy the following guidelines should be followed:

1 Eat less fats Cut down the intake of : visible fats in the form of cream, butter, margarine and fat on meat and fried foods; invisible fat in cakes, biscuits, puddings, pastry and ice cream.

2 Eat less sugar Sugar is not necessary in our diet. Limit the amount of sweets, soft drinks, cakes and biscuits, puddings and jam you eat. Beware of all the hidden sugar contained in manufactured foods.

3 Eat more fibre and more filler foods Eat plenty of breakfast cereals made from whole grains, wholemeal bread, potatoes, rice and pasta, potato skins, pizzas, curries and spaghetti.

4 Eat more fruit and vegetables Try to have some fruit and vegetables at least three times a day. As well as providing fibre, minerals and vitamins, they all contain a good measure of water and provide a lot of bulk without a great deal of calories.

5 Eat less salt There is a positive link between a high salt intake and high blood pressure. Do not add salt to your meals.

6 Drink less alcohol.

7 Control total energy intake and finally, **take plenty of exercise.**

THINGS TO DO

I Which of the following statements are true and which are false?

(i) We should aim to take 80% of our carbohydrates in the form of sugar.

(ii) Protein provides instant energy for the body.

(iii) Polyunsaturated fats are found in fish.

(iv) Athletes need more vitamins whenever they take part in vigorous activity.

(v) You can obtain vitamin C from fresh green vegetables.

(vi) Your intake of protein, vitamins and minerals will increase if you eat more potatoes.

(vii) You can lose up to 8 litres of water a day when training vigorously.

(viii) There is more energy in I gram of fat than in I gram of carbohydrate.

(ix) You must exercise in order to lose weight.

(x) After exercise your levels of glycogen can be restored by eating a carbohydrate rich diet

2 Keep a record of everything you eat and drink for one week. Analyse your intake by attempting to break it down into fats, carbohydrates, proteins, vitamins and roughage.

Calculate your daily kilojoule intake. Do you think it is a balanced diet?

3 Complete the following table.

	Protein	Carbohydrate	Fat	Vitamins	Roughage	Minerals
Milk						
Chicken						
Orange						
Cabbage						
Peanuts						

4 Underline three foods in the following list which are relatively high in protein content:

beef cheese fish lettuce tea

5 Rank the following activities in terms of their energy requirements:

badminton, squash, walking, downhill skiing, golf, swimming, tennis, darts, cricket (batting).

6 You have entered a marathon which is to take place in two months time. Explain how this would influence your diet during training and in the week prior to the event.

7 'The air we breathe and the food we eat are the raw materials which our body converts into energy.' Explain the way in which this happens.

8 State where glycogen is stored in the body. Give one reason why glycogen is stored in the body.

9 Explain how diet and exercise affect weight and how they may contribute to general good health.

10 Interview one of your parents or grandparents. Determine the food and drink which they have consumed during a typical day. Relate this to their activity patterns during this day. Discuss with them the effect this diet and activity pattern will have on their weight.

3 PHYSICAL FITNESS

Aims

To gain knowledge and understanding of:

◆ physical fitness
◆ principles and methods of training

◆ analysis, assessment and evaluation of a variety of training programmes
◆ training programme construction

Fitness means different things to different people. A man who is fit for his work as a taxi driver may be dangerously unfit for a game of squash and a marathon runner may be unfit for lifting weights. If you are asked the question, 'Are you fit?' you should always answer with another question 'Fit for what?'.

Fitness is a blend of a number of physical qualities. We all need these qualities to a greater or lesser extent.

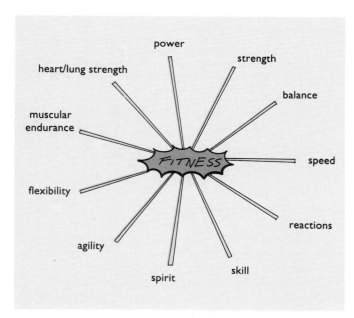

The ingredients of fitness

There is a minimal level of fitness which we all need to maintain:

- We need sufficient energy in the form of food and oxygen to enable the body to work effectively.
- We need muscles which are strong enough to support us and enable us to move ourselves and the things about us.

- We need to be able to move our joints through their full range of movement and so use our body in the way it was designed to be used.
- We need to be able to act skilfully, work efficiently and use the minimum of effort.
- We need to be able to react and move quickly and so protect ourselves in potentially dangerous situations.
- We need to develop sufficient determination and motivation to see things through even if they become difficult.

FITNESS AND EXERCISE

Exercise helps to make you fit. It is good for the heart and it makes you feel good. Fitness and exercise go together. Fitness is an active state. It is achieved by movement and by effort. It cannot be gained by reading about it, thinking about it or seeing examples of it on television.

The cells of the body do not like change. It is the task of the various control systems to keep conditions in the body as constant as possible. This constant state is called *homeostasis*. Homeostasis is threatened whenever we take part in any vigorous activity. The working muscles need extra fuel and oxygen to keep going. All waste products must be removed and any rise in the body temperature must be controlled. A number of body systems respond to physical activity to keep the body working smoothly. If the physical activity is repeated on a regular basis the body systems adapt to cope more efficiently with these demands being placed upon them. This is how the body is trained.

What happens to our body when we exercise?

The circulatory system must circulate the blood (and therefore oxygen) more quickly. It must also get more blood to the areas most in need.

The blood supply to the brain is constant.

The pumping action of the muscles forces more deoxygenated blood back to the heart. This results in greater heart volume. The heart responds by contracting more vigorously and sending out a greater quantity of blood with each contraction.

Adrenalin also causes the heart to beat more rapidly.

Respiratory system causes faster and deeper breathing. The more carbon dioxide in the blood, the more rapidly and deeply we breathe. Exchange of gases is more efficient in the lungs during exercise.

Blood flow is reduced to the areas of the body not in urgent need. It is increased to those areas in greatest need.

The blood vessels to the skin are dilated to allow excess heat to be lost from the body surface. If activity is very severe then even these blood vessels will be constricted. The body temperature then rises very quickly and causes overheating and fatigue.

Blood flow can be increased up to 30 times. The oxygen available to the muscle cells can be up to three times the resting amount for each millilitre of blood.

The working muscles can therefore receive up to 90 times the resting amount.

Anticipation of exercise causes hormonal releases which prepare the body for action.

Adrenalin is released into the bloodstream by the adrenal glands. This stimulates respiratory and cardiovascular systems.

The aerobic production of ATP is much more efficient than if ATP has to be produced without oxygen. There are two reasons for this:

1 The system is able to use stored fat as a source of energy rather than having to rely only on carbohydrate in the form of muscle glycogen. Not only does fat carry twice as much energy per gram as carbohydrate (see chapter 2) but we also have much greater stores of it available. (Stores of muscle glycogen are limited.)

2 The presence of oxygen also enables much greater amounts of fuel to be released from carbohydrate without a build up of lactic acid. A carbohydrate molecule can produce over 12 times the amount of energy if oxygen is present than if the muscle is working anaerobically.

Although carbohydrate can be burned up in the absence of oxygen this is not the case for fat. This means that the muscles will revert to using carbohydrate as fuel whenever the intensity of exercise increases to such an extent that enough oxygen is not available for immediate muscular needs.

The different muscle fibre types are each able to benefit from one or other of the energy systems and they are also involved in particular types of activities. Slow twitch muscle fibres are well supplied with aerobic enzymes and are used when the body is involved in slower, longer lasting activities such as jogging. Fast glycolytic (FG) fibres are not well supplied with aerobic enzymes and are better suited for more dynamic but shorter activities such as sprinting. The fast oxidative fibres (FOG) have some endurance qualities but are also able to carry out rapid and powerful contractions. The body is able to change the muscle fibres being used as the activity changes. The more intense an activity becomes, the more oxygen is used up and the more that fast fibres take over from the slower ones.

The immediate source of energy for the working muscles is from adenosine triphosphate (ATP) and creatine phosphate (CP). As supplies of these high energy compounds are very limited, additional sources of ATP are made available from the breakdown of muscle glycogen. These events take place without a sufficient source of oxygen for the working muscles and therefore there is a build up of lactic acid. The person starts to build up an oxygen debt. It takes about two minutes for the heart and lungs to get sufficient additional supplies of oxygen to the working muscles. Once there is sufficient oxygen at the working muscles then ATP is supplied by the breakdown of carbohydrate and fat. If the physical activity is not too severe then the oxygen debt will be repaid as waste products including lactic acid are removed.

	Rest	Activity
Ventilation	☐ ☐ ☐ ☐ ☐ ☐ ☐ ☐ 8 litres air/min	125 litres air/min
Heart rate	75 beats/min	200 beats/min
Cardiac output each beat	▪ ▪ ▪ ▪ ▪ ▪ ▪ ▪ ▪ ▪ 100 ml/beat	200 ml/beat
Cardiac output per minute	5 litres/min	35 litres/min
Oxygen dropped off at tissues	20 ml arterial oxygen/100 ml blood — 5 ml O₂ dropped — 15 ml venous O₂	20 ml arterial oxygen/100 ml blood — 15 ml O₂ dropped — 5 ml venous O₂
Oxygen utilisation	250 ml/min	5 litres/min
Oxygen debt	—	10 litres

The effects of exercise on the body systems

HOW TO IMPROVE FITNESS

If exercise takes place on a regular basis, the various systems of the body will adapt to be able to cope with the stresses placed upon them. The body can be trained to become stronger, faster and more flexible. All sensible programmes of exercise and training are based on this ability of the body to change itself according to the demands made upon it.

The Principles of Training

A number of guiding principles can help us to decide on the most effective training for any physical activity.

1 The principle of specificity

Wind surfing

The effects of training are very specific. This means that if you wish to build up the strength of your upper arm muscles you need to perform physical exercises which put stress on the particular muscles concerned. Exercising the legs will not help. Heart-lung endurance can only be improved through activity which puts prolonged stress on the heart. In the same way the balance needed for surfing will only be improved by training sessions which are similar to the actual event. You must not assume that an exercise designed to improve flexibility will also improve strength or endurance.

Training effects are so specific that it is perfectly possible for a 110 metre hurdler to have a very flexible trunk and yet be unable to do a back bend. If you want to improve a particular part of your body in a particular way, then you must find a way of stressing it which closely resembles the actual movement you wish to perform. You must also ensure that the same muscle groups are involved and the activity is carried out at the same speed as it will be during competition.

A sprinter must include a large amount of speed work in his training. This will ensure that the fast twitch muscle fibres are fully developed. The slow twitch muscle fibres essential for endurance type activities will only be developed by training which puts prolonged steady stress on the body. Sportsmen and sportswomen who need both speed and endurance must include both types of activity in their training.

2 The principle of overload

To improve the fitness of various body systems we need to overload them

To improve the fitness of the various body systems we need to overload them. This means we need to make them work harder than normal. We call the extra demand on the system 'stress'. We can improve our aerobic ability, muscular strength and endurance as well as our flexibility by gradually increasing the amount of stress which we place upon them. We can increase this stress in three ways:

(i) By increasing the intensity of exercise. This means that we actually work harder, lift heavier weights or run faster.

(ii) By increasing the frequency of exercise. We train more often and allow less time for recovery between training sessions.

(iii) By increasing the duration of exercise. We train for longer periods of time and so prolong the stress situation. Hard training damages muscle fibres as well as producing a shortage of glycogen and potassium in the muscles. Time is needed to allow the muscle fibres to heal as well as to replace fuel supplies in the muscles. It has been found that tissue healing is aided by light training. This is the reason why many athletes do hard and easy training on alternate days.

3 The principle of progression

The effects of training can be seen most easily in the early stages. Almost any increased amount of regular stress will produce improvement in the body parts being stressed. As the body adapts, the intensity of the training will have to be gradually increased if improvement is to be continued. The fitter a person becomes and the nearer they get to their potential limit, then the harder it is to increase fitness.

It is most important that the overload is increased progressively. It is not only muscles which have to adapt to greater stresses being put on the body. Bone, ligaments, and tendons also have to adapt. Their adaptations may take longer than the more responsive muscles of the body. Too much stress too soon can cause breakdown and injury. Too little stress can lead to staleness and boredom.

4 The principle of reversibility

The body will also adapt to less stress. It takes only three to four weeks for your body to get out of condition. Deterioration can be seen most readily in aerobic activity as the muscles quickly lose much of their ability to use oxygen. Anaerobic activities are less readily affected by lack of training. This is because the use of oxygen is not as crucial. Strength gains are lost at about one third of their rate of gain. If muscles are not used they atrophy, that is waste away. Both speed and strength is gradually lost. As muscles become weaker and smaller they become more prone to injury. Weak muscles also take longer to heal following injury.

HOW TO TRAIN THE ENERGY SYSTEMS

We know that each sport places unique demands on the energy systems of the body. A competitor taking part in a Triathlon event will be working aerobically for the vast majority of the activity whilst a 100 metre sprinter may be working almost totally anaerobically. Games players are often involved in short phases of all out effort, that is anaerobic work, interspersed with recovery periods, that is aerobic work. Their training needs to reflect these patterns of activity. It is vital that

we not only know the precise energy demands of individual sports but are also aware of the ways that different training methods can help the body to cope with these demands.

The main difference between aerobic and anaerobic activity is the intensity at which the work is performed. The heart is very sensitive to any changes in work intensity. It will immediately increase its speed and extent of contraction to cope with any additional workload on the body. It is therefore possible to monitor and modify training effects by carefully observing their effects on our heart.

As training intensity is worked out by comparing the heart rate during training with the person's maximum heart rate, a simple formula has been developed in order to estimate an individual's maximum heart rate.

Maximum heart rate = 220 minus your age

As an example, the maximum heart rate of a 15 year old would be calculated as : 220 - 15 = 205.

Competitors in the triathlon

▲ This 15 year old is just starting a training course and wants to build up her aerobic ability. she should train at between 60 - 80% of her maximum heart rate (ie 123-164 beats per minute [bpm]).

At this intensity of training energy would be supplied aerobically and the slow twitch muscle fibres would be providing movement. She would also be helping to build up the respiratory and circulatory systems and toughen tendons and ligaments.

▲ This 15 year old is quite an experienced sportswoman and is able to train at between 80 - 90% of her maximum heart rate (ie 164-185 bpm) for an extended period of time. She is working at the upper limit of her aerobic energy pathways at the anaerobic threshold. She would still be using the slow twitch muscle fibres but also improving the aerobic abilities of the fast oxidative glycolytic muscle fibres which would come into action.

◀ This experienced 15 year old is able to train at between 90-95% of her maximum heart rate (ie 185- 195 bpm). She is developing the short term energy sources and using slow twitch, FOG and fast glycolytic (FG) muscle fibres. If she were to train above 95% of maximum heart rate she would be using anaerobic energy sources and developing anaerobic energy pathways; all the muscle fibres would be in action and skill at full speed would also be improved.

To check that the exercise intensity is right, exercise at the rate you think is right for at least three to five minutes and then check your heart rate over a period of 15 seconds. Multiply by 4 and then see if it is the right level below your maximum heart rate. Adjust your work rate accordingly.

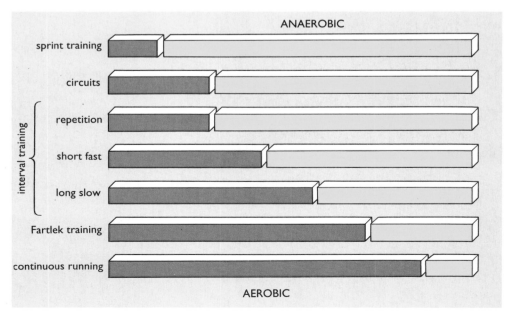

ANAEROBIC

sprint training

circuits

interval training — repetition

short fast

long slow

Fartlek training

continuous running

AEROBIC

Approximate aerobic/anaerobic energy use in a variety of running training schedules

ENERGY TRAINING METHODS

Continuous Training

Continuous training involves exercise without rest intervals. For those who have not done much exercise or who are out of shape then slow continuous running or swimming, working at a rate of approximately 75% of their maximum heart rate, is most appropriate. For those training for specific sporting events the training should be over distances of between two and five times their competition distance. This type of programme trains the body to use fat rather than carbohydrates as a source of fuel. It then makes sense to gradually change to a faster pace of continuous training in which the person works at up to 80-90% of their maximum heart rate. At this rate the person is working at their anaerobic threshold and will find the training more stressful.

Fartlek Training

Fartlek is a Swedish word meaning 'speed play'. This form of running gives an athlete a lot of training over distances far greater than his or her competitive distances. The emphasis should be on the enjoyment of running fast yet within one's self and the physical stress should not be too severe. It should be enjoyable! The extent of aerobic or anaerobic training will depend on how each training session is organised. For the anaerobic threshold to be raised, the fast sessions should last at least two minutes. A typical programme could include:

10-15 minutes jogging or easy running
1 mile run at a steady pace
5 minute rapid walk
10 minute jog with 5 sprints interspersed each over a distance of 75-100 metres
Hard uphill run for 150-200 metres
Jog 1 mile with frequent 5-10 metre bursts
10 minute rapid walk
1-5 sprints over a distance of 150 metres

This type of training can be varied to suit the fitness level of each individual, the degree of aerobic/anaerobic fitness required as well as the time available. This method could be used by cyclists, swimmers or skiers as well as by other sports.

Repetitions

Repetition training involves working at a fast rate for periods of between five and 12 minutes. The athlete then recovers before repeating the exercise. If the activity is performed slower than competition pace then the aerobic system will be developed. If it is near to or at competitive intensity then the anaerobic system will be developed. Repetitions at or above the anaerobic threshold improve the aerobic ability of fast twitch muscle fibres, raise the anaerobic threshold and prepare the body for fast-paced training.

Interval Training

This is an alternating fast and slow training schedule performed over measured distances. The fast periods involve periods of intense work, for example running, cycling, etc. for periods of 30 seconds to five minutes. The slow or recovery periods involve either rest or very light exercise in which the oxygen debt built up during the fast phase can be repaid. Interval training can be planned to improve aerobic or anaerobic fitness or a mixture of the two depending on the following: the length of the fast intervals, the number of fast intervals, the speed or intensity of the fast intervals and the length of the recovery periods.

If aerobic ability is to be developed then work rate should be such that the subject is working at approximately 85% of his maximum heart rate. Equal work and recovery periods of between two to five minutes seem to produce the greatest aerobic improvements.

To increase the intensity of aerobic interval training the subject should work for 15 seconds at a pace above the anaerobic threshold followed by an easy effort (repeated 20-30 times).

A squash player could develop his anaerobic capabilities by repeating intervals of intense training for periods of 30 seconds in order to simulate the length of rallies. The maximum duration of any anaerobic training is 90 seconds. After this the body will return to the aerobic system to allow exercise to continue.

Sprint Training

There are a number of varieties of sprint training but they all involve periods of maximum effort combined with periods of rest. Examples include:
Interval sprinting which involves alternate

short periods of intense effort and recovery phases. For instance a cyclist would sprint for one minute and then ease down for one minute. This could be repeated for 12-15 minutes. During the intense periods the levels of ATP and CP are reduced and there is a build up of lactic acid. The recovery phase allows for this situation to be resolved. Interval training allows for a great deal more high quality work to be performed than if the intense work was continuous. It therefore improves the anaerobic breakdown of glycogen and raises cellular levels of ATP and CP. It also stresses the heart so causing it to become stronger.

Pick up sprint training The basic approach is to start at a jog and build up speed through striding to sprinting and then go back to walking again. The fast phase should be held for 5-15 seconds depending on the specific sports requirements of the subject. The rest periods must allow the subject to recover sufficiently enough for the next effort to be carried out at full speed. The number of repetitions will depend upon the ability and needs of the subject.

Shuttle runs are also excellent for the development of speed.

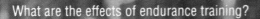

What are the effects of endurance training?

The muscles involved in breathing become stronger. A trained athlete could breathe in and out over 200 litres a minute and sustain this level for up to 20 minutes. An untrained person can breathe in and out 125-170 litres but for only a very short time.

Training will allow you to get closer to your VO$_2$ max (the maximum amount of oxygen which can be taken in and used by the body in one minute).

The number of alveoli in the lungs increases. This allows more oxygen to get into the bloodstream and more carbon dioxide to get out. The muscles involved in breathing become stronger.

Through endurance training the body is able to use more fat and less carbohydrate to fuel a particular rate of exercise. As supplies of fat are plentiful then this is obviously beneficial.

The heart becomes larger with thicker and stronger muscular walls. The heart chambers also become larger.

A fit heart is able to empty its chambers more completely. The stroke volume (the amount of blood pumped out in each contraction) can be double that of an untrained person.

A fit person's heart needs to beat more slowly when at rest. It can cope with hard work readily and will recover its resting rate more quickly than an untrained heart.

The coronary arteries are enlarged.

The number of arteries supplying blood to the muscle cells may be increased.

The arteries become larger and more elastic. There is less risk of the arteries hardening (arteriosclerosis). Blood pressure is also reduced.

Both the quantity and quality of the blood are increased. More red blood cells are produced and, therefore, more oxygen is carried in the haemoglobin. There are lower levels of fat in the blood.

The number and size of mitochondria in muscle cells increase as a result of endurance training. This allows more oxygen to be used by the working muscles.

Muscles develop an increased blood vessel network and so each muscle cell is able to get a greater

supply of blood and therefore oxygen and nutrients.

The muscles can hold greater supplies of myoglobin which increases the store of oxygen necessary for sustaining prolonged vigorous exercise.

Endurance trained muscles therefore use more fat and less muscle glycogen. As less glycogen is used then less lactic acid is produced and the athlete does not feel so tired.

What is flexibility?

Flexibility, mobility and suppleness all refer to the range of limb movement around joints. Most sporting activities demand body flexibility to a greater or lesser degree. Flexibility exercises or stretching are normally a part of most training programmes. There are sound reasons why this should be so.

1 Flexibility exercises performed early in a workout have the effect of warming up and loosening the muscles before they are exposed to vigorous exercise. This helps to lessen the risk of muscle tears and strains. Flexibility exercises should also follow a weight training or heavy resistance programme. This is because the exercised muscles become shorter and tighter when healing unless sensible stretching exercises are carried out.

2 The greater the flexibility of a particular joint the greater the distance over which force may be exerted. Greater flexibility increases the stride length of sprinters and therefore their ground coverage. Swimmers can adopt more efficient positions in the water if they have highly flexible shoulders and ankles.

3 Sportsmen and sportswomen with flexible bodies are less likely to suffer from overstretching injuries. There is a potential danger of extreme flexibility in some sporting activities however. A

rugby hooker with highly flexible shoulder joints would not be an asset to his team.

4 Flexibility exercises also train the agonistic and antagonistic muscles to work in unison. This helps to create skilful movement.

How can flexibility be improved?

Flexibility does not depend on the shape of the person. It can be improved by stretching the muscles and tendons and by extending the ligaments and supporting tissues beyond their normal range of movement. The muscles are overloaded but only to the extent that feels comfortable. Flexibility can be improved in a number of ways:

In **static stretching** the person extends a limb (or limbs) beyond its normal range. The position is then held for at least 10 seconds. After a few seconds rest the stretch is then repeated. This should be continued for at least five repetitions of 10 seconds.

An alternative to the method described above is to briefly contract the muscle immediately after the stretch period. The contraction should be followed by a short period of relaxation before stretching the muscle once more. This method helps muscles to relax and also helps to concentrate the stretch on the connective tissues, joint capsules and tendons.

In **active stretching** the person extends a movement beyond its normal limit and repeats this rhythmically over a period of 20 seconds. For example, the head can be rotated in as large a circle as possible; first in one direction and then in another. The emphasis is on extending the neck muscles. These exercises should be performed slowly in order to reduce the danger of injury. Bouncing or bobbing methods were popular in the past but it is now considered that they increase the risk of muscle pulls. Active exercises involving all the major joints of the body are a sound addition to any warm up before vigorous exercise.

In **passive stretching** joint flexibility is improved by external force caused by partners or coaches who move the limb to its end position and keep it there for a few seconds. It is most important that this type of stretching is carried out carefully. A major injury can occur if the force applied to the person stretching is too vigorous.

STRENGTH

Strength can be defined as the ability of a muscle or muscle group to apply force and overcome resistance. But there are different types of strength. Look at the three photographs below. Each photograph shows strength being displayed, but it is clear that the strength of a tug-of-war competitor is of a different sort to the high jumper or the rower. Researchers have called these different displays of strength, static, explosive and dynamic.

Static Strength

Passive stretching

Tug of war needs static strength

Static strength is the maximum force that can be applied by a muscle group to an immovable object. The length of the muscle remains the same and therefore there is no movement of the limbs on which the muscles operate. Static strength can be of particular importance in activities such as scrummaging in rugby, wrestling and tug-of-war. In all these activities the competitor has to hold his body in a steady position against an opposing force. Static strength can be measured by means of tensionometers and dynamometers. These machines are often available at major weight training centres.

Explosive Strength

High jumpers need explosive strength

Explosive strength or power is a measure of the maximum energy used in one explosive act. It is shown clearly in activities such as throwing and jumping when athletes attempt to project themselves or an object as far and as fast as possible. Explosive strength is readily measured. Leg strength or power can be assessed either by a vertical leap or a standing broad jump.

Dynamic Strength

Rowers need dynamic strength

Dynamic strength is the ability of the muscles to move or support the body mass continuously over an extended period of time. It reflects the endurance qualities of the muscles. Dynamic strength becomes particularly important in activities where maximum effort is required for periods of between 30 seconds and three minutes. Most of the power is obtained in the first few seconds. If the muscular effort is kept up then waste products build up in the muscle cells and the person will feel weaker.

Most sportsmen and sportswomen require all three kinds of strength, although obviously particular types of strength are vital for some sports. Shot putters need explosive strength, rowers need dynamic strength whilst tug-of-war competitors need static strength as well as dynamic strength.

How can strength be increased?
If we apply the four principles of training (overload, progression, specificity and reversibility) to the problem of increasing strength, then we can readily work out a 'strength training' programme suitable for any sport.

1 Specificity
The effects of any strength training programme will be very specific. For example, if very heavy weights are lifted for a small number of repetitions then static strength will be increased. The muscles will not only become stronger but they will also increase in size. If the same exercise is repeated using very light weights, but many repetitions, then dynamic strength will be increased. The muscles will often show little gain in size, but better muscle tone will be noticed. Explosive strength will be increased if the weights are heavy and the exercise is carried out at speed.

Strength training is also specific to the extent that only those muscles which are stressed will become stronger. Any strength training programme needs to work the muscles in the same way that they are worked in the sporting situation. If the movements are performed at high speed during competition then they need to be exercised at a similar speed during strength training. Only in this way will the fast twitch muscle fibres be developed.

2 Overload
Muscles will become stronger if they are forced to work harder than they are used to working. This

can be achieved by either increasing the intensity or the duration of the exercise. Intensity will be increased by using heavier weights or working faster. Duration will be increased by making the muscles work for a longer period of time.

3 Progression

It is important that any overload (or stress) is increased progressively so that the muscles, ligaments, tendons and other connective tissues have time to adapt to the extra stresses being placed upon them.

4 Reversibility

In the same way that muscles adapt to any extra stress being placed on them by becoming bigger and stronger, they will also adapt to disuse or lack of stress by wasting away or atrophying. Muscles need stress to maintain their strength and efficiency.

Strength Training Methods

There are a wide range of strength training methods in common use. They vary in the type of exercises involved, the apparatus used and the actual methods of working. These different strength training methods are related to the various ways in which muscles contract.

1 Isotonic contraction

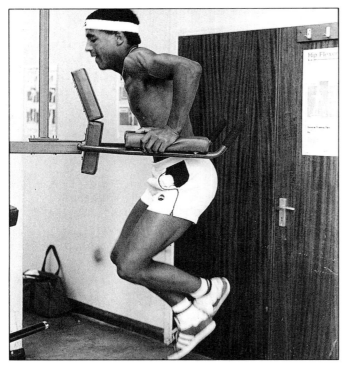

Isotonic contraction of the arm muscles

Isotonic contraction takes place when the two ends of the contracting muscles are brought closer together. The muscle shortens causing movement of the limbs to which the muscle is attached. Isotonic contraction occurs whenever the body, or parts of it, are moving. Isotonic contraction takes place when a muscle is working eccentrically or concentrically. Concentric contraction occurs when the muscle shortens as it contracts. Eccentric contraction takes place when the muscles are under tension as they lengthen. The leg muscles are working concentrically when we walk upstairs. They work eccentrically when we walk downstairs.

2 Isokinetic contraction

Isokinetic contraction occurs when the tension of the muscle remains very high throughout the whole range of movement. It has become possible to improve isokinetic contraction in recent years by the development of variable resistance training techniques involving expensive machinery.

The advantages of variable resistance training are as follows:

(i) It is possible to maintain high resistance throughout the range of movement. This is unlike normal weight lifting where the resistance varies considerably through the range of movement.

(ii) Variable resistance machines allow limbs to be moved at the same speed as the limbs move during competition. This means that the same muscle fibres are being used and therefore developed. This is often not possible using free weights for reasons of safety.

(iii) Research indicates that it is the eccentric contraction of muscles which encourages the soreness felt in muscles after traditional weight training. As weights do not have to be lowered during variable resistance training, no eccentric contraction is involved and therefore there is a lack of muscle soreness after exercise.

The disadvantages of variable resistance training methods are as follows:

(i) The machines are sophisticated and therefore very expensive. To provide for a full range of bodily movements would not only be prohibitive from the cost point of view but the machinery would also take up a considerable amount of space.

(ii) They do not allow for the flexibility that is

possible using free weights. It is not possible to adapt the movements as it is with free weights.

(iii) Athletes do not have to concentrate when using them and consequently get bored with them very much more quickly than with free weights.

3 Isometric contraction

Isometric contraction takes place when the length of the muscle remains the same throughout the contraction. Many of the stabilising muscles of the body work isometrically. They hold parts of the body stationary as other parts move. For example, the deltoid muscles in the shoulder hold the arm steady when an attempt is made to turn a key in the lock of a door.

Isometric contraction of the arm muscles

All methods of strength training attempt to improve muscular strength using one or more of the above methods of contraction. They all have their own particular advantages and disadvantages.

Compared with normal weight training, isometric exercises need little equipment and produce far less fatigue. The basic method to be followed for all muscle groups is as follows. Muscles should be contracted to at least 60% of their total power, but there should be no shortening of the muscle length. A good example of muscles working isometrically is to put your hands on a wall and try to push it over. The tension should be maintained for at least 6 seconds.

There are many disadvantages to isometric strength training. It does not develop cardiorespiratory or cardiovascular fitness. In fact the circulation to the contracting muscles is

stopped. This interferes with the oxygen supply to the working muscles as well as increasing diastolic blood pressure. It is difficult to know if you are contracting to 66% of your maximum. It is also difficult to tell if you are getting stronger. Isometric strength training increases static strength but only at the particular angle at which the muscles are stressed. It does not develop power or muscular endurance at all and there are very few sports which require muscles to be developed in this way.

In brief, isometric strength training is of limited value. It should only be undertaken as part of a complete strength training programme based on isotonic work.

Weight Training

The bar-bell helps to develop the entire body

A wrist roller is used for strengthening the wrist and forearm

Dumb-bells are used for arm and shoulder exercises

Iron boots or leg-bells are used for developing thigh and calf muscles

Different weights used in weight training

Weight training is probably the most popular form of strength training. Weights can be increased progressively. It is easy to overload muscles in a safe manner over a sensible period of time. It is possible to work on different muscle groups within the body. An individual strength training programme can be designed for any person and for any sport. Exercises can be performed concentrically and eccentrically. By holding weights after lifting them a mixture of isometric and isotonic work is possible. Many sports centres now have excellent weight training equipment which is designed with safety in mind. Multigyms and polygyms make weight training safe, enjoyable and highly motivating.

Can I design my own strength programme?

By using the following guidelines, it is easy to work out a strength training programme for any person and any sport.

Analyse the sport in which you want to improve your performance. Decide which muscle groups are of particular importance and select exercises which use these muscle groups in the same way. Be sure to include some exercises which build up the large muscle groups such as the upper and lower legs, the back, the chest and stomach muscles. You must also ensure that you train opposing muscle groups to maintain a balance of strength about a joint.

It is important to plan the order in which you complete your exercises. Start with the larger muscle groups and then go on to the smaller ones. You should also alternate muscle groups in order to avoid local muscle fatigue.

Be sure to warm up and cool down before and after your strength training programme. In the early stages of your programme exercise without weights or with very light ones. Build up stress gradually. It is not necessary to have special equipment in order to develop strength. Partner work, in which a team mate has to be carried or pushed, involves overload or stress. Running up or down steep hills, over sand, in mud or into the wind all involve working against a resistance. This puts extra stress or strain on the musculature which will adapt and become stronger.

You need to be aware of the particular type or types of strength which are an essential part of your sport. Then you can plan the intensity and duration of your programme accordingly. Static strength and explosive strength can be developed through a progressive resistance exercise pyramid system. The idea is to build up to a maximum load

while decreasing the number of repetitions. If we take the bench press exercise for example. This exercise is designed to strengthen the triceps and chest muscles. If we know that the maximum weight we could press in one repetition is 70 kg then we could plan a bench press programme as follows:

Weight	Repetitions
45 kg	10
50 kg	8
55 kg	6
60 kg	4
65 kg	2

As our strength develops over a period of time the exercises will seem to be easier. All of the weights could be increased by 5 kg.

IMPROVING MUSCULAR ENDURANCE

Endurance training improves endurance in both slow and fast twitch muscles. Short term endurance training will improve strength as well as the ability to sustain effort against a moderately high resistance. Intermediate endurance training improves endurance for lesser loads such as an athlete's own body weight in basketball. Long term endurance training improves the production of energy and the oxygen utilisation that is needed for prolonged exertion with a low resistance such as distance running.

As resistance decreases and repetitions increase you move from an emphasis on strength training to endurance training.

Endurance Training Methods

Short term and intermediate endurance can be gained using weights, weight machines, calisthenics or special training devices designed to suit the sport. The main difference between strength training and endurance training is the weight of the resistance and the number of repetitions. You will probably work at 50-75% of your one rep maximum figure. (One rep max is the greatest amount of weight which you could lift just once.) Endurance can improve at a remarkable rate. It can also be lost very quickly. The muscle enzymes produced in long term endurance training are quickly lost during periods of inactivity. It is lost three times more quickly than it is gained.

POWER

When training for power the aim is to move the load as quickly as possible. Power training enhances strength, speed and energy supplies. Resistance should be 30-60% of maximum strength and the activity should be performed as quickly as possible (15-25 reps in three sets three times a week).

It is important to ensure that any exercises match as closely as possible to the actual movements performed in the sport. It is also important to work at the same speed as in the sporting event.

Power Training Methods

Because power is so similar to strength it can be developed using similar training methods. Free weights, weight machines, etc., all lend themselves to power training. Circuit training that emphasises speed is especially effective.

Preload

Power can be developed by using the preload and elastic recoil present in many sports skills. In running for example the strong thigh muscles of the legs are slightly stretched or preloaded before they contract to drive the runner forward. The stretch stores up elastic energy that is quickly released during the contraction. This extra power does not take up much extra energy so it provides more power without any added cost. The same principle applies whenever a muscle is stretched before it contracts. A group of training methods that apply this principle to develop power are sometimes known as plyometrics.

Plyometric exercises

A key feature of plyometric training is the conditioning of the neuromuscular system to permit faster and more powerful changes of direction, such as moving from down to up in jumping, or switching leg positions as in running. Reducing the time needed for this change in direction increases speed and power. Ski jumpers, cross-country and downhill skiers, volleyball players, sprinters and high jumpers can all benefit from this type of training. Plyometric exercises utilise the following movements: bounds, hops, jumps, leaps, skips, ricochets, swings and twists.

Plyometrics place considerable strain on the joints so start any power training using this system on grass or if in the gym on mats.

Building up power can be done in exactly the same way that strength is built up. The only difference is in the speed of the work carried out. Power can be built up and lost relatively quickly.

SPEED

Fast twitch fibres provide more speed than slow twitch fibres and so those individuals with a high proportion of fast twitch fibres will always be at an advantage. It is possible to improve speed however. The secret is to practise the movements at faster than normal speeds. This helps the nervous system to overcome inhibitions and to learn to perform at a faster pace. It is important, however, that improvement of technique should always precede any training emphasis on increasing speed.

Speed training should be founded on a comprehensive programme of strength, endurance and power development. As the competitive season approaches, specific speed work can be integrated into daily practices. It is important to identify the key movement patterns in the sport and to select training methods that will help the athlete to perform these movements faster. In high velocity events such as sprints and the long jump, speed and power must be emphasised as soon as the muscles are ready.

Speed training improves the neuromuscular apparatus and increases short term energy.

Whether or not your sporting success improves as a result of your strength training programme, you should certainly feel stronger and fitter. You should also be able to get the most out of physical activities.

THINGS TO DO

1 You have decided to enter for a marathon. It is to take place in three months. How would you apply the training principles of overload, progression and specificity to produce a training schedule?

2 Give three examples of exercises designed to improve flexibility. State whether the exercises are static, passive or active.

3 The following paragraph concerns the effects of exercise on the body. Complete the paragraph using words from the list below. Each word may be used once, more than once, or not at all.

heart, muscles, oxygen, cardiovascular, increased, lungs, lactic acid, energy, adrenalin, body, respiratory, deoxygenated, decreased, digestive systems.

The anticipation of physical activity causes .... to be released into the bloodstream. This affects both the............................ and the .... systems. During exercise these two systems of the body work together to cope with the increased .... requirements of the .... and to help eliminate waste products such as .... as rapidly as possible from the .... There is also an increased return of .... blood to the .... There is also a redistribution of .... since more goes to the muscles and less goes to the .... The rate and output of the heart is ....

4 Write the letter that gives the correct definition for each word below:

i) **Strength**	A	Ability to move your joints and muscles fully.
ii) **Flexibility**	B	Ability to repeat exercises many times without getting tired.
iii) **Stamina**	C	Amount of force you can exert with your muscles.
iv) **Muscular endurance**	D	Ability to exercise for long periods of time without getting out of breath.

5 As a group, invite a top sportsman or sportswoman to talk to you in detail about their training, what they actually do and the purpose of their activities. Make notes about their training schedule. Later, analyse it in terms of training for stamina, speed, strength, power, and flexibility. Decide, as a group, whether you think the training is appropriate and effective. Discuss any changes you might recommend.

6 'Fitness is specific to a sport.'
Explain what is meant by this statement giving examples from the world of sport.

7 Explain the difference between 'health related fitness' and 'performance related fitness'.

8 (i) Complete a table similar to the one below to record the amount of rest, relaxation and sleep you have in any seven day period.

Dates:	Sleep (Hrs)	Rest (Hrs)	Relaxation (Details)	(Hrs)
Monday				
Tuesday				
Wednesday				
Thursday				
Friday				
Saturday				
Sunday				
Daily average				

(ii) Consider whether you should reduce or increase any of these periods of non-activity or whether you are satisfied with your balance of rest and activity.

9

• TOP BODY PRODUCTIONS •
proudly present the
FRANK AND KEN STEIN AWARD
for the
Best Designed Human Being
for any sport of your choice

To enter this competition just think what qualities your ideal sportsperson needs to have to be the world's outstanding competitor in one particular sport. You should consider physical qualities such as size, body build, strength, stamina and suppleness as well as qualities of personality such as determination, courage and perseverance. Draw a sketch of your individual and think of ways to show on the drawing all the qualities which you consider essential for success. In order to guide the judges you should add the following:

(i) a training programme to enable your competitor to reach top competitive fitness in approximately six months;

(ii) details of how close present competitors come to your ideal.

10 (i) Analyse your own training exercise patterns over a six week period.

(ii) On the basis of your training pattern and considering the demands of the sport in which you are involved, draw up a plan of intent for the next six weeks. Again record your exercise patterns and see how close you come to your intentions.

4 MEASURING PHYSICAL PERFORMANCE

Aims

To gain knowledge and understanding of:

◆ the assessment of sportsmen and sportswomen
◆ the assessment of the normal population

To develop the skills of:

◆ measurement
◆ data analysis and presentation
◆ result interpretation
◆ group work
◆ production of a fitness profile using a variety of tests

We have seen that it is possible for all of us to improve our levels of fitness. Through training we can all become faster, stronger, and more flexible. In activities such as sprinting or weight lifting it is easy to see if we are improving. Our times will become quicker or we will be able to lift heavier weights. It is not quite so straightforward to see if our fitness is improving in activities such as judo or badminton. Tests of fitness have been in existence for a long time but their use both at school and national level has been given greater prominence in recent years.

In this chapter we will see how and why elite sportsmen and sportswomen are tested as well as discover how the assessment of children and young people can be carried out. Through attempting some tests yourself you will gain a greater understanding of how your body works and your particular strengths and weaknesses in terms of fitness.

TESTING THE ELITE COMPETITOR

The British Olympic Medical Centre (BOMC) was opened in 1987 at Northwick Park Hospital and Clinical Research Centre in Harrow, Middlesex. It combines the facilities for full physiological monitoring of the various components of fitness together with a sports injuries clinic. By the end of 1990 it had already tested over 1300 potential Olympic competitors and it has rapidly become a source of specialist advice for elite competitors, their governing bodies and their coaches.

Why test?

1 As a result of testing a large number of elite sportsmen and sportswomen from a wide variety of sports it has become possible to build up a physiological data base and so develop profiles of the successful athlete in specific sports. The information can also provide valuable information about many of the factors which influence a competitor's athletic performance. Squad or team selection in sports such as rowing can also be helped by sensible use of the data gained.

2 By testing the individual sportsman before and after a training programme it becomes easier to assess the value of particular types of training for the individual and to modify the training programme as necessary. It will enable the coach to make training programmes more personal, more specific in their effects and more efficient.

3 For the individual being tested it is possible to:

(i) highlight any individual strengths or weaknesses in order to determine which specific fitness areas need improvement;
(ii) calculate current physical work capacity and help to predict physiological potential;
(iii) assess how much of the components of fitness have been lost following injury, illness or lack of training;
(iv) reveal symptoms related to fatigue and overtraining;
(v) compare their physical fitness scores with other elite athletes in their particular sporting event.

Testing Aerobic Fitness

Aerobic fitness is the ability of the cardiorespiratory system to deliver oxygen to the working muscles. It depends on the efficiency of the lungs, heart and blood and is usually measured in terms of maximum oxygen uptake or VO_2 max. VO_2 max may be expressed as an absolute value in litres/minute (for non weight bearing sports such as rowing or canoeing) or normalised for body weight as ml/kg/minute (for weight-bearing sports such as running).

The VO_2 max for untrained young men can vary between 2 - 4 litres per minute whilst Olympic rowers have been recorded as high as 7.3 litres per minute. International distance runners have reached as high as 92ml/kg/minute. VO_2 max can vary considerably at different times of the sporting season and it is possible to increase your aerobic capacity by up to about 20% through the appropriate type of training.

The BOMC Aerobic Laboratory

The Aerobic Laboratory tests a person's ability to exercise while using oxygen to fuel the working muscles. It is important to use large muscle groups when testing aerobic fitness and also to test in ways which are similar to the type of work carried out by the subject during competition.

The aerobic laboratory has a treadmill, rowing and cycling ergometers as well as a canoeing simulation machine. The subject is set to work on the appropriate ergometer and the work rate is increased at constant intervals until the subject decides that he or she can do no more work. Heart rate, the amount of oxygen consumed and various other measures are recorded using sophisticated equipment. The object is to assess the maximum oxygen uptake (VO_2 max) as part of the overall assessment of aerobic fitness.

There will come a point when the body cannot use any more oxygen (the point of maximum oxygen uptake). If exercise continues then the body starts to provide more energy through the muscles in the absence of oxygen (anaerobic metabolism). The result is a build up of lactic acid in the blood and muscles which soon leads to exhaustion. Regular blood samples can be taken throughout the test and so it is possible to identify the point at which there is a sudden increase in the levels of lactic acid. This point is called the anaerobic threshold, or the OBLA point (onset of blood lactate accumulation) and may be defined as

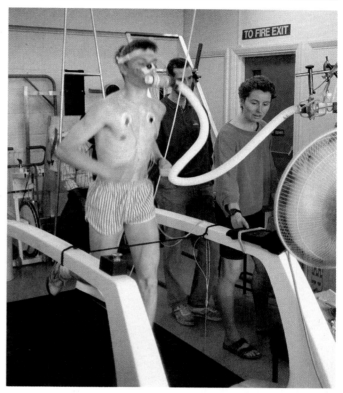

Testing on a treadmill

the rate of work at which plasma lactate accumulates faster than it can be removed.

The anaerobic threshold is normally expressed as a percentage of VO_2 max and may be as high as 95% in marathon runners.

It is known that the best way to improve endurance through aerobic training is to work just below the anaerobic threshold. It is therefore important that sportsmen and sportswomen can assess their own threshold with some accuracy. If they train too far below their threshold then endurance improvement will be minimal; if they train above their anaerobic threshold then fatigue will set in very quickly.

The adult VO_2 max may improve by 20% with training and the anaerobic threshold may be raised from 60% of VO_2 max to 80% or higher. The VO_2 max gives an indication of potential aerobic power available, while the anaerobic threshold gives a measure of the current state of training.

Testing Anaerobic Fitness

Anaerobic power is the rate of production of energy from creatine phosphate and glycolysis. This energy system is used when there is a lack of oxygen at the working muscles. It is involved right at the start of exercise and also when the intensity of exercise is very high. It is probably safer to use the term local muscle endurance as it is almost impossible to identify what is anaerobic and what is anaerobic power in short bursts of energy especially over 30 seconds.

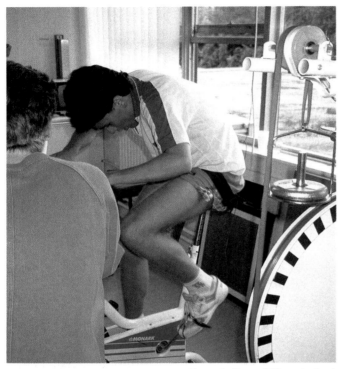

Completing a Wingate test

The BOMC Anaerobic Laboratory measures power in bursts of work carried out at maximum speed in variants of the 'Wingate test'. The centre uses specially adapted cycle ergometers which can be used by the arms or legs in order to simulate the activities performed in the actual sport. The resistance of the machine can be altered to suit the age and sex as well as the sport of the subject. The subject works flat out usually for a period of 30 seconds.

Using the Wingate test it is possible to measure:

Peak power (in watts.);	of particular importance to jumpers and gymnasts.
Time to peak power (in secs.);	of particular importance to bobsleigh crews.
Fatigue rate (in watts per sec of decrease);	a low rate is of particular importance to rowers, kayakers and canoeists,
Total work achieved (kJ);	of importance to many sporting events.

A repeat test, four minutes later, gives an idea how quickly the subject recovers from fatigue. This is an important measure for those sporting activities such as football, squash and hockey which require brief bursts of intense effort again and again.

The total energy expended in the second test is expressed as a percentage of that expended during the first test. Top class footballers and squash players often perform at over 95% on the second test (Fatigue index).

Muscle Strength and Power Testing

The third laboratory contains an isokinetic dynamometer- an elaborate computerised machine that measures muscle strength at a range of speeds, at all angles and when a muscle is lengthening or shortening. It can measure muscles in all four limbs, abdomen and back and detect imbalances in strength that may lower performance. It is important to set the contraction speed to match the speed at which the actions are carried out during the sport.

Strength and Speed Measurements

Measuring muscle strength on an isokinetic dynamometer

Differences in strength profiles of different sportsmen can be explained by different training methods and also by different muscle profiles. Power athletes have a higher proportion of fast twitch fibres than other athletes in for example, the vastus lateralis muscle. They may have up to 95% fast twitch fibres which are metabolically equipped for forceful anaerobic contractions. Fast twitch fibres may be two to four times faster and 50% larger than slow twitch fibres.

The speed of contraction of a muscle is also of particular importance. Using isokinetic dynamometry at velocities ranging from 60-500 degrees/sec, noticeable differences have been observed in elite competitors. At high velocities, rowers demonstrate lower power losses at the knee joint than sprinters. Endurance runners show the slowest decline as velocity increases. The ratio between antagonistic muscles can also be tested using isokinetic machinery. Poor ratios between hamstrings and quadriceps may be related to lower back problems in rowers.

TESTING THE NORMAL POPULATION

It is clearly not possible or even desirable to assess large numbers of the population using the sophisticated equipment and levels of expertise available at the British Olympic Medical Centre. Many educators, however, have felt the need for an effective means of accurately assessing physical fitness in children. This need is based upon the following:

Physical fitness is vital to our health and well-being. We should be able to assess how fit children and young people are in order to ensure that our physical education programmes do actually lead to fitter young people.

For the individual child, the regular assessment of fitness (provided it is carried out in an educationally sound way) should lead to a greater awareness of the importance of keeping fit and an enhanced understanding of how this can be achieved.

EUROFIT - The European Test of Physical Fitness, was designed to satisfy this need. The test battery is the result of ten years of joint work by researchers and government experts in 18 countries involving 50 000 European children. A number of researchers have constructed reference scales for children in their country. The reference scales in the Appendix are based on the assessment of a large number of children (an average of 200 for each age group) in 19 secondary schools in the greater Amsterdam area (W.van Mechelen et al. 1990).

EUROFIT comprises the tests shown in the table.

Full details of these tests plus a great deal of background information is contained in the EUROFIT Handbook which is available from the Sports Council.

Your group will be responsible for the testing of a group of pupils in one of the EUROFIT tests. You must ensure that you read and understand the detailed instructions you will be given for your particular test.

There are some general points which need to be observed by all of the various groups if the results are to be worthwhile.

- Get used to the equipment you are going to use for your testing.

- Go through the test yourself so that you are quite sure of the object of the test and how it should be scored.

- Ensure that the method of scoring is correct and is used consistently for all individuals being tested.

- Your teacher will have certain details about each of the pupils being tested - their name, their age, their weight and their height. Each pupil will also have been given a number. Ask each one being tested their number before they take your test.

- Explain the test clearly to those who are going to attempt it. Demonstrate briefly how it is to be attempted and explain the method of scoring.

- Your teacher should ensure that you have sufficient people to test in order to make your results worthwhile. It is more meaningful to draw conclusions from your results if you have tested 200 pupils rather than 20.

- As far as possible your teacher will ensure that the tests are carried out in the order that they are described in the rest of this chapter. It is wise to carry out the endurance shuttle run on a different day from the other tests. It is particularly important that the balance test is attempted at the start of the testing session and the shuttle run (10* 5m) is attempted at the end.

- It is anticipated that testing will take place at least twice a year, once in September and again

EUROFIT tests

Dimension	Factor	EUROFIT Test
Cardio-respiratory endurance	Cardio-respiratory endurance	Endurance shuttle run Cycle ergometer test**
Strength	Static strength Explosive power	Hand grip Standing broad jump
Muscular endurance	Functional strength Trunk strength	Bent arm hang Sit-ups
Speed	Running speed – agility Speed of limb movement	Shuttle run: 10*5 m Plate tapping
Flexibility	Flexibility	Sit and reach
Balance	Total body balance	Flamingo balance
Anthropometric measures	Height (cm):	
	Weight (kg):	
	Body fat (5 skinfolds: biceps, triceps, subscapular: surprailiac: calf);	
Identification data	Age (years, months):	Sex

** The cycle ergometer test is not used in this battery of tests. Body fat is measured in four areas. Assessment of fat on the calf is not undertaken.

in the following July. The person being tested should be able to see their complete set of test results and your teacher will explain what they mean. It is important that everyone involved in the testing procedures appreciates that it is how individuals compare with their previous test scores and not with their fellow pupils that is of concern. The EUROFIT test scores should not be taken too seriously because they are chronologically age based and cannot take into account maturation and physiological development.

THE EUROFIT TESTS

Endurance Shuttle Run Test

This is a test of cardio-respiratory fitness, which begins at walking pace and ends running fast, whereby the subjects move from one line to another 20 metre distant, reversing direction, and in accordance with a pace dictated by a sound signal, which gets progressively faster. (Few subjects are able to keep going to the end.) The stage at which the subject drops out is the indicator of his/her cardio-respiratory endurance.

For this test you will need a gymnasium or space large enough to mark out a 20 metre track; a 20 metre tape; self-adhesive tape to mark the start and end of the 20 metre track; a tape recorder, preferably allowing adjustment to the turning speed of the tape and a pre-recorded tape of the test instructions (see appendix).

Instructions for the test subject

'The shuttle run test you are about to take gives an indication of your maximum aerobic capacity, that is, your endurance, and involves running along and back a 20 metre track.

Speed will be controlled by means of a tape emitting buzzing sounds at regular intervals. Pace yourselves so as to be at one end of the 20 metre track or the other when you hear a sound. Accuracy to within one or two metres is enough. Touch the lines at the end of the track with your foot, turn sharply and run in the opposite direction.

At first the speed is low but it will increase slowly and steadily every minute. Your aim in the test is to follow the set rhythm for as long as you can. You should therefore stop when you can no longer keep up with the set rhythm or feel unable to complete the one minute period. Note the number announced by the recording when you stop - that is your result or score. The length of the test varies according to the individual: the fitter you are, the longer the test lasts.

To sum up, the test is maximal and progressive, in other words easy at the beginning and hard towards the end. Good luck!'

Scoring

Each successful lap is scored when the subject crosses the end line, with at least one foot, as or shortly before the tone sounds. Failure to reach the end line more than once in succession before the tone sounds, indicates that the subject cannot maintain the required pace. The individual score is then taken as the lap number at which the second successive failure occurred, or as the number of the last completed lap in the case of a subject stopping.

It is essential that subjects are always checked to ensure that the end line is crossed before turning; it is desirable that the individual lap scores are repeated to subjects as they finish, to ensure that the scores are accurately entered on the score sheet. It may be possible to arrange for a partner to keep the score.

Care should be taken that subjects warm down in a suitable manner after completion of the test; watch carefully to ensure that any serious after-effects are observed and treated quickly and appropriately.

Caution
This test is progressive and maximal and therefore individuals suffering from the following conditions should not be tested: heart disease, high blood pressure, respiratory complaints, (such as asthma or bronchitis), joint problems, back pain or arthritis. Those who are recovering from recent illness should also not be tested. It is not advisable to undertake the test within two hours of a meal, or during particularly hot conditions.

The following conditions should apply for the rest of the tests.

- All the tests should be performed with bare feet and in PE or sports clothes.
- No warm ups or stretching exercises are allowed before the tests start.
- Trial attempts should only be allowed if this is specifically stated in the test instructions.
- Those attempting the tests should be encouraged throughout the test time.

*Flamingo Balance***

**The Flamingo balance was not included in the Amsterdam battery of tests and so it does not appear in the reference scales.

For this test of general balance you will need a metal beam 50 cm long, 4 cm high and 3 cm wide, covered with a material securely fastened to the beam. Two supports 15cm long and 2 cm wide provide stability. You will also need a stopwatch which does not automatically zero itself after it has been stopped.

Instructions for the subject

'Try and stay balanced as long as possible on the long axis of the beam while standing on your preferred foot. You bend your free leg backwards and grip the back of the foot with your hand on the same side, standing like a flamingo. You may use your other arm to keep your balance. I will help you to place yourself in the correct position by supporting you with my forearm. The test begins as soon as you release my supporting arm. Try to keep balanced in this position for one minute. Each time you lose your balance (i.e. when you let go your free leg, the one you are holding) or when you touch the floor with any part of your body, the test stops. After each such fall, the same procedure starts all over again until one full minute has elapsed.'

Key points
- You should place yourself in front of the subject.
- Allow the subject one trial in order to become familiar with the test and to make sure that the instructions are understood. The test is carried out after this trial.
- Start the stopwatch when the subject releases the supporting arm.
- Stop the stopwatch as soon as the subject loses balance by releasing his free leg or when he touches the floor with any part of his body.
- After each fall help the subject back to the correct position.

Score

The number of attempts (not falls) needed to keep in balance on the beam for one whole minute.

Should the subject fall 15 times within the first 30 seconds, the test is ended and the subject gets a zero score (i.e. the subject is unable to perform the test). This may happen with children of 6 - 9 years.

Plate Tapping Test

For this test, which assesses the speed at which you can move your upper limbs, you will need a stopwatch, a table which is adjustable in height, two rubber discs and a rectangular plate which are fixed on the table as shown above.

Instructions for the subject

'Stand in front of the table feet slightly apart. Place your non-preferred hand on the rectangular plate in the centre. Place your preferred hand on the opposite disc. Move your preferred hand back and forth between the two discs as quickly as possible, over the hand in the middle. Be sure to touch the disc each time. When I say 'Ready.....start!', perform 25 cycles as quickly as possible. Stop when I give the signal 'Stop!', I will count the score aloud. You do the test twice and the better time is your score.'

Key points
- Adjust the table so that the top is just below the umbilical cord.
- Sit or stand in front of the table; concentrate on the disc chosen by the subject at the beginning of the test and count the number of taps on this disc.
- Start the stopwatch at the signal 'Ready.....Start!'. Assuming the subject starts on disc A, the stopwatch is stopped when he/she touches this disc for the 25th time. Thus the total number of taps on the disc A and disc B amount to 50 taps or 25 cycles between A and B.

- The hand on the rectangular plate stays there during the whole test.

- The subject is allowed to have a trial before the test in order to choose the preferred hand.

- A rest period is given between the two attempts. During this time another subject can perform his first trial.

- You need a partner to assist you with this test. One of you should do the timing whilst the other should count the taps.

- The better result is the score. The score is the time needed to touch each disc a total of 25 times, recorded in tenths of a second.

- If the subject fails to touch a disc, an extra tap is added in order to reach the 25 cycles.

  Example: a time of 10.3 seconds scores 103.

Flexibility

For this test, which assesses flexibility in the lower limbs, you will need a test table or box as shown below, and a 30 cm ruler.

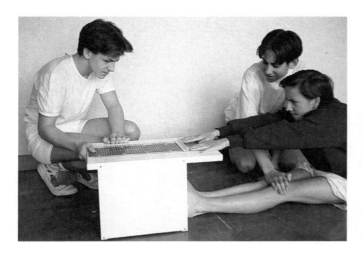

Instructions for the subject

'Take off your shoes and sit down. Place your feet flat against the box, your fingertips on the edge of the top plate. Bend your trunk and reach forward as far as possible keeping your knees straight and slowly and gradually push the ruler in front of you, without jerking and with your hands stretched out. Remain still for two seconds in the farthest position you can reach. Do not bounce. The test will be done twice with the better result counting as the score.'

Key points

- Hold the subject's knees down or use a velcro strap placed around the base board.

- The subject should reach the top edge of the top plate, touching the ruler, before beginning to reach.

- The score is taken from the average distance of the two fingertips.

- The test must be carried out slowly and progressively without any bouncing or jerking movements.

- The second trial should follow after a short rest and the better result recorded in centimetres. As the calibrated surface extends 15 cms in front of the footplate then a person who reaches his toes scores 15. A person who reaches 7 cm past his toes scores 22.

It is also possible to perform this test from a standing position. This is shown in the photograph below.

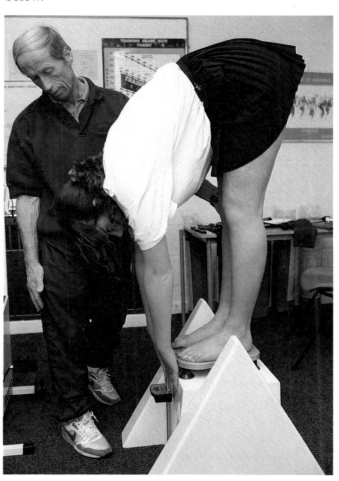

Standing Broad Jump

For this test, which measures explosive strength, you need two judo type mats which have been marked with horizontal lines 10cm apart. These mats are placed parallel to and starting at 1 metre from the take off line on a non-slip surface. Chalk and a tape measure are also required.

Instructions for the subject

'Stand with your feet comfortably apart, and your toes immediately behind the start line. Bend your knees, swing your arms forwards and push off vigorously to jump as far as possible along the mat. Your score will be taken from where your heels land, so try to land with your feet together and don't fall backwards. This test is done twice, with the best score to count. Remember, jump as far as you can, land with your feet level, and don't fall back.'

Key points

- The take off and landing mats must be on the same level and firmly fixed to the floor.

- You should stand alongside the calibrated mat, beside the point at which the pupil is likely to land.

- As soon as the pupil lands, a marker should be placed against the rear heel, and a reading taken.

- The distance is measured from the front edge of the take off line to the point where the back of the heel nearest to the take off line lands on the mat.

- Two trials are allowed, and the better score is recorded.

- A further attempt is allowed if the pupil falls back or if part of the body other than the heel touches the mat.

- The score is recorded in centimetres, for example, 1 m 50 cm = 150 cm.

Handgrip

For this test, which measures static strength, you need a calibrated handgrip dynamometer with an adjustable grip.

Instructions for the subject

'Take the dynamometer in your preferred hand. Adjust the grip so that your first finger joint can curl around the bar. Now hold the dynamometer down by your side, facing away from you. Do not let your arm, your hand or the dynamometer touch your side. Now squeeze gradually and continuously for at least two seconds. Don't swing or jerk the dynamometer. Do the test twice; the better score counts.'

Key points

- The grip dynamometer should be re-set to zero before each test subject.

- The subject should be asked to take the dynamometer in the preferred hand. (If this is not known, the test can be taken with both hands.) The grips should then be adjusted so that the two bars correspond to the distance between the knuckle and the first joint of the middle finger.

- The pupil should hold the dynamometer with the arm extended downwards by the side, and with the dial facing outwards. The arm, hand and dynamometer should not touch the body during the test, and no swinging or jerking action should be allowed. The grips should be squeezed as strongly as possible for two seconds, and a reading taken. A second attempt should then be made, and the best result recorded.

Sit-Ups

For this test, which measures abdominal muscular endurance, you will need two mats, a stopwatch and an assistant.

Instructions for the subject

'Sit on the mat, back upright, hands clasped behind your neck. Your knees should be bent at 90 degrees, and your feet should be flat on the floor, with your knees and feet held in place by your partner. Now lie down on your back until your shoulders touch the mat ..... then return to the sitting position with your elbows out in front so that they touch your knees. Keep your hands clasped behind your neck the whole time. When I say 'Ready ..... GO', repeat this action as rapidly as possible for 30 seconds. I will call 'STOP' after 30 seconds. You do this test only once. Remember, you must keep your hands clasped and touch your knees with your elbows for each sit-up to count.'

Key points

- Kneel at the side of the subject, checking the correct starting position.

- Ensure that the subject's partner sits facing the subject with legs apart, thighs over the subject's feet to keep them on the ground. The partner puts his/her hands in the bends of the subject's knees, thus maintaining a right angle (90°) and the legs still.

- After giving the instructions and before the test begins, the subject executes the entire movement once, to make sure that he has understood.

- Start the stopwatch at the signal 'Ready....start!' and stop after 30 seconds.

- Count aloud each time a complete, correct sit up is performed. One complete sit up goes from the sitting position , to the mat and back to the sitting position, elbows touching the knees.

- Count when the elbows touch the knees. No count means that the sit up was not performed correctly.

- During the performance correct the subject if he does not touch the mat with his shoulders or his knees with his elbows when returning to the starting position.

- The total number of correctly performed completed sit-ups in 30 seconds is the score.

Bent Arm Hang

For this test, which measures arm and shoulder muscle endurance, you will require a horizontal bar of diameter 2.5 cm, set so that the subject when standing below it, can reach it without jumping, a mat underneath the bar, a cloth and some magnesium chalk and a stopwatch.

Instructions for the subject

'Stand under the bar, fingertips on top, thumb underneath, and place your hands, shoulder-wide on the bar with a forward grip. I will help lift you up until your chin is above the bar. Hold this position for as long as possible without resting your chin on the bar. The test ends when your eyes go below the bar.'

10 * 5 Metre Shuttle Run

For this test, which measures running speed and agility, you will need the use of a clean, slip-proof floor, traffic cones, tape, and a stopwatch.

Instructions for the subject

'Get ready behind the start line. On the command 'Ready ..... GO' sprint as fast as possible to the other end line and back again to the start line, crossing both lines with both feet. This will be one cycle, and you have to sprint for five cycles. At the finish of your fifth cycle, do not slow down but continue to sprint across the finish line. This test is done once. Remember, you must cross both lines with both feet, and keep running across the finishing line after five cycles.'

Key points

- Ensure that the subject stands under the bar with his hands shoulder width apart and in a forward grip.

- The height of the bar should be adjusted to the height of the tallest subject. Don't frighten them by making it too high.

- Take the subject by the thighs and lift him into the correct position. A chair or bench may help subjects to reach the bar.

- The watch is started the moment that the subject's chin goes above the bar and is let go.

- Swinging movements by the subject should be stopped; give encouragement.

- Stop the watch when the subject cannot hold the required position any longer as described (eyes above the bar).

- Do not tell the time to the subject during the test.

- Clean the bar between subjects with a cloth. The subjects can chalk their hands.

- The time in tenths of seconds is the score, for example a time of 17.4 seconds, scores 174. A time of 1 min 03.5 seconds scores 635.

Key points

- The test is run over a 5 metre course, in a 1.2 metre lane.

- An area of floor space that is clean, non-slippery and level should be used, ensuring adequate additional space for turning and at the sides. The test area should be marked with tape and cones, with the tape width included within the 5 metre length.

- You should ensure that both feet cross the line at each turn, that the pupil remains in the 1.2 metre lane, and that the turn is made as quickly as possible.

- Each cycle should be called out on completion at the starting end. Verbal instructions may be called to ensure that the lines are crossed with both feet. Practice may be required to ensure accurate timing, and great care must be taken to keep the test area safe and non-slippery.

- The time needed to complete the five cycles is the score and is written in tenths of a second, for example a time of 21.6 seconds scores 216.

ANTHROPOMETRIC MEASURES

Age

We know that each child grows and develops at his/her own particular rate. We also know that scores on particular aspects of fitness tests depend upon physiological maturity as much as upon physical fitness. The reason for keeping a record of a subject's age is not to compare their scores with other people of the same age but rather to see how the individual subject develops over time. One of the aims of the Eurofit group is to assess each pupil at least once a year. This will enable teachers to see not only how individual pupils are developing but also allow them to assess the effectiveness of their health-related fitness programmes.

Height
Test administration

The pupil should stand barefoot and upright on the floor, with heels together and arms hanging comfortably. The back and usually the back of the head should be in contact with the measuring rod. The pupils should be instructed to 'breathe in and look straight ahead'. The measuring arm is then lowered firmly onto the vertex of the head, and the height measured to the nearest 0.5 centimetre.

Weight
Test administration

The weighing scales should be placed on a firm and level surface. Pupils should be barefoot, wearing only light sports clothing. Weight should be measured in kilograms to the nearest 0.1 kg.

Body Composition (Test : 4-site skinfold measurement)*
Test administration

The test requires four skinfold measurements to be taken and the summed result adjusted by a formula to give a prediction of the body density, and so the proportion of fat tissue. Pupils should wear light sports clothing that will allow each test site to be readily reached. You will need to seek the help of your teacher in order to find the exact anatomical positions necessary for this set of tests.

The caliper is used to measure a skinfold at a precise site; the fold consists of a double layer of skin and the underlying fat tissue, but not the muscle. The skinfold is raised by a pinching and rolling movement of the thumb and index finger. The grasp must be large enough to raise a complete double layer of skin and fat, and firm enough to hold throughout the measurement process. A towel may be useful to dry the measurement sites.

When the skinfold has been raised accurately at the site, the caliper is applied so that the near edge is one centimetre away from the pinching thumb and finger, at right angles to the fold. When the caliper trigger is released, and the caliper grips the skinfold, there will be a compressing action for approximately two seconds. The reading is taken as soon as the initial compression ceases, but before further slow compression displaces the fat tissue.

With lean pupils, it may be helpful to draw the calipers out across the skinfold until the muscle is excluded. With obese pupils, firm pinching of the fold may reduce the initial compression effect.

Instructions to pupil

'You will be tested for the depth of fat tissue in four places - the front and back of your upper arm, beneath your shoulder blade, and just above your hip bone'.

Skinfold sites

All measurements must be taken on the same side of the body.

The reading is taken as the sum of the four measurements, in millimetres.

* The fifth area of skinfold measurement (medial calf skinfold) has not been included in the test description. The norms in Appendix 3 have been developed without its inclusion.

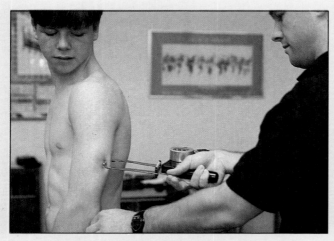

1 ▲ **Triceps** With the pupil's arm hanging loosely, a vertical fold is raised at the back of the arm, midway along a line connecting the acronion (shoulder) and olecranon (elbow) processes.

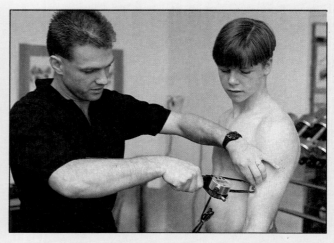

2 ▲ **Biceps** A vertical fold is raised at the front of the arm, opposite to the triceps site. This should be directly above the centre of the cubital fossa (fold of the elbow).

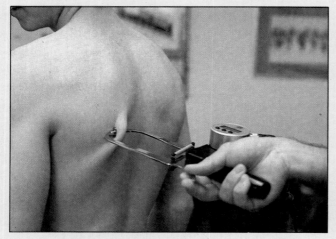

3 ▲ **Subscapular** A fold is raised just beneath the inferior angle of the scapula (bottom of the shoulder- blade). This fold should be at an angle of 45 degrees downwards and outwards.

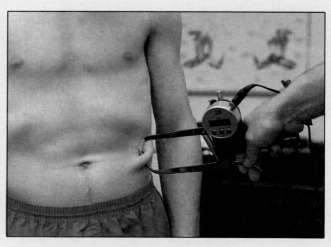

4 ▲ **Anterior suprailiac** A fold is raised 5-7 cm above the spinale (pelvis), at a point in line below the anterior axillary border (armpit). The fold should be in line with the natural folds downward and inwards at up to 45 degrees.

A scoresheet for the EUROFIT Tests can be found in the Appendix.

There are many other health-related and performance-related tests available for use by children, teenagers and adults. Your school may already make use of one or more of them. If used sensibly, they can help each individual to improve his or her general levels of fitness. They should be used individually, however, and not as a form of competition between people.

SEEVIC (South East Essex Sixth Form College) offers a very comprehensive programme of individual assessment as can be seen by the leaflet which they distribute to all of their 1400 students.

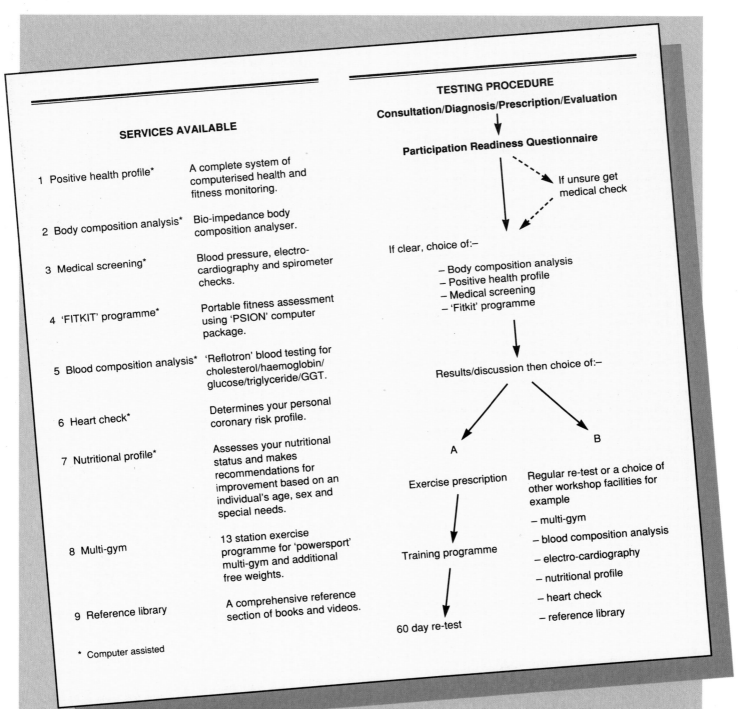

SERVICES AVAILABLE

1 Positive health profile*   A complete system of computerised health and fitness monitoring.

2 Body composition analysis*   Bio-impedance body composition analyser.

3 Medical screening*   Blood pressure, electro-cardiography and spirometer checks.

4 'FITKIT' programme*   Portable fitness assessment using 'PSION' computer package.

5 Blood composition analysis*   'Reflotron' blood testing for cholesterol/haemoglobin/glucose/triglyceride/GGT.

6 Heart check*   Determines your personal coronary risk profile.

7 Nutritional profile*   Assesses your nutritional status and makes recommendations for improvement based on an individual's age, sex and special needs.

8 Multi-gym   13 station exercise programme for 'powersport' multi-gym and additional free weights.

9 Reference library   A comprehensive reference section of books and videos.

* Computer assisted

TESTING PROCEDURE

Consultation/Diagnosis/Prescription/Evaluation

↓

Participation Readiness Questionnaire   ⇢ If unsure get medical check

↓

If clear, choice of:–

– Body composition analysis
– Positive health profile
– Medical screening
– 'Fitkit' programme

↓

Results/discussion then choice of:–

A ← → B

A: Exercise prescription → Training programme → 60 day re-test

B: Regular re-test or a choice of other workshop facilities for example
– multi-gym
– blood composition analysis
– electro-cardiography
– nutritional profile
– heart check
– reference library

The SEEVIC leaflet

THINGS TO DO

1 Explain the following terms:

    (i) anaerobic threshold

    (ii) VO_2 max

    (iii) fatigue index

    (iv) isokinetic dynomometer

2 'Physical fitness is only important to sportspeople.'
'When you are healthy, physical activity is unnecessary.'

Do you agree or disagree with these comments? Give reasons for your answer.

3 Explain why it is important for top-level sportspeople to know exactly how fit they are.

4 As a group, test yourself using the EUROFIT tests. Collect the data and produce a physical fitness report for the group.

5 From the results which you have obtained from these series of tests calculate the following:

    (i) the mean, mode and median scores for the following tests: ▼

TEST	BOYS			GIRLS		
	Mean	Mode	Median	Mean	Mode	Median
Flamingo balance						
Plate tapping						
Standing broad jump						
Hand grip						
Sit -ups						

5 (ii) Construct a frequency histogram for the results which you obtained in the endurance shuttle run and the 10 * 5 metre shuttle run.

6 Using the results which you obtained in the EUROFIT tests, as well as any other data which your teacher may be able to provide, in your group decide which of the following statements are true and which are false:

    (i) Boys are stronger than girls at all ages.

    (ii) Girls are as strong as boys between the ages of 11-13, as shown by their test scores on the standing broad jump and grip strength.

    (iii) You are more likely to obtain a better score in plate tapping if you are a boy.

    (iv) Girls score much more highly on the sit and reach test.

    (v) Girls between the ages of 11-13 are significantly heavier than boys of the same age.

    (vi) Boys of all ages have a significantly lower skinfold score than girls.

    (vii) Your height does not make any difference to the scores you are likely to make on any of the EUROFIT tests.

    (viii) The heavier a boy gets the lower his score will be on all of the EUROFIT tests.

    (ix) Your chronological age is less important than your stage of development in determining EUROFIT test scores.

    (x) You need to score in the top 20% of the EUROFIT scores if you are to become a good sportsperson.

7 Do people who score well in the short shuttle run also score well in the endurance shuttle run? Give reasons to explain your answer.

8 The flamingo balance and the plate tapping test are not included in many tests of health-related fitness. Explain why this should be so.

9 The bent arm hang test is also not used in many tests of health-related fitness. Explain why this should be so.

5 SPORT AND INJURY

Aims

To gain knowledge and understanding of:
- how sporting injuries happen
- how to minimise the risk of sporting injury
- sports medicine

To develop the skills of:
- first aid

The human body is built for movement. We are constantly being encouraged to take part in sport because most sports involve exercise, and we all know that exercise is good for us. However, sport can also have harmful effects. Torn muscles, sprained ankles, broken bones and all sorts of other injuries can result. Some sporting activities are obviously more hazardous than others. Rugby players are more liable to injury than table-tennis players, athletes more than golfers and gymnasts more than swimmers. Most people take part in their particular sport in spite of any possible dangers, although it is clear that sports such as pot-holing, climbing, hang-gliding and so on attract participants because of the element of risk to life and limb.

Why do sports injuries happen?

Sports injuries occur for one of two basic reasons:

1 As a result of sudden or persistent stress on a particular part of the body with which the body cannot cope. In a sport where players come into physical contact with each other, such as rugby league, these stresses happen as a result of tackles, fouls and collisions. They are an accepted part of the game. Some players suffer injury because of their style of play. Others are in danger because of the position they play. For example, front runners in soccer often move with their bodies towards the defenders. They are more likely to get tackles from behind with an increased risk of injury.

2 As a result of damage to the body tissues because of the long term stresses placed on particular body parts within their sport. Professional footballers are again a good example

of people affected in this way. They are often involved in two matches plus training each week for nine months of the year. They are in danger of suffering from overuse injuries affecting the groin, knee and ankle. These may develop into chronic injuries, never really healing and leaving the player permanently less than fully fit. His place in the team and therefore his career may be in danger. Overuse injuries are not only a problem for professional sportsmen and sportswomen. The increasing number of amateurs taking part in distance running with the necessary high training mileage is producing many new overuse injuries. There is also a measurable growth in the number of children displaying signs of overuse injuries gained through sports training.

What should I do if I suffer a sports injury?

This will depend on the type of injury and the availability of skilled help. However, any pain can be eased and the recovery speeded up by the following means.

Stop using the injured body part. You could cause permanent damage.

Apply ice to the injured area. Ice will cause injured blood vessels and surrounding tissues to contract. This will reduce blood flow to the area. The reduced blood flow will give relief and also reduce inflammation by reducing the metabolic and enzymatic functions in the immediate area. Apply ice through a towel or gauze. Remove ice pack after 10/12 minutes. Repeat every 3 hours if necessary.

REST

ICE

COMPRESSION

ELEVATION

ice pack

Keep swelling to a minimum by wrapping an elastic bandage firmly around the area, even over the ice pack. Do not wrap bandage so tightly that the blood supply is cut off. Remove ice pack and bandage after 10/12 minutes to allow skin to warm up and blood flow to return.

Raise injured part of body

ice pack

Raise the injured body part above the level of the heart. The force of gravity will help to drain excess fluid from the damaged area.

The RICE treatment

Skin Damage

Abrasions

These occur when some of the skin layers are scraped off as a result of rubbing the body part against the ground or something rough. For example, mat burns in judo and sliding tackles in soccer.

Treatment

All lacerations should be gently examined to see if there is any damage other than to the skin. Do not poke into the wound.

Apply direct pressure to control bleeding by pressing with your fingers or palm of your hand over a clean dressing. If no dressing is available, squeeze the sides of the wound together with your fingers.

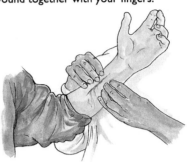

Elevate the limb above the level of the heart unless you suspect the limb is fractured.

Place a clean dressing and padding over the wound. Press down firmly and secure with a bandage. The bandage should be tight enough to control the bleeding but not so tight that it cuts off circulation.

If bleeding continues, do not remove dressing but apply further pads or dressings on top of the original ones and bandage firmly.

If the injury is on a limb and direct pressure does not stop the bleeding, apply indirect pressure to the main artery. Press inwards and upwards, pushing the artery against the bone.

This indirect pressure prevents the blood supply reaching the whole of the affected limb. Therefore this method should only be used as a last resort and must not be applied for longer than 10 minutes.

Do not apply a tourniquet.

Shelter patient from extremes of temperature. You may moisten their lips with water but do not give them anything to drink.

Reassure the patient and seek medical help as quickly as possible.

How to deal with heavy bleeding

If the blood is bright red in colour and is spurting from the wound, then an artery has been cut. This is serious as a lot of blood can be lost in a very short time.

If the blood loss cannot be controlled by direct pressure then indirect pressure must be used. Indirect pressure involves compressing an artery against an underlying bone with the intention of preventing the blood from reaching the wounded area.

There are two pressure points used to control severe bleeding. These are on the brachial artery in the arm and on the femoral artery in the leg.

Blisters

These are caused by repeated friction on the skin. The repeated friction causes a parting of the layers of the skin. The gap is then filled by a tissue fluid (serum) which forms a thin bubble or blister.

Treatment

Small blisters can be covered with an adhesive dressing. Blisters do heal more quickly if the fluid is drained from them. Large blisters can be punctured with a sterile needle and the fluid removed by gentle pressure. Then the blister can be covered by a plaster without removing the skin over the blister. If the blister becomes infected (pain increases, the area reddens and pus appears) then further medical advice is necessary. Infection is the greatest danger arising from skin injuries. All serious cuts or abrasions should be reported to a doctor or hospital for a tetanus jab.

Muscle Injuries

Muscle injuries can be caused by external forces or by internal forces such as tears or strains. They account for approximately 10-30% of all injuries in sport. Muscle soreness is quite normal and may remain for between eight to twenty four hours after exercise. It is more likely to happen if the exercise is new to you. The muscle fibres will have been stretched during the muscular activities. After exercise they swell as they are repaired and replenished. Gentle exercise will help to give relief. Severe muscle injuries should be seen by a doctor on the day of the injury.

Distraction

A distraction strain often occurs in a muscle which works across two joints, for example the quadriceps muscles, which extend the knee joint and flex in the hip joint. As both of these functions cannot occur at the same time, one function, governed by the sensitive neuromuscular unit, is active whilst the other is inactive.

Distraction injuries usually occur in explosive events such as sprinting, jumping or football. This type of distraction strain is often located in the superficially lying muscles, that is rectus femoris, semitendinosus and gastrocnemius muscles. These muscles are subject to stretch and force over two joints, but the muscle fibre orientation may not be able to cope with this.

What is a pulled or torn muscle?

Most of us have seen the sprinter at top speed suddenly in great pain grasp the back of his thigh and desperately attempt to stop running. He or she has probably torn or pulled a hamstring. The muscle fibres have torn because they could not cope with the force which was being applied to them. The pain is very localised and the greater it is the more serious the tear. The possible reasons for torn or pulled muscles include poor training methods, bad technique, overtraining, lack of warm up and poor flexibility.

Treatment

As soon as a sharp localised pain is felt STOP. Continued exercise will cause more damage and increase the recovery time. Follow the RICE treatment (Rest, Ice, Compression and Elevation) for at least 48 hours!

After 48 hours it is important to get increased supplies of nutrients to the damaged muscle. This can be done by applying heat to the area. The blood vessels will open up and increase the blood supply to the area. Do not start to exercise until the pain has gone. When you do start increase the amount of exercise gradually. The length of time a pulled or torn muscle takes to heal will depend upon the size of the tear and the treatment given. Your age is also important. The older you are the longer the recovery time. It is particularly important that you include many gentle stretching exercises in your training programme. This will ensure that the injured muscle does not heal in a shortened position.

What are muscle cramps?

A muscle cramp is a sudden painful contraction of a muscle or group of muscles. It can last for a few seconds or continue for several hours. Cramps can occur at any time. The most common times are either during or following intense exercise. There are many causes of cramp. They include chilling of the body during exercise such as swimming, lack of salt and other minerals, muscle injury and prolonged muscular contraction without movement. A healthy diet including plenty of fruit and vegetables will ensure that you take in sufficient minerals.

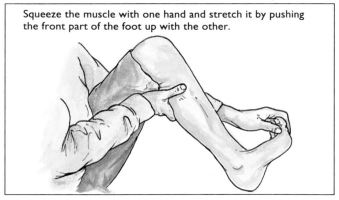

Squeeze the muscle with one hand and stretch it by pushing the front part of the foot up with the other.

Treatment of a calf cramp

Treatment
Stretch the muscle.

Stitch

Stitch is a particular form of cramp which appears to affect the large flat diaphragm muscle which controls breathing. It is common amongst runners who suddenly experience a sharp pain in the upper part of their abdomen. One cause may be a lack of blood getting to the diaphragm. The blood supply is cut off due to pressure from the lungs above (caused by the heavy breathing during hard exercise) and pressure from the stomach muscles below. Other possible causes of stitch include eating just before you exercise or exercising with a full intestinal tract.

Treatment
Stitch can be prevented in two major ways. Firstly by strengthening your diaphragm and stomach muscles. Secondly by avoiding exercise for at least three hours after eating a large meal. If you do get stitch, slow down and bend forward. Push your clenched fist into the area of the pain. The stitch will soon disappear and you will be able to start running again.

Bruised muscles

Hard blows to muscles can result in bruising. These injuries are common in body contact games. The muscle is squashed against the underlying bone and bleeding within the muscles often takes place. The whole area becomes tender to touch with swelling and discolouration. Movement also causes a great deal of pain.

Treatment
RICE.

Are muscle injuries dangerous?
Damaged skeletal muscle has the ability to repair itself very quickly. Myoblasts can be seen around the edges of the damaged tissues within two to three days. Seven to eight days after the injury the contractile properties of the muscle gradually return. At the same time, however, granulation tissue and non-contractile collagenous fibres called fibrocytes are also produced. These fibrocytes shorten and strengthen as the muscle heals and develop into a permanent scar tissue.

Muscle fibres do not regenerate across the scar; the part of the muscle which has been cut off from the motor unit loses its ability to contract and so the muscle is permanently weakened.

This increases the chance of repeated or chronic injuries. There is also a danger that the scar tissue formed on the muscle may attach itself to other muscles, tendon or bone near it. The full movement of joints may then be limited. It is vital therefore that muscles are helped to heal through passive, static and active exercise. In this way the muscle will heal in as long a position as possible and the amount of scar tissue formed will be kept to a minimum. If the muscle heals short, it may limit the range of motion at a joint. Also it is likely to be torn again when under intense pressure.

Muscle injuries are not really dangerous. It is the wrong treatment which can cause problems. Recent muscular injuries (within 48 hours) cannot be run off, heated away or massaged better. Always follow the RICE treatment.

Tendon injury

When muscles contract their force is passed through a fibrous band of tissue called a tendon which is attached to the bone. Tendons are very strong but on occasions have to cope with too great a strain. This can happen through lack of warm up, poorly co-ordinated movements, a blow from an opponent, decreased flexibility, repeated trauma or fatigue. Tendons can be partly or completely torn (ruptured). The most commonly injured tendons are the Achilles tendon at the heel and the tendon in the shoulder.

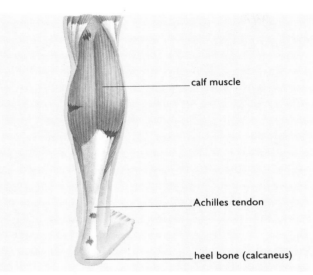

Locations of injuries in the calf muscle and Achilles tendon

Treatment
It is important to apply the RICE treatment immediately and also to get medical advice. If a tendon is only partially torn then it will repair itself. The time needed for healing will depend on the extent of the tear. Complete rupture will involve loss of movement at the joint as well as a great deal of pain. Surgery may be necessary to rejoin the two ends of the tendon and the limb put in plaster for six weeks with physiotherapy to follow. A complete rupture of a tendon is a most serious injury and has finished many sporting careers. Regular stretching exercises can reduce the danger of tendon injury.

Tendonitis

If muscles are kept tight, this will put a strain on the tendons. They may become inflamed and swell causing pain. The pain is felt even when at rest. The pain often disappears when you exercise, only to return again when you rest. Particular sports tend to create problems with certain tendons. For example tennis and javelin throwing can result in damaged elbow tendons (tennis elbow), while sprinters may suffer from damaged Achilles tendons.

Treatment
Continuing to play will only make the condition worse. Stop training at maximum effort and take gentle exercise only until the pain and inflammation disappear. Include plenty of slow, gentle stretching exercises in your training. Strong but flexible muscles will prevent tendonitis.

Injuries to Joint and Cartilage

A joint injury is liable to involve one or more of the following body tissues: bone, cartilage, ligaments, muscles and tendons.

What is a sprain?
A sprain occurs when the ligaments and other tissues around a joint are torn often as a result of a sudden or severe wrenching. The joint is forced beyond its normal range and a great deal of pain is felt. Movement becomes difficult and the area around the joint becomes swollen as blood and other fluids spread from the damaged vessels.

Treatment
Sprains vary greatly in their severity. It is sometimes difficult to distinguish a bad sprain from a fracture in one of the surrounding bones. If there is any doubt, treat the injury as if it is a fracture, that is get immediate medical help. In cases of minor sprain apply the RICE treatment. Ensure that the injured person sees his or her doctor if the pain is still present after 24 hours.

How can a bone become dislocated?
Dislocations occur when one or more of the bones at a joint are forced out of their normal position. This can happen as a result of an external force or through a sudden muscular contraction. Shoulder dislocations may occur in body contact sports such as judo and American football. Basketball players may suffer finger and thumb dislocations. A person suffering from a dislocation will show one or more of the following symptoms:
- They will complain of a severe sickening pain in or around the joint.
- The joint will look deformed and out of place as well as the whole area being swollen.
- The joint will appear fixed with no movement being possible.

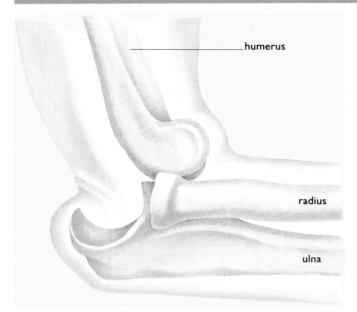

Dislocation of the elbow joint

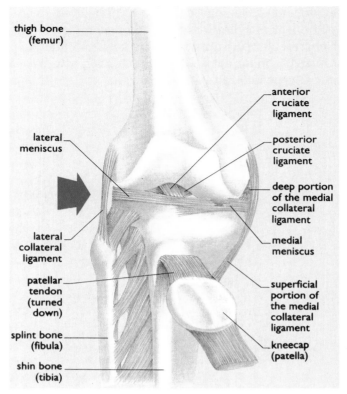

Injuries to the knee joint

Treatment

Support the injured part in the most comfortable position using bandages or slings if available. Then get the patient to hospital as quickly as possible. If you are in any doubt as to the nature of the injury, then treat it as a fracture. A trained physiotherapist or doctor can often manipulate the bones back into place immediately. This should not be attempted by anyone else. There is a real danger of further injury to nerves and other soft structures around the joint.

Dislocations have a tendency to recur. This is because the ligaments protecting the joint become stretched and the whole joint is less stable. This is why it is important to build up the muscles around the joint so that they can help to keep it stable. If joints keep dislocating it is possible for a surgical repair to be done in which the ligaments are shortened.

Why do sportsmen and sportswomen have cartilage trouble?

The two semi-lunar cartilages which work in the knee joint can be damaged as a result of sporting activities. It is a rotational injury caused very often when the athlete turns very rapidly. No other person need be involved. Cartilages can also be injured as the result of a direct blow on the side of the knee joint whilst the leg is still in contact with the ground. The resultant stress tears the cartilage and the knee joint either locks or gives way.

Treatment

If a person's knee locks in a bent position, there is swelling around the joint, and the person complains of a sharp sickening pain, usually on the inner side of the knee, then a knee cartilage has been displaced. Support the injured leg in the most comfortable position. Do not attempt to straighten the leg. Protect the knee by soft padding around the joint. This can be secured by a bandage. Get the person to hospital as quickly as possible, keeping the leg position stable.

In many cases the most effective form of treatment is to remove the damaged cartilage. If the surrounding muscles are exercised immediately after the operation then little muscle bulk will be lost. It is often possible for the sportsman or sportswoman to be fit for competition in six to eight weeks.

Injuries to Bone

Broken bones are a possibility in all fast moving activities particularly if body contact is an essential part of the game. They can be damaged by direct blows, pulls or as a result of too much stress.

Common sites for injuries to bones

Clavicle - the most common fracture found in childhood (10-15% of all accidents) from direct violence or indirect trauma from falls on outstretched hands (riding, gymnastics, team games)

Ribs and thorax - frequent in falls (skiing, bob-sleighing, cycling, motor sports, riding, rugby) and from direct blows to the chest (ice hockey, soccer, rugby, wrestling, judo, boxing, gymnastics)

Upper limbs -

1 *Humerus* - from direct blows and indirect falls (cycling, skiing, gymnastics). Avulsion fractures of the proximal epiphysis in adolescent baseball throwers, or of the tuberosities in throwers, gymnasts or fencers are observed due to the effort of throwing or contraction.

2 *Elbow* - Approximately 7% of all fractures and dislocations occur in the elbow resulting from indirect trauma transmitted through the forearm bones or a direct blow to the radius and ulna against the distal humerus. 60% of fractures in children are supracondylar (often called a gymnastic's fracture) as they result from extension or flexion and may be associated with the brachial artery or the ulna nerve. Throwing may result in avulsions (baseball pitcher, javelin thrower) although many elbow fractures are the result of high speed sports injuries.

Ankle and foot - Safety standards and high skiboots have reduced their injury in skiing - now transferred to knee ligaments. Avulsion fractures of the malleoles are found associated with a sprain in many sports.

Distal forearm, wrist and hand - Age determines the site of fractures.

4-10 transverse fractures of the lower end of the radius and ulna;

11-16 separation of the distal epiphysis;

17-40 Navicular fractures;

After 40 Potts and Colles fractures.

Injuries of the carpals are common.

The metacarpals and phalanges are the most common sites of injury in sports. Mallet or baseball finger is frequently found with an avulsion fracture on the extension tendon at its insertion in 25% of cases (rugby, basketball, handball, volleyball, US football). Dislocation fractures (50% of thumb, 25% of the index fingers), goalkeeper's or gamekeeper's thumb!``

Pelvis - damaged only in motor sports, cycling, skiing, and riding, usually with severe damage to bladder and bowels.

Femur - not common but seen in skiing. Common in the aged population. Avulsion fractures of the apophysis of the lesser trochanter can be observed during a violent contraction in a soccer player, fencer, sprinter, skiier, jumper or weightlifter.

Knee joint - Complex and vulnerable joint. Damaged by direct impact as well as by twisting or angulation movements. Ligamentous injuries are the most frequent and severe.

Tibia and fibula - common.

A closed fracture is one where the skin surface around the bone is not broken.
An open fracture is where the ends of the bone have come through the skin.
A compound fracture is one where the fractured bone has also caused other injuries. All fractures are serious and need urgent medical treatment.

Treatment
Unless you are medically qualified do only what is necessary to comfort the injured person and prevent further injury. Getting the ambulance is a priority.

Steps that may be taken to deal with a suspected fracture are listed overleaf:

1 Do not move the injured person but look for signs of a fracture. These may include:

- pain; sharp, severe and localised
- loss of or difficulty in moving the body part
- deformity at the site of the injury
- swelling and later bruising of the body part
- grating of the bone ends.

The injured person may be able to help you make a diagnosis. Ask him or her about the injury, the pain. He or she may tell you that they heard a crack or snap as they fell.

If there is any doubt in your mind treat the injury as a fracture.

2 Send for an ambulance.

3 Make the injured person as comfortable as possible. Prevent any movement at the site of the injury. This could cause further injury and more pain.

4 If the ambulance is likely to be some time then the injured limb may be immobilised. This can be done by bandaging it to a sound part of the body or using a blow up splint if available. Any bleeding must be treated immediately.

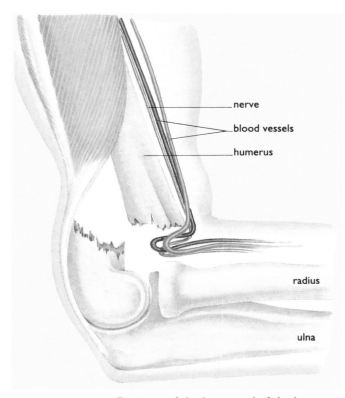

Fracture of the lower end of the humerus

Defending World Champion, Karen Briggs, had her leg broken in her first contest, when her opponent stepped on her leg as she tried to throw her

Stress fractures

A stress fracture is a slight crack in a bone. It is caused in the first place by an excessive force applied again and again to the bone by its attached muscles through their tendons. Some top class international athletes including Sebastian Coe have suffered from stress fractures. Anyone who takes part in a repetitive physical activity such as jogging, rowing, cycling or sprinting, is in danger of developing a stress fracture. It is not the repeated activity itself which is the problem but rather any sudden change in stress on the bone. Bones will become as strong as they need to be to withstand the forces which the muscles, through their tendons, exert on them. Problems arise if the activity is modified in some way or other and the bones are not given time to adapt. If you suddenly change your training programme, your technique of rowing, running or cycling, or even wear a different type of shoe and continue to train hard then the bone can be overstressed and may crack.

Treatment

If you stop exercising the pain will go away, the crack will heal and you can soon start training again. If you carry on hard training however, the crack will become bigger, the pain worse and you could cause a complete fracture of the bone. If you think you have a stress fracture seek medical advice, preferably from a sports medicine specialist.

Unconsciousness

If a player gets knocked out he or she could have a fractured skull, bleeding from the veins or arteries within the skull or bruising to the brain substance. He or she could also have a spinal injury. Even if the unconscious person 'comes to' within a few seconds and insists that they are alright, do not let them continue playing.

Treatment

1 Send for an ambulance or get expert medical help.

2 Keep the injured person rested and covered with a blanket until he or she reaches hospital. If they do not recover consciousness keep a check on their pulse and breathing until the ambulance arrives.

3 Check for spinal injuries. This is most easily achieved by asking the patient whether there is any pain as well as requesting that they move their fingers and toes. The symptoms of spinal injury include severe pain in the back or neck spreading to the arms, leg or trunk, an inability to move the spine, arms or legs and either a tingling sensation or a numbness of the arms and legs.

If there is any possibility of a spinal injury do not move the patient. Wait for the ambulance to arrive and comfort the injured person. Do not give the patient anything to drink as this could delay the hospital giving him an anaesthetic for the next four hours.

If a sportsman or sportswoman receives a hard bang on the head and does not lose consciousness, still keep a close check on them. If in the next few hours they feel sick, drowsy or dizzy, get them to hospital.

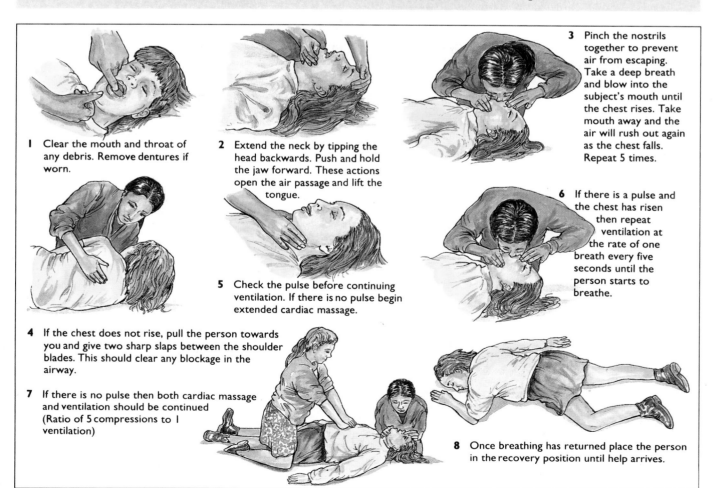

1 Clear the mouth and throat of any debris. Remove dentures if worn.

2 Extend the neck by tipping the head backwards. Push and hold the jaw forward. These actions open the air passage and lift the tongue.

3 Pinch the nostrils together to prevent air from escaping. Take a deep breath and blow into the subject's mouth until the chest rises. Take mouth away and the air will rush out again as the chest falls. Repeat 5 times.

4 If the chest does not rise, pull the person towards you and give two sharp slaps between the shoulder blades. This should clear any blockage in the airway.

5 Check the pulse before continuing ventilation. If there is no pulse begin extended cardiac massage.

6 If there is a pulse and the chest has risen then repeat ventilation at the rate of one breath every five seconds until the person starts to breathe.

7 If there is no pulse then both cardiac massage and ventilation should be continued (Ratio of 5 compressions to 1 ventilation)

8 Once breathing has returned place the person in the recovery position until help arrives.

Mouth-to-mouth resuscitation

What should be done if the injured person has stopped breathing?

1 Send for an ambulance.

2 Feel for a pulse at the wrist or neck. (With death bleeding suddenly ceases from a wound.)

3 If no pulse is felt and there is no breathing start mouth-to-mouth ventilation.

Cardiac Massage

Cardiac massage, (heart massage) should only be attempted if there is no pulse (that is the injured person's heart has stopped beating).

The above descriptions of how to treat sporting injuries are only guidelines. They cannot replace a well run, nationally recognised first aid course. Try and attend one of the courses run by the Red Cross, St. John's Ambulance Brigade or St. Andrew's Ambulance Association.

1 Check for a pulse on the carotid artery. If the heart has stopped beating the skin will be pale and the lips blueish. The arms and legs will be limp and the pupils of the eyes will be dilated.

2 Place your ear on to the chest to listen for any heart beat. If you are sure that the heart has stopped beating then start heart massage.

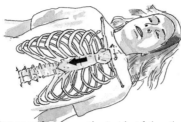

3 Run your fingers up the inside of the rib cage until you feel the tip of the breastbone. Just above this is the massage point.

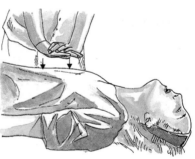

4 Start massage by placing the heels of your hands on top of one another over the lower part of the sternum keeping your arms straight press down firmly to depress the chest wall for about 4–5 cm (1 1/2–2 in). Then rock backwards to release the pressure. Repeat at the rate of 60 compressions a minute.

5 After five compressions the person giving the mouth to mouth ventilation should perform a ventilation. Repeat at the rate of 5 compressions to one ventilation.

6 Check the pulse regularly as each breath is given. Also check if the eyes and lips are returning to normal. Stop heart massage as soon as the heart starts to beat once more.

7 It may be necessary to continue with mouth to mouth ventilation even after the heartbeat has returned. As soon as breathing is fully restored place person in the recovery position. Keep an eye on them until expert help arrives.

Cardiac massage

How can sports injuries be prevented?

It is possible to have a sporting career without suffering a single injury. The risk of injury is linked to the speed of the sport, the implements used and the degree of body contact, as well as other factors.

The type of injury suffered depends on the particular sport. Fractures, bruising and torn ligaments occur regularly in body contact sports. Muscle strains and stress fractures are more common among track and field athletes. Racket players may receive eye and head injuries from racket or ball as well as developing shoulder and ankle strains. There is a lower rate of injury for boxing and judo than for soccer. Most soccer injuries are trivial however (cuts, bumps and grazes) whereas the injuries in boxing and judo may be to the head or joints and therefore potentially more dangerous. Although the injury rate in rock climbing is low, the injuries suffered can be deadly.

All sports put stress on one or more of the body systems. Fit individuals, however, are better able to cope with these stresses. Their bodies are less likely to break down and suffer injury when put under the additional stress brought about through competitive sport. Fitness must include stamina, strength, flexibility and skill.

1 Stamina

When fatigue sets in, skill 'goes out of the window'. Nearly half of the rugby injuries reported happen in the last quarter of matches. This is because as players become physically drained their concentration, speed and their level of skill are all affected. Sportsmen and sportswomen need to develop sufficient stamina to cope readily with all the stresses likely to be put on them. They also need a margin of safety in case of extra stress. This may mean that their training will be more physically tiring than the actual competition.

2 Strength

All muscles act to strengthen joints and protect them from injury. Stronger muscles appear to be able to absorb more energy than weaker ones and therefore are less liable to suffer from strain. Well developed muscles also work as a fleshy shield. This can help to cushion the effects on bone or the abdominal organs. This is particularly important for those who take part in combat sports such as judo and boxing as well as other body contact sports. Any strength training programmes must

Fatal accidents (except by drowning) occurring in England and Wales during sporting and leisure activities in 1988

Category	No. dead	Largest sub-category
Horse-riding	16	Unspecified, **8**
Motor-sports	12	Motor-cycle racing, **3**
Mountaineering	12	Mountain-climbing, **7**
Water sports	8	Diving, **3**
Air sports	8	Aerobatics, **4**
Outdoor sports	6	Mountain/fell walking, **4**
Cycling	3	
Ball games	3	Football, **2**
Angling	1	
Other	13	Weightlifting, **2**

The London Marathon

Between 1981 and 1990:

- One death in over 4.8 million miles.
- Over 185 000 competitors.
- 31 450 stops at St. John Ambulance medical pit stops.
- 177 hospital referrals.
- Total nights spent in hospital by all referrals: 111 (56 of this total was for one person with a fractured femur).

A psychiatrist's view of distance runners:
'Distance running is a socially sanctioned and relatively harmless method for gratifying potentially dangerous narcissistic and masochistic tendencies.'

be checked for balance. It is vital to build up opposing muscles together and not just to increase the strength of one of them. Similarly both sides of the body must be developed; uneven muscular development can be harmful.

3 Flexibility

Flexibility exercises should be part of a warm up programme for all sportsmen and sportswomen. They help to prevent muscle injury by stretching the muscles as well as warming them up and preparing them for the more vigorous exercise to follow.

Strength training alone has a negative effect on joint flexibility but this can be counteracted by combining it with flexibility training.

The flexibility of a particular joint is primarily limited by the tightness of the connective tissue, there are elastic components in both the tendon and the muscle that will stretch. Flexibility decreases with age; therefore more emphasis should be put on older age groups. When the muscle mass starts to increase at 14-16 years of age, flexibility training should be included in all training programmes.

4 Skill

A skilful performer is usually in the right place at the right time. He or she has the ability to select and carry out the most appropriate physical actions often with the minimum of time and effort. Skilled performers are less likely to cause injury to themselves and others. Many sporting injuries are the direct or indirect result of lack of skill: tennis elbow in throwers, many eye injuries in squash and breaks and bruises in soccer, for example.

Not all training is good for you!

Training is necessary to achieve high levels of fitness. It can also be responsible for many injuries. If training puts too much stress on the body or if the body is given too little time to recover between bouts of training, then injury can occur.

Sportsmen and sportswomen can also overtrain. The signs of overtraining include persistent tiredness and loss of interest in training, continual soreness and stiffness in the muscles, joints and tendons as well as numerous minor injuries, frequent colds and so on.

Overtraining can be a problem for complete beginners as well as to experienced professional athletes. The cure is a rest from training. Minor muscle injuries can also occur if you introduce new training methods too quickly into your regular routine. You will be using muscle groups in ways in which they have not worked hard before. They must be given time to adapt.

Age and Sporting Injuries

1 Young people

More and more young people are taking part in competitive sport. This has not only meant that they are engaging in serious fitness training but

also that many of them are suffering from sport injuries. The vast majority of these injuries are preventable and happen because it is assumed that children are just small-scale adults. Those involved in training young people must have an understanding of body growth and development and must ensure that training methods do not put undue stress on the growing skeletal system.

Compared to the bones of adults, children's bones are more resilient and flexible and the ligaments and muscles are more elastic. They also heal more quickly after injury. Bony injuries are potentially more serious however, because of the presence of the growth zones or epiphyseal cartilages in the long bones. These areas of bone growth are softer than fully formed bones and more likely to suffer injury. They must be treated with great care to ensure that permanent joint deformity does not occur.

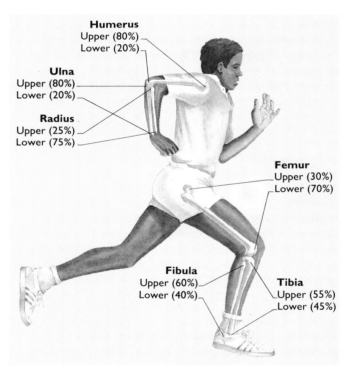

Epiphyseal growth zones and contribution to long bone growth

During adolescence muscles, tendons and ligaments are relatively stronger than the growth zones of the bones. The muscles of adolescents also respond very rapidly to strength training. Skeletal adaptations do not take place as quickly and there is a real danger of the bony attachment of the muscle or ligament being torn away from its origin during strong muscular contraction. These injuries are called avulsion fractures.

Such avulsion fractures are often located in the sensitive growth centres of flat bones, and are most common in the front of the pelvis, and also in the ischium where the posterior hamstring muscles have their origins. Such injuries need to be dealt with by specialists as soon as possible.

Injury is also quite common to the apophyses, the site where muscles and tendons attach themselves to bone. Osgood-Schlatter disease, where the attachment of the patellar tendon to the tibia becomes inflamed and there is some bone disintegration, is particularly common in boys between 10-16 years of age and occurs in a variety of sports including football, gymnastics and athletics.

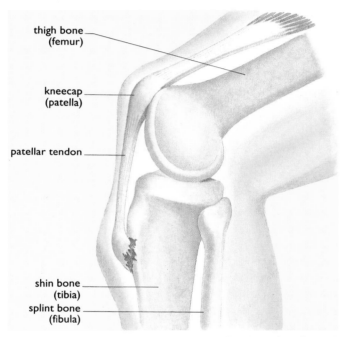

Osgood-Schlatters disease. The bone is inflamed and broken up at the attachment of the patellar tendon to the shin bone

Sever's disease occurs in the attachment of the Achilles tendon to the calcaneous and is common in football. It is often caused through training errors, usually monotonous, repetitive training. Malalignment and a tight Achilles tendon during the growth spurt are also common factors.

Strength training which takes place during adolescence can result in permanent adaptations by the musculoskeletal system. Tennis shoulder, where the shoulder becomes permanently lowered and the active arm therefore relatively longer as well as more muscled is an extreme example of one sided training during adolescence. Gymnasts who train for a number of years bring about

Distribution of injured girls and boys according to type of sport

Sport activity	Number of injured			
	Girls	Boys	Total	%
Soccer	47	131	178	24
Handball	106	18	124	16
Alpine skiing	25	61	86	11
Cross-country skiing	22	42	64	8
Ball (unspecified)	24	16	40	5
Gymnastics	21	19	40	5
Ice skating	21	7	28	4
Horse riding	20	3	23	3
Judo/karate	4	8	12	2
Ski jumping	1	13	14	2
Swimming	8	9	17	2
Volleyball/basketball	12	6	18	2
Roller skating	2	1	3	1
Other	38	51	89	12
Track	5	3	8	1
Total	**359 (47%)**	**399 (53%)**	**758**	

(This study was carried out at the Regional and University Hospital in Trondheim, Norway during 1985-86.)

permanent changes in the vertebral bodies and increased mobility in the pelvis. This increased unnatural mobility might bring problems in later life. Those involved in training programmes for adolescents should ensure that those in their charge develop in a balanced way and one sided and repetitive training should be avoided.

Back injuries are an increasing problem in children's sport. particularly in gymnastics. Many of the lower back pains are the result of spondylosis, a break in the narrow bony neck between the articular processes of the vertebra. This break happens as a result of repeated hyperextension of the lumber spine.

Training with heavy weights should be avoided by most individuals who are still growing. The load on the vertebral column during weight training can be so great that the vertebrae are affected. Only the weight of the body should be used as a load in strength training in young individuals. Not until the skeleton has stopped growing, which in girls happens at about 16 years and in boys 17-18 years, should systematic weight training with heavy weights start.

Flexibility training should take place to counteract the tendency for individuals to lose their flexibility after the growth spurt.

Children are also particularly likely to suffer from overuse injuries such as stress fractures. (See next section.)

As far as endurance training is concerned, evidence shows that there is no loss in effect by delaying systematic physical fitness training until children are in their teens.

2 Young adults

With early adulthood, men and women involved in top level sport are near their peak. As a result their motivation and willingness to train hard is very high. They are likely to suffer from overuse injuries. They are also at their physical peak and so injuries in contact sports tend to be more severe and traumatic.

3 Middle aged people

As men and women progress to middle age the problems of gaining or even maintaining fitness become greater, although in many sporting activities the sportsmen and sportswomen are able to use their skill and experience to counteract lessening physical powers. There is also an increase in ligament and tendon injuries and the joints are liable to suffer from premature arthritis.

4 Old people

Those who indulge in physical activities in old age have normally come to terms with the fact that, although their skill may remain high, their fitness inevitably declines. They are often capable of working within their own level for a prolonged period of time. This explains why a large number of relatively elderly people can happily join the jogging boom. Sudden bursts of effort are no longer possible nor desirable for their body systems.

Are some bodies safer than others?

A person with the wrong body shape for a particular sport is more liable to suffer injury as a result of imposing abnormal stresses on his or her body. An extremely thin person with little or no fat covering or muscle will suffer many bruises in body contact and combat sport. A heavily framed and overweight person will put great stress on the lower joints and heart and lung system if he or she suddenly takes up vigorous physical activity.

We all know that children and young people develop at different rates. One fourteen year old can still be a child in body build whereas another may be almost fully grown.

Competition between them in many sporting activities would appear to be an unequal contest. In a game such as rugby it would appear to be positively dangerous. Yet most sporting competition at school level is organised on an age rather than a size basis. It would be a wise move to look at a more logical way of grouping children in order that only children of approximately the same size and weight compete with each other.

Can the desire for success be dangerous?

No-one likes to be injured, but a nagging injury to a top level sportsman or sportswoman can have implications out of all proportion to the actual injury. Being injured can affect potential earnings, and the desire to get back to the sport may lead a person to restart training before recovery is complete. Injured sportsmen and sportswomen are also loathe to leave a competition when suffering an injury. The adrenalin flowing in the blood dampens down any feeling of pain. Many would sooner accept the help of a pain killing injection which will relieve the immediate feeling of pain but could cause long term damage. Coaches or managers should stop the injured person playing but they are often under pressure for good results and may be tempted to risk the injured player.

Injuries can happen because a person wants to win too much and will do almost anything to ensure victory. Concern has been expressed by numerous bodies about the way that some teachers and parents motivate children before games of soccer and rugby. Similar disquiet exists at the psyching up of individuals before combat activities such as judo.

Can injury be used to advantage?

It is not unusual to see sportsmen or sportswomen with obvious injuries (usually heavily bandaged), perhaps safe in the knowledge that if only they were 100% fit they would have won their event easily. There are others who always appear to suffer an injury just before an important

Overuse injuries

Overuse injuries are not only a problem for professional sportsmen and sportswomen. The increasing number of amateurs taking part in distance running with the necessary high training mileage is producing many new overuse injuries. There is also a measurable growth in the number of children displaying signs of overuse injuries gained through sports training.

Running tends to tighten the posterior lower back muscles and fascias. This increases the chance of lordosis (exaggerated hyperextension of the lower spine) and therefore lower back problems.

Overuse injuries of bones include stress fractures which are most commonly seen in the long bones of the lower leg, fibula and tibia and in the foot but also around the hip and knee. A stress fracture is a partial or complete fracture of a bone which is brought about as a result of repeated stress through activities such as long distance training.

Excessive pronation of the foot (flat feet) can result in foot and lower muscles having to work much harder to compensate for any possible twisting of the lower limbs. These muscles are liable to suffer from overuse injuries as a result.

Muscle imbalance, where one set of muscles is much weaker than those in opposition to it can also cause overuse injuries.

Up to 80% of overuse injuries can be attributed to training errors. These include:

too much distance work;
too high intensity training;
training on hard surfaces;
too much hill work;
faulty techniques which are not corrected;
inadequate or worn out footwear.

The articular cartilage of the knee is particularly susceptible to overuse injury. The cartilage is worn away through a process of softening and shredding.

Stress fractures are most commonly seen in the long bones of the lower leg, fibula and tibia and in the foot but also around the hip and knee. A stress fracture is a partial or complete fracture of bone which is brought about as a result of repeated stress through activities such as long distance training.

Sportsmen and women are more likely to suffer from stress fractures than non sportspersons despite the fact that the thickness, strength and mineral content of their bones are greater.

Tendon injury becomes more likely as the athlete ages. This is because the collagen fibres within the tendon gradually degenerate and become susceptible to overuse injuries.

Bursitis is a common overuse injury around the Achilles tendon, around the knee joint, at the hip and in the shoulder and elbow regions.

A force of up to five times a runner's bodyweight is transmitted through the lower limbs each time that his foot strikes the ground.

A long distance runner who runs 160 km (100 miles) per week plants each foot about 3 million times a year.

It is therefore not surprising that body tissues can suffer from repetitive microtrauma called overuse injuries.

competition only to recover when the pressure is off. It has been argued that, as the competitive and commercial pressures increase, more and more sportsmen and sportswomen are likely to become psychologically injury prone. It certainly appears that injuries increase in direct relation to an increase in stress.

Rules Should be Kept for Safety's Sake

Each sport has its own set of rules. These have been drawn up and changed over many years to keep the sport demanding, enjoyable and safe. The breaking of rules in order to get an unfair advantage over an opponent can result in physical danger. Illegal techniques when used in combat sports can be particularly dangerous, as can some of the more unsavoury tactics used in rugby football union. An increasing number of rugby players these days suffer from serious neck injuries due to intentionally collapsed scrums, a tactic which is against the laws of the game.

A large number of sports have referees or umpires whose job it is to ensure that the game or sporting event is played within the defined rules. It is most important that officials are knowledgeable, alert, and able to keep a firm but unobtrusive control on all that goes on under their care. Many other sports take place in the absence of neutral referees. Activities such as rockclimbing, canoeing, pot holing and sailing can be most dangerous if commonsense rules are not followed.

There are also many unwritten laws in sport. If broken they can lead to injury. Bowling bouncers at tail enders in a cricket match is not considered reasonable by the majority of first class cricketers.

It is particularly important that players keep within the rules in body contact sports

Clothing and Safety in Sport

Sport has become big business in the last twenty years. Each sport has now developed its own specialist clothing and footwear. Some of the advances have been made because of fashion, although most of the specific clothing requirements have developed through a greater awareness of the particular demands of the sport and a heightened awareness of safety. Many of the sporting governing bodies have developed protective equipment to allow participants to

compete in greater safety. Some people still appear unwilling to wear a number of these sensible protections. Their attitude appears to be that only cowards or poor players need protection of this sort. It is astonishing that despite the fact that shin injuries are common in soccer, large numbers of players still refuse to wear shin guards. Sometimes insurance protection is not given unless the appropriate protective clothing and equipment is worn.

There is a danger of relying too much on protective equipment or even using it for the wrong reasons. A bowler may be less cautious if he realises that the batsman has all the necessary safety gear. Serious injury can still occur. The helmets supposedly used for protection in American football are used as battering rams by some players. Both players can be seriously injured. There is a real danger that protective clothing can give a mistaken feeling of invincibility.

Injuries can result from wearing clothes or accessories which are completely inappropriate. All jewellery should be removed before taking part in combat or contact sports and all sports clothing should be checked for potentially hazardous qualities. The wisdom of wearing glasses in some activities is debatable. If glasses have to be worn they should have plastic or toughened glass lenses and they should be kept on by means of a safety tie. There is some disagreement between the experts as to whether contact lenses are a good thing or whether they are potentially dangerous in games such as squash.

It is important to have footwear which is appropriate to the sport and the playing surface. Failure to do so may cause unnecessary injuries. Ensure that shoes fit well. Get the correct width as well as the correct length. Training shoes should have a soft arch support built into them. The sole should be thick enough to cushion the effect of your feet hitting the ground surface repeatedly, but flexible enough to bend with your foot when it moves.

Sporting Equipment

Sporting equipment has been known to break when being used. This can happen because it is worn out, improperly set up or because of an inherent fault in the design. Injuries can result. It may be difficult to predict the snapping of a glass fibre pole, but it also makes good sense to get into the habit of regularly checking sporting equipment. It is also wise to buy well known equipment which is designed to withstand all the stresses of the sport.

Playing Surfaces

Many sporting injuries can be directly related to the surface on which they took place. The vast majority of shoulder, knee and ankle injuries in soccer, rugby and hockey take place when surfaces are hard and dry. There is little give in the ground. Muddy wet conditions often give rise to muscle pulls and strains. Different sports require different playing surfaces. When the hall of a multi-purpose sports centre is used for a number of different sports then this is not always possible

to achieve. Sprung wooden floors are suitable for a wide variety of activities, but as this surface is expensive and does not wear as well as some cheaper harder surfaces, then it is not always used.

Synthetic surfaces are used more and more for outdoor sports and their surfaces give rise to their own group of injuries. Synthetic tracks have undoubtedly led to faster times but the stiffness of the surface can cause joint and tendon problems to develop in athletes who train on them regularly.

The rugby footballer

The rugby footballer needs '... *firstly to develop his endurance so that fatigue does not upset his co-ordination towards the end of the game. He should develop his strength particularly of those muscles which support his limb joints, but also to provide a fleshy 'buffer' against forces which would tend to injure his bones. He should learn the skills of handing off, of sidestepping, and falling on the ball in such a way as to minimise opposing traumatic forces. He should develop his courage and determination, because it is often that the wary, vacillating player is injured in any clash between players. Secondly the player should check his protective clothing. A scrum cap may be necessary to protect his ears, a gum shield for his teeth, jock strap for genitalia, thick socks (and shinguards) for his shins, and boots to protect his feet and ankles from kicks. Lastly he should determine that he will not resort to illegal punching, biting, and kicking in the inevitable physical battles, and hope that his fellow competitors will have a similar attitude to the rules of the game.'*

(Vaughn Thomas: Science and Sport)

Sports Medicine

The steady increase in the number of people taking part in sport has led to a rise in the number of people suffering from sports injuries. A recent national pilot study carried out on behalf of the Sports Council (1990) suggests that there are approximately 1.5 million attendances each year at the Accident and Emergency departments of hospitals as a direct result of sporting injuries. It also suggests that only 24% of those injured in sport actually attend hospital Accident and

Emergency departments and that the total number of restrictive injury episodes could be as high as 4 - 5 million a year.

Most sporting injuries are medically speaking, relatively trivial. Some doctors see sports injuries as self inflicted injuries and show little sympathy. A number of them are also unaware of how to recognise and treat some types of sports injury.

If the injured sportsman or sportswoman goes to the local casualty department then he may well be dealt with by an overworked and understaffed department with little sports injury expertise. Treatment can sometimes be very conservative. 'Rest and come back if it is still painful in a week.' Although rest is helpful for some injuries, many require more than just rest. Early diagnosis may save much unnecessary pain and expert advice may hasten recovery considerably.

One of the major bodies attempting to improve sports medicine in this country over the years has been the British Association of Sports Medicine. BASM is a voluntary body made up of people from the medical profession with a lifelong interest and expertise is the treatment of sports injuries. It provides specialist training in sports medicine, publishes its own journal and acts as a pressure group in order to lobby the Sports Council and Government Ministers to improve the resources for sports medicine in the United Kingdom.

The situation is now improving. An increasing number of sports injuries clinics are being set up and run by National Health doctors and physiotherapists at National Health hospitals. These clinics do not receive any special funding however and staff man them voluntarily. The Sports Council is helping to set up sports injuries clinics open to all at local sports centres, health clinics, local authority centres and individual sports clubs.

Another important advance made in recent years has been the establishment of the British Olympic Medical Centre which is based at Northwick Park Hospital and Clinical Research Centre in Harrow, Middlesex. It is a dual-purpose centre, combining the facilities for full physiological monitoring of the various components of fitness together with a sports injuries clinic. There is no financial charge and bookings are made through the governing bodies of the various sports.

It is able to provide rapid advice or treatment for those injured in sport. As the centre is based in a large hospital it can easily and quickly arrange blood tests, scans and x rays. They are also able to use the hospital's most modern physiotherapy equipment including infra-red lasers to speed healing of chronic soft tissue injuries.

Clinics for those injured in sport are held in the hospital each week under the direction of the consultant orthopaedic surgeon assisted by the Centre's Medical Registrar, nurse and physiotherapist.

Arthroscopy can be used to peer into the knee joint of an injured competitor. Television pictures taken from within the joint with a tiny camera attached to the arthroscope are displayed on a screen beside the operator. Damaged tissue can be repaired or removed with special instruments passed through the 'scope' thereby avoiding the need for major surgery. It is also possible to make use of specialised equipment which can measure the density of long bones as well as the bones of the spine. Cardiologists can also use Multiple Gated Angiography (MUGA) scanning in order to take pictures of the heart as it is actually working under stress. This enables them to learn more about the adaptations of the heart to sustained heavy exertion.

A further positive sign was the setting up of the National Sports Medicine Institute in 1991, at the Medical College of St. Bartholomew's Hospital in London. The NSMI is funded by the Sports Council (£135 000 for 1991/92) and its function is to promote sports medicine through education programmes, research into injuries, develop an accredited network of sports injury clinics and co-ordinate an overall administrative structure within sports medicine.

There are still insufficient sports injuries clinics however. Private enterprise is stepping in to fill the gap. A number of sports injuries clinics have been set up in private hospitals, usually with a highly experienced physiotherapist in charge. Private health associations and insurance companies are also developing sports injuries insurance policies.

Quick, skilled treatment is therefore possible, but it can also be expensive. As most sportspeople are young and not very well off, private insurance is certainly not the answer for all.

This is far from satisfactory. A fit society maintaining fitness through regular exercise needs to be supported by a sympathetic and knowledgeable sports injuries service. The NHS needs to be funded in such a way that sports medicine for all is a reality.

THINGS TO DO

1 Use one of the given phrases to complete each sentence:
  (i) The immediate treatment for severe bleeding from a limb should be to
    A apply a pressure pad to the wound.
    B keep the patient warm.
    C raise the injured limb.
    D find the nearest pressure point.

  (ii) If you suspect a player has suffered a spinal injury you should
    A try to get her up and walking about.
    B move her into the recovery position.
    C not move her but send for an ambulance.
    D ask her to gently stretch and bend her leg.

  (iii) Tetanus may be contracted through
    A loss of consciousness.
    B severe dislocation.
    C a torn muscle.
    D a dirty cut.

2 Complete the following table for treatment to a sprained ankle using the RICE procedure.

	Procedure	Reason
R		
I		
C		
E		

3 During a game a player receives a hard bang on the head and collapses. The player is conscious but feels sick, dizzy and drowsy.
  (i) What would you suspect the player is suffering from?
  (ii) How would you treat the casualty?

4 List four general signs and symptoms of a fracture of a limb.

5 For each of the following incidents, state
  (a) what you believe the casualty to be suffering from;
  (b) how you would treat the caualty;
  (c) what other action you would take.

  (i) During a game of hockey a player receives a hard bang on the head and collapses. The player is conscious but feels sick, dizzy and drowsy.
  (ii) In very cold conditions, a canoeist on a river capsizes. She manages to swim to the bank and hang on. She is very white and has a badly cut forehead.
  (iii) Whilst playing squash, your middle-aged partner finishes a hard rally and collapses. There is no sign of breathing, her lips are blueish and her pupils dilated.
  (iv) After a collapsed scrum in a rugby match, one of the props does not get up. He says that he can't move his arms or legs but the pain in his neck is intense.

6 You are in charge of first aid for a group of six people walking and camping in hilly country for a week. List the contents of your first aid box and explain what other equipment you would take for emergencies.

7 'A good sports medicine service is vital for our international sportspeople.'
  'A sports medicine service is unnecessary when people are dying through lack of money for research.'
  Discuss these two statements and consider the present provision for sports medicine in this country.

8 Have you been injured or seen others injured in your own sporting activity? Explain the circumstances of the injury and how it might have been prevented? What positive steps would you take to prevent future injury?

9 Your friend's younger brother, who is ten years old, is exceptionally talented in a variety of sports. He competes competitively and gets a great deal of support from both of his parents. Recently he has started to complain of pains in his legs but his dad has told him that they are just growing pains. What do you suspect could be the problem? What would you recommend that the boy's father does to resolve this injury problem?

6 DRUGS AND SPORT

Aims

To develop knowledge and understanding of:
- the effects of a variety of drugs on the human body
- how these drugs affect sporting performance
- drug detection worldwide
- sports ethics and drug taking

To develop the skills of:
- primary and secondary research
- group discussion and analysis

The Guardian 13th January 1991

Ben Johnson at the Olympic Games in 1988

Johnson plays deputy

Justice does not come any more poetic than it was for Ben Johnson in Hamilton, Ontario, on Friday night, when the sprinter, whose banishment for the use of anabolic steroids created the sport's greatest scandal in Olympic history, was beaten in his comeback race by an American deputy sheriff who spends his working days steering young people away from the evils of drug abuse. 6ft 2in Daron Counsel was the winner.

This was a return after a life ban which lasted just 29 months. His disqualification in South Korea gave the gold medal to his brilliant American rival Carl Lewis, who has always enjoyed the image of track and field's ultimate Mr. Clean, and the dramas and ironies of Johnson's comeback lurched towards Hollywood extravagence on the eve of the Hamilton race when police in Houston, Texas found Lewis driving with more than the permitted level of alcohol in his blood.*

The fact that both are now seen as being in need of rehabilitation will reduce neither their mutual bitterness nor the clamour to bring them together for a showdown which their sport's hype artists are sure could generate a truckload of dollars. Johnson could still get the estimated £25m that slid out of his grasp after traces of the steroid Stanozolol were found in his urine sample in Seoul. Daron Counsel did say that Ben Johnson 'looked a lot smaller' than he had done two years ago.

Knowing that for seven long years his hurtling speed was fuelled by drugs, many are understandably disgusted by the possibility, sickened by the adulation poured over Johnson in the Copps Colliseum on Friday.

But international athletics is so infested with unrepentent sinners, many of them in blazers, that I cannot entirely blame the Hamilton crowd for welcoming back the prodigal. Forgiveness is forgivable.

Ben Johnson at the World Indoor Championships in 1991

*Carl Lewis was subsequently cleared of this charge.

DRUGS AND SPORT

We must not think however that drug taking is a new evil. Performers have always been prepared to try almost anything to improve their performance or make them feel better. Some historians believe that competitors in the Ancient Olympics took drugs. Galen, a Greek physician of the third century BC, reported that Greek athletes used stimulants, including certain types of mushrooms to enhance their physical performance.

It is known that the Romans gave hydromel (a mixture of honey and water) to their horses in order to improve their speed and endurance in chariot races. The Romans also gave their gladiators various forms of artificial stimulants to give them more courage.

The first major reported use of drugs in human sports took place in 1879 in the sport of cycling. Some riders were suspected of using caffeine, ether, coccaine and heroin to keep themselves going during the first six day cycle race. The first doping fatality was reported in 1890. A British cyclist died whilst under the influence of a stimulant called ephedrine.

Evidence of drug taking was found in the 1950 Winter Olympics in Oslo, but it was the start of the sixties which witnessed a dramatic increase in the number of reported cases of drug taking in sport. Knud Jensen, a member of the Danish 100km time trial team collapsed and died at the 1960 Olympic Games in Rome. Although the cause of death was given as heatstroke, he had in fact been heavily doped with a stimulant called nicotinyl tartrate. This drug is used to increase the supply of blood to the leg muscles. An enquiry into drug taking in Italian soccer in 1961 revealed that eight out of the 36 first division players tested had been taking amphetamines.

It has been suggested that the sudden increase of drug taking in sport at this time was a reflection of the more liberal approach to drug taking among the general population but particularly amongst the followers of pop music. This was also a time when there were many successes and firsts in the pharmacology industry with drugs becoming much more potent and selective in their actions as well as being less toxic. If chemical agents could be successfully used to cure particular physical ailments then some athletes saw the opportunity to use others in order to greatly enhance their physical performance in sport.

What are drugs?

Drugs are chemical substances which, when introduced into the body, can alter the biochemical systems of the body. Drugs are designed to improve imbalances within the biochemical systems which have been brought about by disease. Their use in healthy bodies may not bring about the hoped for physical improvement. Pharmacologists (scientists who investigate drug action) aim to get a drug to be as specific as possible but all drugs possess varying degrees of side effects.

The Use of Drugs in Sport

Drugs, taken for medicinal purposes, are now a part of many people's lives. Instead of a visit to the doctor when suffering from a cold or cough, a stomach upset or a case of athlete's foot, the vast majority will purchase some proprietary medicine from the local chemist. Some of these preparations include such drugs as caffeine, ephedrine and codeine which are included in the IOC list of banned drugs. Though the dose levels of these drugs are low the sophisticated methods used for the analysis of drugs are capable of easily detecting these drugs or their metabolites in urine samples.

If a sportsman or woman is competing in an important event and is suffering from a slight muscle pull or tendon strain then it is not uncommon for them to take an analgesic drug (a drug which relieves pain). This can result in further injury to an already damaged muscle or tendon but it is not usually considered to be giving an unfair advantage over fellow competitors.

Alcohol is a common drug which is taken by millions of people throughout the world and is considered socially acceptable by most cultures. It can alter behaviour to a considerable extent and it has a number of well known short and long term side effects. There is also a worrying growth in the use of drugs for recreational purposes. These include such drugs as marijuana, crack, morphine, cocaine and their derivatives.

As discussed earlier there is a history of sportsmen and sportswomen making illegitimate use of drugs in order to gain an unfair advantage over fellow competitors. Performance enhancing drugs, whether or not they are taken for the deliberate purpose of gaining an unfair advantage in sport are subject to doping control regulations.

The Development of Dope Testing at the Olympic Games

With the sudden growth of drug taking in sport in the early sixties, the IOC took steps to detect and punish drug users. They attempted to test the cyclists participating in the 100km timed team event at the 1964 Olympics in Tokyo but the tests were never completed because of a boycott by a number of the riders. The IOC Medical Commission was formed in 1966 and the first official dope controls took place during the Olympic Games in 1968 in Grenoble and Mexico. The number of dope controls which took place between 1968 and 1984 was 9235 of which 35 were positive.

The doping definition of the IOC Medical Commission is based on the banning of pharmacological classes of agents. The original IOC ruling on doping limited itself to classifying drugs into five categories according to their actions. The most recent rulings also include doping methods. For each of the groups of drugs the IOC lists examples of the drugs which fit into that particular category. To cover the fact that they may have missed particular ones out or that new derivatives of banned drugs are continually being developed, they include the phrase, 'and related compounds'.

International Olympic Committee list for doping classes and methods

(i) **Doping Classes**
   A Stimulants
   B Narcotic analgesics
   C Anabolic steroids
   D Beta blockers
   E Diuretics

(ii) **Doping Methods**
   A Blood doping
   B Pharmacological, chemical and physical manipulation

(iii) **Classes of drug subject to certain restrictions**
   A Alcohol
   B Local anaesthetics
   C Corticosteroids

The mere presence of one of the banned drugs, or their major metabolites, in a urine sample, taken at a sporting event would constitute an offence. For drugs such as caffeine or testosterone, a quantitative analysis is required. The tester will determine whether the amount of the drugs detected is greater than that normally found in urine.

How Sportsmen and Women are Tested for Drugs

Although the responsibility for organising drug testing lies with the governing bodies of individual sports, in this country it is the Sports Council who ensure that all sporting bodies have effective doping control procedures. Financial grants and other Sports Council services would be withdrawn for sporting bodies failing to provide an effective system. There are a number of accredited drug testing centres in this country which carry out the testing procedures for each individual sport. Drug testing centres are set up on site for major sporting events.

Procedures

When drug testing is carried out at a competitive event it is normal procedure to select the winner as well as a number of randomly selected competitors for testing. Athletes are also selected by random for any out of season testing which may be carried out by their particular sporting body. They are usually tested at their place of training.

When selected on a competitive occasion they are notified by an official and are required to sign a form to acknowledge that they have been notified and that they agree to the test. A refusal to sign or attend the actual drug testing is considered to be an admission of guilt and any action taken by the sporting body would be on the basis that the drug test was positive.

The competitor is required to go to the Control Station and can be accompanied by a team manager or other official. A urine sample is collected under supervision. Sufficient urine is collected to provide for both an initial test and for a second test if the first one is found to be positive. Drinks can be provided for the athlete if he or she is unable to provide sufficient urine at the time of testing. This is not uncommon as competitors are often dehydrated at the end of any competitive event. Officials are required to ensure that the urine samples are not substituted for any other samples before they are tested. The competitor observes that both the samples are correctly marked and sealed and signs a form to indicate that he is happy with the way that the samples have been taken.

Sample analysis

The sample is taken from the Control Centre to the testing centre for analysis under strict security and with the minimum time delay. A number of sophisticated analysis techniques are used on the initial urine sample. These techniques make it possible to identify any particular drug or its metabolites even if additional drugs have been taken with the intent of masking the banned substances.

Result of analysis

If the analysis proves negative then the governing body is informed about the result and the urine samples are destroyed.

If a positive result is found then the governing body of the sport will be notified. They will inform the athlete who will usually be suspended from competition until further tests are carried out. The athlete will be given an opportunity to explain why the banned substance was in his or her urine. They can also ask for the second urine sample to be tested. Both the athlete and a representative are entitled to observe this second analysis.

It is then up to the particular governing body to determine how the guilty athlete is to be treated. Any decisions are related to the seriousness of the drug taking as well as to the intent of the athlete. (The IOC give guidance on this matter in an attempt to differentiate between accidental drug and deliberate drug taking.) Some governing bodies have banned guilty competitors for life whilst other ones have limited any suspensions to a period of two years. Any suspended athletes who intend to return to competition following their period of suspension are tested on a regular basis during their suspension.

The Battle Continues

Despite the fact that testing procedures are now very sophisticated and able to detect minute traces of drugs in the body, drug abuse continues to be a problem in sport. This is because many sportsmen and sportswomen think:

- They can avoid detection.
- The benefits outweigh the dangers.
- The cost of being caught is minimal.

There are several steps which could be taken to make it more difficult for sportsmen and sportswomen to compete after taking performance enhancing drugs. These include:

- All governing bodies should set up a system of random testing which would operate throughout the year and not just during periods of competition. This testing must be independent, rigorous and entirely random.
- There should be a World Antidoping Charter for Sport which would ensure that there is an agreed list of banned substances, that drug testing procedures are common throughout the world and that sufficient financial resources are put into drug research.
- Competitors in all sports must be required to make a personal declaration of willingness to undertake tests.
- There should be a commonly agreed punishment system for sports drug abusers and this should be adhered to throughout the world. It must be made clear that taking drugs to enhance performance will not work.

There should be a properly devised education programme which would ensure that young people realise that many of the so called advantages of taking drugs are illusiary and not worth the obvious risks. There should be wide publicity about the effects of drugs, offenders and offences.

STIMULANTS

Stimulants have a direct, stimulating effect on the central nervous and cardiovascular systems. This improves the work level of the athlete as well as reducing the feeling of fatigue. Many stimulants occur naturally. Caffeine, found in tea and coffee, and nicotine, found in cigarettes, are both stimulants. Caffeine accelerates the respiratory and heart rate and decreases reaction time. It appears to increase work output and also speeds up the recovery time from fatigue. It is very difficult to distinguish between its 'normal' use as a pleasant drink and its abnormal use to artificially improve performance. Caffeine was added to the prohibited list of drugs in 1982 but the excess level of caffeine is set at ten times over the amount found in the normal population.

The most widely used manufactured stimulants appear to be amphetamines. They were first prepared in Germany in 1887 and were used to treat nervous diseases. Amphetamines were used for non-medical reasons in both the Spanish Civil War and the Second World War. It was believed that they increased the physical capacity for strenuous tasks which require a great deal of concentration without destroying judgement. They were later used by dieticians as their use tends to lessen a person's appetite for food.

Sportsmen and sportswomen take stimulants because they believe that they will improve their sporting performance. They describe a sense of well being, a reduced desire for food and a feeling of increased mental and physical powers.

Amphetamines certainly do enable people to continue working at high levels for prolonged periods of time. They also have the effect of reducing performance in sporting activities needing a high degree of co-ordination and rapid decision making.

One of the most important effects of stimulants is to suppress the symptoms of fatigue. When reaching the limits of endurance, pain is a warning to the body to stop before damage occurs. If this feeling of pain is suppressed and stress on the body is continued then muscle pulls, cramps

and strains are liable to occur. More importantly, as the body temperature rises, dehydration and heatstroke may occur, sometimes with fatal results. It was found that the British cyclist Tommy Simpson who died during the 1967 Tour de France, died as a result of heat, exertion and drugs of the ergogenic (work producing) type.

A particular group of stimulants are often used in low doses in hay fever and cold remedies. (Examples include ephedrine and pseudoephedrine.) In high doses these compounds can produce mental stimulation and increased blood flow. They can also cause increased blood pressure and headache, increased and irregular heart beat, anxiety and tremor. Medicines containing these drugs should not be taken by competing sportspersons.

Ephedrine, and related substances, were used regularly in the treatment of asthma. They are now regarded as stimulants and therefore banned by the IOC. It is possible for asthma suffers to use salbutamol, bitolterol and a number of other substances in aerosol form. These substances are not regarded as stimulants and do not offend the IOC rulings.

The more an athlete uses stimulants the less

The large scale use of drugs in human sports was first identified in cycling

effect they will have on his or her body. The positive effects he or she seeks can only be maintained by steadily increasing the dosage. The more that is taken, the higher is the risk of suffering from toxic side effects. One side effect is to make the competitor more aggressive and therefore more liable to be too physically committed in body contact sports. This can result in injury to both himself, the opposition or both. There is also a real danger that stimulants will react adversely with any other drugs which the sportsperson may be taking.

NARCOTIC ANALGESICS

Drugs of this type include morphine, heroin, methodone and even codeine which is often taken as a medicant. Narcotics basically put people to sleep while analgesics kill pain. They are highly addictive drugs and their possession is a criminal offence in most countries. They have also been used in high level sport on a large number of occasions.

Cyclists have been known to taken morphine towards the end of a hard day's ride. They receive an initial powerful stimulating effect from the drug which enables them to finish strongly. This stimulating effect is then followed by a longer sedating effect. It is during this stage that the cyclist would sleep and, as a result, be fully fit for the next day's ride. Strict doping controls have now virtually stopped this kind of drug use in cycling.

Codeine causes a particular problem for sports administrators because of its widely accepted use as a treatment for travellers' diarrhoea and other minor complaints. When drug testing is carried out it is difficult to distinguish it from morphine because the body metabolises the two drugs in similar ways. The IOC prohibits the use of codeine whilst a number of national sporting federations allow its therapeutic use.

ANABOLIC STEROIDS

There are some drugs whose main use is during training sessions prior to competition. At this time the body is being heavily stressed. We produce hormones naturally which promote growth and healing. These hormones also help the body repair itself after periods of stress. Anabolic steroids can have the same effect.

There has been quite a long history of the medical use of anabolic steroids. (Anabolic means building up the body; steroids are hormones.) In the early 1940's they were used to treat protein loss and muscle wastage suffered by concentration camp victims and they have also been administered to patients to limit the loss of protein and aid muscle rebuilding after major surgery. Individuals suffering from wasting illnesses such as muscular dystrophy and diabetes can also be helped by their use. Sportsmen and sportswomen have used them in order to help build up their power and recovery rate after training. They often take up to ten times the amount of the therapeutic dosage.

Steroids, which are synthesised male sex hormones, have two sorts of effects on the human body:

1 Androgenic effects

Steroids control the development and maintenance of the male sex organs and the male secondary sex characteristics (for example hair on the chin and a deep voice). The side effects related to taking them artificially can include impotency, infertility, prostate cancer in males and infertility, acne, hair growth and a deep voice in females. Both males and females are likely to suffer a loss in libido or sexual impulse.

2 Anabolic effects

With the increased number of sportsmen and sportswomen taking steroids it is also possible to be more specific on the side effects likely to occur. Anabolic steroids increase the rate of arteriosclerosis in arteries and arterioles and it is the secretion of testosterone in men which is thought to be the major cause of the greater incidence of coronary heart disease in males compared to females in the under 50 age group. There are now several well documented cases of coronary heart disease in apparently fit, healthy athletes aged under 40, who have been taking anabolic steroids.

The increased retention of salt and water not only leads to weight gains amongst steroid takers but also increases the overall workload on the heart as well as leading to hypertension (high blood pressure). It is now clear that taking steroids alters the liver biochemistry and can lead to the formation of tumours both in the liver as well as the kidneys. Steroids aid the rapid healing of body tissues and can make an athlete more aggressive. This can lead to injury if they attempt to lift weights beyond their capability. Tendon damage is also more likely amongst steroid takers. This may be because tendons do not respond as rapidly to strength training regimes as do muscles and therefore may not be able to cope with the increased demands being made on them. It is also thought that anabolic steroids inhibit the formation of collagen which is an important element in ligaments and tendons.

In spite of these real dangers large numbers of athletes are known to take steroids. They are taken for different reasons by different types of sportsmen and women. Some, such as wrestlers and American footballers, may wish to merely increase their overall weight and size. A rugby player or weightlifter may want increased power or dynamic strength whilst middle and long distance runners may wish to speed up muscle repair between hard training sessions. Although most of the early sportmen and sportwomen detected were from the power events in athletics as well as in weightlifting, wrestling and rowing, it is now clear that a large number of sporting activities have their steroid users.

Current research has made it clear that the mere fact of taking steroids does not make an athlete bigger, stronger and more powerful. It does appear however that those who take steroids plus protein supplements, and at the same time undertake hard strenuous exercise, will increase their muscle strength. Steroid takers also appear to develop greater reparative powers in their muscles and associated tissues and may therefore be able to train or compete at a very high level and need only very limited periods of recovery time.

To some extent then it is the increased quality training which gives rise to the greater power developed by steroid takers. Research also indicates that the effects on an individual of taking steroids depends to a large degree on the type of body type the person has. An extremely mesomorphic person will not change to the same extent as one who is more of an ectomorph or endomorph. Muscle strength gains among women steroid takers is much greater than in men because there is a much lower normally circulating level of testosterone in females than in their male counterparts.

Although sportsmen and sportswomen have been taking steroids since the early sixties, it was not until 1974 that the IOC perfected tests for detecting traces of artificial steroids in the body. They were included in the IOC's list of prohibited drugs for the Montreal Olympics in 1976. Only 166 sportsmen and sportswomen in eight different sports were actually tested for steroids. Two American weightlifters were disqualified for having traces of steroids in their body. Cynics suggested that they had got their timing wrong on their dope taking.

Most steroid-taking sportsmen and sportswomen know that their body needs at least two weeks to clear itself of all traces of steroids. During this phase the athlete is likely to suffer unpleasant withdrawal symptoms including depression and a lack of energy. When dope tests were limited to the major international competitions then it was easier to avoid detection. More and more sporting authorities are now trying to insist on random tests. This will increase the chances that the drug takers will be caught.

The chemists working for the athletes have not given up the fight however. They have decided that instead of giving artificial hormones they will give them the natural hormone testosterone instead.

Testosterone

Testosterone is a male hormone produced naturally in the body by both males and females. The greater amounts in the male give him his sexual potency, aggression and competitive urge. As it is a natural compound it is not easy to detect whether additional amounts have been added to the body systems. Athletes are known to have taken anabolic steroids until a few weeks before a big competition. They have then changed to taking testosterone, safe in the knowledge that it will be difficult to detect. It will also have the same effect as the anabolic steroids. The side effects of the additional testosterone are so far unknown. It seems likely that the body will stop producing its own supplies of testosterone after a while. This would leave the athlete chemically castrated. The long term effects on women who take the drug are not known.

The IOC has now decided that there is a natural level of testosterone in the body. Anyone who is found to have above that level is liable to disqualification by their international federation. The normal ratio of testosterone to epitestosterone in the body is 1:1. The IOC says that when the ratio reaches 6:1 then this is a positive result. It has already been claimed by the IOC Medical Commission that some East European athletes are now injecting extra epitestosterone into their bodies to confuse the IOC chemists.

GROWTH HORMONE

Many hormones are involved in the growth and development of humans. We are still not clear exactly how they all interact to produce a fully developed adult but the importance of Human Growth Hormone (hGH) is known to be great. hGH is produced in the pituitary and it releases growth promoting factors, collectively called somatomedins, from the liver and other tissues. Somatomedin C increases cartilage production in the long bones mainly at the epiphyses. As this cartilage is converted into mature bone when the individual reaches the end of puberty, the greater the cartilage production, the longer the bones will become.

hGH has been used in the treatment of individuals suffering from growth disorders for over 40 years and the treatment has always been completed before the person reaches adolescence. Its use has been limited mainly because its only source was from the pituitary glands obtained at autopsy from dead humans. Pharmacologists have now managed to produce synthetic hGH however and it will soon be much more readily available.

There are reports from the United States that hGH has already been used to create taller individuals who would gain a distinct advantage in sporting activities such as basketball, high jump etc., where height is a distinct advantage. It is clear that hGH will increase stature and at the same time increase muscle size. Synthetic hGH is identical to the naturally occuring hormone and cannot be distinguished from it. It is also obvious that as the drug will have to be administered before the sportsman or sportswoman reaches adolescence, detection of it at the height of his or her career will be impossible.

The side effects of taking hGH however are most alarming. It is likely that a person undergoing a course of hGH treatment will develop a condition called acromegaly. The symptoms of acromegaly include hyperglycaemia, enlarged internal organs, thickening and coarsening of the skin, lack of subcutaneous fat, coarsening of facial features and a number of other disturbing symptoms. These side effects will not become obvious until after the person has finished his or her sporting career.

DRUGS USED TO REDUCE ANXIETY IN SPORT

It has long been recognised that physical exercise can be a most effective therapy for anxious individuals and can lead to reduced levels of stress. This is one of the major reasons for wishing to involve more and more adults in some kind of sporting activity. Participation in sport can produce its own stress however and some sportsmen and sportswomen use drugs in order to reduce their levels of anxiety.

The level of anxiety a person exhibits before or during sporting activity depends on the nature of the activity as well as on the personality of the individual. High anxiety is associated with brief and high risk activities. For example downhill skiers and individuals about to go on a frightening funfair ride will exhibit much faster heart rates

Downhill skiers can show high levels of anxiety before a race

than will footballers or tennis players. Research also indicates that footballers show much higher levels of stress before a home game than they do before an away game, presumably because they are expected to win when they are home and they will have the barracking of their own supporters if they do not.

A moderate level of anxiety before a forthcoming event is desirable as it ensures that the person is sufficiently aroused and motivated to perform at their best. As the diagram below indicates, the simpler the task the higher will be the level of arousal that can be tolerated before performance efficiency begins to fall.

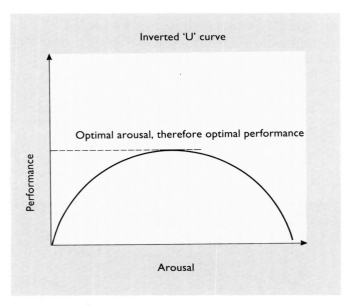

Professional athletes who are regularly subjected to stress get used to dealing with it and are not usually highly anxious individuals. It is clear however that a great many sportsmen and sportswomen need to develop anxiety reducing strategies in order to improve their sporting potential. The majority will develop mental relaxation techniques but some will resort to drugs.

Benzodiazepines

Benzodiazepines have been used in general medical practice as tranquillisers for a number of years and many sportspersons use them for calming or sedative purposes. They are believed to reduce anxiety without affecting judgement and coordination, a real advantage over alcohol. Commonly known derivatives include Librium and Valium. Many of them carry a hang-over effect

however and they are known to affect complex physical performance for up to 24 hours after they have been taken. They are not currently on the IOC's banned list despite being able to induce dependence by their users.

Beta Blockers

Beta blockers are a group of drugs which act on the sympathetic nervous system and prevent adrenaline and noradrenaline being distributed throughout the body. Beta blockers affect both the heart and blood vessels by reducing heart rate and cardiac output. They are used by doctors to control cardiovascular disease. They also have the effect of reducing anxiety by their action of keeping the heart beating slowly during times of emotional stress, by reducing limb tremor as well as limiting the amount of palmar sweating. They have been used with some success by competitors in such sports as ski jumping, motor racing and bob sleighing. Their sedative actions have also been used to good effect in aiming events such as shooting and snooker.

Beta blockers do not appear to affect speed of muscular contraction, strength, power or work capacity but they do affect the energy available for work. They do have a damaging effect on endurance type activities. They can also cause nightmares, insomnia and depression. They were banned by the IOC in time for the 1988 Olympics.

DIURETICS

Diuretics are used to eliminate fluid from the body. They have been used by sportsmen and women to lose weight in a very short period of time in such sporting events as wrestling, judo and boxing. They have also been used to increase urine secretion in an attempt to dilute doping agents likely to be detected within the urine of a doped athlete. As the testing procedures are very sophisticated, these attempts are certain to fail.

Diuretics are used to lose weight in a short period of time

BLOOD DOPING

The idea of blood doping was first raised in the mid sixties. The knowledge that the 1968 Olympics were to be held at high altitude in Mexico City led sports physiologists to wonder how the bloodstream would be able to transport oxygen at high altitude.

One of the experiments conducted in Finland included withdrawing a small percentage of blood from fit volunteers (but not top class athletes) and then storing the red oxygen carrying cells in a frozen state. Tests on the volunteers showed that their athletic performance was impaired. After a month the red blood cells were put back into the blood stream. The volunteers' energy output increased by 8- 10% the first week after the test. This went down to 4% in the second week. By the third week it was back to normal.

The basic idea behind blood doping is that the higher levels of red blood cells in the athlete's blood would increase the oxygen carrying capacity of the bloodstream,. This would in turn improve endurance.

A top class endurance athlete already has a very high concentration of red blood cells in the bloodstream. Recent research has indicated that blood doping of an athlete of this sort could endanger his well being by overcrowding the capillaries and blocking them. It seems unlikely that blood doping is a common occurrence in sport.

A new drug has recently come onto the market which has the same effect of increasing the number of red, oxygen carrying cells in the body. The genetically-engineered drug is identical to the hormone erythropoietin, which controls the formation of red blood cells and it is not possible to tell if an individual has been administered this new drug. Swedish researchers have shown that the taking of erythropoietin can markedly improve the performance of individuals involved in endurance events such as cycling, skiing and long distance running. In 1990 the Royal Dutch Cycling Federation held an investigation into the deaths of several cyclists because of possible abuse of this drug.

The IOC are expected to introduce an upper limit on red blood cells for the 1994 Winter Olympics at Lillihammer in Norway. This presents a real problem, however, because individuals vary in the concentration of haemoglobin which they have in their bloodstream. It is currently not possible to distinguish a person who has a naturally high concentration from one who has a naturally low concentration of haemoglobin but who has taken this new drug to compensate.

PSYCHOLOGY AND SPORT

Success in sport depends on more than just physical ability. Determination, concentration, the willingness to accept a high level of pain, a high degree of aggression and many other qualities are necessary for a successful performer. In recent years there have been a number of reported cases of hypnosis being used to improve sporting ability. Some sportsmen and sportswomen are obviously able to induce a state of self hypnosis, possessing the ability to concentrate so deeply that they become completely oblivious to anything other than the task in hand. Arthur Ashe, an American tennis player of the early 80's used self hypnosis.

Hypnosis would appear to be particularly useful in controlling the stress and worry which can build up in an athlete prior to a big competition. How far hypnosis or any other psychological measures can actually improve an athlete's basic ability is not clear. There is no doubt that it is being investigated.

THE SOCIAL DRUGS

Although only a very small minority of the population will ever consider taking drugs to improve their sporting performance, vast numbers will indulge in the so called social drugs: alcohol and tobacco.

Alcohol

Alcohol is one of the oldest drugs known to man. It has certainly been an important part of life for thousands of years. Historical evidence shows that man has used alcohol for social reasons, as part of religious ceremonies, as a preservative and as a medicine. Its ability to affect people's minds make it a very powerful drug.

The alcohol which we drink is called ethanol or ethyl alcohol and it is obtained either by fermentation or distillation. The process of fermentation involves allowing the enzymes in fruit juices or grain and water to act on the carbohydrates in the mixture and turn it into alcohol. If the products of any fermentation are then boiled, the alcohol is evaporated and collected separately. This process is called distillation. Distilled alcohol is always stronger then fermented alcohol.

Beverage	Source	How produced	% alcohol
Beer	malted barley	fermented	4-6
Wine	grape juice	"	10-12
Brandy	grape juice	distilled	40-50
Rum	molasses	"	40-50
Whisky	malted grains	"	40-50
Vodka	various	"	40-50
Gin	various	"	40-50

What happens when we drink alcohol?

Short term effects

Alcohol is a depressant. The brain is affected very quickly as alcohol is easily absorbed into the bloodstream. Reaction time becomes slower, muscular coordination becomes less efficient.

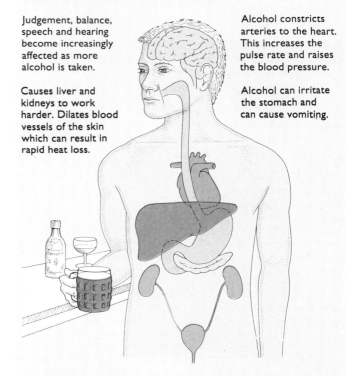

Judgement, balance, speech and hearing become increasingly affected as more alcohol is taken.

Causes liver and kidneys to work harder. Dilates blood vessels of the skin which can result in rapid heat loss.

Alcohol constricts arteries to the heart. This increases the pulse rate and raises the blood pressure.

Alcohol can irritate the stomach and can cause vomiting.

Long term effects

Gastritis in the stomach can develop. This is painful and debilitating.

Digestion is upset if the pancreas is damaged. This can lead to malnutrition and diabetes.

Large quantities of alcohol taken over a long period of time can damage brain cells. Can also cause alcohol dependancy.

Cirrhosis of the liver can develop. This kills liver cells and thus prevents the liver from working efficiently.

Alcohol and sport

Many sportspersons drink socially, often it is part of their particular sporting culture. Although sports such as rugby union, squash and water polo may be particularly noted for their social activities, a vast number of people who participate in a wide range of sporting activities will have a small alcoholic beverage after completing a sporting session. There is some disagreement about the wisdom of light drinking, health and sporting participation.

Small amounts of alcohol increase the flow of gastric juices and stimulate digestion. Men up to the age of 60 develop an increased level of blood pressure as their consumption of alcohol increases. For older men and women however, light drinking is associated with lower blood pressure. There is also some evidence to indicate that moderate drinking may provide some protection against coronary heart disease.

All experts agree that heavy drinking and sport do not go together. It is known that alcohol lowers the muscle glycogen levels. As muscle glycogen is needed during endurance events it is extremely unwise to take alcohol for up to 24 hours before a prolonged sporting event. Alcohol also appears to slow down the rate at which blood lactate levels decrease during and after exercise. This will force the athlete to stop exercising prematurely as well as to lengthen their recovery period.

It becomes more difficult to sustain concentration and motivation after taking alcohol and so not only is sporting performance likely to be diminished but you are much more likely to give up trying to compete or train.

Alcohol dilates the peripheral blood vessels thus causing heat loss from the skin surface and therefore a lower body temperature. This can lead to hypothermia if the athlete is exercising in cold conditions.

Alcohol should also be avoided in hot conditions as its diuretic properties increase the risk of dehydration.

There is complete agreement that heavy drinking and health and heavy drinking and sport do not go together.

Alcohol has been associated with certain sports for a number of years and not just for the social occasions following competition. Sports such as archery, darts, pistol shooting, snooker and billiards require steady limbs and an absence of tremor for real success. Hand tremor is one of the classic indicators of stress. Some turn to alcohol for help.

Alcohol consumption is not banned in archery, snooker, billiards or darts and its use is plain for all to see. Competitors who indulge take small doses of alcohol over extended periods of time. This ensures that they stay relaxed but sober and that their blood alcohol level does not fluctuate. A very small amount of alcohol will adversely affect simple and complex reaction time and so competitors in sports like clay pigeon shooting do not drink in order to be more accurate.

Alcohol is banned in the modern pentathlon, fencing and shooting. Competitors are tested by means of a standard breathaliser. If they are found to have exceeded the limit (50mg/100ml as opposed to the limit for driving a car in this country which is 80mg/100 ml) then they are then subjected to a blood test.

Nicotine

If tobacco had first been discovered in the twentieth century then it is certain that most countries would have controlled its use. The 4000 or so substances which it contains are so obviously harmful to the human body. Yet those people who smoke breathe these substances directly into their bodies.

One of the most damaging substances contained in cigarette smoke is tar. This is thought to be the major cancer producing element. It collects in the lungs of smokers. Tobacco also contains nicotine. This is a powerful drug which has a direct harmful effect on the heart, the blood vessels and the nervous system. It only takes about seven seconds for nicotine to reach the brain. It stimulates the brain by causing the release of chemicals such as noradrenaline, which are usually released in times of stress. The heart beats more quickly due to more adrenalin production. The blood vessels of the skin contract which in turn causes a rise of blood pressure as well as a sensation of cold. People who smoke become dependent on the nicotine. This is why it is difficult to give up once you start to smoke regularly.

The irritant gases and droplets in the tobacco smoke paralyse the cilia (small hairs) lining the bronchial tubes. This prevents them from removing the dust and other particles from the lungs. This in turn can cause the air cells in the lungs to become clogged and so prevent efficient breathing. Tobacco smoke also contains carbon monoxide. This gas is absorbed in the lungs and taken up by the red blood cells. This reduces the blood's ability to transport oxygen.

Smoking or Health

About 30% of the adult population of the world smoke and approximately 80% of children who smoke regularly continue to do so when they grow up. If the children remain as non smokers until they are twenty then they are unlikely to start the habit. About 20% of the smoke exhaled can be recirculated by passive smoking and so we can all be affected even if we do not smoke ourselves. This helps to explain why smoking is restricted in public places in many countries.

The European Commission proposes to ban all publicity for tobacco products in newspapers, posters, radio and films and the use of tobacco logos to promote other goods.

The financial side of smoking

- In 1990 UK tobacco companies sold £7.6 billion worth of cigarettes.
- In 1989/90 the UK government earned £6.04 billion through taxes on cigarettes.
- The National Health Service spends up to £500 million a year caring for people with serious illnesses directly related to smoking.
- UK cigarette companies spend £113.5 million each year on advertising.
- The Government spends about £7.25 million each year to discourage smoking in the UK.
- Tobacco is produced in about 120 countries.
- Tobacco companies spend about £12 million a year sponsoring sporting events. It is estimated that in 1989 364 hours of tobacco sponsored sport were televised on the BBC alone. Cigarette brands were shown on screen for an average of 20 minutes a day.

Smoking or health?

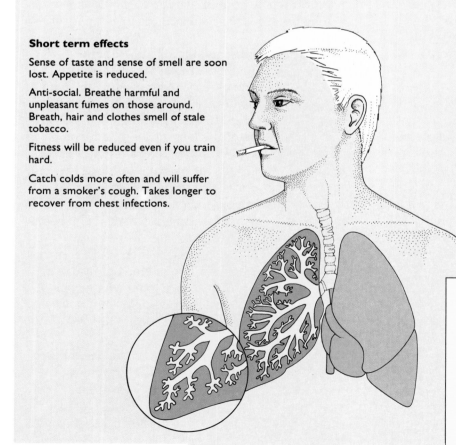

Short term effects

Sense of taste and sense of smell are soon lost. Appetite is reduced.

Anti-social. Breathe harmful and unpleasant fumes on those around. Breath, hair and clothes smell of stale tobacco.

Fitness will be reduced even if you train hard.

Catch colds more often and will suffer from a smoker's cough. Takes longer to recover from chest infections.

Long term effects

Ten times more likely to contract cancer of the mouth or throat.

Up to twenty times more likely to contract lung cancer.

Twice as likely to die of heart disease. Nicotine and carbon dioxide in tobacco damage the heart and blood vessels. Coronary heart disease is the leading cause of death in this country.

Almost certain to suffer from bronchitis. The more cigarettes smoked the higher the chance of contracting the disease.

Smoking can also cause and prevent the healing of stomach ulcers.

- Fitness and cigarettes do not go together.
- Health and cigarettes do not go together.
- Smoking and sport do not go together.
- If you value your health, keep to sport and do not start the smoking habit.

THINGS TO DO

1 Which of the following statements are true and which are false?
   (i) An important effect of stimulants is to suppress the symptoms of fatigue.
   (ii) Boxers will perform better if they are given a tranquilising drug.
   (iii) Analgesic drugs help to build muscle bulk.
   (iv) Women gymnasts might gain from delayed puberty.
   (v) Blood doping is a technique thought to be used by high jumpers.
   (vi) Anabolic steroids can cause liver damage.
   (vii) Testosterone is an artificial sex hormone.
   (viii) Large amounts of alcohol act as a depressant.
   (ix) Nicotine causes the heart rate to increase.
   (x) Smokers are unlikely to suffer from respiratory problems.

2 Complete the following table:

Procedure or drug	Sport where an advantage might be gained
Stimulant	
Anabolic steroids	
Tranquiliser	
Delaying puberty	
Blood doping	

3 A number of examples of illegal drug taking in sport have been given in this chapter. By researching at your local library, find another case which involved a sportsman or sportswoman in drug taking. Give details of the sport in which they took part, the drug used and its supposed advantages, how they were caught and the consequences for their sporting future.

4 Cigarettes, tea and beer contain drugs and many sportmen and sportswomen take drugs for medical reasons. Discuss the problem of defining a drug for sporting purposes and the difficulties involved in detecting the use of drugs internationally.

5 Winning world and Olympic titles is very important to international sportsmen and sportswomen. The temptation to achieve an improved performance by drug taking is considerable. Discuss the dilemma facing the ambitious sportsman or sportswoman, giving arguments both for and against the use of drugs by people in sport.

6 Imagine a discussion between Sebastian Coe, Diego Maradonna and Ben Johnson about the taking of drugs by sportsmen and sportswomen. Work in groups of four, three of you each take the role of one of the above sportsmen whilst the fourth person acts as a chairperson. Consider such things as:

- the pressures on top class performers;
- the rewards for winning;
- the possible long term effects of drug taking;
- their influence on young people.

7 SUCCESS IN SPORT

Aims

To develop knowledge and understanding of:
◆ the variety of body types and their suitability for sport
◆ how the mind is important to sports performance
◆ how sports performance is affected by stress and personality

To develop the skills of:
◆ simple body typing
◆ self analysis
◆ analysis of sporting activities

A study of top sports performers shows that sport not only selects those with outstanding natural ability but also those with particular body types. It is obvious that if you are fully grown, and yet only 1.70 metres tall, then you will not become an international high jumper or basketball player. However body type selection is much more sensitive than this.

Have you got the right body?

Competitors in different sports often have different body types

Body Typing

An American researcher called Sheldon developed a method of body typing called somatotyping. He decided that there were three extremes of body types. He called these three extremes endomorphs, mesomorphs and ectomorphs. In his system it is possible to describe any person in relation to these extremes.

Extreme endomorphs are pear-shaped overall with a rounded head. Their body is wide at the hips and narrow at the shoulders. They have a lot of fat on their body, upper arms and thighs. Their wrists and ankles are relatively slender. They are wider in the front to back rather than the side to side directions. When starved they still keep their basic endomorphic shape.

Extreme mesomorphs are 'wedge-shaped' people. They are wide at the shoulders and narrow at the hips. They have a cubical massive head, broad shoulders and heavily muscled arms and legs. Their forearms and calves are strong relative to their upper arms and thighs. They have a

minimum amount of fat and they are narrow from their front to back direction.

Extreme ectomorphs are narrow at the shoulders and hips. They have a high peaked face with a receding chin and high forehead. They have a thin narrow chest and abdomen and thin spindly arms and legs. They have neither much muscle nor much body fat. Compared to their size they have a large skin area and a large nervous system.

Not many people appear at the end of these extremes of the three different body types. In fact Sheldon thought that all individuals contain parts of endomorphy, mesomorphy and ectomorphy. In somatotyping each person is given a score for each of the basic body types. A scale from one to seven is used. A rating of 2, 6, 3 means a score of 2 in endomorphy (low), a 6 for mesomorphy (high) and a 3 for ectomorphy (low). It is possible to place an individual's score on a chart and then they can be compared with other people.

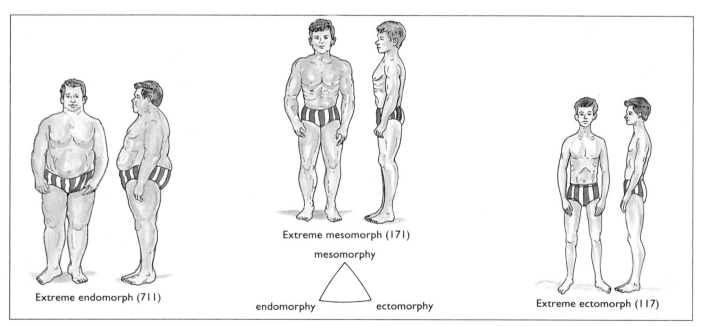

Extreme endomorph (711)

Extreme mesomorph (171)

mesomorphy

endomorphy   ectomorphy

Extreme ectomorph (117)

Somatotyping: the three extremes of body type

The most common somatotypes among the general population are 3, 4, 4; 4, 3, 3; and 3, 5, 2. Almost all extremes can be found however. When somatotyping is carried out on sportsmen and sportswomen they all tend to gather at the upper end of the mesomorph scale.

Professor Tanner examined athletes at the 1960 Olympics. He found that they were mainly high in mesomorphy and ectomorphy with no

scores above 4 for endomorphy.

The table shows the age, height and weight of the athletes who competed in the 1988 Olympic Games at Seoul. As well as supporting Professor Tanner's findings, they also show that the longer the race the shorter and lighter the runner. The throwers are clearly taller and heavier than other athletes. It has also been found that throwers tend to have longer than normal arms for their height.

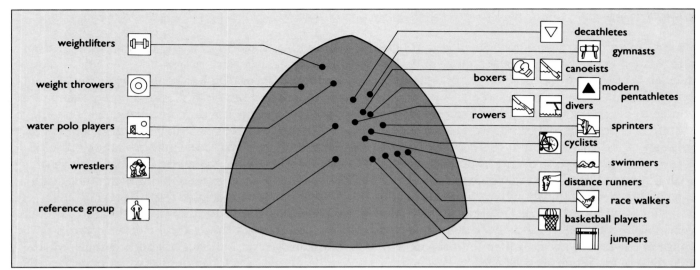

Somatotyping of different kinds of athletes

What does this mean for me?

It is difficult to make an accurate assessment of your body type because it involves a complicated set of body measurements. However you can easily see whether your height and weight would make you suitable for a particular sport.

If you are short then gymnastics, trampoline, the longer distances in athletics, soccer, hockey and so on are a possibility. Boxing, fencing and certain positions in rugby also favour the short person.

If you are tall then high jump, basketball, volleyball, rowing and possibly the throwing events in athletics may be for you. Heavyweights tend to go for the contact sports, weight lifting, throwing events, boxing, wrestling and rugby.

Top level sport selects the more extremes in physique. It is not unusual to see a dozen players over two metres tall involved in a basketball match. Champion gymnasts on the other hand are normally very short. If you were able to see a group of shot putters, divers, basketball players, gymnasts and super heavy weight lifters together, you could easily think that you were looking at more than one species of human being.

YOUR SEX AND SPORTING SUCCESS

One of the most vital factors in deciding your sporting potential is sex. For the first nine or ten years of their lives boys and girls mature at about the same rate. It is difficult to distinguish boys from girls. They have similar body shapes and amounts of bone, muscle or fat. Sporting competition between the sexes is quite fair at this stage.

Boys and girls past the age of eleven develop very differently. Fair competition is then more difficult to achieve.

Girls start their adolescent spurt in height and weight between the ages of ten and a half and thirteen years of age. Boys do not normally start until two years later (twelve to fifteen years). For this period of time girls are often taller, heavier and better co-ordinated than their boy counterparts. Girls usually reach their physical maturity by sixteen years of age. Boys continue to mature until the age of 20 to 21 years.

The anatomical differences between the sexes favour the male in physical activities. The male bone structure is longer, heavier and more robust than the female one. It is also mechanically more efficient in a variety of ways. Women have approximately 5% less bone mass than men. They have a comparatively long trunk and short limbs. The longer and heavier bones of the male give increased weight and the longer levers can develop much greater speed and force in the hands and feet.

The child bearing role of the female requires a pelvis which is broader, flatter and more protruding than that of the male. Consequently the lower limbs are set at a wider and less favourable angle for the transmission of power through the body.

Women are generally fatter than men. An average young male carries about 15% fat. An average young female carries about 25%. Male athletes range between 4 to 15% fat compared

The age, height and weight of competitors in the 1988 Olympic finals

Event	*	Men			Women		
		Age	Height (m)	Weight (kg)	Age	Height (m)	Weight (kg)
100 m	M F R	27.3 25.7 22-29	184.3 180.7 173-189	74.3 73.1 66-80	28.0 25.9 23-31	172.3 170.0 160-181	61.3 59.2 52-70
200 m	M F R	24.0 23.88 21-28	185.3 186.7 182-192	77.3 79.0 76-88	26.7 25.6 23-29	176.7 172.1 168-181	63.3 61.0 57-70
400 m	M F R	21.7 25.0 19-30	188.7 182.3 172-191	78.7 74.7 63-84	23.7 24.5 23-28	172.7 171.0 165-180	60.7 59.6 55-65
800 m	M F R	27.0 26.6 25-29	184.0 184.4 178-193	69.7 69.6 62-76	23.3 23.7 22-27	165.7 171.1 165-179	53.0 55.6 49-61
1 500 m	M F R	23.3 26.2 21-32	174.7 177.2 165-186	61.3 63.0 53-73	28.0 28.0 22-32	166.3 166.6 154-176	55.3 53.5 48-57
1 000 m	M F R				26.7 27.0 21-36	159.3 161.9 154-172	43.0 49.1 41-68
3 000 m	M F R				25.3 25.5 21-29	169.3 165.6 154-173	53.7 51.0 48-57
5 000 m	M F R	26.0 27.0 23-32	177.3 177.2 169-184	62.7 62.9 56-68			
10 000 m	M F R	25.3 26.2 21-29	179.7 175.2 165-185	63.7 61.6 54-76			
Marathon	M F R	28.7 29.0 24-36	180.0 175.9 162-183	62.7 60.4 50-70	28.3 26.6 23-30	165.0 162.0 154.170	49.3 47.6 39-57
100 m hurdles	M F R				25.7 25.1 23-27	173.0 172.5 164-178	60.3 59.5 55-67
110 m hurdles	M F R	25.0 23.6 20-28	185.3 184.5 180-189	78.7 75.6 66-88			
400 m hurdles	M F R	30.7 27.5 21-33	188.0 183.8 182-193	80.5 78.3 71-82	23.7 24.0 22-30	172.7 172.6 165-189	61.3 60.4 57-66

* M=Medalist; F=Finalist; R=Range

The age, height and weight of competitors in the 1988 Olympic finals

Event	*	Men			Women		
		Age	Height (m)	Weight (kg)	Age	Height (m)	Weight (kg)
3 000 m steeplechase	M F R	27.3 28.2 23-34	178.3 180.1 174-188	66.7 67.1 62-72			
Long jump	M F R	28.0 27.0 22-32	187.7 184.9 179-191	78.7 76.1 70-80	25.7 26.0 21-31	176.0 175.1 174-181	64.3 63.1 53-70
High jump	M F R	24.0 25.0 21-31	195.3 194.9 183-202	72.7 76.4 66-85	27.7 25.9 19-30	180.0 180.9 175-190	59.7 62.2 59-67
Triple jump	M F R	24.3 25.8 23-32	183.0 188.2 178-201	75.0 79.0 71-89			
Pole vault	M F R	23.0 24.4 19-33	186.0 184.8 176-193	77.3 76.6 71-82			
Shot	M F R	25.0 27.6 22-33	196.3 194.1 186-200	126.3 123.1 110-140	25.7 27.0 22-33	181.3 180.8 174-188	95.3 93.0 84-100
Discus	M F R	30.3 32.6 27-38	198.0 195.3 190-202	118.7 116.4 108-125	26.3 27.0 24-34	179.0 180.4 175-188	86.7 89.0 81-98
Hammer	M F R	31.3 28.4 24-33	186.0 187.5 180-193	108.7 103.1 82-120			
Javelin	M F R	25.0 26.0 18-32	189-3 188.9 184-196	97.3 96.0 82-105	25.7 26.4 21-32	173.3 170.8 160-180	64.7 69.0 63-75
Heptathlon	M F R				28.0 26.8 23-31	175.3 174.9 168-178	66.7 64.6 57-70
Decathlon	M F R	25.7 26.5 23-30	190.7 188.1 184-201	87.0 88.5 76-93			
20 km walk	M F R	29.3 27.6 21-38	176.7 175.6 168-183	67.3 65.8 54-70			
50 km walk	M F R	30.0 29.2 24-38	175.3 179.1 164-187	63.0 67.1 56-80			

* M=Medalist; F=Finalist; R=Range

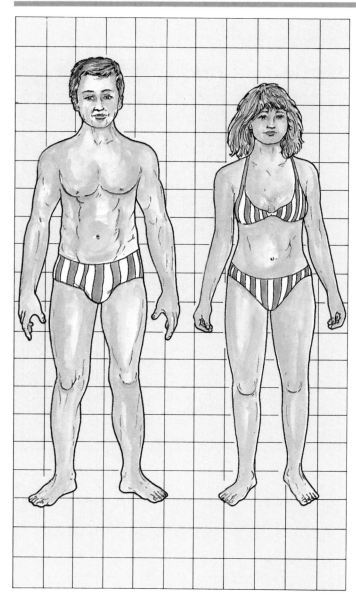

Comparison in size of an average man and an average woman

approximately 27% weaker. These differences exist because less of their body mass is composed of muscle (approximately 36%). During puberty muscle force develops faster than body weight in boys. With girls it remains constant or even declines.

Although training can improve the muscular strength in both sexes, it is the more active production of the male hormone testosterone in the male which ensures that they are stronger. It can be argued that because of their shorter stature, lower body weight, less muscle, more fat and different bone structure women are at a disadvantage against men in physical proficiency. We are talking in general terms however. There are many women who are stronger, faster, taller and more powerful than many men.

Up to the age of 10 girls have an approximately equal oxygen transporting capacity. The male's capacity continues to increase throughout puberty. The female's capacity tends to level off or even decrease after the age of 12. Although female athletes generally have a superior oxygen carrying capacity to inactive men, the best male competitors in sports demanding maximum endurance (speed skating, cross country skiing and orienteering) are better than the best females by at least 30%. These differences seem to be the result of smaller lungs and heart in the female as well as a lower percentage of blood volume. There are also differences in the actual composition of the blood; women have up to 30% less haemoglobin in the blood.

As a result of all these differences it has been estimated that women are about 30% less physically efficient than men.

The Menstrual Cycle

Considerable research has been carried out on the effect of the menstrual cycle on women's sporting success. It is known that women athletes have won World Championships in a number of sports in every stage of the menstrual cycle. Tension often rises before menstruation. In some sporting events (mainly the power events such as the shot put) this increase in tension can actually aid performance. In other more complex events it can lead to poorer performances.

A number of female athletes have successfully competed during the early stages of pregnancy. Evelyn Ashford, of the USA, broke the 100-metre

with 8 to 20% for females. Long distance runners have the lowest percentage of fat in both sexes. The actual distribution of this fat varies between the sexes. In the male fat tends to be found on the upper body. In women it accumulates on the thighs, hips and buttocks. This fact, allied to the different bone structure, explains why women have a lower centre of gravity than men of the same height. Basically they have a stature which spreads downwards.

Women are generally weaker than men. They have on average only 60% of the strength of men. They are at a particular disadvantage in the upper body where their muscles are 45 to 65% weaker than the opposite sex. In the lower body they are world record in 1984 and 40 weeks later gave birth. Liz McColgan, the 10,000 metre gold medalist at the 1991 World Athletics Championships, on the other hand, was not only running up to five miles a day when eight months pregnant, but only stopped jogging ten days before she gave birth. Despite a 48 hour period of labour she was running eleven days after giving birth. Three months later she was recording personal best times.

COMPARING SPORTING STANDARDS

A study of the world records in which it is possible to compare the two sexes shows that, although the men's records are better, the degree of difference is not uniform.

In track athletics the differences are about 10%. Although the female sprinter has less power she also has less body bulk to move. The differences become greater in the longer events because of the differing oxygen carrying capacity of the sexes. Training can obviously help to minimise this difference, but the extra fat of the female has to be oxygenated and carried. This is a built in disadvantage. The exceptionally good times recorded in female marathon running have been achieved by athletes of the most efficient body type who have also managed to shed most of their extra levels of fat. In the jumping events the female's relatively short stature and lower centre of gravity explain why her performances are approximately 16% poorer in the long jump and 15% poorer in the high jump. It is in the throwing events that the relative lack of muscle on the upper body is exposed most clearly. The relatively small difference between the world records is explained by the fact that lighter throwing implements are used by female competitors.

There are some advantages for the female in sport. Their greater fat covering not only helps general buoyancy when swimming but also helps to keep the swimmer's body in a much more efficient position for moving through the water. In events such as channel swimming, this greater fat covering also helps to sustain body temperature. Women also burn fats more efficiently. This could prove an advantage in endurance events such as long distance swimming and running. In activities such as gymnastics, women's natural flexibility can be used to full advantage too.

World records: track, field and swimming: September 1990

Event	Men	Women	% difference
Track and Field			
100 m	9.92	10.49s	5.43
200 m	19.72	21.34s	7.79
400 m	43.29	47.60s	10.20
800 m	1m 41.73s	1m 53.28s	10.20
1 500 m	3m 29.46s	3m 52.47s	9.90
5 000 m	12m 58.39s	14m 37.33s	11.28
10 000 m	27m 08.23s	30m 13.74s	10.23
Marathon	2h:06m :50s	2h: 21m:06s	10.11
4*100 relay	37.79s	41.37s	8.65
4*400 relay	2m 56.16s	3m 15.17s	9.74
High jump	2.44m	2.09m	14.34
Long jump	8.90m	7.52m	15.51
Shot*	23.12m	22.63m	2.12
Discus*	74.08m	76.80m	-3.67
Javelin*	90.98m	80.00m	12.07
Swimming			
100 m freestyle	48.24s	54.73s	11.86
200 m freestyle	1m: 46.69s	1m: 57.55s	9.24
400 m freestyle	3m: 46.95s	4m: 03.85s	6.93
100 m backstroke	54.51s	1m: 00.59s	10.03
200 m backstroke	1m: 48.14s	2m: 08.60s	8.13
100 m breaststroke	1m: 01.49s	1m: 07.91s	9.45
200 m breaststroke	2m:11.53s	2m: 26.71s	3.79
100 m butterfly	52.84s	57.93s	8.79
200 m butterfly	1m:56.24s	2m: 05.96s	7.72
200 m medley	2m: 00.11s	2m: 11.73s	8.82
400 m medley	4m: 14.75s	4m: 36.10s	7.73
4*100 m freestyle	3m: 16.53s	3m: 40.57s	10.90
4*100 m medley	3m: 16.93s	4m: 03.69s	19.19

* Different weights used

Are women catching up?

There is growing evidence to suggest that the differences in times and distances achieved in sport between men and women are becoming smaller. K.F. Dyer in his book 'Catching up the Men' gives a number of reasons to explain why women's records are below men's and argues strongly that they are in fact catching up. His reasons include the following:

- We have carried out less physiological and psychological studies on women in sport than on men.
- Women are not only massively under represented in most sports, but the social and domestic pressures placed on sportswomen make it harder for them to reach the top and stay there.
- Women are very poorly represented in terms of coaches, medical expertise and officials. Most major sporting events, for example the Olympics, World and European Athletics Championships are run almost entirely by men.
- Discrimination against women in terms of available facilities, coaching and so on is still very real in many countries of the world. A large number of countries still only send male competitors to many World events.
- Women have been participating in most sports for only a very short period of time. The numbers competing are often low and this, allied to the fact that they receive fewer qualified coaches, means that the standards achieved are relatively low.

Dyer argues that if the above points are remedied then the best women's results will approach those of men. He gives the comparison between male and female sporting records in East Germany where the women were given as much time, expertise and high expectation as their male counterparts. The difference between the male and female records was as low as 6% in many sporting events.

Successful female competitors in sporting events requiring strength and power do tend to possess more masculine attributes than those who are less successful. The same is true for men however. There is such variety in the sports available that most people, male or female, endomorphic, mesomorphic or ectomorphic can find a particular sport to suit them. Whether the women are catching up the men in terms of records is not so important. What is crucial is that they have equal opportunity to take part in sporting activities and are given every encouragement to do so. A change in attitude is of paramount importance.

See Chapter 15 for a fuller discussion on this issue.

RACE AND SPORT

In 1991, a football league club chairman said in a television interview *'That's the trouble with black players. I don't think too many can read the game … when you're getting into mid-winter in England, you need a few of the hard white men to carry the artistic black man through'*.

These comments caused a storm of protest and eventually the chairman apologised. Nevertheless they show clearly how stereotypes exist today.

A brief glance at sport might lead to the conclusion that sport is free of racism. Many black sportsmen and sportswomen are household names. Black athletes and footballers are essential to national teams. However a more detailed examination suggests otherwise.

In the USA black sportsmen first made their mark in boxing, with Jack Johnson winning the world heavyweight title in 1908. Later the rules were changed and it was not until 1937 that a black boxer was again allowed to challenge for the title. Jessie Owen's world records and huge success in the 1936 Olympics encouraged black athletes. Baseball, American football and basketball gradually attracted black players, but they were only allowed to play at the top level in the post 1945 era.

In Britain there was a similar development with boxers leading the way, although black boxers were not allowed to box for a British title until 1948. Athletes followed and in recent years black footballers have risen to the top. Albert Johannesson played for Leeds in the 1960s. Clyde Best for West Ham in the 1970s and in 1979 Viv Anderson became the first black player to represent England. Today about one third of the members of the Professional Footballers' Association are black.

An analysis of the positions occupied by black football league players on the field shows only a small number in mid field or defensive positions and rarely in goal. The majority are likely to be forwards.

Positions of Afro-Caribbean football league players

Position	Percentage	
	1985/86	1989/90
Goalkeeper	0.9% (1)	0% (0)
Fullback	19.8% (22)	15.8% (24)
Centreback	12.6% (14)	15.2% (23)
Midfield	15.3% (17)	12.5% (19)
Forwards	51.3% (57)	56.5% (86)
	N=111	N=152

Source: Sport, Racism and Ethnicity

This follows a similar pattern noted in American football where traditionally black players have been in running back and wide receiver positions rather than at quarterback. Also in baseball black players have usually taken outfield rather than starting pitching positions. It seems that white players, rather than black players, are far more likely to occupy the centrally important positions in these team games. It could be argued that this is due to the persistent stereotype held by those selecting teams which links black players with speed and power rather than intelligence and judgement. A similar situation has been found in British rugby union and rugby league where black players are over represented in wing positions. Australian Aborigines playing rugby league have had similar experiences. The qualities associated by the coaches with wing positions have corresponded to the dominant aboriginal stereotype.

There is no doubt that in some sports today, black competitors achieve success quite out of proportion to their numbers within the total population. These sports also tend to attract black competitors in far larger numbers than other sports. To try to account for both the high participation and success rates we can look at the two major factors which affect people taking part in sport, namely ability and availability of the sport.

It has been claimed that black sportsmen and sportswomen have a 'natural ability' which gives them an advantage in sport. However this claim does not stand up to scientific investigation. It is not possible to show that black people have any physical advantage at all over competitors of other races. Indeed the whole idea of examining a race has been discredited since genetic heritages are

never pure. Black sportsmen have reached the highest levels in a wide variety of sports requiring very different abilities, for example tennis, boxing, marathon running and American football.

Getting involved in sport is closely linked to where a person lives, their cultural background and their social situation. Rowing is most likely to be taken up by young people who attend public schools situated near rivers. The way black people have been treated by society in the USA and UK has determined their social status. In both countries racism and racial discrimination have worked to exclude them from many areas of employment. Career opportunities have not been the same as for their white peers. They have usually been offered work only in areas of least importance to society. They have lived mainly in urban areas. As a result their financial and social situation has generally prevented them from involvement in sports requiring expensive equipment and a well developed, traditional club system. They have been attracted to sports like boxing, athletics and football which require a minimum of equipment and organisation. Consequently it has been in these sports that they have found the successful role models to follow.

In the past schools have helped to continue the black stereotype of athletic prowess and academic failure. Academic expectations have not been as great for black pupils as for their white peers. They were encouraged to develop their sporting talent, sometimes at the cost of their academic studies. Once set on a sporting career, black youngsters had little to fall back on if sports success did not follow. Even for successful sportsmen and sportswomen, fame is shortlived and without good advice many champions have quickly returned to poverty and obscurity. Today in education, all pupils are encouraged to develop their talent to the full, both in academic and sporting areas.

Whilst there are many black competitors in different sports, there are very few in managerial, coaching or administrative positions. Although nearly 12% of the British Olympic team for Seoul was Afro/Caribbean or Asian there were only two black officials. In spite of the large number of black professional footballers, no black football league manager has yet been appointed. This situation can be investigated by looking at the people who have the power to appoint and the qualifications they hold important for the post.

Historical, social and cultural factors are more important than physical qualities when explaining black involvement in sport. Further it seems likely that when discrimination declines, career opportunities expand and financial circumstances improve, fewer young black people will need to opt for the sporting dream.

This analysis is particularly relevant for people of Afro-Caribbean descent and is largely about the sports performance of men. Black women have achieved high levels of success in many sports especially athletics, but hardly at all in professional sports. Chapter 15 examines the reasons for women's second class citizenship in sport.

In Britain today, people of Asian origin have taken little part in sport at the highest level. Sports does not have a very high priority in Asian communities and Asian women in particular have a very low sports participation rate. The Sports Council is now attempting to involve such groups through intervention and outreach work. This situation also would seem likely to be due to social and cultural influences rather than lack of physical ability.

THINGS TO DO

1 Write the letter that matches the definition for each word below.
   1 Endomorph
   2 Mesomorph
   3 Ectomorph

   A Thin, narrow shoulders and hips.
   B Fleshy, pear shaped and plump.
   C Muscular with broad shoulders and narrow hips.

2 Write the somatotype score that is most likely to fit a top class sportsman in the sports listed below.
   1 Heavy weight lifter   A 3-5-3
   2 Cross country runner   B 2-5-4
   3 Basketball player   C 2-3-6
   4 Gymnast   D 6-5-2

3 The following paragraph concerns early physical development. Complete the paragraph.
   Until the age of about ..... boys and girls mature at the same rate. They have similar body .... At this age sporting competition between them is quite .... Girls start their adolescent spurt between the ages of ..... and ..... Boys normally follow ..... years later. Girls usually reach physical maturity by ..... years of age. Boys may continue to .... until they are older. After puberty competition in activities requiring .... and .... is usually unfair.

4 Explain why women are at a disadvantage in many sports compared with men. Use the following terms in your answer:

   musculature, oxygen carrying capacity, height, weight, fat, pelvic girdle.

5 An individual's choice of sport is usually influenced by his or her body build. Describe the body build and likely sports associated with sportsmen and sportswomen having the basic body types of mesomorph, ectomorph and endomorph.

6 Obtain the height and weight of each member of your school or year athletics team. If possible see if you can obtain a group photo of them. Show this photo to someone who does not know the pupils and see if they can correctly identify the event in which each of them takes part. Within your group see if you can give approximate somatotype ratings.

SPORT AND THE MIND

A large number of sporting activities are listed here. Read through them and pick out those in which you have already gained some degree of success as well as those in which you would anticipate being successful if given the opportunity to participate.

Very few of us could honestly say that we would

Gymnastics Skiing Basketball Climbing Trampoline Ice-skating Soccer Potholing Swimming Sprinting Rugby Archery Diving Middle distance running Volleyball Badminton Dancing Throwing events Cricket (batting) Cricket (bowling) Wrestling Jumping events Sailing Hockey Judo Weight lifting Canoeing Golf Squash Tennis Table tennis Hang gliding Parachuting Gliding Horse riding wish to try all of the above activities, or if we did, that we would expect to achieve a high degree of success in all of them. This is not surprising. We know that to play a successful game of rugby requires different physical abilities than to complete a good round of golf. Similarly a skilful gymnast would not normally become a top class cross country runner. The fact that sportsmen and sportswomen differ with regard to their physical abilities, however, does not fully explain why some of us spend hours pursuing one particular sport, yet would not consider trying another.

Our final standard of performance in any sport is dependent on a number of factors.

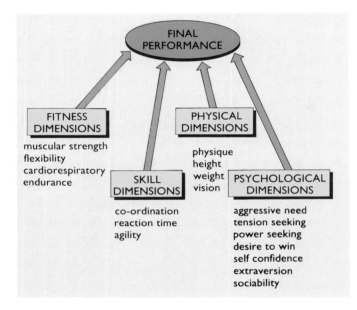

We have looked in some detail at our physical abilities, fitness and skill levels earlier in the book. We must now concentrate on the part which the mind plays in physical activity and sport.

People who work in the field of sports psychology attempt to find answers to the following questions:

- What type of person is attracted to competitive sport?
- Why do people choose one sport rather than another?
- What effect does long term sports involvement have on the individual?
- Why do sportsmen and sportswomen with apparent equal physical abilities differ in the degree of success they obtain from sport?
- Why do people behave in the way they do when involved in a sporting activity?
- What type of person becomes a champion?

Why take part in sport at all?

Most children are introduced to sport during their school days. They have little choice about whether or not to take part. Nevertheless sport is popular with almost all age groups and at all social levels.

Why Sport?

As a safety valve
Using sport as a way of getting rid of excess energy or aggression in an acceptable manner.

For aesthetic reasons
Where pleasure is experienced from the actual physical movements involved in sport.

For health and fitness
To maintain fitness or to improve it.

For the pursuit of excitement
Where the body is temporarily out of control or where there is a great deal of physical and so psychological danger.

For company
The sporting occasion enables people to meet and make friends with people of similar interests.

- Do you take part in sport for any of the above reasons?
- Can you think of any other reasons why you or other people take part in sport?

SOMETHING TO DO 1

1 Construct a questionnaire to find out why people take part in sport. Each member of the group should get it completed by 20 active sportsmen and sportswomen. What conclusions can you come to?

   • It is quite common for a person to start in a sport for one reason, but then pursue it for another. Did you find any examples of this happening in your survey?

2 Set up a similar survey to find out why people do not take part in sport.

STRESS AND SPORT

Some people are attracted to a particular sport because of the qualities within the sport itself. Sports can be rated not only according to the degree of physical energy and strength required for success but also according to the differing demands they place on the mind. We need to discuss the meaning of stress before looking at how it can affect the individual in sport.

In this discussion we will define stress as 'the rate of wear and tear on the body'. We are all being constantly exposed to stress in one form or another. Whenever the balance of the body or mind is upset the body attempts to adjust in such a way that this balance is restored. Stress exists when one or more of the body systems is out of balance. Stress is such a normal and essential part of our life that we are only occasionally aware of it. Experiments have shown that individuals need stress. People exposed to a completely stress free state soon show a great desire to get back into the stressful world.

Too little stress is unhealthy. Too much stress is harmful because the individual becomes unable to cope with it. Sport can be seen as a stress situation and it is possible to discuss sports according to the type and amount of stress they create in the individual.

The degree of aggression displayed in any sporting activity will vary according to a number of factors. In a game of soccer there are times when only indirect aggression is shown (for example, when shooting at goal) and other times when direct aggression is necessary (when

Different sports create different types and amounts of stress

tackling an opponent for example). One would also expect that the same player would show different levels of commitment, hence aggression, when involved in a training session, or kick around in the local park, to when he is in a championship final.

It must not be assumed that the amount of physical effort matches the degree of aggression involved. Games of chess can often be most aggressively played without a single blow being struck.

SOMETHING TO DO 2

Using the above descriptions as a guide, fit the following sports on the scale below:

Swimming	Skiing	Snooker
Squash	Throwing events	Basketball
Parachuting	Sprinting	Volleyball
American football	Croquet	Boxing
Darts	Table tennis	Rugby
Cricket (batting)	Cricket (bowling)	Climbing
Hockey	Karate	

...

Degree of aggression

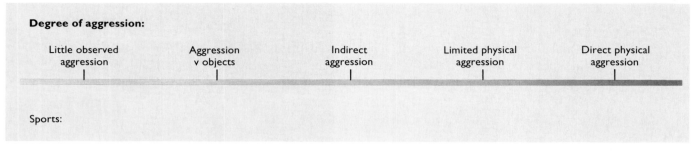

Degree of aggression:

| Little observed aggression | Aggression v objects | Indirect aggression | Limited physical aggression | Direct physical aggression |

Sports:

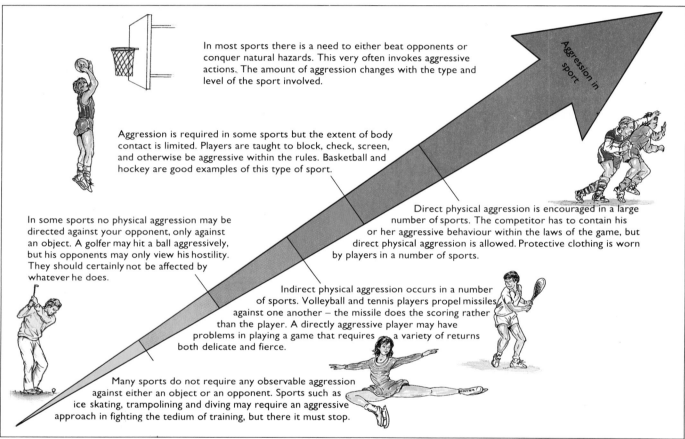

In most sports there is a need to either beat opponents or conquer natural hazards. This very often invokes aggressive actions. The amount of aggression changes with the type and level of the sport involved.

Aggression is required in some sports but the extent of body contact is limited. Players are taught to block, check, screen, and otherwise be aggressive within the rules. Basketball and hockey are good examples of this type of sport.

In some sports no physical aggression may be directed against your opponent, only against an object. A golfer may hit a ball aggressively, but his opponents may only view his hostility. They should certainly not be affected by whatever he does.

Direct physical aggression is encouraged in a large number of sports. The competitor has to contain his or her aggressive behaviour within the laws of the game, but direct physical aggression is allowed. Protective clothing is worn by players in a number of sports.

Indirect physical aggression occurs in a number of sports. Volleyball and tennis players propel missiles against one another – the missile does the scoring rather than the player. A directly aggressive player may have problems in playing a game that requires a variety of returns both delicate and fierce.

Many sports do not require any observable aggression against either an object or an opponent. Sports such as ice skating, trampolining and diving may require an aggressive approach in fighting the tedium of training, but there it must stop.

Effort and Accuracy Stresses

Sports vary in the degree of effort and accuracy needed for successful participation.

SOMETHING TO DO 3

Complete the table, using the above information as a guide. (The maximum score awarded is 5.)

Event	Skill	Endurance	Power
Archery	5	2	2
Shot	4	2	5
Marathon			
High diving			
Pole vault			
Hockey			
Table tennis			
Swimming			

Effort and accuracy stresses

High skill
High power
Low endurance

Accuracy of prime importance

Stress is not only physical. Remember how tired you felt after you completed your last examination. You can often feel mentally and physically drained despite having taken part in no physical activity.

Start 14 M | Finish 12 M

All out power
High in skill
Low endurance

High skill
High in power
Low endurance

Low skill
Low power
High endurance

Degree of Social Support

Whenever sportsmen or sportswomen take part in competitive sport then they take the risk of being beaten and therefore demoralised to some extent. Sports differ in the degree to which individuals are exposed to defeat and also in the amount of emotional support that participants are likely to receive. It is how the individual competitor views the importance of the event that determines the amount of stress he or she feels.

An individual athlete competing against an unknown opponent may feel completely isolated and perform badly. Some sportsmen and sportswomen may like this isolated feeling, however, and react favourably to it.

More often an individual athlete at least has the support of his or her coach who can help to maintain morale when the going gets tough. Obviously partners in a doubles team tend to give each other emotional support.

Members of a sporting team such as basketball and team rowing will receive more emotional and physical support and will tend to be not so vulnerable to either aggressive opponents or partisan crowds.

In large team games, such as soccer and rugby, the individual player is always supported by 15 - 20 others around him whether he is playing at home or away.

Members of a basket ball team give emotional and physical support to each other

All of the above are generalisations. It is easy to think of situations when a soccer player playing on his home ground in a winning team could nevertheless feel isolated and threatened.

SOMETHING TO DO 4

You are the coach of a squash player who is due to play in a tournament. You cannot go with him or her. Suggest as many ways as possible of ensuring that he or she does not feel alone and unsupported.

Space and Time Uncertainty

It is also possible to group sports according to the degree of control the sportsman or sportswomen has over the proceedings. The scale would range from sports in which there was a great deal of uncertainty (for example, tennis doubles) to sports in which almost all the conditions are controlled, as in an event such as shot putt.

SOMETHING TO DO 5

Using the above description as a guide, place the following sports into one of three groups:

  (i)   high uncertainty;
  (ii) medium uncertainty
  (iii) low uncertainty

Trampoline	Hurdles
Discus	Rugby
Swimming	Clay pigeon shooting
Squash	Pot holing
Sailing	Sailing
Cricket (batting)	Hockey
Table tennis	Bowling
Soccer	Pole vault
Diving	

There are other ways of looking at the different types of stress present in sport. See if you can think of other ways of grouping sports.

PERSONALITY AND SPORT

Do people behave consistently and do they behave differently from each other?

We can all think of one or more boy or girl in our form, year or our school who is always talking and always wishing to be the centre of attention. We can also think of others who seldom talk in class, who keep their thoughts to themselves and who get on with their work with the minimum of fuss. People do seem to behave differently from each other. One of the skills in life is learning to anticipate how others will behave in all sorts of situations. If we could not predict a person's behaviour then life would be very difficult for us. If we know a person is friendly, awkward, touchy, easy going or quick tempered then we will treat them accordingly.

Psychologists have attempted to classify people's personality in a more accurate way. Even so, their results seem to show that our commonsense categories are usually quite sound. Eysenck, for example, places individuals on two different scales according to their answers to a personality questionnaire. One scale is the introversion–extroversion scale, whilst the other is the neuroticism–stability scale.

The majority of us are neither complete introverts nor complete extroverts but lie somewhere between the two extremes. The same applies to the neuroticism–stability extreme. Extreme extroverts would have the following

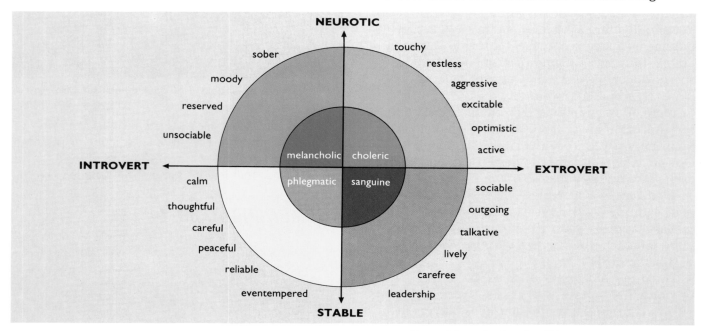

Eysenck's scales for classifying people's personalities

characteristics: the ability and the need to express themselves, their ideas, etc., high self-confidence in new situations, high opinions of themselves and their ideas. They would also be socially outgoing and tend to be the leaders of any group.

Extreme introverts would tend to show the opposite characteristics: little wish, or ability to express their ideas, very quiet when in a group, with no wish to expose themselves or their ideas in new situations.

With the help of a personality questionnaire it is possible to place individuals at particular points on a personality chart.

Sports psychologists have used a wide variety of personality questionnaires as well as other methods in order to assess the personalities of sportsmen and sportswomen. Thousands of people have been tested, some young, some old, some top class sportsmen and sportswomen and others who take part in spite of their lack of sporting ability.

A number of interesting conclusions have been suggested by these psychologists. It must be stressed, however, that often the results from one test are contradicted by the results from another. Their findings include the following

- Extroverts tend to produce better sporting results when they are highly aroused. Introverts perform better at a lower level of arousal. The idea of arousal needs to be understood.
- Pupils representing their school in netball, soccer or any other sporting event work much harder, get more involved and become more physically exhausted when they play in the final of a cup competition than if they are playing in a friendly unimportant game. Some people do not play their best in a friendly game because they cannot get excited or keyed up. Others play below their best in a very important game because they are too excited and too concerned to play well.
- People produce their best work when their tension level (or arousal level) is at a particular point. Both above and below this level, their performances will not be as good.
- Different people perform most effectively at different arousal levels. Introverts reach their peak performance at a lower level of arousal than extroverts.
- Extroverts seek sports in which high states of arousal are most likely to occur. They are therefore more likely to take part in team

games than in individual sports.
- Although introverts will work hard in training sessions and unimportant matches, they are prone to get 'worked up' or become too tense in important matches. The reverse will be true for extroverts. Whilst it may be difficult to get them really involved in training sessions or practice matches, they will usually play at their best in the really important matches.
- Introverts perform better in fine physical skills where confined and precise movements are required. They probably excel in sports such as fencing, rifle shooting, archery and rock climbing.
- Extroverts perform better at gross physical skills, that is movements using the whole of the body in a relatively unlimited manner.
- Extroverts prefer sports in which there is plenty of activity and uncertainty. Hence such sports as cross country running and long distance swimming, in which there is little variety in what the sportsman has to do, tend to be more attractive to the introverted person. There are a number of sports in which action is restricted. For example, in rifle shooting the competitor lies stationary for a long period of time often in unfavourable conditions and with little body movement. Rock climbing, pot holing and similar sports also demand close constricted movement. These types of activities would be more likely to appeal to the more introverted person.
- Research experiments have shown that extroverts can tolerate more pain than introverts. Sports which are likely to involve physical pain, for example, body contact sports such as boxing, wrestling, judo and rugby should therefore be more suitable for extroverts.
- In general, the most successful sportsmen and sportswomen tend to be stable extroverts, although there are exceptions to this general rule. It is certainly true that the more neurotic a person is the less likely they are to take part in sport.

Despite the great amount of research which has been carried out in the last thirty years, we still know very little about sport and the mind. People with the wrong 'body types' as well as the 'wrong' personality characteristics still manage to do remarkably well in sport. Other people apparently gifted both physically and mentally fail to make it to the top. Perhaps this uncertainty about sporting success gives sport its great appeal.

Even if you have the wrong type of body, the wrong type of personality and your sporting prowess is not very high, then you can still get great enjoyment and satisfaction out of taking part in sporting activity.

THINGS TO DO

1 List the sports that you enjoy taking part in, in order of preference. Now list your reasons for enjoying each sport. Try to analyse your answers and see what it is that you find attractive about sport. Compare your answers with others in your group.

2 Research suggests that solitary sporting activities are likely to attract
   A introverts
   B extroverted mesomorphs
   C all endomorphs
   D all mesomorphs.

3 The success and interest shown by an individual in a particular sport is often related to his personality and body type. Discuss this statement and give examples from different sports.

4 Use one of the given words to complete each sentence:
   (i) Games involving body contact and with the risk of pain tend to attract
       A introverts
       B neurotics
       C extroverts
       D conservatives

   (ii) Indirect aggression against opponents occurs in
       A Rugby
       B Soccer
       C Tennis
       D Golf

   (iii) An extrovert sportsman is usually
       A Rather quiet and shy
       B Very sociable and the centre of attention.
       C Friendly in a restrained way
       D Retiring and unfriendly

Sport in society

Part 2

8 THE HISTORY OF SPORT

Aims

To develop knowledge and understanding of:
- the development of individual sports and sport in general
- the influence of social history on sports development
- the reasons for change in sport

To develop the skills of
- secondary research, historical and cultural
- primary research
- interviewing

People have always played. The desire to play is very strong in the human race. Children learn through play. Adults use play for relaxation and enjoyment.

In ancient times, people who had enough time and energy left over after work relaxed together. They developed different forms of play. Throughout the centuries these recreational activities changed. The type of activity which people chose was related to their way of earning a living. Those in privileged positions in society had the time and resources to take part in a variety of activities. For most people the opportunities were few and the activities simple.

People of different countries have found different ways to play. One tribe of North American Indians used the head of an enemy as a ball. In the Far East games like chequers have always been popular. The cruel sports of bear baiting, cock fighting and hare coursing have entertained many Europeans. Today American football combines the violence of the battleground with the tactics of the chessboard.

To look at the history of sport is to look at the social history of a society. Sport reflects the society in which it is found.

SPORT AND SOCIETY

Throughout history there have been many obvious links between each society and its sport. As the Roman Empire declined so did its sport. The events in the arenas became more and more bloody and violent. In mediaeval times military training influenced sport. The knights took part in tournaments and jousting. All other men were expected to practise archery. The public schools in Victorian days saw games as a means to develop moral values. 'To play cricket' came to mean to behave in an acceptable way. The Berlin Olympics of 1936 were used by Hitler to publicise the achievements of his Nazi government.

Sport also reflects the situation of those taking part. In eighteenth century England, only the upper classes were able to hunt, shoot or fish. They alone had access to the necessary land or water and their position was reinforced by the Game Laws. For ordinary people these sports were out of reach. The nearest they could get to them was to poach and this carried heavy penalties.

There were two important influences on the development of sport in Britain over the last two centuries:

1 The industrial revolution brought with it the most unpleasant social conditions. Gradually workers in the cities turned to sport for relaxation.

2 Schools introduced children to organised physical activities. The public schools led this movement with great emphasis on games. In the state-run schools only drill was given at first. Eventually a much wider range of activities was taught in all schools.

The influence of the ancient Olympic Games cannot be ignored. They inspired the revival of the Olympic movement, which has been very important to modern sports development.

Discus thrower in the second century AD

THE ANCIENT OLYMPICS

A man called Koroebus is recorded as the first Olympic winner. His victory was in a foot race in the earliest known Olympic Games. These were held at Olympia in Greece in 776 BC. Religious ceremonies and games had been held there before that time, but irregularly. From this date the Games were held every fourth year. They took place continuously for over a thousand years, until at least AD 261. This is remarkable since the Greek city states were often at war. During the period of the Games a sacred truce was strictly observed.

The Games were not just athletic meetings. They were religious festivals of great importance. The Olympic Games were always held in honour of the god, Zeus. They were not the only games of the time. In fact over one hundred cities held athletic competitions. The Olympic Games were one of four famous Crown Games, so called because crowns or wreaths were awarded to the winners.

The Olympics were the most spectacular and important games. As their fame spread, more and more competitors and spectators attended. The athletes prized victory in the stadium at Olympia above everything. Originally the Games only lasted one day, but this was gradually extended to five. This allowed time for making sacrifices, registering the athletes, taking the oath and prizegiving. People also came to see special works of art produced for the Games. One of these was a gold and ivory statue of Zeus, one of the seven wonders of the ancient world. Some of the great thinkers, including Socrates and Plato, also attended the Games and public debates took place.

Only Greeks and citizens of Greek colonies were allowed to take part. At first all competitions

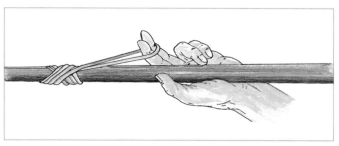

The method of holding a javelin by a thong

This is probably how jumping weights were used

were for men, but later boys took part. They usually competed naked. Women and slaves were not even allowed to watch the Games. Separate athletic meetings were held for women although eventually the other three Games included women's events.

The Crown Games

Name	City	Timespan	God	Crown
Olympic	Olympia	4 years	Zeus	Olive
Pythian	Delphi	4 years	Apollo	Laurel
Isthmian	Corinth	2 years	Poseidon	Pine
Nemean	Nemea	2 years	Zeus	Wild celery

The Ancient Olympic Programme

The three main running events were:
1 Short sprint (stade), one length of the stadium (200 m).
2 Double sprint (diaulos), two lengths of the stadium (400 m).
3 Long distance race (dilichos), many lengths (about 4 800 m).

In 708 BC the wrestling and pentathlon events were added. Boxing was included in 688 BC, followed by chariot races in 680 BC. The pankration, added in 648 BC, was the roughest and toughest of all sports. Competitors could punch, grapple, kick and throw. These events formed the basic programme. Other events were included at different times, for example the races in armour.

The pentathlon covered five events, the long jump, discus, javelin, short sprint and wrestling. Three wins were needed for victory. In the long jump, strange weights called halteres were carried in each hand. It is thought they helped gain extra distance. The discus was larger and flatter, but is believed to have been thrown in a way similar to that used today. To increase the distance achieved by the javelin, a thong held in the hand was wound around the shaft.

The three physical contact events were very popular. Boxers wore no gloves, but bound leather thongs around their hands. They fought until one gave in or was knocked out. Wrestling, like the event today, continued until one wrestler forced his opponent's shoulder blades against the ground. In the pankration, the crowd's favourite event, a submission or knockout decided the winner.

Chariot racing was held on a separate track, called a hippodrome. Races were very exciting and usually dangerous, especially at the turning posts at the ends of the stadium. On one occasion a record number of 41 chariots started a twelve lap race with only one completing the course!

The famous marathon race was not held at the ancient Games. The Greeks and Persians fought a battle at Marathon in Greece, in 490 BC. Afterwards, a runner was sent to Athens to give the news of a Greek victory. The story says that after delivering his message, he collapsed and died. The modern marathon race, first run in 1896, was to commemorate the original feat.

The Importance of the Ancient Games

About a hundred years ago, excavations at Olympia uncovered the ruins of a large sporting and religious complex. The sacred area contained the temples, including that of Zeus with its statue. Other buildings found were the Gymnasium, the Palaestra (where the wrestling and boxing took place) and the Baths. The stadium was close by containing a rectangular track, about 200m by 30m. Up to 10 000 spectators could squeeze onto the slopes surrounding the stadium.

In the early Games, competition was friendly and fair. As they became more important, so did the winning. Athletes found trainers and specialised in one event. They trained very hard, even following special diets. Many cities offered valuable prizes to the winners. Civic receptions were arranged; rewards included money and pensions. Pindar of Thebes became famous for writing victory poems.

The decline of the Games was gradual. The importance of winning, the large rewards given to winners and the singlemindedness of the athletes all changed the Games. There was bribery and corruption.

In the second century BC Greece was conquered by the Romans. Although they kept the Games going they did not understand the Olympic spirit. Cruel events were introduced, eventually leading to contests between gladiators and fights with animals. In AD 393, the Christian Emperor Theodosius abolished the Games. He claimed they were a pagan festival. The sacred site of Olympia was very soon destroyed. First there were the invaders, then an earthquake, followed by a flood which buried the remains under mud and water. It remained lost for many centuries. It was not until 1896 that De Coubertin was able to rekindle the Olympic spirit.

Pierre de Coubertin

Baron Pierre de Coubertin was born in Paris on January 1st 1863 into a rich and influential family. His great interests in life were sport and education. He was very impressed by the way sport was used in English public schools. Gradually his idea to re-establish the Olympic movement emerged.

At a conference in Paris in 1894, 79 delegates from 12 countries agreed to restore the Olympic Games. He saw the Games as a way of making sport popular. By the time he died in 1937 he had achieved greatness by turning a simple idea into a reality.

The Olympic movement faced criticism from the start and has done ever since. Much of the criticism has been directed at the International Olympic Committee. This is the supreme body of the movement. De Coubertin chose the members of the original committee. Since then they have themselves chosen new members when required. He wanted members to be trustees of the Olympic idea and above politics and group interests.

THE EARLY DAYS OF SPORT IN BRITAIN

Before 1700, sport in Britain was mainly a local affair. The games and competitions were controlled by the people involved. They decided on the rules. Travel around the country was difficult and not attempted by many people. Regional variations in the activities were not very important. Most competitors were from the locality.

Patronage

In the eighteenth century social position was fixed. People knew their place in society. A system of patronage existed. This meant that wealthy people were able to support talented people who were poor. The rich employed musicians and artists to work for them. Patronage was also found in sport. Indeed it was necessary as the financial rewards for sportsmen were very limited. The Duke of Cumberland was patron to Jack Broughton, the prize fighter. The Duke of Dorset was one of the main patrons of the Hambledon Cricket Club. Royal patronage of horse racing allowed the early development of modern thoroughbreds.

Gambling and the Rules of Sport

Gambling was a popular activity throughout eighteenth century society. It helped the development of a number of sports. However it also encouraged unfair practice and the involvement of criminals. Prize fighting was developed mainly as a sport for people to bet on the result. By the 1820's so many fights were fixed in advance that it lost the support of the upper class and gradually faded away.

As it does now, horse racing had gambling as its prime purpose. It was very popular and well organised. The Jockey Club was founded at Newmarket in 1750. It was soon sorting out problems and making rules to control betting.

In 1743 the first rules for boxing were drawn up, known as Broughton's Rules. They were an attempt to see that both the fight and the gambling were fair.

Surprisingly cricket also owes much of its early increase in popularity to gambling. Wagers were staked on the outcome of games. As with other sports, this showed the need for rules and regulations. The first laws date from 1744 and by the end of the century they had spread throughout the country.

In the same year, golf laws were agreed upon. This was to enable wagers to be laid fairly between players.

Gambling at this time was officially illegal for the lower classes. It was also strictly limited for the upper classes. Of course it was impossible to enforce as many politicians were heavy gamblers. The idea of sport as a relaxing form of leisure for the lower classes was not considered. It was assumed that the spectators' motive was gambling. Therefore the activity was undesirable.

Many sports were based on cruelty to animals

Violence in Sport

Society was used to physical violence and brutality in the eighteenth century. Public hangings drew large crowds. Law and order relied on severe punishment as a deterrent. In the armed forces and schools corporal punishment was widely used. Many sports were based on cruelty to animals, for example badger baiting, dog fighting and hare coursing. Bare knuckle prize fights were only won when one fighter was unconscious. Physical violence was also part of football, cricket and horse racing. For most people, violence and cruelty were accepted as normal in both sport and ordinary life.

The first law to prevent cruelty to animals was not passed until 1822 and two years later large scale prize fighting was ended. Even today fox hunting and boxing continue.

THE FOUNDATIONS OF MODERN BRITISH SPORT

The Victorian period was one of great change and development. Victorian inventiveness gave Britain a headstart in the industrial revolution. The British Empire provided the raw materials and ready markets for the 'Workshop of the World'. Sport and recreation were caught up in the national drive to organise, improve and develop. The foundations of modern sport were laid in this period. These sports were exported very successfully and greatly influenced the whole pattern of world sports development.

Changing Social Conditions

The industrial revolution changed the distribution of the population. In every area, people moved towards the towns and cities. In 1800 only 30% of the population lived in towns. By the end of the century this had grown to 75%. This change caused many social problems for the towns. Work was usually indoors in factories and offices. The hours were long, the work often hard and boring. There was a great need for physical recreation away from work.

At this time most of the popular sports were linked with the country. Apart from the obvious field sports of hunting, shooting and fishing, sports such as horse racing, cricket and prize fighting usually took place in the country. Only the cruel baiting sports were staged regularly in towns and these were banned early in the century. Ordinary people turned to public houses for recreation and entertainment. Some pubs organised rat killing competitions using dogs. Others had shooting galleries or running tracks for contests. Some landlords arranged boxing matches. In the second half of the century, sport became more widely available and the influence of the public houses faded.

93 384 fans attended the FA Cup Final in 1936

For most working people life was hard. Work occupied six days a week with Saturday a full working day. Nevertheless many people attended sporting events whenever they could. By the 1870's most workers only worked until lunchtime on Saturday. This gave a great impetus to sport, which had already developed in many different forms.

The working class particularly identified with soccer. Teams became the centre of attention for local people. Large crowds attended matches on a regular basis. In the Midlands and North of England industry and soccer developed together. The Football Association was formed in 1863 and the FA Cup first played for in 1872.

The great following that soccer attracted allowed players to be paid. It very soon became a professional sport. Amateur soccer continued but most amateurs could not compete with the professionals. Only one amateur team, the famous Corinthians, could beat professional sides. Their success continued until 1914.

Horse racing has always attracted large crowds mainly for the gambling. When the country cricket teams played in the towns they too were sure of high attendances.

Education and Public Schools

Until the middle of the nineteenth century, the public schools actively discouraged most sporting activities. Sport was thought to be a waste of time. Also teachers worried about the drinking and unruly behaviour that usually went with sport.

However, later in the century, this attitude changed. Sport was strongly encouraged as a form of physical religion, often called 'Muscular Christianity'. Dr. Arnold, the headmaster of Rugby School, is often given credit for the games cult. In fact it had already started and the fame of his school helped it to spread.

Spectator sports, such as horse racing, prize fighting and animal baiting were forbidden. Sports requiring a lot of physical effort were very popular, as were team games. Games like cricket, rugby and soccer were thought to develop concern for others, unselfishness and leadership. Above all, such games were believed to prepare the young men for their future careers.

The Old Etonians played Old Westminsters at cricket as early as 1768. Apart from cricket, the public schools had little effect on sport outside the schools until the middle of the nineteenth century. At this time professional cricket coaches were appointed and the standard of play improved.

The new games of rugby and soccer were developed by the public schools. In the early days the rules varied from school to school. There were two basic forms, 'the handlers' and 'the dribblers'. Competition between schools presented many problems. The Football Association after 1863 standardised the rules of soccer.

Rugby, according to legend, originated when William Webb Ellis picked up the ball and ran with it at Rugby School in 1823. The game developed at many schools and the Rugby Football Union was formed in 1871.

The first university boat race, between Oxford and Cambridge, took place in 1829. The interest shown by the public helped popularise rowing.

At the beginning of the nineteenth century, pedestrianism was very popular. It was a form of long distance running and attracted large crowds who came to gamble. Athletics, as we know it today, developed much later at the universities. The students drew up rules for the events and in 1864 the first university match was held.

Many other sports including hockey, swimming and mountaineering owe much to the early influence of public schools and universities.

The Oxford Boat, 1829

Drill in the schoolyard

For the mass of children outside the public school system, education was very different. The elementary schools lacked the facilities, equipment and staff to provide a wide range of physical activities. The Education Act of 1870, making schooling compulsory, resulted in the building of more schools. However only exercises and drill were recommended and these were for disciplinary and health reasons. Gradually Swedish gymnastics, involving rhythmic exercises, were introduced and later some games and other activities. The different views about physical education, held by public and state schools, continued until recent times.

The Transport Revolution

The improvement in transport throughout the country had far-reaching effects on sport. During the eighteenth century improvements in the road network enabled keen spectators to travel to major sporting events.

These changes were small when compared with the arrival of the railways. At first, those who took part in field sports feared the railways would ruin the country areas. However the railways allowed them to travel elsewhere to practise their sport. Scotland, in particular, benefitted in this way. Poachers too were pleased, as the railways helped them get their game to market more quickly!

Until the arrival of the railways, sports had been unable to develop nationally. From the late 1860's, excursion trains took spectators to regattas, prize fights, race meetings, cricket and soccer matches. Horse racing had taken place on a regional basis because of the problems of transporting the horses. The railways enabled

horses to be taken anywhere in the country. Even at this time, the local inhabitants complained about the excursion trains bringing undesirables who committed crimes in the town.

Cricket too had been limited to regional competitions. In the thirty years from 1846 a number of representative teams toured the country. They encouraged cricket and only stopped when the County Championship began in 1873.

After overcoming its early problems with rules, soccer flourished. The Football League was founded in 1888 with teams competing from all over the country. This was only possible because players and spectators could travel so easily on the railways.

Strangely enough, the railways helped to keep prize fighting alive. The sport had officially been banned, but excursion trains were still organised. A game of hide and seek usually took place with the police and magistrates. The organisers often presented the fight in a field by the railway.

International sport was also affected by the introduction of the railways. Travel across other countries became easier and safer. The revival of the Olympic Games in Athens in 1896 was only possible because athletes were able to travel to Greece.

The arrival in Britain of teams from other countries made many sports review the British standards of play. Rowing suffered in this way and had to admit that the best of British rowers had been beaten by 'colonials and Americans'.

The first England versus Scotland soccer match was played in 1872. The cricketers had started earlier with a tour of North America in 1859 and of Australia in 1861. The first serious Australian team played in England in 1878 and in 1882 they beat England at The Oval. The following famous obituary notice then appeared in the Sporting Times:

'In affectionate remembrance of English cricket ... the body will be cremated and the Ashes taken to Australia.'

The first England cricket team to tour America in 1859

BRITISH SPORT TODAY

The Sports Council encourages participation in sport in Britain. In 1988 it planned, within five years, to encourage an extra 1.25 million women and 750 000 men to take part in sport. This looks like an ambitious target. However the growth of sport has been so great this century that it could be achieved.

Most people agree that satisfying leisure time activities are important for everyone. Very few jobs today need a great deal of physical effort. Many are boring and repetitive. Physical recreation plays a vital part in maintaining good health. Opportunities to take part are open to everyone.

It was very different before the First World War. Although working conditions had improved, working hours were still long with Saturday morning usually included. Many jobs left people too tired to think of taking part in sport. There was still much poverty and the expense involved in sport was too great for many. Some sports were still only available to the rich and privileged.

After the war, the Education Act of 1918 allowed local education authorities to provide playing fields, swimming baths, camps and centres for physical training. The National

Playing Fields Association was formed in 1926 to provide more sports facilities. In 1935 the Central Council of Recreative Physical Training was established to promote sport and recreation. It was renamed the Central Council of Physical Recreation after the Second World War. This Council was responsible for the post-war development of sport until the formation of the Sports Council in 1972.

Most people in Britain suffered a long period of hardship after 1945. Following the great war effort, sport was slow to develop again. However the expansion of sport in the last 30 years has been quite remarkable. It is related to changes in society which are themselves complex.

Social Change

Social conditions improved for most people in Britain during the twentieth centry. Work became less demanding both physically and in terms of hours worked. Improvements in medical care, diet and sanitation raised the general health of the population. Labour saving devices and better transport saved people time. All these factors helped the development of physical recreation. After the Second World War the standard of living greatly improved. Most people had more money to spend on leisure. This allowed more people to take part in sports needing expensive equipment. Attitudes towards sport also changed. Today newspapers and television reflect the great public interest in sport. Many sports stars are household names. The current emphasis on healthy living has also encouraged people to take part in physical recreation.

Education

There were many changes after 1945 in physical education in State schools. Most importantly the subject was accepted as a vital part of all pupils' education. The importance of early experiences in the primary schools was stressed. A wide variety of different activities was offered both in lesson time and out of school at all ages. The basic skills were taught and a positive attitude encouraged towards taking part in sport. The importance of lifelong physical recreation was emphasised by physical education teachers. Government sponsored bodies such as the Health Council and the Sports Council did much to promote physical recreation.

Multipurpose sports halls and leisure centres were often developed on school sites. In the future, reductions in working hours and high levels of long term unemployment will make the provision of sports facilities very important.

More recent changes in education may reduce its importance in encouraging active physical leisure in the future. As Physical Education is one of the last foundation subjects to be implemented it will face strong competition for curriculum time from other subjects. Falling school rolls have allowed local education authorities to sell off sports grounds which at the moment are not needed. In some schools, particularly in the primary area, there has been a strong move against competitive sport. The major games especially have suffered. During the teachers' unions pay dispute many staff stopped out of school activities. After the dispute was settled, teachers' hours were fixed and many staff did not resume their activities. The effects of Local Management of Schools may also reduce the resources put into sport as schools struggle to balance their budgets.

There are two other important changes outside education. Sports and leisure centres are increasingly expected to run at a profit. This may make sport available only to those who can pay. The Government has decided not to increase the grant (in real terms) given to the Sports Council. This means less money to develop sport, unless the Council can find money from other sources.

For the future, sport for young people will have to rely less on state subsidy and local authority support. It will depend more and more on private enterprise and commercial sponsorship.

Sport in a Technological Age

Before the Second World War, radio reported the major sporting events live. It enabled people to enjoy the sport, regardless of where it was held. Radio commentaries made sport more popular.

Today television has been responsible for the development of interest in many sports. Show jumping, skiing, snooker and darts have gained popularity helped by television coverage. Falling attendances at football matches were blamed on over-exposure on television. American football, Japanese Sumo wrestling and Australian rules football have been successfully introduced on television. One satellite television channel shows

only sport from around the world. Events such as test matches, world championships, cup finals and major tournaments appear to dominate television at the time they take place.

Bobsleighing is a modern high-tech sport

The development of technology earlier in the century encouraged sports using machines such as motor and cycle racing. More recently power boat racing, hang gliding and windsurfing have become popular. Improvements in sports surfaces, including all-weather tracks and pitches, have helped other sports. For most sports, advances in clothing and equipment have improved performances. Sometimes new equipment has changed the sport considerably, for example the fibre glass pole in pole vaulting.

Commercial Interests

A whole leisure industry has grown up around sport. This includes builders of specialist facilities, sports centre employees, equipment and clothing manufacturers and retailers.

Closely linked to the media and the leisure industry is sponsorship and commercial interests in sport. Because of the popularity of sport, many companies are willing to sponsor sport in return for the publicity. This extra injection of money has enabled sport to develop. Indeed many sports now need sponsorship to keep their activities at the present level. However sports are now more selective in the sponsorship they accept. Many avoid products harmful to good health, such as alcohol and tobacco. Sponsorship has in many cases enabled top amateurs to concentrate full-time on their sport. Most sports have changed their rules to allow these performers to receive payments and rewards. Few sports separate amateurs and professionals, most performers are now called players or competitors.

Sport for Everyone

Not all sports have always been open to everyone. In the past women were excluded from the majority of sports. Gradually they have overcome prejudice and now participate in most sports. It is no longer seen as unfeminine to take part in sport. However women do not usually compete with or against men.

In the nineteenth century, all aspects of life, including sport, were closely linked to the class system. The field sports of hunting, shooting and game fishing were limited to the upper classes. Fencing, squash, hockey, horse riding, skiing and sailing were middle and upper class sports. The working class dominated cycling, wrestling, weight lifting and coarse fishing. Soccer, cricket, swimming, athletics, boxing and tennis attracted people from all classes.

There were exceptions. Golf had always been played by everyone in Scotland, but largely by the middle and upper class in England. Rugby Union was played by the working class in Wales, but by the middle and upper class in England. Rugby League's home had always been in the working class areas of the North of England.

As the class divisions in society broke down or changed, so most sport became available to those who wished to take part.

In Britain, sport continued to develop largely independently of government control. This is both its strength and its weakness.

There is a lack of central planning to ensure smooth development of sport throughout the country. The different sports bodies run their own affairs. Co-operation between sports is usually limited. The Sports Council attempts to co-ordinate all sport in Britain.

Independent sports bodies are free to control their own sport as their members decide. They are therefore able to resist political pressure. This independence has always been at the heart of British sport throughout two centuries of development. It has been, and still is, jealously guarded.

THINGS TO DO

1 Copy and complete the following paragraph:

The Ancient Olympic Games were held at .... in .... From 776 BC the Games were held every .... years for over .... years. The Greek city states were often at .... During the period of the Games a .... was strictly observed. Apart from the athletics, the Games were also important as .... festivals. They were held in honour of the God........................... The athletes usually competed .... The Olympic Games were one of four famous .... Games.

2 The Modern Olympic Games were first held in 1896.
   (i)   Who was responsible?
   (ii) Where were they held?
   (iii) What do you know about them?

3 In what ways were the English public schools important for the development of sport in the nineteenth century?

4 Explain why working class participation in sport was limited in the nineteenth century.

5 Explain how the following affected the early development of sport in Britain:
   (i)   patronage
   (ii) gambling
   (iii) the Industrial Revolution
   (iv) improved transport

6 Suggest ways in which education has assisted the growth of sport since the Second World War.

7 Choose one sport or activity which has increased in popularity in recent years. Explain the reasons for its growth, taking into account such factors as television, sponsorship, costs, lifestyle, etc.

The following assignments cannot be answered without a good deal of research. You will need to go to your school or public library to gather the information you require. Ask for help and guidance from your teacher.

8 Imagine you are an athlete competing at one of the ancient Olympic Games. Write a letter home describing your journey to the Games, your experiences there and any adventures you had. Give as much detail about life at the time as possible.

9 Great sporting moments of the past might include Michael Powell's world record long jump, Olga Korbut's Olympic gymnastic performance on the beam and Boris Becker winning Wimbledon at seventeen.

Produce your own picture quiz of famous sporting events from the past using photographs you have been able to collect.

For each photograph ask:
(i) What has happened?
(ii) Who was involved?
(iii) When and where did it take place?

10 The following list of sporting clues will help you to identify a recent year. See how many clues you need before you can correctly identify the year:

Clue 1 – England win a test match in the West Indies.
Clue 2 – Scotland beat favourites England at rugby to complete the Grand Slam.
Clue 3 – Douglas beats the invincible Tyson.
Clue 4 – Martina wins Wimbledon for the ninth time.
Clue 5 – World javelin record for Britain.
Clue 6 – Cameroon beats Argentina sensation.

Compile your own sporting headlines, photographs, champions, for a particular year into a set of clues which you can use to test your friends' sporting knowledge.

11 Choose any one sport and find out all you can about its origins. Try to discover the first set of rules, who produced them and the date. See if you can find early drawings or photographs of early competitors showing the clothing worn.

12 Choose any famous sportsman or sportswoman who achieved fame before 1960. Try to find out how he or she trained for their event. Compare these training methods with those of today's sportspersons.

13 Interview a relative or friend who attended a famous sporting event before you were born. Record their memories of the event on a tape recorder. Ask them about the excitement, the competitors involved, the crowd, any memorable incidents and the atmosphere on the day.

Examples could include:

The 1966 World Cup Final
The 1948 Olympics
Virginia Wade winning Wimbledon
Jim Laker beating the Australians
Tony Jacklin winning both the British and American Open Golf Championships
Kuts versus Chattaway

14 In pairs, construct a conversation between two famous sportsmen or sportswomen of past and present in the same sport. For example, W.G. Grace and Ian Botham or Lotte Dodd and Martina Navratilova talking about the way they played their sport.

15 Arrange to interview a person who was at school before the beginning of the last war (1939).

Draw up a checklist of questions to ask about school sport, clothing and footwear worn, equipment used, facilities available, staff involved and any achievements.

Turn your interview into a report for your local paper entitled 'School Sport 50 Years Ago' or similar.

16 Investigate your own family sporting history. First you will need to draw up your own family tree. Then question all the relatives that you can contact in order to find out information about their particular involvement in sport. List the activities they took part in together with any successes they achieved. Do not forget to include yourself in this investigation!

9 AMATEUR AND PROFESSIONAL

Aims

To gain knowledge and understanding of
- the historical development of amateurism and professionalism
- the status of sportspeople today
- eligibility for international competition

To develop the skills of
- secondary research
- primary research
- interviewing

Labelling sportsmen and sportswomen as amateurs or professionals has only happened during the last century. Athletes competing in the ancient Olympics did not have to show that they were amateurs.

In the early nineteenth century, the word amateur was closely linked with a person's social position. Only slowly did it become a matter of rewards received and time given up to sport. The famous cricketer Dr. W.G. Grace made a great deal of money from his sport. However, since he was a doctor by profession, he remained an amateur.

Today the situation is complicated in many sports which in theory still remain amateur. It is possible for many top amateur sports competitors to devote themselves full-time to their sport, to receive rewards of various kinds and to retain their amateur status. Around the country the thousands of people who happily take part in sport in the traditional amateur way have little interest in status. Increasingly competitors at all levels are being helped financially, whether it is a trust fund for an international athlete or a set of sponsored kit for the local netball team.

Perhaps the only honest way forward is to do away with amateur and professional sport and to declare all sport open. This would allow those seeking rewards to do so and also allow competition freely between all players in a particular sport. However, if rewards are paid directly to players without the involvement of the governing bodies, control of sport might pass to commercial enterprises.

TRADITIONAL DIFFERENCES BETWEEN AMATEURS AND PROFESSIONALS

Amateurs

Amateur sportsmen and sportswomen take part in sport because of the enjoyment and satisfaction they get from the activity. Taking part is more important than the result of the game or competition. They train and compete in their own time, usually after work or at weekends. They are not paid.

Above all, amateurs make their own decisions about sport. They choose to play. No-one can force them to take part. Sport is quite separate from their work. It is a leisure time activity.

Professional sportsmen and sportswomen are paid to compete in sport

Amateur sportsmen and sportswomen take part in sport for enjoyment and satisfaction

Professionals

Professional sportsmen and sportswomen are paid to compete in sport. Winning is all-important. The more successful they are, the more money they earn. They usually train full-time and devote themselves to their sport. Sport is their work. They sign contracts and must take part in competitions.

THE STATUS OF PLAYERS IN DIFFERENT SPORTS

There are amateurs in all sports in Great Britain. In many sports there are also professionals. Some sports do not distinguish between amateurs and professionals. They call their sportsmen and sportswomen 'players' and we say the sport is 'open'.

The situation in 1988

	According to the rules of his sport, is a competitor allowed:						
	1 To be a professional in any other sport?	*2 To coach his sport for payment?*	*3 To be paid for time lost from his business?*	*4 To write, broadcast, lecture or appear on television for payment?*	*5 To receive money from advertisements?*	*6 To receive expenses for competing?*	*7 To receive prizes or money for competing?*
Association football (FA)	Yes	Yes	Yes	Yes	Yes	Yes	Yes
Athletics (AAA)	No	No unless employed	No	Not without permission	Only through trust funds	Yes	No
Cricket (TCCB)	Yes	Yes	Yes	Yes	Yes	Yes	Yes
Golf (R and A)	Yes	No	No	Yes, provided instruction in playing golf is not included	No	Yes - out -of-pocket expenses may be paid. Not now confined to team events	Playing for prize money is not permitted, accepting prizes (max value £170) is allowed
Lawn tennis (LTA)	Yes	Yes	Yes	Yes	Yes	Yes	Yes
Racing (Jockey Club)	Yes	Yes, subject to approval of Stewards of Jockey Club	No	Yes	Yes	No, other than specific expenses approved by Stewards of Jockey Club	Trophies only
Rowing (ARA)	Yes	Yes	Yes	Yes	No	Yes, out-of-pocket expenses only	Prizes only. Cash prizes must go to club
Rugby Union (RFU)	Yes (excluding Rugby League)	Yes, but only players up to age of 21	No	No	No	Only out-of-pocket expenses	No money, but trophies or mementoes to value of £50
Equestrian sport (BEF)	See Bye-laws to IOC Rule 26	Yes, with the agreement of his NF under certain conditions	Yes, providing a competitor has a contract with NF and/or sponsor. Payment through NF	Yes	Yes, but only if the competitor has a contract with his NF and advertiser. Payment must be through NF	Yes, but as for 4 and 5	Yes, but prize money has to be paid to the owner of the horse
Skiing (BSF)	Yes	Yes	Yes	Yes	Yes, but is paid into trust fund	Yes	Yes, but no more than SFr2000

Source: The Palmer Report

In some sports the links between amateurs and professionals are very close. They may even compete together. In other sports the amateurs have no contact at all with the professionals.

What is the situation today?

Amateur sports

It is estimated that 22 million people participate in sport in Britain. The vast majority are amateur in the strictest sense of the word. That is, the sport is played for the enjoyment and love of the game and not for any financial reward. It is thought that about 6.5 million are registered with clubs. The rest do not feel the need to be officially registered, though they are all to some extent affected by decisions of those governing the sport.

The international governing bodies of each sport draw up rules to decide who is an amateur in their sport. They decide if professionals may compete with amateurs. Unfortunately there is no agreement between the sports on the definition of an amateur. This makes the situation very confusing. For example, amateur athletes are allowed officially to receive appearance money and to advertise products. The money is passed through their association and placed in a trust fund, to be available to them after they have retired.

Different countries and sports look at the rules differently. The Olympic Movement has a set of rules which participants must obey. Sports in the Olympic programme must agree to these rules. It is well known that many Olympic competitors are not really amateurs. They work at sport like professionals. Avery Brundage (President of the IOC 1952-72) explained the problem of agreeing on an amateur definition in 1966 by saying *'I have been endeavouring to establish a uniform amateur definition for many years, but when you are dealing with 25 to 30 sports in 120 different countries in a score or more languages, it is not easy'*.

Professional sports

There are a number of sports from which performers can earn a lot of money, whether as prize money for taking part or through endorsement of products. Some well-known celebrities have formed themselves into limited companies. They are able to market themselves and sell their company's products world-wide. Examples of sports from which competitors can earn money are:

Badminton	Golf
Basketball	Horse racing
Bowls	Motor cycling
Boxing	Motor racing
Cricket	Rugby league
Cycling	Surfing
Darts	Table tennis
Equestrianism	Tennis
Football	Yachting

Some of these sports are 'open', but others (for example golf) have both a strong professional and amateur status.

Nick Faldo is a professional golf player

Often professional sports have player associations. For example, the Professional Footballers' Association looks after the interests of its members. It may discuss ways of improving the game for players and the sport with national and international governing bodies (the FA and FIFA).

In Britain the number of professional players able to support themselves from their sport is very small.

Open sports

Some governing bodies of sport do not distinguish between amateurs and professionals. These are known as 'open' sports. They permit sportsmen and sportswomen to compete together regardless of whether they are paid or play for pleasure. The sports include:

Angling   Speedway
Bowling   Squash
Cricket   Tennis
Equestrianism   Ten pin bowling
Mountaineering   Yachting

The danger for open sports and sports involving professional participants is that the international and national governing bodies may be by-passed by groups of competitors and commercial organisations whose only consideration is high financial rewards. It is necessary, therefore, for the international governing bodies to represent all players, both professional and amateur. This enables a balance to be made between participants at local level and promotion of excellence at the higher level, often involving television companies and commercial sponsors.

AMATEURS AND PROFESSIONALS AT THE ANCIENT OLYMPICS

The modern Olympics have been for amateurs only. They are based on the ancient Games and it is often assumed that they were for amateurs. The truth is quite different. The athletes were in our terms, professionals. The true amateur spirit, of fairplay and friendship, was not always seen either. Today eligibility for the Games has moved away from definitions of amateurism.

All athletes expected to receive prizes for winning. These were usually in the form of money, pensions or goods, such as jars of olive oil. Athletes differed in the amount of time spent in training and the quality of the training. In the early years of the Games, it was only the athletes from wealthy families who could afford to take part. Money was needed to pay trainers and coaches, the cost of travel, day to day living expenses during training, an adequate diet and the additional expense of horses and equipment in equestrian events. The records show the winners to have come from amongst the wealthy and privileged class.

Change came gradually. Talented boys were encouraged and supported, if necessary, by their home city. Cities spent generously on athletes and sports facilities. This included financing the public gymnasium where full-time athletes trained for competition. Although successful athletes won prizes, they still needed money from their cities to live.

As the number of games increased, so did the number of professional athletes who competed. Gradually all free born groups in Greek society, not just the wealthy, were represented amongst the athletes.

Winning was very important at the Games. The prizes were only awarded to the winners. A winner of an Olympic event could charge a large fee for taking part in local games festivals at a later date. This 'appearance money' helped the athlete to support himself.

However the Games held at Olympia were special. Unlike other Games, no prizes were awarded for winning. The glory and fame to be gained was thought sufficient to attract all the very best athletes. This was true. Winning at Olympia was prized above all else.

There was no distinction between athletes, apart from their ability. The words amateur and professional were not used.

AMATEURISM AND PROFESSIONALISM AND THE GROWTH OF BRITISH SPORT

In the early days of sport in Britain rewards and prizes were not a problem. They were offered to all who took part and accepted if won. Betting was often part of the sport, sometimes with wagers between the competitors. There was nothing wrong with making money out of sport.

People who were upper class were able to spend time playing sport. They could afford the equipment. They were able to join clubs. They also were able to travel to where sport took place. These sportsmen were called 'gentlemen amateurs'. This referred to their social position. It was not so easy for the working class to play sport. They had none of these advantages.

Class distinctions were very strong in society at the time and were also found in sport. For example the Henley Regatta was only open to amateur oarsmen. The rules stated that you could not be called amateur if you worked as a mechanic, artisan or labourer.

Until quite recently, the word 'gentleman' was used to distinguish the amateur cricketers who played in county matches from the professionals who were called 'players'. The 'Gentleman' versus

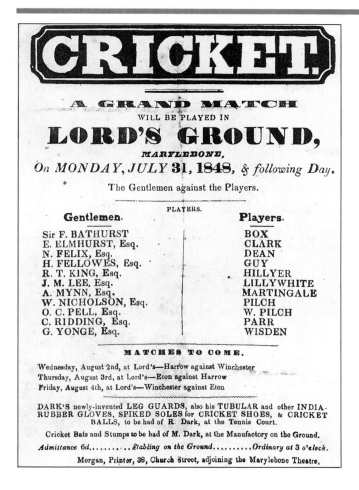

CRICKET.

A GRAND MATCH
WILL BE PLAYED IN

LORD'S GROUND,

MARYLEBONE,

On MONDAY, JULY 31, 1848, & following Day.

The Gentlemen against the Players.

PLAYERS.

Gentlemen.	Players.
Sir F. BATHURST	BOX
E. ELMHURST, Esq.	CLARK
N. FELIX, Esq.	DEAN
H. FELLOWES, Esq.	GUY
R. T. KING, Esq.	HILLYER
J. M. LEE, Esq.	LILLYWHITE
A. MYNN, Esq.	MARTINGALE
W. NICHOLSON, Esq.	PILCH
O. C. PELL, Esq.	W. PILCH
C. RIDDING, Esq.	PARR
G. YONGE, Esq.	WISDEN

MATCHES TO COME.

Wednesday, August 2nd, at Lord's—Harrow against Winchester
Thursday, August 3rd, at Lord's—Eton against Harrow
Friday, August 4th, at Lord's—Winchester against Eton

DARK'S newly-invented LEG GUARDS, also his TUBULAR and other INDIA-RUBBER GLOVES, SPIKED SOLES for CRICKET SHOES, & CRICKET BALLS, to be had of R. Dark, at the Tennis Court.

Cricket Bats and Stumps to be had of M. Dark, at the Manufactory on the Ground.

Admittance 6d...........Stabling on the Ground..........Ordinary at 3 o'clock.

Morgan, Printer, 36, Church Street, adjoining the Marylebone Theatre.

'Players' match was played annually until 1962. The idea of the gentleman in sport still survives in a few ways. For example, in football 'ungentlemanly conduct' is penalised.

During the second half of the nineteenth century the popularity of sport grew. Many people in the middle and working classes wanted to compete and play sport.

By the 1880's, competing for a money prize or making any sort of a living out of a sporting activity had become the principal cause of disqualification from taking part as an amateur.

Clubs who had used the Henley Regatta definition of an amateur, changed their rules. The Amateur Athletic Club did so in 1881, allowing anyone to take part, providing they were not paid. The Football Association, in 1882, stopped payments to players, other than expenses and any wages actually lost. Other governing bodies founded at this time immediately made rules about payments to players. By 1890, players were no longer called amateurs because of their social position. They remained amateurs as long as they did not receive payment or reward from their sport.

The distinction between amateurs and professionals also arose from the employment of professionals at clubs. There had been professionals in some sports for a long time. They were usually players of a high standard who coached members and looked after the grounds and equipment. In sports such as cricket, golf and horse racing the professionals were controlled by the governing bodies. They made rules for everyone involved in the sport. The Football Association decided to control the professional game in 1885. The popularity of the game and the business interests involved forced this decision.

In golf there were no difficulties in dealing with the amateurs and professional players. The Royal and Ancient Golf Club of St. Andrews has controlled the sport for all players. Professionals have almost always reigned supreme. However amateurs, if they are good enough, may compete against professionals in the major national 'Open Championship'.

In cricket and football, amateurs have always been allowed to play in the same team as professionals, providing they were worthy of a place. The distinction between amateur and professional players was abolished in 1962 for cricket and in 1975 for football.

In 1968 the Wimbledon tennis championships became 'open'. Until this time many of the best players were amateurs who received large amounts as 'expenses'. The role of the professional was still largely that of a teacher.

Other bodies like the Rugby Union decided to have nothing at all to do with professionals. Even those rugby clubs only paying their players expenses for loss of wages, were expelled. These professional rugby clubs formed themselves into the Northern Union, later the Rugby League, which became very popular in the North of England.

The two codes have remained quite separate ever since. Over the years there had always been stars of the Union game who changed to the League code where they could earn a living. This caused bitterness between the administrators of the two games. The Union game remained exclusively amateur. However, during the 1980's, the increasing popularity of the sport and the use of trust funds by other amateur sportspeople, resulted in pressure from the top players to allow them to be rewarded. In 1991 the rules were relaxed to let players seek rewards outside the game. However the practical application of the rules has varied from country to country. This caused some arguments between the Rugby Football Union and England players.

A good working relationship exists between the Rugby Football League, representing the professional game, and the British Amateur Rugby League. They are able to organise their sport for the benefit of both the paid and unpaid players. It has been agreed that amateur players can play the professional game. Also at the end of their paid careers, professional players can be reinstated in amateur rugby league.

Hockey has no professional players in Britain. However, the pressure on international players to take a professional approach is very great. At the Seoul Olympics the Great Britain team took the gold medal. One of the stars of that team, Sean Kerly, gave up his job as a sales executive before the Games to train full-time. He explained that he was unable to work and give sufficient attention to his Olympic training.

Sean Kerly on the attack for Britain

The governing bodies which used the word amateur in their title, like swimming, boxing and athletics, also decided to reject professionals completely. Professional boxing is today controlled by the British Boxing Board of Control. There are no professional swimmers competing in Britain. In athletics, there are only a few professional competitions in the North of England and Scotland.

Trust Funds and Sponsorship Contracts

Governing bodies of traditionally amateur sports have in recent years developed ways to safeguard the eligibility of their competitors whilst allowing them to receive financial rewards. At the same time they have kept control of their sport by insisting that all payments should be channelled through or authorised directly by the governing body. There are two methods - trust funds and sponsorship contracts.

Athletics became the first amateur sport to set up trust funds in 1981. It has since been joined by boxing, swimming, gymnastics, canoeing, judo, skiing, surfing, triathlon, water-skiing and skating.

Trust funds

When an athlete has more than £5 000 in his or her athletic fund, a formal trust may be set up. This involves the British Amateur Athletics Board (BAAB), the competitor and trustees. Payments are made from the fund for the competitor's training and competition expenses plus assistance towards equipment and living expenses. On retirement from competition the competitor will receive the balance of the fund, less a small amount deducted by the BAAB.

Sponsorship contracts

No trustees are involved, instead there is a contract between the governing body, the competitor and the sponsor. The British Equestrian Federation (BEF) has used this method. All payments by the sponsor pass through the BEF. The BEF is therefore able to ensure that the sponsorship is suitable and complies with eligibility rules.

Sports Scholarships

'The most useful help received was via the American system. These scholarships are effective because they allow competitors to be both educated in the formal sense and to develop their sporting potentials. I am horrified that youngsters in my sport neglect their education and their future in order to devote themselves only to swimming.' Duncan Goodhew, Olympic swimmer and medallist.

Other top British sportsmen and sportswomen have found the American sports scholarship system very attractive. They have had the opportunity to train, compete and study at the same time. In American colleges sport is highly competitive and big business. Sports departments may be funded by the income from their teams.

Very few British universities offer sports scholarships. Sadly many highly talented

Duncan Goodhew at the start of the 100m breaststroke final which he won at the 1980 Olympic Games

sportsmen and sportswomen fail to develop their talent whilst studying in higher education.

Bath University set up the first British sports scholarships in 1976. Since then it has given 18 scholarships and 20 bursaries. The scholarships enable studies to be extended over an extra year. The bursaries are a grant of up to £500. The scheme aims to help students reach high sporting standards and also succeed in their degree courses. Students need the usual degree course qualifications and must keep up with their studies. Combining top level sport with full-time academic study requires commitment and dedication. Today, the universities of Newcastle, Oxford, Stirling and Swansea offer similar schemes.

Talented school sportsmen and sportswomen may have problems too in dividing their time between academic study and training for sport.

PROBLEMS OF PROFESSIONALISM

The people who controlled sport in the second half of the nineteenth century faced many problems. Sport was developing quickly. People from all classes were becoming involved. Payments and rewards needed controls. Business interests were growing.

It was obvious that rules and regulations were needed. There were worries that professionalism could not be prevented from bringing major problems.

Unfair Practices

Professional teams would need to win to survive. To do this they would need the best players. They might be tempted to use unfair means to sign players. Matches could be fixed in advance and opponents paid to ensure the right result. For professionals the result is usually the most important factor.

In the early years of the nineteenth century, one or two outstanding cricketers had been bribed to arrange results. Bribes had also been accepted at athletics meetings. It was not always the professional sportsmen who were involved. Professional gamblers played a large part.

Over the last century, there appears to have been little corruption. In professional football a few players and managers have been unfairly approached by rival clubs. In a rare case in the 1950's, a number of first division football players fixed a vital league match and were banned for life. There have been allegations that some professional boxing matches have been fixed in advance.

Recently the most serious form of cheating has been from competitors taking drugs. Drug taking and illegal payments are not just limited to professionals. It has been claimed that many international athletes receive illegal expenses and some take drugs. A major sports shoe company admitted that it paid international rugby union players to wear its boots.

The pressures on top amateur sportsmen and sportswomen to win are often as great as those on professionals. The pressures to use unfair practices are therefore just as great.

Unfair Competition

Sportsmen and sportswomen who devote all their time and energy to their sport are likely to reach a higher standard than those who just play for fun in their spare time. It was thought that amateurs would be no match for full-time professionals. Then the amateurs would fade away and take no part in sport. Many people believed that this had happened at the ancient Olympics and had caused their decline.

Certainly amateurs were soon unable to compete in most sports at the highest level. There were exceptions, especially in cricket. In the early years of the FA cup, amateur football teams took part in many finals, but not after 1883.

The fact that there are professionals in a sport does not seem to have discouraged amateurs from playing the sport. Indeed the high standard of professional play seen on television may have encouraged people in recent years.

Different sports have reacted differently to the problem of unequal competition. In cricket all distinctions between amateurs and professionals were removed in 1962. The widespread, but illegal, payment of players in senior amateur football leagues led the FA to remove distinctions between amateurs and professionals. The Amateur Cup was replaced and Britain withdrew from the football tournament in the Olympic Games.

For many years the Lawn Tennis Association allowed amateur players to receive expenses which enabled them to train and play around the world. Today competitions are open to all. Only the full-time professionals can reach a high enough standard to compete at top level.

In amateur athletics and swimming, the time spent on training by international competitors is very great. Professionals would be unable to do more. These 'amateurs' work full-time at their sport. They may be supported financially by the Sports Aid Foundation, their families, local firms or other sponsors. Some may attend college, living on scholarships. In some countries, athletes are openly supported by the State, in theory as students or members of the armed forces.

Top amateurs act as professionals in terms of their time and commitment. For this reason many people claim that all sport should be declared open. This would allow those who wanted payment to receive it, if they were good enough.

Professionals usually beat amateurs at sport, if they are allowed to compete together. This fact has not prevented the steady increase in the number of amateurs in all sports.

Traditional Values

In the nineteenth century a lot of sport was played at public schools and universities. Those educated in this way had a special view of sport. They had learned ways of playing where social rules and traditional attitudes were very important. The idea of *'gentlemanly conduct'* was understood by all the players. *'Fairplay'* and *'good sportsmanship'* were essential parts of the game. The rulemakers were worried that working class players would not be able to keep this spirit alive

Harrow School football team, 1867

if they were paid as professionals.

As sport increased in popularity, people from all classes in society took part. Traditional attitudes were maintained in most sports. Sometimes extra rules were written to ensure competitors behaved in acceptable ways.

There has been no evidence to show that professionals in competition have a poor attitude compared with amateurs. The antics of the top professionals are reported in detail in the media. Anyone watching amateurs in action will soon find that their sportsmanship is far from perfect. Whether or not the players are amateurs or professionals there will always be great differences between the attitudes and sportsmanship of individuals.

During the last century professional sport solved its own problems. Amateur sport learned to live alongside professional sport. The main problem has been at the top level of amateur sport - how much financial help should the best amateurs receive? Many answers have been tried by different sports. It has been a major difficulty in Olympic competition, until recently.

THE OLYMPIC GAMES AND AMATEURISM

Baron Pierre de Coubertin was the founder of the modern Olympic Games. As such he is usually thought of as a defender of the amateur ideal. However, his words and writings show this to be mistaken. He was upset about the constant arguments about who was allowed to take part in the Olympics. He said *'we ought to put an end once and for all to this confusion between 'Olympism' which is mine and 'amateurism' which is other people's affairs.'* Above all he was concerned with the Olympic spirit and he said the rest was of no importance. In 1919 he wrote *'On the pretext of preserving the doctrine of pure amateurism, disqualifications were pronounced against supposed professionals whose sporting spirit and disinterestedness remained greatly superior to those of so many duly qualified false amateurs'.*

For more than ninety years, the International Olympic Committee (IOC) has made rules about amateurism. The Committee wanted only true amateurs to take part in the Olympic Games. In the early days of the modern Olympics, the IOC allowed governing bodies to check that their athletes were amateurs. However it was soon clear that different sports had different ideas about rules for amateurs. This meant that some athletes had unfair advantages.

At the Stockholm Olympics of 1912, Jim Thorpe won both the pentathlon and the decathlon. The King, in presenting him with his gold medals, said 'You are the greatest athlete in the world'. Later it was discovered that Thorpe had received small payments for playing baseball in the past. His title was taken away and his name removed from the records. Seventy years later the IOC relented and reinstated his name on the role of Olympic honours.

The IOC believed that sportsmen and sportswomen should not use their sport to make a living or any form of profit at the time. Over the years many sets of rules have been issued and changed later. The Olympic ideal is of a competition between part-time sportsmen and sportswomen competing purely for enjoyment. Many people believe this ideal to be out of date. Winning at the highest level is now too important.

In recent times the high standards of performance at the Olympic Games have encouraged many competitors to train full-time. This has resulted in a move towards 'open' Olympics. In 1988 in Seoul, changes to the eligibility rules allowed fully fledged, highly paid professional tennis players to take part. They competed for the honour of winning the gold medal with no financial rewards.

Jim Thorpe, June 1912

Tennis professional, Steffi Graf, competed in the 1988 Olympics

Today the responsibility for eligibility for the Olympic Games lies with the International Federation for each sport. These rules vary from sport to sport but they must be approved by the IOC.

Participation in the Olympic Games

Rule 45 of the IOC refers to the eligibility code. It is short, but there are a number of important bye-laws.

    IOC = International Olympic Committee
    IF = International Federation
    NOC = National Olympic Committee

Rule 45– Eligibility code

To be eligible for participation in the Olympic Games a competitor must comply with the Olympic Charter as well as with the rules of the IF concerned as approved by the IOC, and must be entered by his NOC.

Bye law to rule 45

1 Each IF establishes its sport's own eligibility criteria in accordance with the Olympic Charter. Such criteria must be submitted to the IOC Executive Board for approval.

2 The application of the eligibility criteria lies with the IFs, their affiliated national federations and the NOCs in the fields of their respective responsibilities.

3 All competitors in the Olympic Games shall:

  3.1 respect the spirit of fair play and non-violence, and behave accordingly on the sportsfield;

  3.2 refrain from using substances and procedures prohibited by the rules of the IOC or of the IFs;

  3.3 respect and comply with all aspects the IOC Medical Code.

4 No competitor who participates in the Olympic Games may allow his person, name, picture or sports performances to be used for advertising purposes during the Olympic Games.

5 The entry or participation of a competitor in the Olympic Games shall not be conditional on any financial consideration.

A COMPARISON BETWEEN AMATEURS AND PROFESSIONALS IN SPORT TODAY

Why do people take part in sport?

Amateur sport exists because people enjoy taking part in sport as a leisure time activity. (The reasons have already been discussed fully in the earlier chapter on 'Success in Sport'.) Some find the event very satisfying, for example flying through the air on a trampoline, moving smoothly along on a bicycle or hammering a squash ball against the wall. Others get most of the enjoyment from being with people they like. They often join a club for this reason. Tennis and rugby clubs are well known for their social events. There are many other reasons for taking part in sport. The excitement of doing something dangerous as in mountain climbing or driving a racing car. The satisfaction from being very accurate as in bowls, golf, darts and snooker. Some people just enjoy the thrill of competing against others or beating their own best previous performance.

Professional sportsmen and sportswomen will only exist as long as people are prepared to pay them for their services. These services include playing the sport for the public to watch and coaching or teaching groups and individuals. Also companies are willing to pay professionals to use them and their sport in advertising the company and its products. In addition, most sports support a small number of professional administrators who run the day to day work of their central offices.

A few years ago the future of professional football was being questioned because of falling attendances. If the public is not willing to watch football live in large numbers, then the money to pay players will decrease. This is likely to result in either fewer full-time professionals or the players becoming semi-professional. This means they would accept less money for playing and find a job outside football to supplement their income.

Some years ago, county cricket was also in a difficult financial position. Only small crowds watched the three day games played during the week. The introduction of one day games played at weekends, together with regular television coverage of the Sunday matches, made cricket more popular. Increased sponsorship followed and greatly improved the finances of the counties and their players.

In some sports a professional is available to coach for a fee. At golf clubs the professional is expected to be available to help all the players from beginners to competition winners. Similarly, squash and tennis clubs often have a professional available to give lessons.

Professional coaches of this type will only make a living if people want their help. Coaches are also employed to improve teams in professional sport. Their livelihood depends on the success of the team they coach. If their team fails they may need a new job.

Some amateur sports, for example swimming and athletics, employ professional coaches to be responsible for the best performers and for developing outstanding youngsters.

Many companies are willing to pay successful players and teams to advertise their goods. The amount of money earned through sponsorship is linked directly to the amount of success of those players involved.

Today amateurs take part in sport freely, at their own level. The professionals must always chase success, for without it they will be unable to survive.

The Attitude of Sportsmen and Sportswomen

Gary Lineker has a very hardworking and dedicated attitude to his sport

When people talk about sport, they sometimes refer to '*a professional attitude*'. Such an attitude is usually unwelcome in amateur sport. It comes from the traditional differences between amateurs and professionals. Amateurs take part for enjoyment and satisfaction. For the professional, the result is all important, a 'win at all costs' attitude is therefore a possibility. Because of this it is sometimes thought that all professionals will stop at nothing to win.

Obviously this is not true. Professionals, as a group of people, have a variety of different attitudes to the way they try to win. Whilst some will stop at nothing, others will show good sportsmanship and be considerate towards their opponents.

A 'professional attitude' can be a compliment to a player when it refers to such things as very thorough and careful preparation for a competition and a hard working, dedicated approach to the sport.

Amateurs are expected to have a different attitude. Since they do not rely on winning to pay their wages, they are not expected to take the result of the competition so seriously. However a wide variety of attitudes are seen, including winning at all costs.

The top amateur in international competition cannot be expected to take part with the same attitude towards winning as the tennis player having a game with a friend in the park.

In practice it is best to look at the individual person involved in the sport, rather than his or her status as an amateur or professional. Professional rugby league is a very physical and often violent game. Amateur rugby union matches can also be described in the same way.

There are no general rules. There are as many different attitudes towards sport as there are people taking part.

Time Given Up to Sport

The amount of time given to sport by a competitor will depend on the level of competition rather than whether the player is an amateur or professional.

Ordinary amateur sportsmen and sportswomen will take part in sport during their leisure time. That is after work when other necessary activities are finished. To improve, more time is needed for practising and training. By devoting evenings and weekends to sport, it is possible to reach high standards. However, the responsibilities of a family or demanding job may make it difficult to find the time necessary to improve.

To increase the time devoted to sport, working hours may be reduced and loss of earnings made up in other ways. Sponsorship and grants may be obtained by those showing exceptional ability or promise.

Top international amateurs solve the problem of finance and time in a variety of ways. In Britain, enough sponsorship is available for them to train full-time. Others accept college scholarships which allow them ample time for training as well as studying. In some countries sportsmen and sportswomen may be in the armed forces or in government jobs which allow them the time and facilities necessary to train at their level.

Evelyn Ashford; a highly paid sportswoman with an amateur track official

The full-time professional has all day to prepare for competition. The standard of play is far higher than any ordinary amateur, working all day, can produce. Professional golfers, tennis players and football players, competing regularly in top class tournaments, will be far superior to amateurs or even part-time professionals. However, because most sports are unpredictable, there are occasions when the unexpected happens and unlikely winners emerge. This is one of the attractions of sport.

The Palmer Report

In 1988 the CCPR published the report of a committee which investigated amateur status and participation in sport. They received evidence from the governing bodies of sports and from individual sportsmen and sportswomen. Their conclusions are summarised as follows:

1 All legal sources of revenue for governing bodies and individual competitors are acceptable.
2 There will never be enough finance from spectators, sponsors and the media to provide adequate income for governing body, competitors and officials.
3 The goodwill of voluntary officials should not be abused.
4 Governing bodies must continue to exert control and influence over the direction of their sport.
5 Trust funds and sponsorship agreements are recommended to preserve eligibility.
6 Information and financial advice to competitors should be readily available.
7 The concept of payment is now accepted in spite of the word 'amateur' still being used in governing body titles.
8 British sporting hopefuls are going to American colleges because of the lack of sports scholarships in Britain.
9 British universities and institutions of higher education should be able to provide opportunities for aspiring athletes to compete, train and study.
10 No concessions are made to outstanding school athletes who endeavour to obtain high academic and sporting standards simultaneously.

The committee found that people are concerned about eligibility to take part in sport, rather than the traditional idea of amateur status. In most sports the labels 'amateur' and 'professional' are now out of date. Full-time training is necessary in nearly all sports for the highest level of competition. Properly controlled financial support can provide positive benefits for individuals and the governing body of the sport concerned. Above all, international federations and governing bodies must be responsible for moulding the direction of their sport.

THINGS TO DO

1 Which of the following statements are true and which are false?

   (i)   Athletes in the ancient Olympics were always amateurs.

   (ii) In the last century amateur status was linked to social position.

   (iii) Rugby union players can now receive payment for playing their sport.

   (iv) Amateur and professional boxing have the same governing body.

   (v)   Athletes may only draw on their trust funds when they retire.

   (vi) W. G. Grace was a professional cricketer.

   (vii) Governing bodies of sport are always involved in trust fund arrangements.

   (viii) The Olympic Charter specifically bars individuals who receive money for playing sport from competing in the Olympic Games.

2 Explain the historical background for the 'ungentlemanly conduct' rule in Association Football.

3 'Trust funds have been set up for athletes.' Explain how both the athletes and the governing bodies of sport benefit from these arrangements.

4 What are the traditional differences between amateur and professional sportspersons with regard to:

   (i)   attitude to sport;

   (ii) rewards;

   (iii) time spent on sport?

5 Imagine you are a professional sportsperson in the sport of your choice. You have been invited to speak to a meeting of talented young sportspeople on life as a professional performer. Prepare a five minute talk describing the advantages and disadvantages of your chosen career.

6 As a group, invite a professional sportsperson to your school or college. Prepare a number of questions to cover the following:

   (i)   school sports career;

   (ii) joining the professional ranks;

   (iii) future prospects, advantages and disadvantages of being a professional in their chosen sport.

7 It has been suggested that all sports should be 'open'. What advantages and disadvantages would this involve?

8 'First is first, second is nowhere.'

   (i)   Do you agree with this comment when talking about sport?

   (ii) Discuss whether the comment is more likely to come from an amateur or a professional sportsperson.

10 ORGANISATION OF SPORT IN BRITAIN AT NATIONAL LEVEL

Aims

To gain knowledge and understanding of
◆ the structure of national sporting organisations and their international links
◆ the specific aims of these organisations

To develop the skills of:
◆ practical research
◆ group work including role play
◆ oral presentation

The development of sport in Britain has not followed a regular pattern. Individuals, groups and clubs have always been free to develop their sport as they liked. At both local and national level the Government has never really involved itself directly.

Today the Sports Council has overall responsibility for sport in Britain. The affairs of each sport are controlled by a governing body for that sport. The governing bodies are all members of the Central Council of Physical Recreation (CCPR). The CCPR tells the Sports Council how the governing bodies as a group feel about the development of sport.

The governing bodies of sport represent all those who take part in their sport and they are members of the international sports federations. This membership allows competitors to take part in international matches. The governing body's membership of the British Olympic Association allows teams to be sent to the Olympic Games.

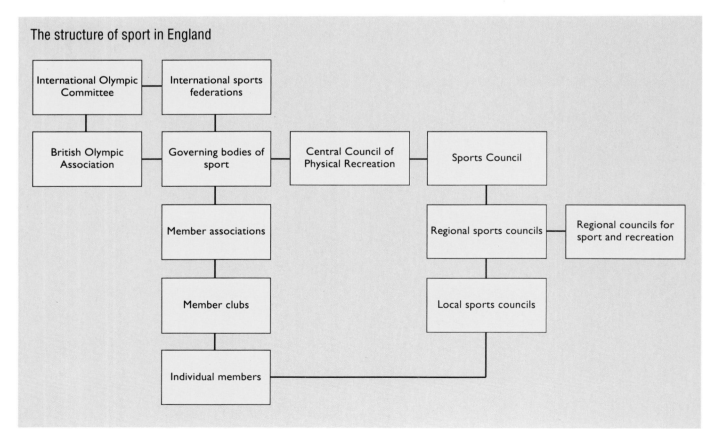

The structure of sport in England

THE SPORTS COUNCIL

Background

In 1935 the Central Council of Physical Recreation was founded. It had two main purposes:

1 To encourage people to take part in all forms of sport and recreation.
2 To give governing bodies of sport a place to discuss matters of interest to them all.

The CCPR developed this work and built national sport centres. Regional offices were started to help develop sport in each area.

In 1966, Mr. Dennis Howell, the Minister for Sport, created an advisory Sports Council to help the Government on sporting matters. The CCPR worked closely with this advisory council. In 1971, Mr. Eldon Griffiths, the new Minister for Sport, decided to give the Sports Council much greater power to influence sport. Most importantly the new Council was given an annual grant by the Government to develop British sport.

The CCPR transferred all its property, staff and other assets to the new executive Sports Council. However, the governing bodies of sport decided to keep their independence. The CCPR has continued as an organisation where the governing bodies may discuss their common problems and interests. The CCPR now acts as a consultative body to the Sports Council, advising it of the views of the governing bodies.

The London Marathon

Structure

The Sports Council is an independent body, founded by Royal Charter in 1972. It has overall responsibility for sport in Great Britain and a particular responsibility for sport in England. There are separate Councils for Scotland, Wales and Northern Ireland. All four Councils work closely together to see that they have a similar approach to sporting matters. Senior representatives meet as a UK affairs committee to harmonise policies. On international matters the Sports Council co-ordinates the views of the four Councils to give a British view.

The Sports Council is made up of a Chairman and 14 members. These people are all appointed by a Government minister responsible for sport.

In order to develop sport throughout the country, there are nine regional offices. Here the Sports Council staff are able to plan according to the particular needs of the area. They also give technical and advisory services to local authorities, voluntary sports bodies and other organisations.

This may be done through the Regional Councils for Sport and Recreation which are independent bodies bringing together regional interests. The Sports Council provides a secretarial and administrative service to these Councils.

Local sports councils have been set up to bring together all those involved in sport in a particular local community. By discussing the local provision for sport and the problems, the community may be able to provide what is needed for local people.

Aims

The four main aims of the Sports Council are:

1 To increase participation in sport and physical recreation.
2 To increase the quality and quantity of sports facilities.
3 To raise standards of performance.
4 To provide information for and about sport.

1 Participation

Sport and physical recreation are enormously popular yet the actual number of people taking part is low - 58.9% of all men and 37.2% of women (1986 figures). The Council plans to increase the number of people taking part in many ways. Examples include:

- giving regional participation grants to help local organisations get local people into sport;
- running campaigns to persuade people to take up sport;
- paying for development staff to help governing bodies to increase the number of people taking part in their sport;
- organising programmes, such as Action Sport, to promote sport through various agencies.

2 Facilities

Between 1982 and 1987, 135 new swimming pools and 350 sports halls were built. By 1992 another 150 pools and 500 sports will be needed. Present facilities could be used better, for example by opening up more school facilities for use by the local community, by providing lighting and introducing artificial surfaces.

The Council's programme includes:

- the development of new or improved sports facilities by giving grants, especially in areas of need;
- research into standard designs for sports buildings;
- designing, building and testing new ideas, for example, artificial surfaces;
- finding good practice in facilities and management and spreading the ideas;
- paying for research into what facilities are needed both locally and nationally.

Plas Menai Water Sports Centre – a new sports facility

3 Standards of performance

At the end of 1990 Britain held 87 world titles in 31 different sports. Success depends on coaching, motivation and facilities. Success at international level encourages others to take part in sport. Council action includes:

- running five centres of excellence - Crystal Palace, Bisham Abbey, Lilleshall Hall, Holme Pierrepont and Plas y Brenin;
- offering support (often financial) to governing bodies of sport to help them develop excellence programmes, improve standards of coaching, compete internationally and provide facilities and equipment;
- providing money for the National Coaching Foundation to train more coaches;
- encouraging the private sector to sponsor top class sport;
- financing and running the campaign against drug abuse in sport.

4 Information

The Council is the country's main centre for information and data about sport. Knowledge about sport from home and abroad is collected and passed on to others.

For example, the Council:

- provides a National Information Centre and a network of nine regional centres at the regional offices;
- briefs journalists, politicians, government staff, students and the private sector;
- researches and publishes sports data, including such subjects as the economic impact of sport and the long-term demand for facilities;
- runs the largest annual conference/exhibition for recreation management.

Who pays for the Sports Council?

The Government gives the Sports Council an annual grant each year. In 1989/90 this was £42 million. The Council also raises money in a number of other ways, including:

- sponsorship to support, for example, participation campaigns and excellence training grants. It also funds a sponsorship advisory service for the governing bodies of sport through the CCPR;
- commercial activities including publishing and endorsement of selected goods and services;
- running the National Centres as effectively as possible to generate income.

Sporting Campaigns

Sport is a natural part of active leisure whether you compete for championships or just for fun. In Britain today many people are unable still to take part because of lack of facilities in their area.

Sport for all – 50+

More details are contained in the Leisure chapter.

In 1972, the Sports Council started its 'Sport for All' campaign. It encouraged people of all ages and abilities to take part in some form of physical activity during their leisure time. It also attempted to increase the facilities available. Local authorities, private and commercial organisations were asked to try to extend the opportunities for people to take part in physical recreation. The campaign is still running. At intervals a particular emphasis has been placed on the campaign.

1982 'Sport for All - Disabled People' to coincide with the International Year of Disabled People.

1983/4 'Sport for All - 50+ : All To Play For' aimed at people in the older age group.

1985/6 'Ever Thought of Sport?' to encourage 13-24 year olds to take part in sport.

1987/8 'What's Your Sport?' was built on the previous campaign by providing detailed information on sports opportunities.

1991 'Year of Sport' to coincide with a wide range of international events held in Britain, including the World Student Games.

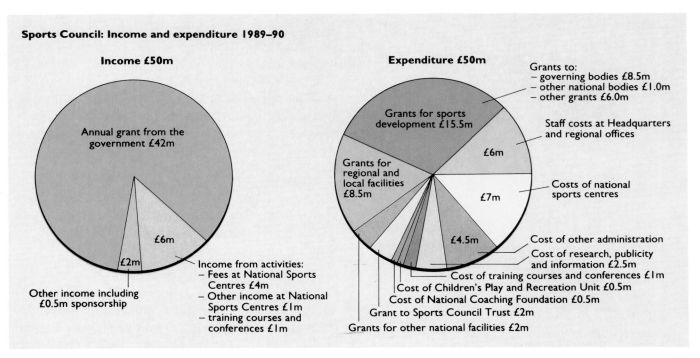

Sports Council: Income and expenditure 1989–90

Income £50m

- Annual grant from the government £42m
- £6m
- £2m
- Other income including £0.5m sponsorship
- Income from activities:
  - Fees at National Sports Centres £4m
  - Other income at National Sports Centres £1m
  - training courses and conferences £1m

Expenditure £50m

- Grants for sports development £15.5m
- Grants for regional and local facilities £8.5m
- £6m
- £7m
- £4.5m
- Grants to:
  - governing bodies £8.5m
  - other national bodies £1.0m
  - other grants £6.0m
- Staff costs at Headquarters and regional offices
- Costs of national sports centres
- Cost of other administration
- Cost of research, publicity and information £2.5m
- Cost of training courses and conferences £1m
- Cost of Children's Play and Recreation Unit £0.5m
- Cost of National Coaching Foundation £0.5m
- Grant to Sports Council Trust £2m
- Grants for other national facilities £2m

Policy Statements

In 1982 the Council published its plan 'Sport in the Community : The Next Ten Years'. The aims included an increase in participation, more and better facilities and improved coaching. Much was achieved but there were problems. In 1988 progress was reviewed and a new plan produced 'Sport in the Community : Into the 90s'. Again this aimed at improving both facilities and participation. However it also wanted to target young people and women, especially any who were unemployed, from ethnic minorities or disabled.

Further details of these plans are given in the Leisure chapter. Information on the national sports centres is given on page 168.

THE CENTRAL COUNCIL OF PHYSICAL RECREATION (CCPR)

The Sports Council is a government body whose members are appointed by a government minister. In contrast the CCPR is a non-governmental organisation whose officers and executive committee are elected by the whole membership.

- National sports centres

0   64
miles

The Sports Council's regions and national sports centres

Aims

The CCPR is made up of nearly 250 national sports organisations representing a vast number of sportsmen and sportswomen throughout the UK. Its main aims are:

- To improve and develop sport and physical recreation.
- To support the work of the specialist sports bodies.
- To be able to give its views to the Sports Council and others concerned with sport and physical recreation.

Organisation

In order to achieve these aims it has organised itself into six divisions. Each division includes sports of a similar type. They are:

Games and sports
Major spectator sports
Movement and dance
Outdoor pursuits
Water recreation
Interested organisations

The CCPR is democratic. Each division elects its own committee and these six committees in turn elect members of the executive committee to run the CCPR.

Within the divisions, organisations with similar interests can meet together and talk about problems that affect them all. They may also plan future action and the best way to develop their sports. The Council is able to bring together all the views of its members and to make them public whenever necessary.

The CCPR watches developments carefully in such areas as education and community provision. It has close contacts within the press, radio and television and can make its voice heard quickly. Some of the many problems the CCPR has recently looked at include sponsorship, parliamentary legislation, international sports contacts, youth and sport, school and sport, sport and recreation for the disabled, medical aspects of sport and recreation, loss of playing fields and sports grounds.

Services: As an independent, voluntary body, the Council only has a very small staff. They give advice on such matters as sponsorship, publicity, legal and accounting problems. The money needed to run the CCPR comes from the Sports Council, members' donations and sponsorship by commercial and industrial organisations.

Sponsorship: The Institute of Sports Sponsorship aims to encourage sponsorship of sport by commercial and industrial organisations. The Council's links with the Institute help it to bring together sporting bodies and potential sponsors. The CCPR has undertaken to expand its Sports Sponsorship Advisory Service. This service helps governing bodies sell their own product to commercial partners. The Sports Council has agreed to provide the finance.

Awards: In 1982 the Council created a special Community Sports Leaders Award (CSLA). The aim is to develop the qualities of leadership, responsibility and self-confidence amongst the voluntary helpers of sports clubs and youth groups. The CSLA is a structured training scheme and leads to awards at three levels - Preliminary, Basic Expedition Training and Higher. By 1990 2 500 courses had been organised with 30 000 awards made. To raise money for the CSLA, the British Sports Trust was founded. It is supported by many well-known people from commerce, industry, Parliament, the media and sport.

The CCPR, together with the British Sports Trust, is involved with the Colson Fund. This Fund provides financial assistance to help handicapped young people take part in sport and recreation.

Above all, the CCPR serves the governing bodies of sport in the UK. It is their organisation and their voice. Their views are passed onto the Government, the Sports Council, local authorities and the nation as a whole. It believes that sport and recreation are important to the life of the country and that people of all ages should benefit.

GOVERNING BODIES OF SPORT

In Britain, many people who take part in sport belong to a club or similar organisation. These clubs usually specialise in one particular sport. They are independent, relying only on their members to run them and decide their future. Club members also take on the important jobs of organising, coaching and officiating at competitions. Usually these clubs come together with similar ones to form local associations. In turn the local associations are part of county or

The Colson Fund provides financial assistance for handicapped young people to take part in sport

regional associations. These large associations then join to form the governing bodies of the sport in Britain. The governing bodies are members of the CCPR.

The governing bodies have much to do. Their main task is to see that everything goes smoothly for their sport throughout the country. Competitors have to obey the rules of the sport and the competition. The governing body must make the decisions when serious problems arise. They may change the rules if they think this may help their sport. However if rules are changed they must see that the new rule does not break any of the rules of the international federation for their sport. It is the international federation which makes the rules and regulations to control international competition in each sport.

Each governing body works hard to develop its sport. More people are encouraged to take part, particularly youngsters, the handicapped and pensioners. It is also the responsibility of governing bodies to choose competitors to represent Britain in international tournaments. They must see that their top sportsmen and sportswomen get the best coaching and training. Everything must be done to help them when travelling and competing abroad.

Tennis coaching

THE NATIONAL COACHING FOUNDATION (NCF)

The NCF was set up in 1983 at Leeds Polytechnic. It aimed to bring together the coaching already going on in many sports and to expand coaching services. Although it was set up and funded by the Sports Council, it is now run by an independent committee. This committee is made up of representatives from the Sports Council, CCPR, BOA, British Association of National Coaches, the sports sciences, sports medicine and the network institutions of higher education.

The NCF has a network of National Coaching Centres at colleges throughout the country. Courses are run to develop coaching skills and improve knowledge about performance at national, regional and local level. Study packs, booklets and videos have been produced on a range of topics.

In 1991 The Sports Council published a review of coaching and coach education in the UK called 'Coaching Matters'. It urged governing bodies of sport to include coaches in policy development and produced a seven point plan to improve coaching.

INTERNATIONAL COMPETITION

The International Sports Federations (ISFs) control all sport that takes place between different countries. They are responsible for the rules of the sport and the rules of their own competitions. The governing bodies of sport in Britain must be members of the international federation for their sport. This allows their sportsmen and sportswomen to take part in international competition.

Olympic Competition

The International Olympic Committee (IOC) is the final authority on all questions concerning the Olympic Games and the Olympic Movement. The aims of the IOC are:

(i) to promote the development of those physical and moral qualities which are the basis of sport.

(ii) to educate young people, through sport, in a spirit of better understanding between each other and of friendship, thereby helping to build a better and more peaceful world.

(iii) to spread the Olympic principles throughout the world, thereby creating international goodwill.

(iv) to bring together the athletes of the world in the great four yearly sport festival, the Olympic Games.

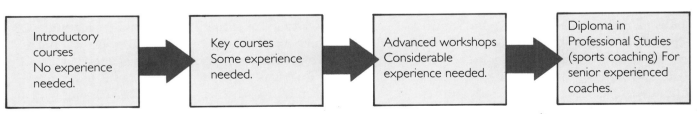

NCF Coaching development programme

The opening ceremony at the 1988 Olympics in Seoul

The Olympic organisation contains two other very important groups:

1 The International Sports Federations who are responsible for all matters relating to their own particular sport.

2 The National Olympic Committees (NOC) which represent the IOC and promote the Olympic Movement in their own countries.

Today eligibility for taking part in the Olympic Games is the responsibility of the International Sports Federations. Their eligibility rules must be approved by the IOC. The national governing bodies in each country must ensure their competitors are eligible under these rules.

In order to take part in the Olympic Games, governing bodies of sport must conform to the rules of the IOC and also be members of the National Olympic Committee of their country.

British Olympic Association (BOA)

The British Olympic Association (BOA) is the name for the National Olympic Committee in Britain. The IOC states exactly what the National Olympic Committees must do.

The BOA has three main functions:

(i) to organise British participation in the Olympic Games.

(ii) to develop interest throughout Britain in the Olympic Games and Olympic Movement.

(iii) to assist the governing bodies of Olympic Sports in the preparation of their competitors.

The British Olympic Association enters competitors for the Olympic Games and the BOA is in control of the team at the Games. The behaviour of all members of the team is also the responsibility of the BOA. The BOA must make all the arrangements for travel, accreditation, transport, insurance, health-care, accommodation, food, training venues, publicity and entertainment.

In 1988 a team of 100 went to the Olympic Winter Games in Calgary - with their bobsleighs, luge sleds and skis. Almost six times that number later went to the Seoul Olympics together with boats, horses, canoes and other equipment. In all

£2.5 million was the cost to the BOA in 1988. This money was raised through the British Olympic Appeal, with donations from industry and the public, as well as sponsorship.

Recently the BOA has expanded its services to education and the press. The aim has been to spread the Olympic message through schools and the media.

In 1987 the British Olympic Medical Centre at Northwick Park Hospital was opened. It tests Olympic competitors and undertakes research into the fitness of top class sportsmen and sportswomen. Further details are contained in the chapter on 'Physical Fitness'.

National Olympic Committees are forbidden to become involved with affairs of a political or commercial nature. Governments cannot put members on the committee. They must be completely independent, making their own decisions, only subject to the rules of the IOC.

This independence was illustrated when the British Olympic Association, under the leadership of Sir Dennis Follows, refused to withdraw the British team from the Olympic Games to be held in Moscow in 1980. The British Government wanted the team to stay at home, but the BOA resisted all political pressure and the team competed. However some governing bodies withdrew their teams and a number of individuals refused to attend.

The Sports Council, CCPR, BOA and the governing bodies of sport together control sport in Britain. Sport in the past has developed to meet the needs of sportsmen and sportswomen. The independence from direct government influence has always been jealously guarded.

THE NATIONAL SPORTS CENTRES

There are eleven national, residential sports centres managed by the four Sports Councils.

Priority of use is given to national team training and competition and the training of leaders and officials. At other times the centres are open to all. Courses are provided to improve personal performance as well as to introduce beginners to new activities. Residential accommodation is available in each centre together with conference facilities. Centres are now focussing on marketing their facilities and courses.

ENGLAND

Crystal Palace National Sports Centre Norwood, London.
International sports centre for many sports.
Activities include: Swimming, diving, basketball, gymnastics, judo, badminton, squash, boxing, fitness, weightlifting, athletics, indoor football, sports injuries clinic.

Holme Pierrepont National Water Sports Centre and Country Park Nottingham.
Activities include: Rowing, canoeing, angling, sailing, board sailing, power boating, sub-aqua diving, long distance swimming, water skiing, white water canoeing.

Bisham Abbey National Sports Centre Marlow, Bucks.
LTA National Tennis Centre.
Activities include: National Strength and Fitness Centre and Olympic weight training base. Tennis, weightlifting, dance, squash, soccer, rugby, hockey. .

Lilleshall Hall National Sports Centre Newport, Shrops.
FA football school and injury and performance testing centre.

Activities include: Football, gymnastics, archery, cricket, volleyball, squash, tennis, golf, bowling, orienteering.

Plas y Brenin National Centre for Mountain Activities Capel Curig, N. Wales.
Activities include: Rock climbing, mountaineering, sea and river canoeing, orienteering, skiing, dri-skiing, multigym.

SCOTLAND

The Scottish National Water Sports Training Centre Cumbrae, Ayrshire.
Activities include: Dinghy and board sailing, offshore cruising and racing, sea canoeing, sub-aqua diving.

Inverclyde National Sports Training Centre Largs, Ayrshire.
Activities include: Gymnastics, movement, squash, weight training, human performance laboratory, golf, floodlit synthetic pitches and courts.

Glenmore Lodge National Outdoor Training Centre Aviemore, Invernesshire.
Activities include: Downhill skiing, ski mountaineering, ski touring, Nordic skiing, hill walking, mountaineering, snow and ice climbing, mountain rescue, rock climbing, kayaking, Canadian canoeing, dri-skiing, multigym.

WALES

National Sports Centre for Wales Cardiff.
Activities include: Basketball, gymnastics, judo, badminton, cricket, squash, swimming, multigym, weight training, tennis, artificial pitch.

Plas Menai National Watersports Centre Caenarfon, Gwynedd.
Activities include: Dinghy sailing, windsurfing, cruising, power boating, canoeing, mountain activities.

N. IRELAND

The N. Ireland Centre for Outdoor Activities Tollymore, N. Ireland.
Activities include: Mountaineering, rock climbing, inland, sea and open canoeing, outdoor adventure.

THINGS TO DO

1 Complete the following table:

Sport	Governing body
1 Football	The Football Association The Women's Football Association
2	
3	
4	
5	
6	

2 Which of the following statements are true and which are false? Place a T opposite true statements and an F opposite false statements.

(i) The CCPR built national sports centres.

(ii) The Sports Council was founded by Royal Charter in 1980.

(iii) One aim of the Sports Council is to raise standards of sports performance.

(iv) There is no separate Sports Council for Wales.

(v) The National Coaching Foundation is financed directly by the Government.

(vi) 'Sport and Leisure' is a weekly paper published by the Sports Council.

(vii) The governing bodies of sport are members of the CCPR.

(viii) The IOC is represented by the National Olympic Committees.

(ix) Sport in Britain is controlled by the Government.

(x) The British Olympic Association is responsible for the Olympic team.

3 (i) Choose one sport and explain the links between local clubs, regional associations, the governing body, the CCPR and the international sports federations.

(ii) Explain why British sports organisations might be unwilling to accept money from the Government.

(iii) Do you think the Government, local authorities and other organisations should increase their spending on sport at the present time? Should they have other priorities? Give reasons for your answer.

4 Find out all you can about the national organisation of sport in another country. Compare their organisation with our own. Do you think, from your research, that international sports success is linked to the national organisation of sport? Give reasons to explain your answer.

5 Complete the following sentences:

(i) In order to develop sport in Britain, the Government gives a large grant to the
....

(ii) The organisations which are responsible for the control of individual sports in Britain are ....

(iii) In Britain the organisation which is responsible for all matters relating to the Olympic Games is the ....

(iv) People over fifty have been encouraged to become involved in sport through a campaign called ....

(v) The 'Ever Thought of Sport?' campaign in 1985 was aimed at ....

(vi) The ultimate authority on Olympic matters is the ....

6 Plan a visit to your nearest National Sports Centre to find out what is offered to top sportsmen and sportswomen and in which sports? Also see what is available for those wishing to take up new sports or to improve their sports skills. Is the centre 'user friendly'? Prepare a report on your visit. Add photographs if possible.

7 Imagine you are a top competitor in your favourite sport. You have begun to realise that retirement is quite close! Find out how you could remain involved in your sport as a coach, administrator or manager.

ORGANISATION OF SPORT IN BRITAIN AT LOCAL LEVEL

Aims

To gain knowledge and understanding of:

◆ the provision of local sports facilities
◆ the financing of local sports facilities
◆ how the providers of local sports facilities actually carry out their work

To develop the skills of:

◆ obtaining information from a variety of sources including questionnaires and interviews;
◆ map compilation and graphical representation;
◆ presenting an effective report using a variety of methods

In the past sport at local level usually consisted of many small groups of people taking part quite independently. Clubs were small, the facilities were basic and the organisation was limited. There was no central organisation at this level to plan and co-ordinate all sports development.

With the formation of the Sports Council things changed. Regional offices were established. Regional Councils for Sport and Recreation were formed and local sports councils encouraged. Gradually many local authorities established separate leisure or recreation departments as the demand for active leisure increased.

Today facilities are provided by a number of different bodies, as shown opposite.

The providers decide who may use their facilities and what charge, if any, will be made.

LOCAL AUTHORITIES AND THEIR SPORTS FACILITIES

England and Wales are divided into administrative areas. Each area has a system of local government. In most of the country there is a two tier system of county councils and district councils. These two types of council are the local authorities who between them provide a variety of essential services for the community. In the large centres of population, the metropolitan district councils and the London boroughs provide all the services themselves. In addition to the county and district councils there are also small local councils

Provider	Facilities	Availability
County councils	Schools	Pupils only – also dual use
	Colleges	Students only – also dual use
	Youth centres	General public (but age limit)
	Adult education centres	General public
District councils	Leisure centres	General public
	Swimming pools	General public
	Parks and recreation grounds	General public
Parish councils	Village halls	General public
Others: Industry/Commerce	Various	Employees only
Private clubs	Various	Members only
Commercial enterprises	Various	General public
Spectator sports	Various	Elite competitors only
Community associations	Various	Members only

called parish, town or community councils who have powers to provide services.

Each local authority has a number of departments. The departments each deal with a particular part of the authority's work. They are run by full time professional staff. All major decisions are made by committees of councillors. Councillors are elected to represent the residents of an area of the authority. They take on their council responsibilities in addition to their normal work.

The Chief Executive is a kind of general manager for the council. Each council will have a treasurer's department to control the spending of the authority. There will also be a number of departments which provide a service to the public such as housing, social services, environmental health etc.

The responsibility for sports provision will depend on where you live. In areas with county and district councils, it is the county's statutory responsibility to provide educational sports facilities. The district council has a non-statutory responsibility for leisure provision in the area. District councils in the metropolitan districts and London borough councils are responsible for both educational and leisure sports provision in their particular areas.

In all areas, parish councils may provide some sports facilities such as village halls. They may also have some influence on local provision for recreation, for example in the use of playing fields.

The education department has the greatest responsibility for sports provision in terms of the number of staff and facilities. The schools must provide physical education at the different levels - nursery, primary and secondary. Facilities such as gymnasia, halls and fields are needed, together with equipment and apparatus suitable for the age groups involved. Skilled staff must be provided to offer the children a full programme of activities. Similarly facilities and staff are needed for physical recreation at colleges of all kinds. Youth clubs and adult classes often use the sports facilities provided for the schools. Sports centres may be under the control of the education department, the leisure department or jointly controlled.

The leisure or recreation department has responsibility for providing facilities and promoting activities outside the educational system. This may include the provision of swimming pools, leisure and sports centres, outdoor activity centres, parks and recreation grounds. Sports Development Officers may be appointed to encourage sport amongst a wide range of different groups in the area for example 'New Horizons' for the over fifties and 'Action Sport' for young people.

The treasurer's department allocates the money that each local authority department is given for the year. Each department must plan

how best to use the money. They must see that they do not overspend. If a new swimming pool is wanted or extra land drained for pitches, the department responsible must either receive more money from the treasurer's department or reduce spending elsewhere. Grants from the Sports Council and other organisations are sometimes available for major projects.

The planning department produces detailed plans for developments of all kinds. New housing areas will need provision for recreation and sport. With the increasing demand for leisure facilities of all kinds, long term planning to meet these needs is very important. More outdoor facilities like golf courses and football pitches may be required. Indoor facilities for squash, badminton and general activities may be provided within a new sports centre or by developing the facilities of a school for the whole community to use. The department will work closely with leisure officers to ensure that proposed developments will meet future needs.

The local authorities are very important providers of a whole range of sports facilities. In the past many of these facilities were heavily subsidised from public money. This policy is now changing due to the introduction of compulsory competitive tendering.

Local Authorities and Compulsory Competitive Tendering (CCT)

Government policy has directed that many of the services run by the local authority should be put out to competitive tendering. This means that firstly the local authority draws up a very detailed description of the service. Then commercial organisations can offer to take over the service at a certain price. The department of the local authority which has been providing the service can also bid for the work. This is called the Direct Services Organisation (DSO). One of the first services to be subject to CCT was the collection of refuse. Private firms now undertake this work for some local authorities.

CCT was extended to the management of selected local authority sport and leisure facilities in October 1989. It includes some sports centres, swimming pools, golf courses, athletic grounds, tennis courts, pitches for team games and many more types of facility. Some of the management functions are the collection of and accounting for charges, cleaning and maintaining facilities, supervisory activities, providing instruction, catering, securing premises and promoting facilities. The role of the local authority is changing to become 'enablers' and 'monitors' of provision rather than actual 'providers'.

There is still debate about the advantages and disadvantages of CCT. On one side people say that competition for the contracts will bring savings to the local authority and a better standard of service to the customer. Others argue that there is an inbuilt bias against the DSO winning the contract and that the service offered will be more expensive for the customer and restricted to activities that 'pay their way'.

Certainly managing sports and leisure services is different from services such as rubbish clearance. It is 'people orientated' where relationships between staff and customers are very important. CCT is not the same as privatisation. The local authority still owns the facilities and will have control over how they are used. For example, the local authority can decide on pricing, programming, opening hours and the quality and standard of service it requires.

The Sports Council and CCT

The Sports Council believes CCT provides local authorities with an opportunity to shape the future development of their leisure services. Therefore it is vital that the level and type of service is specified in detail for each facility. At the same time integration of the facilities is necessary to provide a co-ordinated service to the whole community. Above all 'Sport for All' should continue to be a major influence. Thus opportunities should be safeguarded for the key target groups - the young, the old, the disabled, the unemployed, women with young children and ethnic minorities.

Leisure and Recreation Departments

With the coming of CCT these departments are being reorganised because the DSO will be competing alongside contractors for management contracts. Therefore the departments must carefully distinguish between their client and contractor roles. An example of the new structure is shown below.

Some facilities and activities are not included in CCT legislation. These include joint use facilities (used by education and the community) and facilities on educational premises, both indoor and outdoor.

SPORTS FACILITIES NOT PROVIDED BY THE LOCAL AUTHORITY

In many areas most sports facilities are provided by the local authority. There are nearly always however, other facilities which are provided by different organisations. Usually, these organisations control and limit who can use the facilities in some way. They are companies, private

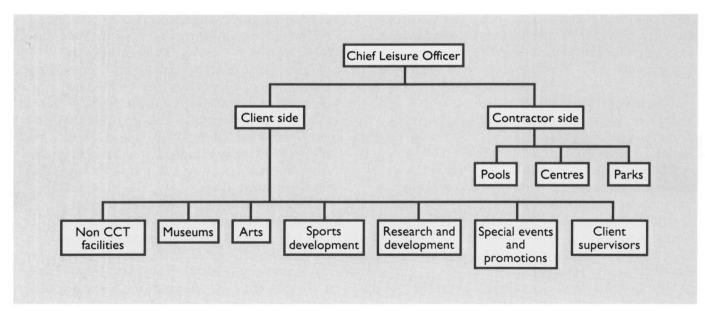

Structure of leisure and recreation departments

clubs and commercial organisations. In some cases facilities are restricted to the top sportsmen and sportswomen who compete before the paying public.

Facilities for Employees

Some facilities are provided by companies and businesses solely for the use of their employees. The company pays all the expenses of the upkeep of the buildings, pitches, courts and greens. Sometimes a small charge is made for using the facility, but usually it is free. It is seen as a way of encouraging people to work for the company. If teams are also organised, time off work would be given usually to play the matches and perhaps also to train. Employees might see success on the sports field for the company as improving their career prospects. An enjoyable social life linked to the company is likely to improve the workforce's morale.

Private Clubs

There are many private clubs which concentrate on one particular sport or activity. Often started by a group of enthusiasts, the club will attract those who have a strong interest in the sport, whether angling or archery, wrestling or road running. The facilities needed will vary with the sport of course. Many of these clubs are too small to own their own facilities. Bigger clubs, and those that cater for more than one activity often can afford their own facilities and clubhouses. They may sometimes get grants to help them, but they usually have to charge people to cover the everyday costs of running the club. Subscriptions, a charge everytime you play and fund raising help to produce the money needed. The facilities are usually only for members and guests. Some clubs encourage anyone to join, others are very selective in their membership.

Commercial Enterprises

Commercial organisations offer the public sporting and leisure facilities at a price. They have to make a profit to stay in business, so prices are quite high. They usually try to offer good value to encourage people to use their facilities. They may provide facilities which the local authority does not, and for which they believe there is a demand.

Horse racing – a popular spectator sport

Health and beauty centres may be combined with saunas. Fitness centres may use a gymnasium with weight training and other exercise equipment. Popular activities where facilities are in short supply may also attract people, for example squash courts, golf driving ranges and snooker halls. Ice rinks and dance centres may attract people for social rather than sporting reasons. Where there is a public demand, but no facilities, commercial enterprise may step in. Not all commercial enterprises in sport are successful.

The 1960's saw the rise and fall of ten pin bowling. Skateboarding in the 1970's followed a similar path, although both had recovered to some extent by the early 1990's.

Spectator Sport

Facilities may also be provided for professionals and top amateurs to entertain the public. The public pays to watch the sportsmen and sportswomen in action. Professional footballers and tennis players, amateur athletes and rugby union players all compete before large crowds. At race tracks, dogs and horses race for their owners whilst providing an opportunity for the public at large, and those present, to bet on the outcome. At other tracks and circuits, speedway riders, racing car drivers, motor cyclists and stock car drivers thrill the crowds who pay to see them take risks at high speed. The top racket games players compete before large crowds as do golfers, swimmers, gymnasts and boxers.

Sometimes the arenas and sports areas used are available to the general public or club members at other times. The Crystal Palace athletics track is open to all and members of the Wimbledon Tennis Club can use most of the courts. Some grounds are kept exclusively for a particular sport and the competitors involved.

REGIONAL SPORTS COUNCILS

In addition to its London headquarters, the Sports Council has nine regional offices. The Eastern Region, for example, comprises Bedfordshire, Cambridgeshire, Essex, Hertfordshire, Norfolk and Suffolk.

The regional staff work closely with all agencies concerned with promoting sport and physical education in the region. They carry out the plans of the Sports Council.

The Sports Council gives grants to local authorities, commercial concerns and voluntary organisations for the provision of sports facilities. The Eastern Council for Sport and Recreation (ECSR) suggests the priority to be given to each request. Funds are also available to promote sport. Priority is given to schemes involving large numbers of participants, particularly groups identified by the Sports Council and ECSR.

The regional council works with the National Coaching Foundation's network of centres in the region. It also makes annual awards to individuals and organisations for service to sport.

A diary of events, quarterly newspaper and other information are produced regularly for the region. In addition, a full-time information officer is able to provide up-to-date details of courses and events.

REGIONAL COUNCILS FOR SPORT AND RECREATION

In England there are 10 such Councils, for example the Eastern Council for Sport and Recreation (E.C.S.R.) is responsible for Bedfordshire, Cambridgeshire, Essex, Hertfordshire, Norfolk and Suffolk. Membership comes from four sources:

(i) Local authorities - each District Council and County Council is represented.

(ii) Governing bodies of sport and recreation - representatives are chosen at the conference of Eastern Counties Sport and Recreation.

(iii) Minister's nominees - appointments are made by the Minister of Sport.

(iv) Other bodies concerned with sport and recreation - including Countryside Commission, Forestry Commission, East Anglian Tourist Board, Anglian Water, landowning and farming interests, the TUC and the Armed Services.

These organisations represent the main providers and users of sports facilities. Through the ECSR they are able to discuss the needs of sport and recreation and plan for the future in the region. In doing this they take into account the Sports Council's and other organisation's national and regional plans. They also give advice on the use of resources, assist in the allocation of Sports

Council grant aid and promote and protect sport and recreation opportunities.

In recent years the ECSR has tried to increase participation by promoting sports leader courses, improving access to sporting opportunities to all sections of the community and improving publicity. Apart from encouraging the building of new facilities, the ECSR has promoted dual use, joint provision and conversion of buildings for sports use.

The work of the ECSR is carried out by three committees - participation, facilities and capital grants - with a co-ordinating committee and working groups.

The ECSR has no funds of its own and depends on the Sports Council to provide a secretarial and administration service.

LOCAL SPORTS COUNCILS

The Regional Sports Councils cover too large an area to be familiar with the needs of all the local communities in their region. Many communities have formed local sports councils to deal with their own particular problems.

They have aimed to encourage local people and organisations interested in sport to get together. The involvement and support of the local authority is essential. The following should be considered for membership:

Sporting bodies	– Individual sports clubs
	– Leagues
	– Industrial sports clubs
Education	– Physical education adviser
	– Physical education teachers
	– Youth and community
	– Adult education
Local authority	– Recreation officer
	– Local councillors
	– Parish councils
Health authority	
HM Forces	
Community associations	
Playing fields association	
Local media	

The Local Sports Council is largely advisory. By bringing together all those interested in local sport, views may be exchanged, problems discussed and plans drawn up for future development. To be effective, the Council will need to set objectives and these may include some of the following:

• To assess the sporting needs of the area.

• To advise and help with the organisation of courses for beginners, personal performance, coaches and leaders.

• To advise on facility needs.

• To co-operate with the LEA to encourage school leavers to continue with sport.

• To organise competitions, events and social activities in the interests of sport.

• To encourage efficient planning for the future development of sport.

It is hoped that those who provide the facilities will gain a better understanding of the views of those who use them. This will enable future sports development to be made in the best interest of the community.

The Council may promote its work through festivals of sport, promotional booklets, mass participation events, coaching courses and 'taster' opportunities for new sports. It may also support the national 'Sport for All' campaigns at the local level, help develop coaching expertise through the NCF courses, promote the CCPR Community Sports Leaders courses and encourage the dual use of facilities.

THE LEE VALLEY PARK

There have been a number of imaginative schemes to develop large areas of land for leisure use. The Sports Council's national sports centres offer a wide variety of activities at all levels. The National Parks allow leisure pursuits in natural surroundings.

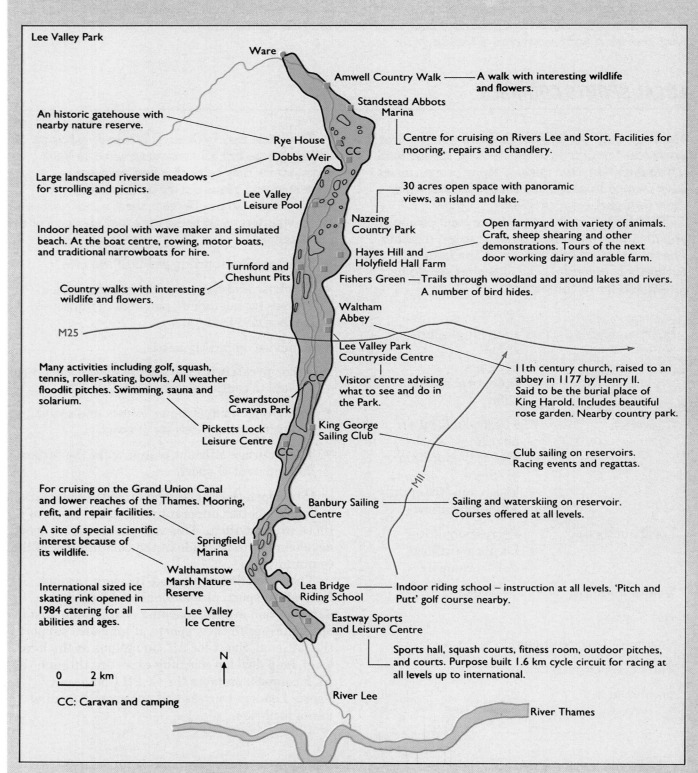

Lee Valley Park

Ware

Amwell Country Walk ——— A walk with interesting wildlife and flowers.

Standstead Abbots Marina

An historic gatehouse with nearby nature reserve.

Rye House

Dobbs Weir

Centre for cruising on Rivers Lee and Stort. Facilities for mooring, repairs and chandlery.

Large landscaped riverside meadows for strolling and picnics.

Lee Valley Leisure Pool

30 acres open space with panoramic views, an island and lake.

Nazeing Country Park

Open farmyard with variety of animals. Craft, sheep shearing and other demonstrations. Tours of the next door working dairy and arable farm.

Indoor heated pool with wave maker and simulated beach. At the boat centre, rowing, motor boats, and traditional narrowboats for hire.

Hayes Hill and Holyfield Hall Farm

Turnford and Cheshunt Pits

Fishers Green ——— Trails through woodland and around lakes and rivers. A number of bird hides.

Country walks with interesting wildlife and flowers.

Waltham Abbey

M25

Lee Valley Park Countryside Centre

Many activities including golf, squash, tennis, roller-skating, bowls. All weather floodlit pitches. Swimming, sauna and solarium.

Visitor centre advising what to see and do in the Park.

11th century church, raised to an abbey in 1177 by Henry II. Said to be the burial place of King Harold. Includes beautiful rose garden. Nearby country park.

Sewardstone Caravan Park

King George Sailing Club

Picketts Lock Leisure Centre

Club sailing on reservoirs. Racing events and regattas.

M11

For cruising on the Grand Union Canal and lower reaches of the Thames. Mooring, refit, and repair facilities.

Banbury Sailing Centre

Sailing and waterskiing on reservoir. Courses offered at all levels.

A site of special scientific interest because of its wildlife.

Springfield Marina

Walthamstow Marsh Nature Reserve

International sized ice skating rink opened in 1984 catering for all abilities and ages.

Lee Valley Ice Centre

Lea Bridge Riding School

Indoor riding school – instruction at all levels. 'Pitch and Putt' golf course nearby.

Eastway Sports and Leisure Centre

Sports hall, squash courts, fitness room, outdoor pitches, and courts. Purpose built 1.6 km cycle circuit for racing at all levels up to international.

N

0   2 km

CC: Caravan and camping

River Lee

River Thames

One of the most ambitious and far-sighted projects is the Lee Valley Park. It combines formal sport, leisure facilities and activities with the natural environment. The Park follows the course of the River Lee from Ware in Hertfordshire, southwards for almost 23 miles to London's East End.

It offers the whole family a great variety of activities all the year round. These include water based activities such as sailing, angling, cruising or rowing or countryside pursuits such as picnicking, walking or riding. There are very many sports on offer at the different centres and family holiday facilities include narrowboats, riverside chalets or camping and caravanning sites.

The Park is being developed and managed by the Lee Valley Regional Park Authority, established in 1967. Much of the land was derelict. It has been transformed with modern leisure facilities and a sensitive approach to the management of land adding to the natural water scenery. Landscape improvement and nature conservation remain as major features of the development programme.

The swimming pool at the Lee Valley Park

THINGS TO DO

1 On an outline map of your area mark in all the sports facilities including parks and open spaces, sports and leisure centres, swimming pools, school halls and gymnasia, youth clubs' facilities, private and professional clubs' facilities, arenas for major events, golf courses, bowling greens, cricket pitches and hard surface areas for games.

Remember to use a key, with a special set of symbols. Different colours might help.

Analyse your results.

(i) Which facilities need expanding or improving?
(ii) Does your area need new facilities for any sport?

2 Make a survey of people's interest in sport. For example, interview twenty four people, four from each of the following different age groups: 10-19, 20-29, 30-39, 40-49, 50-59, 60 plus. Make a note of each person's sex and ask each person the same set of questions.

(i) Do you take part in physical recreation in your leisure time?

(ii) If the answer is yes, follow up with questions about what sort of activities they take part in, how regularly, at what time of day, how much it costs and which facilities they use.

(iii) If the answer is no, follow up with questions about alternative leisure time activities and reasons for not taking part in physical recreation.

Collect in all the results for the group and see if you can draw any conclusions or spot any trends. You might find it helpful to link your findings to a sports facilities' map.

3 Make a study of your local sports centre. Find out:

(i) how it is organised, the name of the manager and his or her assistants, coaches and instructors, whether or not they are full-time or part-time employees.

(ii) how you become a member, the total number of members, their age and sex, the cost of membership.

(iii) the number and types of activities offered. Produce a chart to show the programme run by the centre.

(iv) the financial organisation of the centre, how much it costs to play different sports, what happens to the money and how the centre is paid for.

(v) whether or not a special effort is made to attract housewives, the elderly, the disabled, single parent families or school leavers.

4 Imagine you are a member of a local group which is campaigning for a new swimming pool or golf course or cycle track or shooting range or similar facility. Choose one project and explain how you would go about organising support. Write a letter to the Sports Council, local authority or other body explaining your case and asking for help.

5 Suggest one sport which could be introduced into your area on a profit making basis. Explain why you think it would be a sound commercial venture. Describe what you would do to make it attractive and successful.

6 Draw up a table to show which sports have facilities in your area, and who provides them.

7 Find out from your local authority if there is a recreation department or whether responsibility for physical recreation is spread out amongst many departments. Invite a speaker to explain to you how local physical recreation is funded and organised. You may be able to ask about future plans as well as about the decision making process. Ask about CCT and the implications for the Sports Council's key target groups (for example women, unemployed, ethnic minorities).

8 Explain the advantages and disadvantages of CCT for sport and leisure provision.

9 Imagine you are a member of the local sports council which has just received an offer of £10 000 from a retired businessman to promote sport in your area. The only requirement is that a detailed plan, with full explanation of the proposed activities, is sent to him as soon as possible. Within your group of six people prepare an action plan.

12 SPONSORSHIP IN SPORT

Aims

To develop knowledge and understanding of:

◆ the need for sponsorship of sport in all its forms

◆ the advantages and disadvantages of sponsorship for sport and the sponsor

◆ trends in sponsorship - the influence of the media

To develop the skills of:

◆ primary and secondary research

◆ simple statistical analysis

Sports sponsorship usually means that a commercial organisation gives financial help to an individual, a team or a sport in general, in return for publicity for their product.

In recent years two particular needs have contributed to the great increase in sponsorship. The increasing popularity of sport has given rise to higher standards of performance. To achieve these higher standards, extra money is needed by the individual or team and by the sport in general.

At the same time, since sport has become a major interest in society, the business world has looked for ways to be connected with it. It has been found that sponsorship is a successful way for companies to reach a large number of people.

Today sponsorship is available throughout the sporting world. It is not only the champions who are sponsored. Local teams and groups can also find sponsors. There are also many sponsored achievement and coaching schemes to encourage young people. Most major sports championships and international sporting fixtures have a sponsor.

It should be remembered that every company that sponsors sport does so in order to increase its business. Advertising is a very powerful force in the world today. It is usually the company which offers the greatest amount of money that gets the sponsorship agreement. Of course individual competitors and the sport in general will also benefit from sponsorship.

INDIVIDUAL SPORTSMEN AND SPORTSWOMEN

The professional world champions and those sportsmen and sportswomen in the highest rankings are heavily sponsored. Companies want their products to be linked with people of outstanding ability. They hope that the public will then associate their product with excellence. The public often forgets that players advertise certain products, rather than others, because of the money they are paid.

For the top professional players, sponsorship just adds more money to their usually very healthy bank balances. For the younger, up and coming, players sponsorship money will help them buy the best equipment, travel to tournaments they need to play in and help them in their training.

Without sponsorship of some sort, international amateurs could not find the time to devote themselves to their sport. Sponsorship pays their living expenses and all the costs of being a top competitor. These include money for equipment, clothing, travel, accommodation and food, together with the expenses of training and competition.

For those amateurs who have trust funds, the balance of the sponsorship and other monies in their fund will be available to them when they retire from sport. Obviously for some star performers this will be a very large amount of money.

For anyone other than a top competitor, sponsorship depends on the person's potential in sport. Young people showing promise may be given clothing and equipment free by companies. They may have their travelling expenses paid for a period. Some sportsmen and sportswomen are employed by companies sympathetic to their sporting life. They may be allowed time to train and compete without loss of pay.

TEAMS AND GROUPS OF SPORTSMEN AND SPORTSWOMEN

Successful professional sports teams are able to attract sponsorship in a similar way to individual competitors. Any money received is shared between everybody in the team. The manager or coach is usually included and the club as a whole may also benefit. This money increases the players' earnings. If the money is linked to winning a trophy it may only happen once. However, if the team is sponsored because of its generally high standards and achievements, then the sponsorship may last for a much longer period.

Amateur teams who are sponsored may find it easier to get together for training if expenses are paid. Equipment and clothing may also be supplied. Travelling and hotel expenses both at home and abroad may enable the team to get the competition it needs.

In most cases, the top amateur teams receive help in order to reach higher standards. They are the flag bearers for their sport. For some sports, sponsorship support is given to teams and groups at different age levels.

As with individual competitors, the sponsors are keen to have their name linked with a successful team or group of people. However some sponsors are willing to support junior teams and others with potential. They try to let the public know how they are helping sport, even if their name is not really prominent.

COACHING AND ACHIEVEMENT SCHEMES

Most young children are very proud and happy when they win a competition or achieve a certain standard in a sport or activity. Receiving a reward can encourage further effort towards higher standards.

Many sponsors now help sport by encouraging the young and other people who want to improve

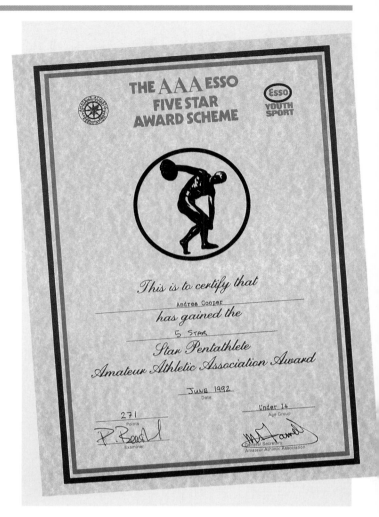

their skills. The schemes usually involve achieving standards at different levels. Those who are successful receive a certificate or badge. Some of the schemes are national ones, like the Five Star Award scheme in athletics. The schemes are popular in schools. The swimming awards are given for a wide variety of performance including distance, speed, style and survival skills. Other sports are encouraged by similar schemes. Sponsors pay all the costs of the administration of the scheme as well as providing the badges and certificates.

The sponsor gets publicity when the certificates and badges go home to parents with the sponsor's name prominent. The sponsors also hope to get credit from the public for encouraging young people to take part in sport and to improve their ability.

Apart from achievement awards, most sports offer coaching and teaching courses which lead to official recognition. Sometimes a sponsor will pay for running such courses. These awards are for adults in clubs, schools or sports organisations.

Sporting events are a good opportunity for sponsors to put their names before the public

SPORTING EVENTS

Sponsors are attracted to a number of different types of sporting events.

Single events, occurring once only, such as international fixtures, championship finals or invitation competitions are very popular. For the sponsor this is a good opportunity to put their name before the public. If the event is being televised the publicity will reach an even bigger audience. When top class teams or famous individuals are taking part, the sponsors will be more interested. In recent years, in some major athletics fixtures, well-known athletes have dropped out at the last minute. This has not pleased the sponsors.

For major events, the sponsors pay all the expenses of the individual competitors or teams and all the costs of organisation and administration. This allows the sport running the event to keep any profit made from gate money, television fees, etc.

Sometimes companies will sponsor a league or a knock out cup competition. These competitions may be local or national and may involve a series of matches over a long period of time. The league or cup is then known by the sponsor's name, for example in football there is the Barclays' League and in cricket the Britannic Assurance County Championship.

Sponsorship of this sort is of great value to the sport. Without the money sponsors provide, many of the events would not be held. This is particularly true when overseas competitors and teams are involved since their expenses are usually considerable. The sponsor gains a great deal of publicity. Their name is displayed prominently around the arena or ground.

When a company is considering sponsorship of a particular sport, it will need to know the level of public interest in the sport, the likelihood of radio and newspaper publicity and the likely attendance at any event taking place. However, the most important factor is the likelihood of television coverage and the estimated television audience.

Market Trends

It is essential that companies have full details of market trends, growth areas and television coverage details before committing themselves to sports sponsorship. A company called Research Services Limited, through its computerised analysis of sponsor exposure on television, produces such up-to-date advice.

In 1990 virtually all major events in the sports calendar had sponsors. The sponsors continued to extend their contracts for long periods of time and with ever-increasing sums of money.

The continuing popularity of sports sponsorships was shown by an 11% increase in sponsorship expenditure in 1990. There were over 2 000 major sponsors, with fewer withdrawals (27 in all) than in 1989. The average major deal was for three and a half years and over 70 companies had committed over £1 million each.

During 1990, companies agreed more than 600 new and extended contracts with £70 million in total. Between 100 and 120 companies account for about half this total. The market is steady at the top end with major sponsors. Some effects of the early 1990's recession were evident at the other end of the market with sponsorship involving £10 000 or less.

The current prices show the increase in the value of sponsorship without taking into account inflation. The indexed figures show the real increase in sponsorship each year since 1981. This is steady at 3 to 4% per year.

In the six months January to July 1990, 22 companies signed agreements worth over £2 million and another 34 for between £1 million and £2 million.

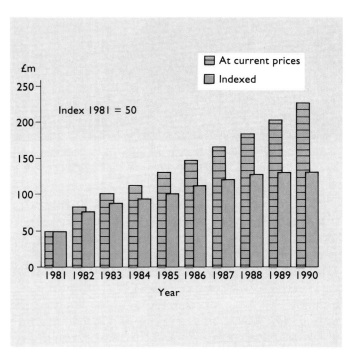

Estimated total UK sports sponsorship

The Whitbread Round the World Yacht Race

Sponsorship details: January - July 1990

Top 10 Sponsorship Deals (*Source*: RSL Sportscan)		
Embassy	£11m	7 years – World Snooker Championship
Whitbread	£10m (estimated)	Next 'Round the World' Yacht Race
Bells	£7.5m	5 years – Golf : The Scottish Open
Barclays	£7m	3 years – English Soccer League
Rothmans	£6m	Entry in 'Round the World' Yacht Race
Scottish Brewers	£5m	5 years – Glasgow Rangers FC
Cornhill	£4.5m	5 years – Cricket 'Test Series'
Fosters	£4.5m	4 years – Motor Racing : Silverstone Grand Prix
Philip Morris	£4m	3 years – World Cup Yachting Event
Lombard	£4m	5 years – RAC Rally

Sports sponsorship growth areas

(a) Youth

There has been a marked increase in sponsorship of youth sport. More and more companies realise the advantages of a young, lively, relevant image. Examples:

Bull Computers: Cricket - £1.4m-3 years - Development of young players

Raleigh: Cycling - £150 000 - World Junior Championship

(b) Women's sport

To date companies have not realised the sponsorship potential of women's sport. At present there is a lack of television and press exposure. However, millions of women both play and watch sport. Examples:

Fisons: Hockey - £100 000 - 10 years - Ipswich Womens' Club

Vauxhall: Tennis - Ladies National League

(c) Disabled and handicapped sport

This is the ethical, supportive side of sponsorship. Examples:

British Telecom: £30 000 - 1 year - British Sports Association for Disabled

Royal Mail: Sponsor Ian Haydon - Disabled athlete

(d) National team and events

(i) National. Examples:

Minet: Hockey - £185 000 for GB team Olympic preparation

Johnson & Johnson: Netball - England team, travel and accommodation

(ii) Initiatives and support. Examples:

British Telecom: £50 000 for 1991 World Student Games

Heineken: £150 000 for triathlon

Sponsorship of clubs

This sponsorship continues across many clubs, including football and cricket. Most recent development has taken place at rugby union and rugby league clubs. Hockey, swimming and athletics clubs are starting to approach commercial firms. Examples:

Athletics: Eastern Electricity – £100 000 – Harringay AC and Essex Ladies Club

Cricket: Ansells Brewery – £180 000 – 3 years – Notts County Cricket Club

Minet sponsored the Great Britain hockey team's preparation for the Olympics

Hockey:	Guytech – £80 000 – 5 years – Glasgow Western Womens Club
Rugby Union:	Bass – £250 000 – 3 years – Gloucester Rugby Club
Swimming:	Telescan – £50 000 – Wigan Wasps Club
Soccer:	Goodyear Tyres – £250 000 – 3 years – Wolves Football Club

Sponsorship of people

This includes both genuine sponsorship of an individual and the contracts to endorse goods or services.

(i) Promotion and endorsement. Examples:

Tennis:	Fila - £1.9 m - 3 years with Monica Seles
Snooker:	Bostik - £250 000 - 1 year with Stephen Hendry

(ii) Individual sponsorship. Examples:

Athletics:	General Portfolio - £20 000 with Peter Elliott
Judo:	Transline Systems - £30 000 with Karen Briggs

THE INSTITUTE OF SPORTS SPONSORSHIP (ISS)

The Central Council of Physical Recreation (CCPR) believes that the work done by governing bodies of sport is limited by lack of finance. Through its association with the Institute of Sports Sponsorship, it provides a liaison and advisory service. This enables contact to be made between sporting bodies and their potential commercial partners. The ISS has commercial companies as members. It advises them about sponsorship opportunities at local, national and international level. It then arranges contacts with officials from the sport concerned. The ISS will help its members to understand what it is possible to achieve through sponsorship and how long this will take. Since sponsorship is only one factor in marketing, it is difficult to be precise about its effect. Nevertheless the ISS will advise on techniques for the evaluation of such things as television, press and radio coverage. In this way it will help its members get value for money from sports sponsorship. Above all, the ISS encourages sponsorship and aims to improve the benefits for both sponsors and sport.

THE SPORTS AID FOUNDATION (SAF)

The Sports Aid Foundation, set up in 1976, is a completely independent body, managed by a board of governors and trustees. 'Giving Britons a better sporting chance' has become its slogan. It assists British sportsmen and sportswomen to succeed in international sport. Also through the Sports Aid Trust disabled athletes and talented youngsters are helped to achieve their sporting potential.

Its main function is to raise funds to distribute to the outstanding competitors. They receive grants, according to their personal needs, towards the cost of preparation, training and competition. These expenses have to be approved by their governing body. By removing any money problems, individuals can concentrate on improving their sporting performance. The money is collected by fund-raising projects and from commercial, industrial and private sponsorship.

The SAF was set up to enable our top amateur competitors to train in the same way as state and college sponsored athletes elsewhere in the world. Of Britain's 48 medallists at the 1988 Olympic Games, 46 had received SAF grant aid at some point in their careers. In the three years before the Seoul Olympics, £1.19 million was provided, which allowed support for British competitors at all levels and not just those of the highest calibre. In 1988, 2 363 sportspeople received grants in 46 sports, not all of them Olympic sports. Among those to benefit were the Seoul gold medalists - Adrian Moorhouse (swimming), Malcolm Cooper (shooting), Mike McIntyre and Bryn Vaile (yachting), Steve Redgrave and Andy Holmes (rowing) and the Men's Hockey Team.

SPONSORSHIP AND TOBACCO

Some years ago a major row broke out when it was known that the State Express Tobacco Company was contributing to the Sports Aid Foundation. In fact they offered a lot of money to the fund. They challenged Britain's sports stars to reach targets and so gain extra money for their sport. The tobacco company was to receive a lot of publicity in return for its money.

Some sportsmen and sportswomen returned their grants in protest. Geoff Capes, the shot putter, said *'This is a contemptuous manoeuvre to associate a dangerous and addictive drug with athletics and myself'.*

Many people objected to a tobacco company being linked with sport when smoking had clearly been shown to be a health risk.

Others argued that sport needed financial help and should take money from wherever it could get it. They also pointed out that sponsorship is accepted from companies that make weapons, alcohol and drugs. These products may bring problems comparable to smoking hazards.

The Sports Council issued the following statement: *'The association of sport with smoking through sponsorship and advertising is incompatible with the main aims of the 'Sport for All' campaign - that of helping to improve the fitness and health of people.'*

Nevertheless, tobacco and alcohol sponsorship of sport has continued at a high level in a limited number of sports.

THE FOUNDATION FOR SPORT AND THE ARTS

This is a new trust founded in 1991 by the football pools companies. The Pools Promoters Association (PPA) will donate £40 million each year, with a further £20 million coming from a reduction in the pools betting levy. Approximately two-thirds of the total amount will be used for sport, excluding league football and horse racing which benefit from other arrangements. The foundation is run by a board of five trustees with advice from the PPA, Sports Council and CCPR representatives. The board hopes to link in the grants to sporting bodies with funding from other sources. Exact plans are still being developed. It is hoped that this money will help many sports groups with financial problems and will also help to stimulate vital new projects.

Nevertheless, welcome as the money is, some people claim it would be much better to have a national lottery. Britain, alone in Europe, has no national lottery. It has been estimated that a single, nationwide government-authorised lottery could benefit sport, art and the environment by £1.1 billion a year. Thus about £300 million could be allocated to sports development, giving an opportunity to build modern facilities like the rest of Europe. The PPA claims that such a lottery would merely divert money from pools, charity

lotteries, bingo and bookmaking. This would place jobs in jeopardy and reduce the £1 billion received by the Government in duty and tax on gambling. Also at risk would be the £40 million given to football league clubs each year, currently being used to implement the Taylor report on grounds.

However in a number of European countries and also in Australia, a national lottery runs happily alongside other betting games with benefits for all concerned.

TELEVISED COVERAGE OF SPORT

After many years of increase, the total amount of sport shown on the four British channels has declined recently. The figures for 1990 show BBC1 and BBC2 continuing to reduce their hours devoted to sport, whilst ITV and Channel 4 have again increased their sports coverage. The 1984 and 1988 figures were inflated by 202 hours and 500 hours of Olympic Sport. Similarly, the Football World Cup, Commonwealth Games and other major events distort annual figures.

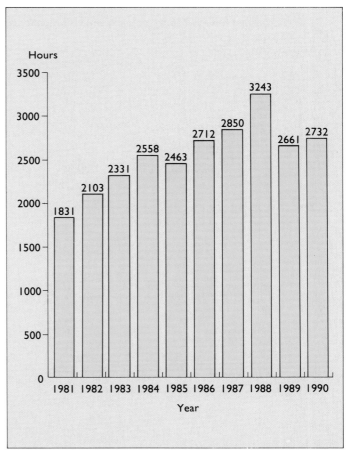

Total hours of sport on television

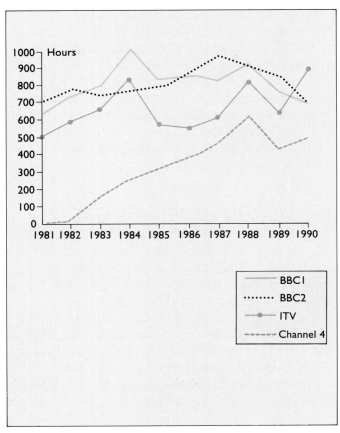

Scheduled hours of sport on each television channel

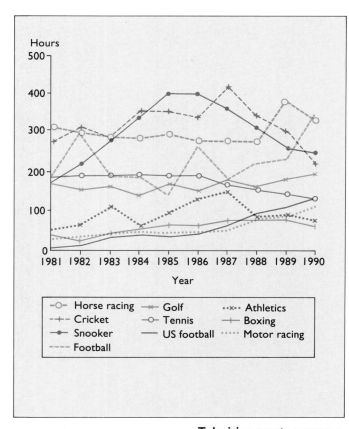

Television sports coverage

Total television coverage by sport (1990)

For 1990, the football figures include World Cup coverage and the Commonwealth Games make a four yearly entry in the list. American football continues to rise in the list, whilst popular sports absent from the list are darts, bowls, rugby league, cycling and gymnastics.

		Hours	%
1	Football	347.47	12.82
2	Horse racing	331.29	12.22
3	Snooker	243.57	8.99
4	Cricket	216.25	7.98
5	Golf	190.23	7.02
6	American football	129.20	4.77
7	Tennis	127.34	4.70
8	Commonwealth Games	113.30	4.18
9	Motor racing	102.15	3.77
10	Athletics	72.40	2.68
11	Rugby Union	66.15	2.44
12	Boxing	55.10	2.03
13	Wrestling	53.35	1.97
14	Ice skating	49.44	1.83
15	Equestrian	42.25	1.56

Source : RSL Sportscan   **Total television coverage by sport (1990)**

Top 15 Television sports audiences in 1989

The figures for 1990 were totally dominated by the Football World Cup, with the largest audience of 21 386 000 for the semi-final match between England and West Germany. The highest place for a non-football event was 17th for boxing's Benn v. Ewbank fight with 9 456 000 viewers.

In 1991, the FA Cup Final Spurs v. Nottingham Forest had an audience of 14 940 000 and the European Cup Winners' Final 13 060 000 (Manchester United v. Barcelona).

	Channel	Date	Sport	Event	Audience
1	BBC 1	26/2	Boxing	Tyson v. Bruno	12 066 000
2	BBC 1	8/4	Racing	Grand National	11 972 000
3	BBC 2	9/7	Tennis	Wimbledon Men's Final	11 114 000
4	BBC 1	20/5	Football	FA Cup Final	9 059 000
5	BBC 2	8/7	Tennis	Wimbledon	8 970 000
6	ITV	26/5	Football	Liverpool v. Arsenal	8 860 000
7	ITV	3/5	Football	Everton v. Liverpool	8 398 000
8	BBC 2	9/7	Tennis	Wimbledon Women's Final	8 263 000
9	BBC 1	1/7	Athletics	Bislett Games	7 963 000
10	BBC 1	3/12	Snooker	UK Championships	7 884 000
11	BBC 1	26/12	Results	Final Score	7 648 000
12	BBC 1	15/4	Results	Final Score	7 307 000
13	ITV	15/1	Snooker	Mercantile Credit Classic	7 267 000
14	BBC 1	2/1	Results	Final Score	7 223 000
15	BBC 1	9/12	Football	World Cup Draw	7 156 000

Source : RSL Sportscan   **Top 15 television sports audiences in 1989 age 15+**

**Gary Mabbutt and
Bryan Robson display
their trophies**

American Football - A Success Story in Britain

In terms both of media coverage and popular interest, American football was the fastest growing sport of the 1980's. Just compare 1980 with 1990. At the beginning of the decade only two hours of television coverage a year was shown, almost no-one played the game and not many more knew the rules. By the end of the decade, over 100 hours of American football were shown on television, there was a fully developed British League sponsored by Coca Cola, the National Football League of America played an annual pre-season game at Wembley (attendance 70 000), and had announced a London franchise (the Monarchs) for its new 'World League'. In addition, the sport had gained extensive press coverage (nationally and in new specialist weeklies and monthlies) and two satellite stations between them scheduled 10-15 hours of action each week during the season (including live transmission of college games).

How can we account for this remarkable expansion of items?

It is believed that it is the only major sport where television created interest, rather than interest leading to television (Channel 4).

It had immediate appeal for a number of reasons, but especially because its image (tough, American, glamorous, superstars) was found to be attractive, particularly to younger working class men.

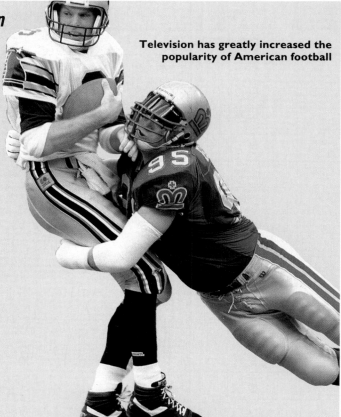

Television has greatly increased the popularity of American football

In 1986 Budweiser took over sponsorship of the fragmented British leagues. In 1989 they pulled out and were replaced by Coca Cola in a three year £1 million deal. There are also many regional companies who sponsor individual teams. The future now looks secure.

Channel 4 Television

Channel 4 has been responsible for introducing and popularising a number of sports. The success of American football in Britain was largely due to Channel 4. They have also introduced Sumo wrestling from Japan, the cycling classic, the Tour de France, and most recently of all in 1991, Kabaddi from India. Other foreign sports introduced include baseball and Australian rules football. Many of the minor British sports including volleyball and basketball have been featured, together with Gaelic and Celtic sports like hurling and curling. This commitment to minor sports continued in 1991 with a wheelchair basketball series. Channel 4 continue to be committed to women's sport, covering cricket, netball and volleyball. In 1991 the Women's Football Cup Final and England v. Scotland were both shown.

Kabaddi:

Kabaddi is a simple game played throughout Asia. Nothing is required apart from a piece of even ground about the size of a badminton court. Both men and women play the game in teams of seven players. The object is for one player at a time to advance into the opposition's half and touch as many players as possible before returning to his/her own half without being caught. All the while he/she must chant the word 'Kabaddi' and hold his/her breath. In practice it is a mixture of British bulldog and tag! Agility and quick reactions are required, together with strength, stamina and tactical skill. In 1990 it was included for the first time in the Asian Games held in Beijing, China.

The Darts Crisis

Suddenly dropped by television in 1989, the game of darts has fallen on hard times. During the seventies, through television, it became increasingly popular. In the eighties it was suddenly everywhere. The World Championships in 1983 were watched by a television audience of 8.6 million.

The stars of darts became household names - Eric Bristow 'The Crafty Cockney', 'Jocky' Wilson and John 'Stoneface' Lowe. Tony Green, the darts 'Master of Ceremonies' was admired for his cry of 'Wun hundred an' aye-tay!'. Darts progressed from providing a living for no-one to making a handful of men millionaires and enabling others to earn substantial amounts.

The reasons for dropping darts from television were closely linked to the audience it was attracting, which was largely 'downmarket'. Without television coverage the sponsors withdrew and in 1991 only the Embassy World Championships on BBC2 were broadcast.

SPORTS SCHOLARSHIPS

Universities in the USA have a highly developed and very competitive inter-college sports system. To attract top sportsmen and sportswomen they offer sports scholarships. These pay all the student's fees and living expenses while at university. In return the student is expected to achieve sporting success for the university.

In theory the student is at college to study, but in practice sporting achievements are the priority.

Kabaddi: Tamil Nadu v West Bengal

Failure at sport can mean the removal or reduction of the scholarship. A number of British sportsmen and sportswomen have benefitted from these scholarships. Excellent facilities, first-class coaches and top level competition are provided.

The Sports Scholarship Foundation helps British students gain scholarships at American colleges.

In the past, in Eastern European countries, Cuba and some of the developing countries many top competitors were officially at college or in the armed forces for the duration of their sporting career. Also in these countries, children with sports potential were selected to attend sports schools from an early age. Sport was state controlled and everything was done to ensure international success for their sports stars. Following the reunification of Germany in 1990, the highly successful East German development system for young sportsmen and sportswomen was dismantled. The turbulent events in Eastern Europe have affected the state system of sport in a number of other countries.

In Britain no comparable system exists. In the past some universities would appear to have taken more notice of a student's outstanding sporting record than of their academic achievement. This has not been general practice.

Some top sportsmen and sportswomen in Britain have been attracted to colleges to train as teachers of physical education. There they have the opportunity to maintain their training at a high level. Also they have access to good facilities and coaches. However many have not taught after qualifying.

The British Universities of Bath, Newcastle, Oxford, Stirling and Swansea offer help to gifted sportsmen and sportswomen. The universities still require the same academic entry standards for all students. However the sportsmen and sportswomen may be allowed extra time to complete their courses. Sponsorship may also be available to help the student continue with his or her sport whilst studying.

ADVANTAGES OF SPONSORSHIP

For sport

1 Sponsorship in professional sport provides another source of income for the players and the sports organisation.

2 For amateurs sponsorship gives help in raising standards of performance. Individuals may be able to devote themselves full-time to their sport without the need for regular employment. Sponsors may cover all the costs of training and competition.

3 Most amateur sports organisations are short of money. Without sponsorship they would not be able to operate many coaching and training schemes. Major events are expensive to organise and without the help of sponsors many would not take place.

For the sponsor

1 The sponsor gains publicity by being linked with a popular, wholesome activity like sport. The name of the company or product is prominently displayed. The media may refer to the sponsor, the event may be named after the sponsor and television pictures can hardly avoid the sponsor's name.

2 Companies may reduce their tax through sponsorship. However any advantages gained this way depend on how the money is given to sport.

3 The company may gain public esteem by being keen to support British sporting achievements.

DISADVANTAGES OF SPONSORSHIP

For sport

1 Once sponsorship is accepted, the sport comes to rely on it. Then there is the danger of collapse if the sponsorship is removed. This gives the sponsor a potentially powerful hold on the sport. This is especially true if a large amount of money is involved and few alternative sponsors are available. Sponsors may be able to change the way a sport is conducted. Some sporting events in Europe have been held at unusual times in order to be available on American television at popular times.

2 There is the possibility that less popular activities which attract little or no sponsorship

may actually decline, as the cost of maintaining their activities increases.

3 A governing body may make an agreement with a sponsor which is then binding on its sportsmen and sportswomen. Competitors may be forced to wear clothing or use equipment which is not of their choice. Their name may also be associated with a product without them first being consulted.

For the sponsor

1 The main difficulty is assessing the effectiveness of the publicity received in return for the money given to sport. If it is not seen as worthwhile the sponsor will pull out. Usually agreements between sport and sponsor are only for a limited period.

2 The sponsor may withdraw support if the image of the sport or reputation of the individual suffers in any way.

3 For the best publicity, sponsors need successful people and worthwhile causes. Regular losers and doubtful issues attract few sponsors.

4 Since sponsorship in sport continues to increase, it would seem that generally companies see it as a worthwhile investment.

Summary

If we accept that amateur sport today needs outside financial support, we must ask from where it should come.

Sponsorship by commercial and industrial companies is one answer. Government aid is another. Both mean that the individual governing bodies, teams and individual sportsmen and sportswomen give up some of their cherished independence. This is especially true of government aid. A sponsor may be rejected, but who rejects government influence once it has arrived?

The problem is how to bridge the gap between complete state sport and a commercial takeover of sport.

THINGS TO DO

1 Explain what you understand by sponsorship in sport.

2 Complete the chart below:

Sport	Sponsor	Details
Soccer		
Motor racing		
Athletics		
Cricket		
Gymnastics		

3 Complete the following sentences:

(i) It is possible for top amateur sportsmen and sportswomen to obtain grants from ....

(ii) In the past Eastern European sportsmen and sportswomen were sponsored by ....

(iii) Many people object to sports being sponsored by cigarette companies because ....

(iv) In the USA sports .... are often offered by ....

(v) An example of sponsorship helping school children is the .... scheme.

4 Which of these statements are true and which are false?

(i) Companies sponsor sport to increase their business.

(ii) Players advertise products for financial gain.

(iii) Companies prefer to be linked to average competitors.

(iv) Amateur competitors may not be sponsored.

(v) Companies prefer sponsored events to be televised.

(vi) The Government supports the Sports Aid Foundation.

5 Give reasons why each of the following might look for sponsorship:

(i) an individual.

(ii) a sport.

(iii) a major events' organiser.

6 You are a talented young athlete. Write a letter to a local company asking them to sponsor you. Explain the benefits that you both might gain.

7 As Chairperson of the Sports Aid Foundation you have been asked to speak to a large group of business people on the advantages of sponsorship from the point of view of the sponsor. Prepare notes for your talk.

8 Imagine you are a sponsor with £100 000 to spend on sport. You could spend it by sponsoring an individual, a team, a particular sports event, schemes for young people, or in other ways. Explain what you would hope to gain through your sponsorship and how you would decide on the form of sponsorship.

9 If the Government banned all commercial sponsorship in this country, explain how this might affect sport.

10 For one week, study in detail all the sport shown on television. This is best done in a group with different people allocated to different days or sports. Try, between you, to see as many of the programmes as possible. Your analysis could be presented as a visual display using graphs, tables, diagrams, photographs and reports, including personal comment.

13 LEISURE AND SPORT

Aims

To gain knowledge and understanding of:
- the meaning of leisure
- how the Sports Council encourages sport for all in leisure time
- the economic importance of sport-related activity

To develop the skills of:
- obtaining information from a variety of sources
- analysis and interpretation of information
- interviewing

If we listed the things we did during any one day we would include a great variety of activities. We could put most of them under the simple headings of work, bodily needs, duties and leisure. Some activities would appear in everyone's list, for example sleeping, eating, washing and dressing. We have to do many things to stay healthy.

Work is necessary to earn a living. This takes up a large period of time for many adults. People who spend their day looking after the home and children would include this time as work. Pupils might consider time at school as work. Some activities are closely linked to work. For example, travelling to a job, a teacher marking homework at home and a mechanic reading about car engines in his spare time.

There are also a number of things which we feel obliged to do. These include duties towards the family, pets, house and garden. For example washing up, taking the dog for a walk, mending a leaky tap, mowing the grass, weeding the garden and writing letters.

If we take out of our day the time required for bodily needs, our duties and for work and work linked activities, we are left with free time for leisure activities. The amount of choice we have varies with the activity. We have little choice about staying alive and healthy, more choice about work and duties, and the greatest choice about what we do in our leisure time.

It is not always easy to put activities neatly under the different headings. For example, reading a book for enjoyment on the train to work combines a leisure activity with a work linked activity. Having a meal at a restaurant in the

evening combines a bodily need with a leisure time activity. Also it is not so much the activity but whether or not it is freely chosen that counts. Grass cutting may be hated and therefore a duty, or enjoyed and therefore a leisure activity.

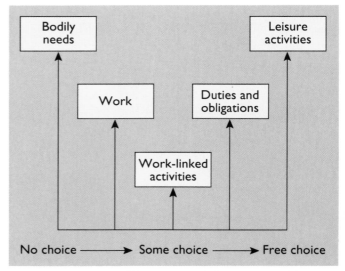

The amount of choice in our daily lives

LEISURE AND WORK

We use the word leisure in two ways. It can mean a period of free time which is left over after work and everything else we have to do is finished. It is also used to describe an activity or something we do. A leisure activity is freely chosen. Most leisure activities take place during leisure time.

In Britain many adults have a pattern to their life set by the need to work regular hours in an office or factory. Leisure time is concentrated into weekends and evenings. Working overtime will reduce opportunities for leisure. People on night and shift work may find advantages in having their leisure time when most people are working. The introduction of flexi-time has allowed some workers to plan their work around their leisure.

The dividing line between work and leisure is not clearcut for everyone. A worker on the production line in a factory with a monotonous, routine job will leave the work behind at the end of his or her shift. Leisure time is seen as free time for enjoyment and satisfaction, quite the opposite of work.

In contrast, a social worker or doctor may have no clear end to the working day. People who have interesting, absorbing jobs are likely to choose freely to continue with work linked activities in their leisure time.

There is a link between taking part in sport and different types of work. Semi and unskilled workers are less likely to take part in sport than professional, non-manual and skilled workers.

For everyone the amount of leisure time will continue to grow. The last thirty years have seen a great increase in leisure time. People in work now have more leisure hours than working hours. There are many reasons why we are becoming a leisure society:

1 Working careers have got shorter as people continue their education longer and retire earlier.

2 People live longer in retirement.

3 Paid holidays have increased.

4 Working weeks have got shorter.

5 Housework takes less time.

6 Unemployment, short-time and part-time work have increased.

The Value of Physical Recreation as a Leisure Time Activity

It is, of course, quite right that people should be free to choose their own leisure time activities. They may be bee keepers, stamp collectors, Red Cross members, train spotters or voluntary workers at an old people's home. All these activities have great value for those involved. Some also have great value for the community. Physical recreation is different and offers different benefits.

Is physical recreation more important than any of these activities?

One of the most important benefits of exercise is to improve physical fitness.

'Present day living is the enemy of the human body. When our ancestors came down from the trees a million or two years ago, they lived an active hunting life, running to catch their food, fighting off predators, struggling to keep warm at night. Modern cities make no such demands on us. Many of us ride to work in our cars or on public transport, work all day at a desk, then slouch in front of the television at night. It's not surprising that our bodies become flabby, stiff and fat.

So the main reason for improving your physical fitness is simply to get more joy out of life. Your body was meant to be used, and when you have given it back its strength and vitality, you will develop a happier, more confident outlook on life as a whole.

The other reasons for taking physical exercise are more sobering. Just as when you leave your car in the garage and don't take it out for a regular spin, the tyres go flat, the bodywork rusts and the battery runs down, so the body that is not exercised begins to degenerate. Unfit, overweight people have a greater than average chance of arthritis, breathing trouble, low back pain and accidents. And there is a lot of evidence that people who do not exercise have a greater chance of developing one of the big killers of our time - heart disease and high blood pressure. Unfit people only live half a life and all too often it ends abruptly...' *Reproduced by kind permission of the Health Council, London.*

Apart from the benefits of exercise, physical recreation offers the opportunity to meet other people. Whether rambling across the countryside, playing tennis at a club or jogging in a fun run, people are able to join in with others. They have the activity as a common interest. This helps to stimulate conversation and encourages friendships to develop.

We are not solitary beings and most of us suffer if denied company for a long period. People can be very lonely even in large cities. Sports and other activities are a way for people to get together - casually as at a swimming pool or more regularly through clubs or regular classes. The success of the London Marathon and other marathons has shown that even the traditionally lonely sport of distance running has its social side.

The success of the London Marathon has shown that even long distance running has its social side

In modern life stress is one of the greatest dangers to health. Worries about work or unemployment, difficulties in the home or just the problem of keeping up with all the demands of modern life, can make people ill. Physical recreation will not usually solve any of these problems.

However it will enable the individual to relax physically and mentally for a while. This break from pressure may itself be beneficial. It may also allow a fresh look to be given to the problems.

PHYSICAL EDUCATION AND LEISURE

PE in school encourages a positive attitude towards sport and physical recreation as future leisure activities

Physical education, like all subjects in the school curriculum, is concerned with the general education of pupils and their development towards maturity. In normal physical education lessons the work centres on physical activities of many kinds.

It is hoped that all pupils will master the basic skills in a wide variety of activities. The subject also encourages the development of a positive attitude towards sport and physical recreation as future leisure activities. The value of regular exercise for good health is explained to pupils.

Physical education aims to give young people physical skills, an understanding of the value of fitness and good health and a desire to be involved in physical recreation. This is the relatively easy part. The difficult part is getting young people at work to continue with sport and making it a lifelong habit.

The statistics from the Sports Council and others show that the school to work gap is difficult to bridge. This is especially true for girls. To combat the problem some schools have made special arrangements. These include linking local sports clubs closely with the school and taking senior pupils to local sports centres.

Alternative leisure activities are too attractive for many young adults. Television, discos and pubs are often more appealing that sports centres and playing fields. Many sports are often, in practice, dominated by a single sex group. Social pressures to take part in activities with the opposite sex are very strong for young people. In the future, the greater involvement of both sexes in most sports may help to encourage more participation.

PHYSICAL EDUCATION, SPORT AND EDUCATIONAL REFORM

Educational reform brings fresh opportunities and new challenges. Schools, local authorities and sport will be affected in a number of ways by the 1986 and 1988 Education Acts.

1 National curriculum

Physical Education has been included in the National Curriculum as a Foundation Subject. As such, attainment targets and programmes of study have been set. Assessment procedures will be needed to check what the pupils achieve in relation to the targets. PE teachers will not have total control over what is taught, only how it is taught.

The National Curriculum for PE will be introduced to schools in 1992. Detailed proposals were completed in August 1991. They consisted of a set of statements saying what each pupil should be able to show they can do at the end of each key stage. There are four key stages covering the years 5 – 16.

Examples of statements include:

By age of 7	'practise and improve their performance.'
By age of 11	'practise, improve and remember more complex sequences of movement.'
By age of 14	'evaluate how well they and others have achieved what they set out to do, appreciate strengths and weaknesses and suggest ways of improving.'
By age of 16	'develop and apply their own criteria for judging performance.'

The main emphasis in these attainment targets is on participation, but they also include planning and evaluation of activities.

The programmes of study for years 5 – 11 should include six areas of activity – athletic activities, dance, games, gymnastic activities, outdoor and adventurous activities and swimming. In years 11 – 14, all pupils should experience all these activities, except swimming, at some point. They should experience at least four areas of activity in any one school year, one of which should be games and one either dance or gymnastic activities.

At the 14 – 16 stage, all pupils not taking GCSE PE should study at least two activities. The choice given to pupils will depend on what the school is able to offer both on and off site.

What is taught to young people at school has a lasting influence. It is hoped that sufficient time will be allocated to physical education in schools. This will enable teachers to produce a nation of physically literate adults who enjoy an active lifestyle.

2 Local management of schools

Management of schools has been moved from the local authority to school governors and the headteacher. Schools are given their own budget to control, based largely on the number of pupils in the school. In general the governors manage the community use of the school premises. However, the local authority still controls the use of schools for Adult Education and the Youth Service.

The governors decide which school facilities are to be made available to the local community and local sports clubs. Also they decide the charges which apply. The need to increase income may lead to increased charges but greater availability of school facilities.

In the past local authorities have paid for schools to use such off-site facilities as swimming pools, sports halls and recreation grounds. School budgets will influence the extent to which schools use these facilities in future.

3 Open enrolment:

Schools are in competition with one another to attract pupils. Wider use of school facilities will involve parents and the community in activities on school sites. This will help enhance the school's reputation and recruitment potential. The quality of physical education in the school and the amount of extra-curricular activity offered will help market the school.

TAKING PART IN SPORT AND PHYSICAL RECREATION - RECENT TRENDS

People take part in sport and physical recreation in many different ways and at a great variety of places. Some people take part very regularly whilst others have no set pattern of participation. This makes collecting exact figures very difficult. Surveys also have to rely on people giving honest answers!

The General Household Survey is a national social survey which has included questions on leisure since 1973. Up to 1986 people were asked to remember the physical recreation activities in which they had taken part during the four weeks before the interview. In 1987 they were given a prompt card with likely activities listed to help their memory.

In 1987, 61% of adults said they had done at least one activity in the four weeks before interview, compared with 46% in 1986. This increase may be partly due to the use of a prompt card. There were large increases in the number of people taking part in cycling, keep fit/yoga and walking two miles or more. 78% said they had done at least one activity in the twelve months before interview. Easily the most popular form of physical recreation was walking. Next came snooker/billiards/pool and then swimming.

Participation is linked to gender, age and social class. Overall men outnumbered women in sports participation with only keep fit/yoga and horse

Participation rates in sports in the four weeks before interview

Persons aged 16 or over	%
Walking	37.9
Snooker/billiards/pool	15.1
Swimming: indoor	3.5
Swimming: outdoor	10.5
Darts	8.8
Keep fit/yoga	8.6
Cycling	8.4
Athletics – track and field	0.5
Other running (including jogging)	5.2
Football	4.8
Golf	3.9
Badminton	3.4
Squash	2.6
Table tennis	2.4
Fishing	1.9
Tennis	1.8
Cricket	1.2
Water sports (excluding sailing)	1.1
Horse riding	0.9
Self defence (excluding boxing)	0.8
Ice skating	0.8
Sailing yachts/dinghies	0.6
At least one activity	61

Source: HMSO: *General Household Survey* 1987

'Top ten' sports for men and women. Rank order for the four weeks before interview (1987)

All aged 16 or over	Men	Women
Walking	1	1
Snooker/billiards/pool	2	5
Swimming (indoor and outdoor)	3	2
Darts	4	6
Cycling	5	4
Keep fit/yoga		3
Golf	6	
Football	7	
Running (excluding track, including jogging)	8	7
Weightlifting/weight training	9	8
Fishing	10	
Tennis		9
Badminton		10

Source: HMSO: *General Household Survey* 1987

riding having more women than men. For most activities there was a decline in participation with age. Some activities, such as golf, sailing and walking, showed smaller differences with age. Taking part is linked to social class. 78% of people in the professional class compared with 42% of the unskilled manual group took part in at least one activity in the four weeks before interview. However there were exceptions to this pattern; for example the skilled manual group had the highest rate for taking part in darts and fishing.

THE SPORTS COUNCIL'S PLANS

Nearly half the population takes part in some form of sport and recreation, and many more watch on television. There are a vast number of bodies providing opportunities to take part in sport. Examples include national organisations, local authorities and sports clubs. Sport is important to the nation in many ways - for good health, for social reasons, for national morale, for enjoyment and satisfaction and for the jobs it supports and consumer expenditure involved.

It is the task of the Sports Council to try to organise much of this activity to avoid unnecessary duplication and wasted effort.

THE NEXT TEN YEARS

In 1982 the Sports Council presented a new plan called 'Sport in the Community - The Next Ten Years'. This plan wanted to encourage participation and increase sports facilities. It aimed for:

- A 70% increase in women's participation in indoor sports and a 35% increase in outdoor sports.
- A 15% increase in men's participation in sport.
- More and better facilities for a wide range of sports.
- Improved coaching, and better training and competition venues to help achieve international success.

By 1988 achievements included:

- Nearly 1 million extra women had been attracted into indoor sport.
- 600 000 more men were taking part in indoor sport and 400 000 in outdoor sport.
- Participation by middle-aged and older people had increased considerably.
- Many 'healthy lifestyle' activities showed an increase in participation (swimming, keep fit, jogging, cycling).
- The target of 50 new pools had been exceeded by 100.
- Support for coaching had improved considerably with the setting up of the NCF.
- National Sports Centres had received major improvements.

Problems remaining included:

- Fall in number of women taking part in outdoor sport.
- Relatively little success in attracting young people into sport.

- Less than half dry indoor sports facilities provided.
- Lack of co-ordination in helping people on ladder to sporting success.
- No national indoor arenas. Top level facilities for many sports remain poor.
- Resources of Council inadequate to meet the needs of communities and those seeking high standards.

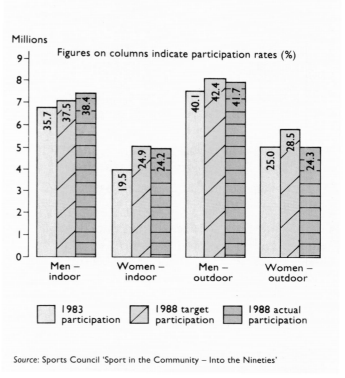

Source: Sports Council 'Sport in the Community – Into the Nineties'

Revised participation targets and assessments of achievement 1983 – 1988

INTO THE NINETIES

In 1988 the Sports Council updated its plans for the next five years in the light of progress in the previous five years. It published 'Sport in the Community : Into the Nineties'.

The Council was concerned with the development of two groups in society. The larger group is generally well-off and takes advantage of the sporting opportunities. The smaller group is generally poor and the benefits of increased leisure and 'Sport for All' have passed it by.

The Council also believes that the development of major facilities is controlled by the amount of Government money made available to local authorities.

There are three themes for increasing community participation:

- encourage an extra 1.25 million women and 750 000 men into sport.
- give particular emphasis to young people and women, especially any who are unemployed, from ethnic minorities or disabled.
- encourage the provision of: 500 new sports halls, 150 new swimming pools, improvements to playing fields, new artificial pitches, more safe routes for cyclists and joggers, improved access to sports sites in countryside and on water.

There are three themes for those aiming for the higher sporting level:

- encourage clear links between coaching, sports medicine, sports science and other support services.
- encourage the building of major national facilities for competition and training.
- encourage regional and local plans for developing talent.

To achieve these targets the Council would support and co-ordinate the efforts of all the bodies involved. In appropriate cases financial help would also be provided. The Council would need an extra £11 million to finance these plans.

SPORTS COUNCIL CAMPAIGNS: 1972 'Sport for All'

This campaign aimed to change how people thought about sport. It showed that sport was of value to everyone in the community. It hoped that the public response would put pressure on public bodies to provide sporting opportunities. Above all it promoted sport as a desirable social idea. As such it encouraged participation by all sections of the community in sport and physical recreation.

Initially the campaign attempted to provide the best possible opportunities for the greatest number of people. Gradually evidence emerged of lack of success with some groups of people. Only then were policies agreed to target these groups.

The aims of the campaign fit into a number of broad areas:

- To increase participation of the public at large.
- To improve performance at every stage.
- To establish the principle that providing opportunities to take part in sport is a social service.
- To bring the social benefits of participation to a wider population.
- To create wider opportunities for enjoyment of leisure time through physical activities.
- To improve the quality of life.
- To promote the idea of better health through regular physical activity.

Over the years special emphasis has been placed on targetting particular groups or following special themes. In 1975/6 'Sport for All the Family Year' put a special focus on family recreation. In 1979 the 'Sport for All - Come Alive' campaign emphasised positive health through regular exercise.

The success of these campaigns is hard to assess. The Sports Council starts the campaign, but it is up to other agencies in the community to develop the ideas. The regional councils for sport and recreation are in a powerful position to promote them. However it is the local group leaders who determine whether the idea is put into practice or ignored.

DISABLED PEOPLE AND SPORT

1981 was the International Year of Disabled People, organised by the United Nations. This focussed attention on disabled people, both their special needs and the contribution they can make to society.

The Sports Council added its own campaign 'Sport for All - Disabled People'. This had a number of aims:

1 To make people aware of the needs of the disabled and to give an understanding of their problems.
2 To encourage the disabled to take part in a wide variety of physical activities.
3 To encourage mixing of the able bodied and disabled for the benefit of all.
4 To involve the disabled in physical recreation and the world at large.

Above all the aim was for disabled people to enjoy sport for its own sake.

The Council hoped to stimulate interest that would continue in the future. A variety of events was organised, including the International Disabled Children's Games at Gateshead.

Three particular groups were thought to have been neglected and need special attention. These were people with a mental handicap, those with progressive diseases and the elderly disabled.

The success of such campaigns is difficult to assess. Certainly there was great public interest in the achievement of Neroli Fairhall at the 1982 Commonwealth Games. Competing for New Zealand, she won the gold medal for archery, having been confined to a wheelchair since a motorcycle accident in 1969. She was the first paraplegic to win a major title in open competition. In Britain great encouragement has been given to wheelchair athletes by their inclusion in a number of long distance races. For those disabled athletes talented at sport, there is the opportunity to compete in the special Olympic Games for the disabled.

SPORT FOR THE OLDER PERSON

In January 1983, the Sports Council launched a nationwide campaign aimed at older people. Called 'Fifty Plus - All to Play For' it aimed to get hundreds of thousands more people between the ages of fifty and sixty to take part in some form of active sport or recreation.

To encourage people to become involved, a series of attractive, colourful leaflets was produced, saying:

'Playing's better than watching and it'll bring out the best in you. You're never too old to start, so take up something now, you've got all to play for.'

The leaflets also answered important questions about health check ups, which sports to try, how to get started and above all the advantages of physical recreation.

At the same time local and regional Sports Councils, together with other groups, organised many different events especially aimed at the 50 plus age groups. The whole campaign stressed not only the physical benefits from activity, but the social advantages of getting out of the house and making new friends.

YOUNG PEOPLE AND SPORT

1985 saw the Sports Council link its own campaign with that of the International Year of Youth. The 'Ever Thought of Sport?' campaign was jointly sponsored by Weetabix. It was aimed at the 13 to 24 year old age group, especially those who had given up sport on leaving school. It tried to capture the imagination of young people and involve them in sport during their leisure time. The campaign was supported by good promotional literature with both television and radio exposure.

AN INFORMATION CAMPAIGN

As a follow-up to the 'Ever Thought of Sport?' campaign, 'What's Your Sport?' was launched in 1987. Sponsored by the Milk Marketing Board, this was the biggest campaign of its type yet seen. Linked to television commercials, viewers were invited to send for a 'sports pack' of information. This information was provided by a wide range of organisations. It was hoped to set up a permanent information system for people in their own locality. Over 100 000 enquiries were received and 1 200 local information points set up within a year.

In 1989, the second phase of the campaign 'Milk in Action for Women' was launched. It aimed to encourage all women to take part in physical activity whether they saw themselves as 'sporty' or not. On the opening day sports centres around the country invited women to come in and sample a wide range of activities. Follow up schemes were designed to keep their interest.

'Bring a Friend into Sport' was the theme of the day. Active women from local clubs were asked to bring along at least one woman who did not take part in sport. This 'sisterly' practice had worked well in the Reebok Running Sisters Network in which women runners had helped inactive women to start running.

YEAR OF SPORT

The Sports Council declared 1991 the 'Year of Sport' to coincide with a wide range of international events held in Britain. Centre stage was the World Student Games and around it 120 sporting bodies created a special programme of events from 'Come and Try It' days to major championships. There were sports festivals, inter-town challenges, fitness roadshows, with a special week of sport in support of Comic Relief. People were encouraged to enjoy a healthy active lifestyle by involving themselves with the activities offered.

SPORT AND DEPRIVED AREAS

The whole country was shocked by the riots in Brixton, Toxteth, Moss Side and other inner city areas of Britain in 1981. The Scarman Report examined the problems. Sport was not prominent in the report.

However, in the Toxteth area of Liverpool, the Government offered £1 million for sports facilities, if the same amount was raised from private or voluntary sources. This was achieved and the Sports Council was asked to administer the scheme. Included were many improvements to pitches and playing areas, a new sports hall, water adventure centre and a large supply of equipment to help 69 clubs throughout Merseyside. This £ for £ programme was extended for a longer period and to other inner city areas.

The offer of government help may be seen as recognition of the important role sport can play as part of leisure in inner cities. Sport indeed may help to reduce social problems in deprived areas.

The Sports Council has its own programme to help special areas. In 1976 grants were allocated to areas of special need. Demonstration programmes for areas of unemployment were begun in 1980. The Action Sport scheme for London and West Midlands inner city areas was established in 1982. £3 million over a three year period was provided to train sports motivators to go out into the streets. They aimed to get those people who normally miss out on sport involved in some sporting activity.

This scheme was very successful and expanded nationwide over the following years. The emphasis was on people, not facilities. It captured the imagination and within months many local authorities were setting up 'action sport' teams of their own. Above all the scheme showed the value of sports leadership in inner cities. This particular approach brought sporting opportunities for participation to the disadvantaged.

In 1989 a report on 'Sport and Active

Recreation Provision in the Inner Cities' was published. The three main conclusions were:

(i) Those providing facilities and other sporting opportunities must help motivated local people to become closely involved with sports provision.
(ii) Proper training, recruitment and career structure must be set up for outreach workers, sports leaders and coaches.
(iii) Resources must now be directed at people, with less emphasis on facilities.

THE RUNNING BOOM

Hardly anyone in Britain can have failed to notice the great increase in interest in running and jogging. Day and night the runners are out in the streets and on the paths. Gone are the old plimsolls, the long shorts and the baggy tracksuits. The new image is of purpose-made running shoes, well cut shorts and fashionable rain suits. Although still male dominated, runners of both sexes, old and young are pounding out the miles.

The London Marathon, thanks to television, has become an internationally famous event. In 1991, 23 000 runners finished the course. The sight of so many runners competing together has encouraged many people to have a go. No doubt the distressed state of some of the finishers has convinced others of the advantage of the fireside and television.

The demand for races is now very great. Over one hundred marathons are held each year. Long distance running beyond the marathon is also increasing in popularity. In 1983 the Crane brothers from Britain ran the length of the Himalayas, a distance of 2 027 miles, in 101 days. Only eight weeks later Richard Crane was first in the Quadrathon. This consisted of a two mile swim, 32 mile walk, 100 mile cycle ride and a full 26 mile marathon. Few people would wish to push themselves to the limits of their endurance in this way. However, judging from entries for all races from fun runs through to marathons, there appears to be no end to the present running boom.

CYCLING TAKES OFF

Not so long ago the image of the cyclist was all cloth cap and bicycle clips. Apart from a dedicated band of racing cyclists, few people rode bicycles from choice.

Today, following the creation of the mountain bike, all this has changed. The riders are likely to be young and fit, men and women alike, dressed in fashionable bright coloured, skin-tight bike wear. The image is of fitness, freedom and fashion.

In the mid-eighties annual sales in Britain were down to 1.5 million - everyone wanted four wheels not two. However, by 1990 sales had risen to 2.25 million and in 1991 were expected to exceed 2 million for the fifth year running. Between 50 and 60% of bikes sold now are mountain bikes.

The success story of the mountain bike started in California, where sturdy bikes were used to ride the rough mountain trails. Soon Japanese companies perfected the technology which allowed the bike to be mass produced with sophisticated gearing, pedalling and braking mechanisms. In Britain 'Muddy Fox', the first company to sell the bikes, sold 30 in 1981 but its turnover in 1989 was £13 million!

The marketing of the bikes has been a major feature of their success. The advertising has portrayed a glamorous image. Bikes were shown in exciting places, emphasising the fun and freedom they gave. Riders were dressed in colours and styles associated with other leisure sports like skiing and windsurfing. The leisure bike has captured people's imagination.

The popularity of the bikes has been helped by the exploits of some adventurers. Nicholas

Cycling has become a very popular sport since the creation of the mountain bike

and Richard Crane, for example, in 1984 rode up the highest mountain in Africa, 5 894 m Kilimanjaro. National and World Championships are on the race calendar and have produced a new group of sports stars.

The once-threatened cycle industry is not sitting back on its success. There is great pressure to improve braking, suspension and performance.

SPORT AND THE LEISURE INDUSTRY

The leisure industry has grown up to meet the needs of people who have money to spend on their free time interests. Today this industry is big business. It is largely made up of enterprises run for profit. Some leisure facilities like parks, libraries, galleries and museums are provided by local or central government. Many theatres, orchestras, ballet and opera companies also receive government grants.

For the private enterprise part of the industry to survive, the public must be willing to pay for its products or services. Although the overall demand is growing, fashions change.

Sport has always been an important part of the leisure industry. It too has been affected by changes in public demand. Interest has declined recently in such activities as darts and table tennis. Ten-pin bowling has recovered from a decline in the 70's to increasing popularity today. Cycling has leapt in popularity.

THE ECONOMIC IMPACT OF SPORT

The growth of sport as a leisure-time activity has turned it into a major industry. People are spending more of their income on sport as part of leisure.

Public money has been put into sport through the Sports Council and local authorities. It has been justified by the personal, social and health benefits of taking part in sport. To this should be added another reason - the contribution made by sport to economic wealth. The Sports Council asked the Henley Centre for Forecasting to look into the economic impact of sport in the United Kingdom. They produced reports in 1986 and 1991.

Consumer expenditure on sport related goods and services

	1985 prices £m	1989 prices £m
Admission	121	233
Sports goods	375	722
Bicycles	28	43
Boats	290	1 190
Participants sports, subscriptions, ad hoc admissions	533	990
Clothing and footwear: Sales Repairs and laundry	725 46	1 884 34
Travel	416	343
Magazines	66	38
Books	3	63
Newspapers	266	319
BBC licence	95	136
Skiing holidays	243	373
Sub total:	3 207	6 368
Gambling : Football pools horse racing	385 774	495 1 999
Total:	£4 366m	£8 862m

Selected categories of consumer's expenditure

	1985 £m	1989 £m
Motor vehicles	9 916	17 363
Beer	8 347	10 677
Cigarettes	6 115	7 244
Electricity	4 860	5 787
Furniture	4 639	6 005
Sport, including gambling	4 366	8 862
Bread	4 051	5 575
Gas	4 046	4 424
Menswear	3 981	5 412
Spirits	3 861	4 641
Wines and ciders	3 847	4 500
Sport, excluding gambling	3 207	6 368
DIY goods	2 616	4 655
Newspapers/magazines	2 273	2 949
Pets	1 278	2 014
Records	783	1 653

The comparison between 1985 and 1989 shows the rising importance of sport. The sports sector has grown faster than most other consumer expenditure categories. The real increase in expenditure for sport, including gambling, was 67.9% over the four years.

UK employment in selected sectors in 1985

Construction	968 000
Transport	878 000
Mechanical engineering	803 000
Food, drink, tobacco	620 000
Postal services and telecommunication	432 000
Sport-related economic activity	376 000
Chemicals and man-made fibres	352 000
Agriculture, forestry and fishing	336 000
Electricity, gas, other energy and water supply	336 000
Motor vehicles and parts	291 000
Coal, oil, natural gas extraction and processing	282 000

Sport-related economic activity (1985 Prices)

Income

VAT & excise duties
£770m
Betting duty
£537m
Income tax & NI
£951m
Rail fares (to British Rail)
£22m
Corporation Tax
£163m

£2 443m

Income

Central Government
Grants
£425m
Grant from Urban
programme
£24m
Sports Council
£10m
Fees & charges from public
£134m
Rates paid by firms and
institutions
£120m
other
£25m

£738 m

Central Government

Expenditure

Rate Support Grant
(sport-related
component)
£425m
Grants to
Sports Council
£37m
and Urban Programme
£24m
other
£59m

£545m

Expenditure

Direct spending on labour
and other running
expenses
£531m
Sport-related component
of education expenditure
£300m
Administration
£90m
Urban programme
£24m
other
£45m

£990m

Local Authorities

These statistics from the reports show clearly the importance of the sports sector to the economy as a whole. There is a complex economic relationship between the state, the voluntary and commercial sports sectors, individual consumers and other parts of the economy.

CLOTHING AND EQUIPMENT FOR SPORT

The clothing and equipment trade is a very important part of the leisure industry today. Some brand names are immediately recognised throughout the world for their sporting connections. Companies go to great lengths to advertise their products. Professional and amateur teams and players wear clothing and use equipment with the manufacturer's name clear for all to see, especially television cameras.

Today, not only is sports wear acceptable as ordinary casual clothing, it is very fashionable. Sports shoes, track suits and sweat shirts are seen in every high street. This merging of sportswear and ordinary clothes has greatly benefitted manufacturers. There is a great range of modern styles in attractive colours to suit all sports and interests.

Equipment for sport is also available in great variety. Again companies are anxious to have the top players using their equipment. In games such

as tennis and golf, star players are paid large sums of money to use particular brands of goods. For international sportsmen and sportswomen requiring large, expensive pieces of equipment like boats, canoes, cars and cycles, financial help is needed. The purchasing of expensive equipment does present a severe obstacle to some up and coming sportsmen and sportswomen in particular sports, and sponsorship is essential.

TELEVISION AND SPORT

During our leisure time we may have the choice of watching television or playing sport. Then sport and television are in direct competition. However television has also done much to help the development of sport.

Since 1927 the BBC has broadcast radio commentaries on the major sporting events including the Boat Race, the Grand National, the Derby, the FA Cup Final and more recently Wimbledon and Test matches. The sports commentators have also played their part in popularising sport. John Arlott (cricket) and Eddie Waring (rugby league) became almost inseparable from their games.

Some sports, such as show jumping, snooker and American football, owe their present popularity to the exposure they received on television. Other sports have benefitted greatly from television, including ice skating, gymnastics and athletics. Channel 4 has been very important in bringing new sports to the viewing public. In particular American football, but many others of which Kabbaddi is the latest.

A number of people have protested at the overall amount of sport seen on television. This happens regularly when major sporting events are televised, especially when the competition takes place over a number of days.

Television helps sport in many ways:

- Interest may be stimulated and viewers may become participants or spectators.

- Exposure on television encourages sponsors to invest in the sport.

- Minority sports can be publicised.

- Sports personalities may emerge and develop a following.

NEWSPAPERS, MAGAZINES AND SPORT

Most newspapers include a sports section which contains reports of events, comments, sports news and articles on fitness. Despite the great interest in sport in Britain, there is no national daily newspaper devoted to sport. In France, L'Equipe is the daily sports paper.

Although many articles are factual and descriptive, some rely on sensationalism. Indeed some sportswriters have been criticised for both building up sports stars and teams and then pulling them apart when they have failed. There is no doubt that sports writers have a great deal of influence on the opinions of sports fans.

As with newspapers, there is no national magazine which deals with all sports. Interest centres around one sport or a group of similar sports and there are many magazines.

HOOLIGANISM – AN UNWANTED BY-PRODUCT

Hooliganism, vandalism and violence associated with crowds at professional football matches have grown over many years. This behaviour seems to have its roots in society in general rather than in sport. It finds a convenient expression through sport. Football would often appear to be far away from the minds of those involved. Violence on the field is not directly linked to violence amongst the crowd.

Although the problems are caused by only a small minority of those present, their effect has been considerable. Visiting supporters are escorted to and from their transport and segregated in the ground. Some fans have been killed and many innocent people injured, both in and around the grounds. Even the players on the field have been attacked with darts and other objects. Damage to shops and public transport has been very serious. On some match days shops have been boarded up, pubs closed and public transport withdrawn.

The hooliganism has not been limited to Football League and Cup matches. After one England versus Scotland match at Wembley Stadium the pitch was torn up, goal posts pulled down and the whole area terrorised outside the stadium. Abroad England's fans have earned a dreadful reputation. Many countries have now imposed strict controls on these fans.

The Football Association and clubs often appear powerless to control the hooligans, although a whole variety of measures has been tried. Some people have blamed television and the press for giving the hooligans too much publicity.

They say this encourages hooliganism.

A major effect of violence and hooliganism has been to reduce attendances at matches, especially amongst young people and families. However, the four seasons since 1985/86 have all shown a healthy upward trend in attendances, as the amount of hooliganism has declined.

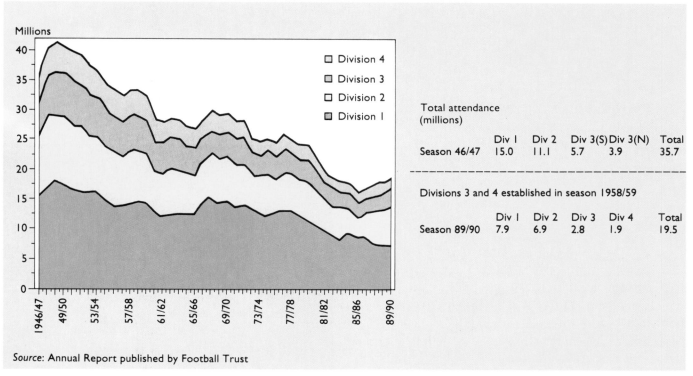

Total attendance (millions)					
	Div 1	Div 2	Div 3(S)	Div 3(N)	Total
Season 46/47	15.0	11.1	5.7	3.9	35.7

Divisions 3 and 4 established in season 1958/59

	Div 1	Div 2	Div 3	Div 4	Total
Season 89/90	7.9	6.9	2.8	1.9	19.5

Source: Annual Report published by Football Trust

Football league attendances 1946/47 – 1989/90

MILLWALL IN THE COMMUNITY

In June 1986, Millwall Football Club faced a crisis common to many football league clubs in the 80's. Falling gates, high wages and over-reaching ambition combined to bring the club to the brink of extinction, at a time of outright public disdain for football. Millwall had an added problem - its supporters' reputation for hooliganism and violence.

The club was saved by businessmen fans who believed in the club and the community it served. Traditionally the club had recruited from London and South East England. The club already had a Community Development Officer, whose job was to open up the club to the local community. In 1987 Lewisham Council became the club's sponsors in a £280 000 four year deal. Many new links with the community followed.

A creche was made available on match days and complimentary tickets given to community groups. The Lionesses, the women's football club, were encouraged and given use of the club's pitch and facilities. John Stalker, the former Assistant Chief Constable of Greater Manchester, advised on improving relationships with the police. Players went into primary and secondary schools to coach groups of children. Sports editors were visited by the Vice Chairman who explained what Millwall was trying to achieve.

In the year up to April 1991, 40 schools were visited with 1 500 boys and girls aged 8 to 11 years taking part in the schools' coaching programme. The holiday and after school coaching programme attracted 1 600 participants. All the players took part in the fun run, together with another 500 runners. The club provided up to 40 placements for students on work experience. Millwall's work with young offenders was highly commended.

The Club Chairman, Reg Burr, said *'Our wish, our task, our commitment was to return Millwall to the people. We wanted to bring football home'*.

SPORT, ENTERTAINMENT AND THE SPECTATOR

When is an activity sport and when is it entertainment? Circus acrobats, trapeze artists and high wire walkers are not usually called sportsmen and sportswomen. Nevertheless some of the tricks they perform would be difficult for Olympic champion gymnasts. The Harlem Globetrotters are professional basketball players who developed a highly successful show around their game. They sometimes seemed to be both sportsmen and entertainers.

In professional wrestling, the wrestlers excite the crowd with a series of violent attacks on each other. The whole show often appears to be stage-managed, but considerable skill is still required.

You can see that it is sometimes very difficult to separate sport and entertainment. One important factor is the importance of the spectators. Activities which have the spectators very much in mind are likely to be closely linked to entertainment. If spectators or an audience are not very important for the activity, then it is more likely to be called sport.

Professional Sports

Professional sport must always be linked to entertainment. Entrance fees paid by spectators are necessary to provide money to pay the professional performers. People pay to watch a sporting event for the entertainment value of the match or competition. They expect to enjoy it, as well as to see a high level of skill and exciting play.

Giant Haystacks is a professional wrestler who attracts large crowds

It seems likely that most professional tennis and golf players would play the game even if they were not paid. Although they must concentrate first of all on their game, they must not forget the importance of the spectators.

Amateur Sports

In contrast to professional sport, most amateur sport depends only on the people taking part. They compete together because they enjoy the sport and get satisfaction from being involved.

However, rugby union players and amateur athletes who play or compete at international level are in a special position. They can attract thousands of spectators to fill stadiums. The audience is important to give the event the right atmosphere. Also the spectators pay a lot of money to see the event. This money goes to the organisers and the governing body of the sport. Large crowds encourage sponsors to support the sport.

Performing

Every sport has its own set of rules, forms of play and codes of conduct. These are so much part of the game that they are not thought about by those involved in sport. However, if a sport is worried about its entertainment value, changes may be made to attract more spectators. In trying to establish professional soccer in the USA, attempts were made to play the game in a number of shorter periods to suit television. Also rule changes were tried to make it a higher scoring game.

The pressure to win can be very great for professionals and top amateurs. Codes of conduct have to be strict to ensure the event's attractiveness for spectators and sponsors.

Sport has its own standards of play or performance. This allows teams and individuals to be compared with others at present or in the past.

In entertainment the action can be framed to ensure the audience enjoys it. In sport the action is largely under the control of those taking part. However, sportsmen and sportswomen are increasingly controlled by agents, coaches, managers and trainers. The American footballer has little freedom of action compared with the long distance runner. The professional wrestler may be considered more an actor on a stage, than a sportsman.

THINGS TO DO

1 Make a detailed survey of the next seven days of your life. Keep a record of the time you spend on each of the following activities: sleep, rest, watching television, attending school/college, study, sport, leisure. Compare your survey with others in your group.

2 Make a survey of sports coverage on television or in the newspapers for the next week. Breakdown the information into individual sports and the time allotted to them.

3 (i) We talk of *leisure time* activities. What do we mean by leisure time?
 (ii) Is leisure time likely to become greater in the future? Give reasons for your answer.

4 Water sports, squash and golf have increased considerably in popularity in recent years. Give your reasons to account for the increase in their popularity.

5 A lot of sport is seen on television.
 (i) Give two reasons why this might increase participation in sport.
 (ii) Give two reasons why this might create a nation of non-participants.

6 Imagine you are an active sportsman or sportswomen suddenly disabled, but still able to compete in some sport. Talk about your disability and explain how you intend continuing to play sport. Describe the problems you need to overcome and where you could turn for advice and help.

7 You have been invited to speak at a meeting of local sports officials on the topic 'Leisure in the future'. Prepare notes using the following headings as guidelines:

Work patterns, travel facilities, coaching and teaching needs, provision of facilities, the dangers of inactivity.

8 The circus trapeze artist and the Olympic gymnast both have great skill. The circus act is called entertainment and the gymnastics is called sport. Is there a difference between sport and entertainment? Discuss your answer using a number of different activities.

9 Place the following activities on a line labelled sport at one end and entertainment at the other:

ice dance, ballroom dancing, synchronised swimming, professional wrestling, circus acrobats, international rugby, hang gliding, tobogganing, ten pin bowling

10 Your favourite leisure time activity is not at present included in the Olympic programme. Write a letter to the Chairman of the IOC explaining why you think your activity should be included in future Olympics.

11 'The professional wrestler may be considered more an actor on stage than a sportsman.'

Discuss this statement.

12 Find out which particular sporting activities are provided for the disabled at your local sports centre. Contact the manager to ask permission to carry out a survey to see how 'user friendly' it is to disabled people. You will need to draw up a checklist of items to include amongst other things - access, entrance, signs, assistance, corridors, changing rooms, spectating areas. If possible contact any disabled person who uses the centre to find out what they think.

13 In your group, design and carry out a survey in order to assess the following for your area - the average amount of leisure time for adults, the sports participation levels by age, the leisure spending patterns of the different age groups. Produce a visual display to show your results.

14 Conduct a debate in your group on the motion 'The Government should spend a much larger amount of money on sport and leisure facilities than it does at the moment'. You will need to appoint a Chairperson and you will need people to propose and support the motion and others to oppose it. Questions from the floor should be allowed before a vote is taken on the motion.

14   SPORT AS A CAREER

Aims

To gain knowledge and understanding of:

- the life of a professional sportsman or sportswoman
- careers in sport other than as a participant
- advantages and disadvantages of careers in sport

To develop the skills of:

- communication
- role play

When we talk about careers in sport we usually think of the pop star life style of some of the top sports stars. We must remember that these are the lucky few. The rewards for the majority of professional sportsmen and sportswomen are much less. It is possible to work in sport apart from performing. Most of these jobs do not make the headlines, although they are essential to sport.

To succeed as a professional performer in any sport you need a number of qualities, including a lot of natural ability, a willingness to work hard, a determination to succeed and some luck! Failure may be caused by any number of things. Laziness, lack of desire to win, loss of form, illness or injury are some reasons. Of course age catches up with all players, even the greatest. Although many

Paul Gascoigne is injured after challenging Gary Charles in the 1991 FA Cup Final

Nigel Mansell has won many trophies

sportsmen and sportswomen start out on the ladder to success, few achieve their dreams.

Professional players usually only have a short career in sport. There are always eager young players waiting their turn. Players should be prepared for the day when they have to look for a new career.

Many young people who are keen on sport are not good enough to become professional players. There are still many opportunities for them to be involved in sport when choosing a career. Although being a professional player appears very attractive, a career in sport brings its own special problems.

The major sports that support professional performers in Britain are football, rugby league, cricket, tennis, golf, boxing, speedway, horse racing and racing motorcars and motorcycles. Professionals are also to be found in squash, badminton, basketball, cycling, bowls, showjumping, billiards and snooker, darts, table tennis and ice skating.

Soccer

There are very many talented schoolboys and the competition to be taken on by a professional club is very strong. Although quite a lot of boys sign 'associated schoolboy' forms, few are offered apprenticeships. Only the very best eventually sign contracts. There are about 2 000 full time professional players at present in Britain.

Boys still at school need their parents' permission to sign associated schoolboy forms. They then have regular training sessions and play matches for their club outside school hours. At sixteen they may be signed as a trainee on a two year Youth Training Scheme contract. This means they work full-time at the club and attend a day-release course at a college. They train with the senior players, take part in youth matches and help with the many chores at the club. Contracts are only offered to the very best trainees at eighteen, the others have to leave the club. Players who are rejected by league clubs may find places in a club in the numerous semi-professional leagues. The players are part-time footballers who combine a normal job with evening and weekend matches, for which they are paid.

In 1984, the Football Association established a School of Excellence at Lilleshall National Sports Centre. Sixteen outstanding boys of 14 or 15 are selected each year. They live at the centre, develop their skills under the best coaches and attend a nearby school for normal lessons during the two year course.

Rugby League

Rugby league players in Britain are usually only part-time professionals with a regular job outside football. Few players are able to make a living from the game although the number is increasing. They train and play in the evenings, and at weekends. It is a hard life. The rugby is fiercely competitive, making the players' other jobs often difficult to cope with.

Rugby league players are usually only part-time professionals

Scouts from the professional clubs look for young talent in amateur rugby league and rugby union sides. Only the very best prospects are offered a signing-on fee and a contract.

In Britain the professional game is mainly played in Cumbria, Yorkshire and Lancashire. In recent years new teams have been formed in the South, for example Fulham Rugby League Football Club has established a sound base for the sport in London.

Cricket

During the season, from April to September, cricketers are fully employed. Matches follow one after the other, including weekends, and there are few breaks. A lot of travelling is also involved.

The eighteen county cricket clubs in Britain employ about 350 players. Good schoolboy players are spotted in representative games. They are then invited to junior coaching courses and to play for county colt or junior teams. If they are taken on by a county, they will play in the second eleven at first.

A very high level of skill is essential to be a professional cricketer. Long hours of practice are needed to develop the players' ability. Many players continue playing the top level for far longer than in most other sports. Financial rewards are not great unless you are an outstanding player. During the winter many players have to find other jobs. Top players may play or coach abroad.

Golf

The glamorous world of the golf superstar is not typical of the life of most golf professionals. The majority work at golf clubs or driving ranges. To be a professional at a club, a handicap in a low single figure is necessary, together with a willingness to accept poor pay during the early years. 'The Pro' gives lessons to club members and runs the club shop. There is usually an assistant who learns about the business side of the club and also coaches members. Hours are long, especially in the summer, and include weekend work.

Most golf professionals work as coaches at clubs or driving ranges

In order to play in the tournament circuit, a PGA players' ticket is necessary. This may be applied for, if you have a handicap of less than two. It allows you to enter pre-qualifying competitions which lead to tournaments at the top level.

The tournament golf player has many expenses to meet, including travelling, hotel and living expenses. In order to make a living the golfer needs to win prize money regularly.

Horse Racing

To ride a race horse, at sixteen a boy must weigh under seven stones (45 kilos) and a girl under eight stones (51 kilos). There are two routes for becoming an apprentice. A school leaver might gain a place at the British Racing School at Newmarket or the Northern Racing School at Doncaster. He or she would need to be over sixteen, light and fit. After completing the course, successful apprentices will be offered to a trainer. Alternatively a young person might go direct to a trainer and be accepted as an apprentice.

National hunt jockeys ride over fences. They are heavier than flat racing jockeys. There is no formal training scheme although a form of apprenticeship for 'Conditional Jockeys' has been introduced. Their careers start later at about seventeen or eighteen and usually develop from experience jumping fences in point-to-point racing. They all start their careers with a trainer.

Jockeys work hard especially early in their careers. They have to get used to the travelling as well as riding and stable routines.

Young jockeys are often apprenticed to a trainer

Tennis

To become a professional tennis player, you need to be very good. However, ability is not enough on its own. Hours of daily practice are needed to improve your game.

Progress for the young player depends on winning tournaments. The successful player may be asked to join the county training squad. Promotion is then through the regional squad to national level. The very best may be invited to the National Tennis Centre at Bisham Abbey National Sports Centre for intensive coaching. Only when players are in the British top 20 will they be invited to tournaments where prize money will cover their expenses.

There are about 80 professional players in Britain at present. Although the life seems glamorous, it involves a lot of travelling at home and abroad. The rewards are very high for those who reach the top. The less successful must still win enough prize money to pay for their living and playing expenses.

Other Sports

Only a few major professional sports have been looked at in detail. It is noticeable that most of the professional players are men. Only in tennis and golf are women professional players found in numbers.

Athletics in Britain is still an amateur sport. However the rules on amateurism have been changed to allow athletes to earn money. This is done by building up a trust fund from sponsorship, appearance money and other income. Living and competition expenses may be paid from the fund. At the end of their amateur career the fund is available to the athlete.

Professional athletics has been attempted in the past. It has not yet been really successful. Usually it has failed and left a number of athletes financially better off but disqualified from amateur competition.

Apart from athletics, a number of other amateur sports have a trust fund system including boxing, swimming, gymnastics and judo.

Today many top amateur sportsmen and sportswomen receive generous financial help which enables them to concentrate full-time on their training and competitions without having to work. Although still remaining amateurs, in many ways their career is sport.

THE ADVANTAGES AND DISADVANTAGES OF PROFESSIONAL SPORT

To most young people it is very attractive to be able to work at something you enjoy doing and get paid for it. Professional sportsmen and sportswomen seem to have an ideal life. Although usually young, they earn a lot of money, often travel about the world and are in the public eye. However this world is reserved for the lucky few, and for each of the stars there are many other professionals in the same sport whose life is quite different. They may have failed to reach the top for any one of many reasons.

Most sports involve the risk of injury. Accidents outside of sport and serious illness can also affect a player's career. Any long break from training or competition will influence performance for some time.

Apart from illness, accident or injury, players may find that they are not good enough to reach the highest level. They may not fulfil their early promise.

For those at the top, there is the pressure of the ambitious players below who are anxious to take their place. Being in the limelight, especially at a young age, may bring its own problems. The demands of press and public can be very great.

In professional sports, rewards are related to success. Players have to look for new careers half way through their working lives.

Teaching

Most physical education teachers work in secondary schools teaching a wide variety of games and physical activities. Physical Education is a foundation subject in the National Curriculum. They often teach a classroom subject as well. Some work in primary schools with younger children and teach the whole range of subjects. Others provide health, fitness and leisure programmes for students at colleges.

There are, in addition, opportunities to teach at diploma and graduate level also in colleges.

All physical education teachers qualify by completing a degree course at college. Apart from an active interest in sport, the basic requirements are usually five GCSE passes at Grade C or above (including English and Mathematics) and three passes at GCE 'A' level.

The work of the PE teacher is demanding and varied. The ability of the young people being taught will range from very poor beginners to junior champions. Apart from being good at sport, the PE teacher must be keen to work with young people and be able to get on well with them.

Above all the teacher must be committed to educating young people through physical activities.

Coaching

Coaches work with individuals or small groups of sportsmen or sportswomen and concentrate on improving performance.

Professional coaches earn their living as coaches or trainers and to keep their job they must be successful. They always work with players who are very able. They are often ex-players who have given up the game because of injury or age.

Only the very best coaches in amateur sports are paid for working full time and usually by the governing body of the sport. Most amateur sports coaches are people who are prepared to devote their own time to helping others improve. Full time coaching jobs are also found with local authorities, outdoor centres, holiday camps, private hotels, leisure centres and large sports clubs.

All coaches need to understand their sport thoroughly. They must be good at handling people with different personalities. Above all the sportsmen and sportswomen must have complete confidence in their ability to help them. In each sport there is a training course for coaches to take.

The National Coaching Foundation aims to bring together all the coaching groups in the different sports. It offers courses at various levels up to a Diploma in Professional Studies (Sports Coaching).

Recreational Management

Leisure facilities continue to expand - today there are over 1 500 sports centres in the country. These facilities all need trained staff to manage and run them. A recreation manager plans and directs the sporting activities at a sports complex. To do this well involves leadership, good organisation, and an understanding of business as well as a commitment to sport. Centres are usually based on a large central hall together with other specialist facilities such as squash courts, swimming pools and fitness rooms. Cafeterias and bars may also be on the site.

The manager and his assistants timetable the various sporting activities, organise major events and co-ordinate the use of the centre by groups such as clubs and schools. Also they employ staff, ensure the building is kept clean and well maintained, order equipment and publicise the events and classes taking place. Increasingly the centres owned by the local authority will be expected to make a profit. Managers need to run their centres as businesses.

Apart from the managerial staff, centres employ part-time coaches and instructors to take classes. Attendants are needed to look after equipment and office staff help to ensure the centres run smoothly.

As well as GCSE qualifications, young people will find the BTEC Diploma and CGLI Certificates in Recreation and Leisure Studies helpful in starting a career in sports centres. Coaching qualifications in different sports are also an advantage. To move up to management, a diploma in management studies or a degree in recreation management is a great asset.

With the growth of the leisure industry have come many commercial enterprises - gymnasiums, health and fitness centres and specialist sports clubs. The private facility manager is under great pressure to increase membership and make the club more attractive and profitable all the time. Therefore business skills are extremely important.

Working in Outdoor Pursuits Centres

Full-time wardens and instructors work at the centres which are run by local education authorities, the Outward Bound Trust and similar organisations. The centres are usually found in remote areas where they can offer their special activities. Courses are residential with groups often staying a week or more.

Instructors must have special qualities. Apart from being experts in their own activity, they must use their enthusiasm to enable others to enjoy demanding activities.

Some centres employ only qualified teachers. Nationally recognised qualifications, together with experience in their sport, are essential for instructors.

Instructors have to be experts in their own activity and encourage others to enjoy demanding activities

Officials in Sport

When we see a soccer referee surrounded by angry players or hear a tennis player swearing at an umpire, we usually wonder why people do those jobs. The official does not have an action-replay in front of him to check to see if he has made a mistake. He must rely on his own judgement. It can be a very lonely job with both players and spectators upset by a decision.

Most referees, umpires and other officials are part-time. This is true of both amateur and professional sport.

Fitness requirements vary with the sport. Rugby referees, cricket umpires and trampoline judges have different fitness needs. The main requirement is concentration and being ready to make an instant decision. Officials must know the rules inside out and be prepared for anything to happen. A wrong decision could mean disaster for some competitors. In professional sport, the decisions of officials can affect a player's livelihood.

All sports have a ladder for officials to climb. Governing bodies set written, oral and practical examinations. As the official gains experience, progress is made from the junior sections to senior sport and more demanding competitions.

In most cases the reward for this difficult and responsible work is just a small fee and expenses. It is one way to become very involved with a sport without actually taking part as a competitor.

Sadly there are usually more complaints than thanks.

Administration

All sporting organisations need administrative and office staff to ensure that activities run smoothly. Governing bodies have a head office from which the day-to-day running of the sport is controlled, new plans developed and major events organised. Professional sporting organisations, like any other business, need company secretaries, accountants and general managers. In many sports today a great deal of money is handled from a variety of sources, particularly sponsorship. The Sports Council through its headquarters and regional offices employs more than 500 people, developing sport nationwide. Sports administration staff need a sound knowledge of the sport in which their organisation is involved together with professional qualifications.

The Sports Trade

With the increase in leisure time has come a great expansion in the range and style of sports products and clothing available. Career opportunities exist in the industry manufacturing these goods from research into new products to selling them to the shops. Sports shops and sports departments of major stores also need people with an interest in sport together with business understanding.

Reporting Sport

The national newspapers and large local papers have their own sports desks. The specialist reporters start their careers on local papers, covering all types of sport. To be a reporter you need to be able to write quickly and clearly. Your reports must be interesting and accurate. You need to be in the right place at the right time.

The sports commentators on television seem to lead a very exciting life, always dashing off to another top event somewhere in the world. In fact, hours are often especially long and hard. Most commentators are trained journalists.

For radio commentary, the job is even harder in some ways. The commentator must describe, not only the action taking place, but also the whole sporting scene. It must be brought to life for the listener.

Medical Aspects of Sport

Doctors are called upon to deal with a wide variety of injuries resulting from sport. Because of the demand, some hospitals now have specialist departments just for injured sportsmen and sportswomen. A number of private sports injury clinics have been set up around the country.

Physiotherapists are also much in demand. They use exercises, electrical treatment and manipulation to return players to fitness. Many work in hospitals. Some work privately and charge patients a fee for treatment.

Before specialising in sport, all doctors and physiotherapists must first obtain professional qualifications. Osteopaths, who aid recovery from injury by manipulating bones and joints, are becoming more widely used. They do not work for the NHS but work in private practice.

Machines and Animals

Amateur riders who use machines of various sorts look after them themselves. This can be a big job, it depends whether the machine is a car, dinghy or cycle. They all need regular attention to see they are in first class condition for competition.

Professional rally and racing car drivers have a team of mechanics to keep their cars in the very best condition. Only the top professional cyclists and motorcyclists have full-time mechanics.

When animals are involved in sport, they too must be in the best possible condition. Race horses are very valuable animals and must be well cared for by the stable lads. Grooms look after horses used for show jumping.

Working with animals means having a special feeling for their health and happiness.

Ground Staff

All playing areas need regular care to see that they are in good condition for competition. This is a highly skilled job. Famous areas like the Wimbledon grass courts and the test match wickets must be looked after very carefully.

Clubs and local authorities employ many ground staff throughout the country. It is an active, outdoor type of job requiring work to be done in all weathers. For the golfer the quality of the grass is a vital factor and for tournament preparation the best greenkeepers are much in demand.

Professional rally and racing drivers have a team of mechanics to keep their cars in the very best condition

Summary

Professional sportsmen and sportswomen must be prepared for fierce competition all the time. Only the best and most determined will survive and reach the top. A talented youngster therefore needs a tough, competitive nature to stand a chance.

However many players will be satisfied to be part of the professional sport. With limited ambitions as players, they may be able to devote more time to developing a second career in or out of their sport.

For those interested in sport, but not outstanding performers, there is a very wide choice of careers in work related to sport. There is also ample opportunity for people to be involved in sports clubs and organisations, quite separately from earning a living.

THINGS TO DO

1 Which of the following statements are true and which are false?
   (i) There are about 10 000 full-time professional footballers in Britain.
   (ii) Cricketers usually have very short careers.
   (iii) To be a golf professional you need a handicap of five or less.
   (iv) A jockey's apprenticeship must end by the age of 23.
   (v) You need to be a top class sports performer to become a PE teacher.
   (vi) Sports centre managers always have a degree in recreation management.
   (vii) Age is the enemy of all professional players.
   (viii) All referees and umpires are ex-players.

2 From the following list, choose a person involved in sport and arrange to interview them. Find out all you can about their work - the qualifications needed, the rewards and problems involved.

   Professional coach, trainer or manager; physical education teacher; instructor at a swimming pool, health club, leisure centre, youth club or outdoor activities centre; manager at a leisure complex; groundsman; top class referee or umpire; sports journalist; physiotherapist; mechanic for a motor sport; full time sports administrator; sports retailer.

   Do you think you would like their job? Give your reasons.

3 George Best and Bobby Charlton were both outstanding soccer players. However their careers were very different in a number of ways. Explain why young people usually find a career in sport very attractive. Discuss also the problems and difficulties that a sporting career might bring.

4 Apart from being paid to play, suggest other ways in which a professional sportsman or sportswoman might increase their earnings.

5 Produce a drawing to show the people involved in a professional soccer match. Include the following in the drawing:

   Gateman, spectators, police, groundsman, players, injured player, doctor, physiotherapist, referee, linesman, manager, coach, substitutes, St. John's Ambulance personnel, press box, journalist, camera man, photographer. Try to produce a drawing for another sport to show all the different people involved.

6 Complete the following table about professional performers:

A	Qualities needed to achieve success	1	Determination to reach the top
		2	
		3	
		4	
B	Reasons for failure to succeed.	1	Serious injury causing retirement
		2	
		3	
		4	

7 Visit your local sports centre, swimming pool or leisure complex to find out how many people work there and what responsibility they each have. Think of a way to show how the staff are all ultimately responsible to the general manager. Find out what qualifications, if any, are necessary for each type of job. Try to find ways to show your results in the form of diagrams and charts.

8 People who report sport on television, radio or in newspapers are usually trained journalists. Attend a major sports meeting yourself and write your own newspaper report in advance of the printing of the newspapers. Collect a variety of professional reports and then compare and contrast them with your own. Consider the different ways in which all the reports, yours included, are agreed or differ about what took place.

_15 WOMEN AND SPORT

Today, as in the past, most women have fewer opportunities in life compared with men. They are expected to run a home and bring up children. This may often be in addition to a full or part-time job. Therefore they have less free time. Also their choice of leisure time activities is more restricted than for men. Over a long period of time women have demanded changes in society to give them equal status with men. Social change has gradually given women greater opportunities to plan their own lives. Nevertheless the battle for equal opportunities with men is still being fought.

As the expectations of women have changed, so their participation in a variety of activities, including sport, has increased. Previously many sports were not open to them. Today women can take part in almost any sport, although only in a few do they actually compete on equal terms with men. There is still much discrimination and prejudice against women taking part in sport. However, people's attitudes are changing slowly.

The way forward is being shown by the top sportswomen. An earlier chapter has shown that in most sports the gap between the achievements of the best men and the best women is closing. Indeed it is claimed that women will be better than men in some endurance events by the turn of the century. In the 1988 World Triathlon Championships in Hawaii, Paula Newley-Fraser came 11th overall. Open to both men and women, the event consisted of a 2.4 mile swim, a 112 mile cycle ride and a full marathon!

WOMEN AND SPORT BEFORE 1918

The great development in sport in Britain before the First World War hardly involved women at all. It is true that women were accepted at Wimbledon in 1884 and a year later Martine Bergman-Osterberg founded the first PE college for women at Dartford. However women were not invited to the Paris Congress organised by Pierre de Coubertin, nor were they allowed to compete in the 1896 Olympic Games which followed. At the Paris 1900 Olympic Games unofficial tennis and golf events for women took place. In 1904 at St. Louis there was a women's archery competition, but it was not recognised by the IOC! In 1908, in London, 43 women competed in figure skating, tennis and archery.

To understand why women had such difficulty in being equal partners with men in the development of sport and physical recreation, it is necessary to look at social issues.

Very few working class women had the money, the time or the energy to take part in sport of any sort. For the mass of girls attending State schools, physical activity consisted of drill and informal playground games. Towards the end of the century drill was replaced by Swedish gymnastics due largely to the effort of teachers from Dartford College. From the start women's sport had a strong middle class character. In the nineteenth century as the middle classes prospered, they were able to take part in various games and recreations. However, the women were often showpieces wearing extravagant, expensive clothing. Women's clothing was a symbol of a life of leisure and prevented them doing anything vigorous! They played croquet, skittles, quoits and some racket games, and were seen at races, regattas and cricket matches. Women were thought of as weak physically, without much energy and unsuited to vigorous exercise. In contrast, sport with its aggression and competitiveness was seen as a symbol of masculinity.

In the 1880's tennis became very popular. Nevertheless women players had to fit the ideas of the time. They played in heavy dresses with petticoats and were expected to play in a leisurely fashion. At this time women also took to golf, although often it was little more than pitch and putt. Costume for golf remained very restrictive and it was usually played for social not sporting reasons. The arrival of cycling as a popular activity gave women two new freedoms. Within limits they were able to cycle wherever they liked and also they escaped from their restrictive clothing into looser fitting and lighter clothes.

Cycling became a popular activity for women in Victorian times

Men viewed with suspicion all women's sports which emphasised freedom and spontaneity. The rules of participation reflected the roles of men and women at the time. Many governing bodies of women's sport were founded around the turn of the century - badminton, cricket, golf, hockey, lacrosse, netball, punting, skating, swimming and tennis. Much of this sport took place separately from men and traditional feminine behaviour was expected at all times.

WOMEN AND SPORT 1918-39

This was a period of great change. During the First World War women took on many jobs previously only done by men. After the war many people had a different attitude towards women and their role in society. Women took part in sport in increasing numbers. Many rejected the old restrictions based on a view of women in the role only of wife and mother. It became easier for women from the working class to take part in sport as living standards rose.

In 1920 in the Olympic Games at Antwerp, 136 women from 20 countries took part in tennis, swimming, archery, figure skating and yachting. The IOC continued to exclude women's athletics from the Olympic programme. In 1922 the International Women's Sports Federation (IWSF) organised their own Women's Olympics. It was held in Paris and consisted of eleven athletic events in one day. A crowd of 30 000 saw the events.

The Winter Olympics started in 1924 and from the beginning included women. The IOC formally allowed women's athletics in the 1928 Olympics, with five track and field events. Unfortunately, some of the runners in the women's 800 m collapsed after the race. This strengthened opposition to women's sport.

During the inter-war years, a number of sportswomen caught the public's imagination. Suzanne Lenglen did so in tennis. She won her first Wimbledon singles title in 1919 at the age of 20. Suzanne Lenglen was a glamorous French woman who wore a short sleeved blouse, a short pleated skirt and white stockings. On court she dashed around, leaping and stretching for shots around the court. Although she initially shocked many people, she established new standards of play, dress and behaviour for women tennis players.

Suzanne Lenglen

In 1928 at St. Morritz, Sonya Henje won the first of three successive victories in the figure-skating. She became world famous as a skilful and exciting performer before becoming a film star.

Babe Didriksen in the 80m hurdles final at the 1932 Olympic Games

'Babe' Didriksen was an outstanding all-round sportswoman. She first achieved fame in 1930 when she broke the world javelin record at the age of sixteen. She could compete in as many as eight athletic events and also took part in baseball, basketball, tennis, swimming and diving. She was a notable amateur golfer and later turned professional.

In 1930 the Women's League of Health and Beauty was founded in London with 16 members. By 1939 there were 166 000 members in England and the movement had spread to many other countries.

WOMEN AND SPORT SINCE 1945

During the Second World War, Britain again needed to call upon women to work in the factories and fields. Many more women became used to earning their own income. When the men returned home again, many women continued to work and have done so increasingly over the decades that followed.

In spite of the post war problems, the 1948 Olympics were held in London. The 'Flying Dutchwoman', Fanny Blankers-Koen won four track gold medals. The 'blond haired mother of two' was given the headline 'Fastest Woman in the World is an Expert Cook'!

The great social changes of the 'Swinging' Sixties gave women greater confidence and more independence and freedom to control their own lives. There was publicity for the feminist view of society.

The 1960 Rome Olympics saw a large increase in women taking part - 610 out of a total of 4 736. The women's 800m returned to the programme after a gap of 32 years. It was followed by the 400m in 1964, the 1 500m in 1972 and the marathon and 3 000m in 1984. 1988 saw the 10 000m for the first time but the steeplechase, triple jump, hammer and pole vault are still not open to women. However, in the UK Championships the triple jump was introduced in 1990 and the hammer in 1991.

The most successful sisters in Olympic history, Irena and Tamara Press, were suspected of drug taking. They retired suddenly when sex testing was introduced into athletics in 1966, giving rise to more suspicion about their gender.

Olga Korbut at the 9th European Gymnastic Championships in 1973

The child-like gymnast Olga Korbut shot to fame in the 1972 Munich Olympics. She captivated audiences worldwide with her ability and innocence. Four years later the gymnast Nadia Commaneci produced near perfect scores at the age of 14. However, questions were being asked about the possible use of drugs on young gymnasts to delay the onset of puberty.

The 1970's saw the emergence of the powerful East German women's teams in athletics and swimming. At the 1976 Olympics they won 20 out of a total of 28 gold medals in both sports. Again questions were asked about drugs, but this time the subject was the use of steroids.

Billie Jean King started the women's professional tennis circuit, having become dissatisfied with the treatment of women in professional tennis competitions. Many girls and young women were trying to join boys' teams and to play sports which had previously been male only. At the same time the boom in fun runs, jogging and marathons saw women running with and against men.

In 1981 the first woman was appointed to the IOC. A decade later Britain had two members - the Princess Royal and Mary Glen Haig. At the Seoul Olympics 2 476 women and 7 105 men took part.

Activities such as aerobics, dance and weight training have promoted images of a modern ideal women - fit with a well proportioned and conditioned body, and therefore attractive to men. Advertising has exploited this image by using sportswomen to sell products. The 'glamorous, glitzy, shock-haired queen of Seoul' - Florence Griffiths Joyner - was in great demand after winning her gold medals.

Naomi James has sailed singlehanded around the world

Today sport is big business in a commercial sense. Undoubtedly there are more opportunities for women to take part in sport. Women as sports participants are not only the target of the Sports Council, but also of sports business people.

Women compete directly with men in many equestrian sports, such as show jumping, three day eventing, flat racing and steeplechasing. Mixed doubles are played at the highest levels in tennis and badminton. In ice skating mixed pairs provide some of the most popular events. Most marathons are now open to both men and women runners. Nevertheless, in the vast majority of sports women compete quite separately from men. For such sports as diving and trampolining it would be hard to give sound sporting reasons for separate competition.

Few sports now ban women completely. Although many women compete at judo and karate, few so far have seriously attempted to wrestle, box or play rugby. Women's cricket is a long established minority sport. In 1972 the Football Association officially recognised women's football.

Despite old fashioned views about what is or is not suitable for them, women are now playing in nearly all sports at different levels. This quiet revolution has accelerated in recent years. It is based on the view that women themselves should be quite free to choose their own leisure time activities.

There is no doubt as we enter the 1990's that girls and women still have many disadvantages to overcome in order to take part in physical recreation on an equal basis with men.

In 1990 the Council of Europe ran a seminar called 'Women and Sport - Taking the Lead' at which 19 countries looked at ways to encourage women to take up leadership roles in sport.

Zina Garrison is a good role model

The media, especially Channel 4, has promoted strong images of successful sportswomen. The Sunday Times Sportswoman of the Year Award has shown further good role models of performers, coaches and officials. Helen Rollason, a former PE teacher, in 1990 became the first women ever to host Grandstand, the BBC's flagship sports programme.

The Sports Council has recognised the need to target women in its 'Sport for All' campaign. The formation of the Women's Sports Foundation in 1984 and its development has given women a voice to challenge the discrimination they face in sports and recreation at all levels.

SPORTS ACHIEVEMENT

As we have seen in earlier chapters, there are many physical reasons why, at present, most women are unable to compete on equal terms against men. It must be remembered, however, that the best women in some sports can now beat good men in those sports. When women are given the same sporting advantages as men, their performances increase considerably.

It may be that social pressures are more important than physical limitations in determining a women's sporting success. People learn the values, attitudes and expected behaviour of the society in which they live. Although it is a lifelong process the child's early experiences are very important. In our society there have been different expectations of boys and girls from an early age. Boys have been taught sports skills and encouraged to be competitive. In contrast girls have often been encouraged to learn the skills of housekeeping and to accept a passive role.

In the secondary school, the games dominated physical education programme has appealed to boys. The majority have found the subject attractive, an opportunity to show off their developing masculinity. This has not been so for girls, many of whom have rejected the games approach and with it physical recreation in general. In recent years the development of many non-competitive, movement based activities for girls has increased participation and interest.

In the past there was a dilemma for girls. They did not believe that they could be sexually attractive and sportswomen at the same time. This view was reinforced by society in general. It

Jarmila Kratochvilova has a very muscular body

is no wonder that many girls avoided physical activity of all kinds.

Today attitudes in society are changing. Women now feel free to take part in sport of all kinds without their femininity being threatened.

Removing the Barriers

The Southern Council for Sport and Recreation has produced its own plan for encouraging more women into active physical recreation.

The Council found a number of barriers:

Tradition and perception

- Traditionally sport has been male dominated.
- Social conditioning and sexual stereotyping have been the main factors which prevent women's participation in sport.
- Image and identity of sport have worked against greater involvement by women.
- Sport, in particular competition, is linked with muscularity.

Caring role in society

- 'A woman's place is in the home.'
- Women should care for husbands, children and ageing relatives.
- This role makes a regular commitment to sport very difficult.

Finance

- Working at home is not paid employment, therefore women can feel that they are not entitled to their own leisure time.
- When financial resources are scarce women's sport tends to get a low priority for the family expenditure.

Transport and access

- In the majority of cases the man uses the car in connection with his employment.
- Access to facilities via public transport is critical.
- Links between the facility and the public transport are also important - unlit passages, dark subways.

Recognition of these Barriers Leads to Greater Attention to Women's Needs

Welcoming atmosphere

The design of facilities, outside and inside, should be more welcoming. Facilities should be light, bright, clean and well-signposted, and staff should be more welcoming and less intimidating.

Programming

Sessions attracting women with different lifestyles should be carefully timetabled, for example mothers with toddlers from 10.00-12.00; older women from 14.00-16.00; working women lunchtime and evening; family sessions at the weekend.

Childcare

This is an obvious need where women with responsibility for young children are participating, that is family changing, babyfeeding and creche facilities. Cleanliness in all these areas is vital.

Women-only sessions

Many women tend to doubt their physical capabilities and do not want to make fools of themselves in front of men. They prefer to try out new sports and acquire new skills in purely female company. Other considerations, such as modesty, need to be taken into account, especially in the case of older women and women whose culture or religion has a strict dress code.

Women instructors

When women are beginning or learning a new activity, many prefer to be taught by a woman.

Balance of competitive and recreational sport

Much of the view that sport is not appropriate for women relates to the idea that women are not competitive and that it is unfeminine to want to win. However, many women do like competitive sport as it gives them standards to achieve and the motivation to improve.

Widening of horizons

Women also need to try more adventurous and challenging activities. In a Sports Council demonstration project in Cambridgeshire, a women's Sports Motivator worked with local Women's Institutes and encouraged over 2 000 women to take part in gliding, sailing and windsurfing.

Social area

Women welcome the opportunity to relax after sport with their friends, have coffee or a drink, a chat and perhaps a bite to eat. They do not feel comfortable about going off to the pub in the same way that sportsmen do.

Advertising

Often women do not hear about courses that are just right for them. Providers need to advertise their programmes and facilities. One of the best ways of reaching women and girls is through word of mouth, for example outside supermarkets and schools, through mother and toddler groups, and through friends, husbands and boyfriends.

Women are not all the same

It is wrong to think of women as one target group all with the same needs. Some prefer competitive, others non-competitive sports; some prefer activities in mixed groups, others women-only sessions. Centres need to find out what women in their area need, and plan their activities for them.

Women and sports participation

A 1983 survey found that only 25.0% of women compared with 40.1% of men were active in outdoor sport. The figures for indoor sport were 35.7% for men and 19.5% for women.

The Sports Council has made great efforts to improve the level of participation by women in sport. Their 1982 plan for 'The next ten years' aimed at a 70% increase in women's participation in indoor sports and a 35% increase in outdoor sports.

By 1988 an extra one million women had been attracted into indoor sport (24.2%). However, the number of women taking part in outdoor sport (24.3%) had fallen by 100 000 over the same period of five years, 1983-1988.

The 1988 'Into the 90's' plan aims to encourage an extra 1.25 million women into sport, especially those who are unemployed, from ethnic minorities or disabled.

The growth in women's indoor participation has been spread across all age groups. The decrease in outdoor activities has been greatest amongst young women. A 1986 survey showed an increase in swimming, keep fit/yoga, cycling, athletics (including jogging). The benefits of increased participation are not being shared by all women.

Many local projects have been aimed especially at women. They have taken careful account of activities offered, time of sessions, use of female staff and provision of creches. The National Sport for All 'Milk in Action for Women' (1989) campaign invited women to sample a wide range of activities.

The Sports Council also promotes programmes for ethnic minority women, closer liaison with women's organisations, financial support for women sports officers and various publications. It aims to see that women feature in all its programmes of work. Special attention will be given to the unemployed, young mothers, single parents and ethnic minority groups.

WOMEN AND SPORT – AN ALTERNATIVE VIEW

The Sports Council's approach has been criticised for labelling women 'as having a problem' with regard to physical recreation. Making women a 'target group' may encourage stereotyping. It could be more helpful to carefully identify what women themselves see as their needs. Policy making teams are likely to be largely male. There is then a danger of trying to make women fit into sport as it is, rather than using community recreation, with women staff, to find out how provision at local level can be changed to meet women's own preferences.

Historically sport has been developed by men and for men. The male dominated sports club or sporting facility does not fit the culture of women.

Women themselves need to take more responsibility for the further development of sport. There needs to be a dramatic increase in women in the leadership positions. However, women are too often seen as having the major share of responsibility for the family and home. They are at a considerable disadvantage, therefore, in trying to find the time and energy to be involved in policy making and leadership in sport.

Also the male model of sports leadership is hierarchical, elitist, exclusive and autocratic. This is in sharp contrast to a feminist approach which is likely to be supportive, co-operative, inclusive and democratic. The dilemma for the woman is whether she should adopt the male values in order to reach the top or maintain her own values and be ignored.

WOMEN'S SPORTS FOUNDATION (WSF)

The WSF is a national, voluntary organisation, founded in 1984 by a group of women. They wanted to provide a voice to challenge the discrimination faced by women and young girls in sports and recreation at all levels. Their aim is to promote the interests of all women and girls in and through sport and to demand equality of opportunity.

The WSF draws its membership from those involved professionally with sport and recreation, students, sportswomen and others who are concerned at the problems that women often face in sport.

The WSF tries to use the expertise and strengths of its members in various ways. Some campaign for improved and equal media coverage of women's events. Others help produce resource packages which include a 'Guide to Careers in Sport and Leisure for Women and Young Girls'.

The WSF works in partnership with organisations such as the Sports Council, the

CCPR and the British Association of National Coaches. A quality newsletter is produced, together with a series of leaflets and posters on women's participation in sport.

The WSF believes that for far too long sportswomen have had to contend with tensions between their roles as females and athletes, and that this must change!

WOMEN AND PHYSICAL EDUCATION

Teacher training for Physical Education in England started with women only colleges. Some 40 years later the first college for male PE students opened. However, the philosophy, teaching methods and course content developed along different lines. In the 1970's the reorganisation of teacher training colleges led to mixed courses for all PE students.

It is suggested that, following the merging of male and female colleges and courses, women's influence in the PE profession has declined. A number of reasons have contributed, including the closing of specialist colleges, the loss of many all girls' schools, the pressure for PE to become more academic and the move towards scientific analysis. Whilst men have been appointed to

A female coach in action

former women's colleges, women have not been appointed to the same extent in former men's colleges. This has led to women being under-represented in this area.

The current movement towards mixed teaching of PE in schools may also disadvantage girls. It is likely that boys will dominate the lesson, getting more of the teacher's attention, taking up more space to practise and retaining more possession of the ball in team games due to their physical size and strength. Girls' experiences of mixed PE may leave them disinterested and uninvolved. Equality of opportunity at secondary school should take into account girls' and boys' different earlier experiences. Girls may lack skill and confidence to compete on equal terms.

It is essential that all students training to teach are aware of the way education often discriminates against girls and women. This is especially important for PE teachers as research suggests they are likely to hold the least sympathetic attitudes towards equal opportunities.

WOMEN AND COACHING

At the 1988 Olympics in Seoul, 66% of the competitors were male and 34% female. Yet, 92% of the coaches were male and only 8% female.

Many women in Britain coach at the beginner level but few in more senior coaching positions. Traditional attitudes are found at all levels of coaching, for example at the local club often 'Dad' coaches the youngsters and 'Mum' organises the refreshments.

One major problem for women is that coaching is seen from a male point of view. In general the male coach is likely to appear forceful and decisive. Therefore successful women coaches are likely to be those who adopt this style. However, the more democratic style favoured by many women may produce equally good results, if it is not rejected.

There are three main routes in which women get involved in coaching: senior competitors whose playing days are ending; women who get involved through their children's sport and women physical education teachers. Getting women into coaching is not organised. Many senior competitors just disappear from their sport. Mothers are usually left to watch their children from the sidelines. The

reduction in out of school activities will reduce the impact of PE staff.

Many women lack the confidence to try coaching and find the image of the confident male coach a deterrent. Those who do coach at an introductory level often do not progress.

The National Coaching Foundation provides a service to all coaches, designed to fit in with the technical programme provided by National Governing Bodies. The director of the NCF, Sue Campbell, believes action is needed on a number of fronts to ensure women play a full part in coaching.

WOMEN AND SPORTS ADMINISTRATION

In 1980, Linda Whitehead became the first full-time paid officer of the Women's Football Association (WFA). In 1989 she was voted the Sunday Times Sportswoman Administrator of the Year. She realised that the long hours of sweat, toil and frustration in promoting women's football had paid off for both her and the sport.

She has fought for the right of all women as individuals to be given the opportunity to do what they want and not what society tells them they should be doing.

In the early days she received little support, although that has improved considerably in recent years. However, although ideas are changing, she is still fighting the view of football as the exclusive preserve of men. Numerous Football League clubs still operate a ban on women in the boardrooms.

She believes that women administrators should adopt a higher profile. This will demonstrate that women make excellent professional administrators and also encourage more women to follow. However on occasions where injustice exists she believes in taking on the people concerned.

WOMEN AND LEISURE MANAGEMENT

Recently more women than ever before have been opting for a career in leisure management. Although statistics for colleges and lower management positions may be improving, the higher managerial positions are still dominated by men. In 1990, only 15% of the membership of the Institute of Leisure and Amenity Management were women.

The leisure profession is a hard discipline. It involves unsocial hours and late nights. Success depends not only on enthusiasm and commitment but the ability to manage, to negotiate, to persuade and to influence.

Women are as capable as men in performing the skills required in leisure management. Their greatest problem is the conflict with the demands of family life. The busiest time for leisure participation is after five and at weekends. Therefore, children of female leisure managers will continue to be at home when their mother is working. For many women the rewards of the work are not great enough to make up for the problems caused.

WOMEN AND SPORTS JOURNALISM

At the 1988 Seoul Olympics 120 British journalists and photographers covered the Games. Two of them were women! A stranger to Britain who looked at the sports pages of the national papers, or switched on to the main sports programmes on television, would probably think sport was reserved for men!

In the world of journalism, women have excelled, but sport still remains male dominated. There are many difficulties to be overcome for a woman wishing to write about sport.

As apprentices, women are not usually given an opportunity to work in the sports department. Breaking into sport is difficult. Men have developed networks of contacts over the years. Press boxes have long been considered as reserved for men only.

Combining a career in sports journalism and family life can cause problems. Evening and weekend working are common practice. This can cause conflicts.

The governing bodies themselves need to supply the media with information about women coaches and officials as well as competitors. A positive image of women in sport and reporting sport is essential.

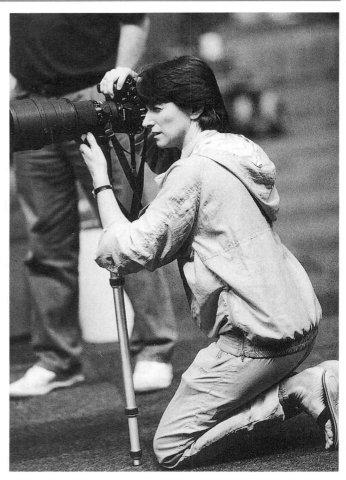

There are very few female sports photographers

The Women's FA Cup Final, 1991; Millwall are in blue, Doncaster in yellow

THINGS TO DO

1 List the Olympic athletic events in which women do not compete. Find out if this list is any different for the UK championships.

2 Women play soccer and compete at judo. Should they box, wrestle and play rugby? Are there good reasons why women should be banned from any sporting activities? Using a variety of sports as examples explain your views on the subject.

3 Carry out a recreation survey on women in your group. Prepare a checklist of physical recreation activities. Find out which sports are most popular and most disliked, both in terms of participation and watching. Ask questions designed to discover the reasons for these likes and dislikes. Analyse your results together with those of men in your group to see if there are any underlying trends or explanations.

4 Make a list of sports in which women at present do compete with men on equal terms. Suggest other sports which you believe might also be included. Give reasons to support their inclusion.

5 Which of the following statements are true and which are false?
   (i) Before puberty boys and girls can compete together on equal terms.
   (ii) After puberty girls are at a disadvantage in sports requiring precision.
   (iii) Women's bodies contain a higher proportion of fat compared to men.
   (iv) More women than men take part in indoor sport.
   (v) In endurance events, women are likely to approach men's world records soon.
   (vi) Women can compete with men on equal terms in most equestrian events.
   (vii) There are women professional hockey players.

6 As a group, discuss the ways in which you might try to discover how women in your local community use their leisure time. If you use a questionnaire you will need to decide what sort of information to gather. You will also need to ensure you have a representative sample of women. Collect your data and display your results visually. Analyse and discuss your results. Prepare a report for your local sports council.

7 Consider your school, college, sports club or leisure centre and draw up a checklist to see if there are disadvantages in being a women in sport. Write a report suitable for presentation to the headteacher, principal or manager of the institution.

8 Analyse the sports coverage in a newspaper over a week. Compare the amount of space devoted to men's sport with women's sport. Similarly compare the number of photographs of men and women. Present your results in the form of bar graphs or pie charts.

16 INTERNATIONAL SPORT AND POLITICS

Aims

To gain knowledge and understanding of:
◆ the links between sport and politics
◆ the present and past problems caused by political influences on sport

To develop the skills of:
◆ secondary research - historical and political
◆ analysis and problem solving
◆ role play

In spite of wars, the ancient Olympic Games were held every four years, without a break, for over one thousand years. The modern Olympic Games have been cancelled three times in 1916, 1940 and 1944 because of two world wars. In recent years many problems have threatened the continued survival of the Games.

In 1956, Mr. Avery Brundage, President of the International Olympic Committee, said, '*By their decisions these countries show that they are unaware of one of our most important principles, namely that sport is completely free of politics*'. He was referring to the countries who had decided not to compete in the Olympic Games in Melbourne. They withdrew because of the fighting that had taken place earlier in Hungary and Suez.

However, the history books tell a different story. They show that international sport in the past has often been influenced by politics. Today the links between sport and politics are very complex. Decisions by governments do prevent many sportsmen and sportswomen from competing together.

When he founded the modern Olympic Games, Pierre de Coubertin hoped that they might help countries to get on better with each other and so help progress towards world peace. World sport today often has the emphasis on winning at all costs together with badly behaved competitors, teams and spectators. We might wonder if sport helps understanding between nations at all.

SUCCESS IN WORLD SPORT

All over the world the top sportsmen and sportswomen want to compete against the best from other countries. At international level competitors are more than just individuals having fun playing sport. As representatives of their nation, they carry extra responsibility for success. In team sports, teams are automatically associated with the country they represent.

Victorious English football team with the World Cup in 1966

The failure or success of teams and individuals at international level may have considerable effects after the competition. The World Cup for soccer is of special importance. Following England's success in 1966, Alf Ramsey the team manager was knighted. Eight years later, following England's failure to qualify for the finals, Ramsey was sacked!

Sometimes the strength of the desire to win on the part of competitors and spectators alike is so great that the sporting occasion starts to fall apart. The rules are broken, cheating occurs and spectators misbehave. The natural human desire to win may be made stronger by political pressures to bring the nation victory at all costs. It is no wonder that in these situations the framework of the sports event may crack and violence may break out. Sport at the highest levels has become a very important activity to the people and nations involved. The idea of it being basically for enjoyment is often forgotten.

However it must be remembered that there are great moments of true friendship and sportsmanship between sportsmen and sportswomen from countries with very different political systems. There are many friendly and fair contests that go unnoticed by the papers and television. These moments are a great credit to those involved. They make sport worthwhile.

If people must compete to be superior, it is best they do so in sport where victory is never for all time and recovery from defeat is always possible. The individual, the team or the nation lives to fight another day.

NATIONAL POLICIES TOWARDS SPORT AND POLITICS

Western Europe, Britain, USA, 'Old' Commonwealth

In the last century the development of sport in these countries was haphazard and piecemeal. Progress depended on groups of individuals with an interest in a particular sport. They got together to sort out rules and improve competition amongst themselves. The organisations they formed were usually completely independent of their government. They made decisions based on the needs of their own sport and provided their own money to run the organisation. During this development governments were usually happy to allow the associations to control their own affairs. Some sports became professional and today they are very much influenced by big business and commercial interests, especially in the USA.

However, since the last war, and particularly in the last twenty years, these governments have become more involved in world sport.

Firstly, they have given money to sport to improve facilities, coaching and administration. Such help has made the sporting associations less independent than they were. Secondly, the governments have been able to put pressure on sports associations to try to stop them playing against some nations or in certain countries.

In recent years the Western world has seen the rapid growth of sponsorship, the disappearance of the 'true' amateur in spectator sports and the commercialisation of the Olympics.

These changes have moved the control of spectator sport away from sportspeople towards business people.

Eastern Europe, Soviet Union, Cuba, Third World Nations

Nations in this group saw sport as an official state activity to be controlled and directed in order to achieve the aims of the government. In these countries, sports organisations were either taken over from the original voluntary bodies or were set up in the first place by the state. In both cases the links between sport and the state were so close that the government controlled all national decisions. Of course international rules and regulations had to be followed. All the money required for facilities, coaching, competitions and organisation was provided by the government. It also paid the teachers, coaches and other people involved. Outstanding sportsmen and sportswomen were spotted at an early age and sent to schools for sport.

Professional sportsmen and sportswomen did not exist. State help allowed outstanding competitors to stay in the armed forces or at college for as long as their sporting careers lasted. Great importance was given to winning by national teams. Success in sport was seen as a way of showing the world that their sports system and way of life were the best.

In recent years there have been massive political changes in the Soviet Union and Eastern Europe. The collapse of communist party rule has seen these countries moving towards Western style democracy. Sport is in the early stages of moving from state control to a new pattern of organisation.

The amount of control the politicians have over sport depends on the way sport is organised in a country, particularly who provides the money to run sport. The organisation of sport may have grown naturally, been set up by the government or developed in another way. Whatever their history, many countries have quite different views about how much influence politics should have on sport.

POLITICAL PROBLEMS AFFECTING WORLD SPORT

To understand the events that have occurred and the present problems, it may be helpful to look at some examples under three headings:

1 Human Rights

– The way different governments treat other nations and groups within their own country.

South Africa Apartheid has not allowed people of different races to compete together. In the past only whites represented their country. This resulted in South Africa being barred from most world sport. Recently the apartheid laws have been removed and South Africa is again joining world sport.

Soviet Union There has been harsh treatment of dissidents, Jews, Christians and other minority groups. Military occupation of Hungary, Czechoslovakia and Afghanistan has taken place. The latter caused the boycott of the Moscow Olympics. There have been many political changes in recent years.

2 National Identity

– Conflicts between nations and claims to represent certain countries.

People's Republic of China and Taiwan The island of Taiwan is considered to be part of mainland China. Both the mainland communists and the island nationalists claimed to represent the Chinese people. The problem has now been resolved and both compete together.

Israel Israel is not recognised by most Arab countries. Usually they refuse to compete in international sport with Israel. A peace treaty between Egypt and Israel has been signed. Israel is willing to compete against Arab countries.

3 Propaganda

– The use of world sport to publicise a cause to a world audience.

Hitler Hitler used the 1936 Olympics to show Germany's strength and the superiority of their athletes. Jesse Owens and other black athletes proved troublesome!

Black Americans They protested at the medal ceremonies in Mexico (1968) and in Munich (1972) to show their dissatisfaction with the treatment of black people in the USA.

The list above is not, of course, complete containing only some of the major problems. Sadly, it is certain there will be more to add in the future. Some of the problems outlined will now be examined in detail.

Apartheid and Sport in South Africa

The population of South Africa is dominated by nearly 21 million black people out of a total of less than 30 million for all races (1989 figures). The minority groups include Asians, coloured people of mixed race and white people of mainly Dutch and British origin. The white minority rules the country. Until recently government policy has been for separate development for the different racial groups, known as apartheid.

This policy has resulted in discrimination against non-whites in sport. The facilities and opportunities for sport have been inferior for non-whites. Spectators have been segregated. Teams have been limited to players from one racial group only. Whites alone have been chosen for national teams. Such open discrimination, admitted by the South Africans, resulted in their expulsion from most international sports associations.

An all-white team represented South Africa in the 1960 Rome Olympics, but the IOC withdrew its invitation for the Tokyo Games. In 1970 South Africa was expelled from the Olympic movement. The Olympic charter states that 'Any form of discrimination with regard to a country or a person on grounds of race, religion, politics, sex or otherwise is incompatible with belonging to the Olympic Movement'.

In 1968, England's cricket tour to South Africa was cancelled when Basil D'Oliveira was forbidden entry. He was a former resident of South Africa, classed as 'coloured', now selected by England for the tour.

In 1969-70 the all-white South African rugby team needed special security precautions throughout their British tour. Political pressures from the British government forced the MCC to cancel the 1970 tour of Britain by the South African cricket team.

Although the 1974 British Lions rugby team toured South Africa and many other international, as well as Lions, teams have followed, opinion was split over the issue. Some people believed that by continuing to play against South Africa apartheid might be changed by argument, and also that isolation would just make white South Africans more determined to work things out for themselves. Others believed that by competing against South Africa, apartheid was being supported and recognised. Only by isolating South Africans from world sport would they be likely to change their ways.

Before the Olympic Games of 1976, a New Zealand rugby team toured South Africa. There were many protests, especially from black African countries. These countries threatened to boycott the Montreal Olympics unless New Zealand was banned from taking part. The IOC refused to give in to the pressure, claiming that rugby was not an Olympic sport. The boycott that followed was supported by most black African nations. New Zealand's argument was that they were opposed to apartheid. However, they did not feel that the government should interfere with the right of individuals and groups to travel about the world freely and play sport.

At a meeting of the leaders of the Commonwealth in 1977, a declaration on apartheid in sport was made, known as the Gleneagles Agreement. In it apartheid in sport was condemned. The governments again stated their full support for the campaign against apartheid. They left individual governments to *'take every possible practical step to discourage contact or competition by their nationals with sporting organisations, teams or sportsmen from South Africa or from any other country where sports are organised on the basis of race, colour or ethnic origin'*.

To discourage sporting contacts with South Africa the United Nations special committee against apartheid in 1981 published its first 'blacklist' of sports performers who had worked in South Africa.

During England's cricket tour to the West Indies in 1981, Guyana refused to allow Robin Jackman to enter the country because of his links with cricket in South Africa. The tour did continue after the West Indies decided that participation by individuals in South African sport, was outside their control. However the event that did most damage to international cricket was the 1982 'rebel tour' to South Africa by a team of English international players. The players involved were banned from international cricket for three years.

Following the 1984 England rugby tour of South Africa, some countries wanted to exclude England from the Commonwealth Games to be held in 1986. They claimed that England did not do everything possible to prevent the tour and therefore broke the code of conduct agreed in Brisbane in 1982, which clarified the Gleneagles Agreement.

Zola Budd

In January 1984, at the age of 17, the white South African, Zola Budd shattered the women's 5 000m world record. Three months later she left for London and two weeks later became a British citizen. It was generally believed that such haste was to enable her to run for Britain in the 1984 Olympics. For the years she was in England many regarded her as a symbol of racism and she was hounded by the anti-apartheid movement. Others considered her an athlete unfairly caught up in a political situation not of her making. After the controversial fall of her rival, Mary Decker, in the Olympic final, Zola continued to run for Britain before returning to South Africa in 1988.

The Commonwealth Games in 1986 in Edinburgh were boycotted, by 32 nations, because of Britain's refusal to apply economic sanctions to South Africa. The inclusion of Zola Budd in the England team was also considered a factor. This boycott was effective in undermining the Games. It devalued the actual competition and caused serious financial difficulties for the organisers.

In 1988 the England cricket tour to India was cancelled after visas were refused for a number of players with South African connections. In 1989 the International Cricket Conference decided that any cricketer with 'sporting contact' with South Africa should be banned for life from test cricket. This did not deter Mike Gatting, the former England Captain, from leading a rebel tour in 1990. However the tour was a fiasco. Massive demonstrations allowed little cricket to be played and the cricketers quickly returned home.

In 1990, President De Klerk announced the unbanning of the African National Congress and the release of Nelson Mandela from prison. A year later the dismantling of apartheid was started with the repeal of key laws. Moves to end South Africa's sporting isolation began immediately. Talks started to ensure that each sport was run by one non-racial organisation. Also the National Olympic Committee was reconstituted on non-racial lines. The IOC formally readmitted South Africa to the Olympic Movement in July 1991. There was speculation that South Africa would compete in the 1992 Olympics in Barcelona. Some people have expressed concern at the speed with which South Africa is being readmitted to world sport. They say it will take some time to give people of all races equality of opportunity in every aspect of life, as well as sport. They would prefer to wait until a new government is elected under a non-racial constitution.

Hitler and the 1936 Olympics

The Games of 1936 were given to Berlin in 1931, two years before Hitler came to power in Germany. Later the Nazi Government agreed that they would follow the Olympic Charter and that the German Jewish athletes would not be at a disadvantage. Persecution of the Jews in Germany had begun and there was wide publicity for the racial views of the Nazis. However the world as a whole seemed not to want to believe the stories told. Opposition to the Games did continue, especially in the USA which had many Jewish and black team members. Eventually a full American team competed, but only after a close vote.

Hitler was determined to turn the Olympics into a display to show the world the strength of the German nation and the superiority of the Aryan sportsmen and sportswomen. The first victory went to a German in the shot putt and he received public congratulations from Hitler in his box. In the 10 000m Finnish runners made a clean sweep and they were also congratulated by Hitler. However, there were no personal congratulations for the two black Americans who came first and second in the high jump or later for the victories of Jesse Owens.

Jesse Owens competing in the 1936 Olympic Games in Berlin

It is ironic that the hero of the Nazi Olympics should be a black, American athlete. Before the Olympics Jesse Owens was already famous. On one afternoon in May 1935 he had set five new world records. At the Games he won the 100m, 200m, long jump and completed the 4 x 100m relay team. Above all he and the other black athletes rejected Hitler's idea of Aryan supremacy.

Speaking years later, Owens made it clear that he was well aware of the German disapproval of his success. The great personal friendship he had with his rival German long jumper, Luz Long, helped him to ignore it. It should be remembered that at this time the colour bar in the Deep South of the United States was strongly enforced. Owens' comments remind us of this:

'But I knew prejudice after I became Olympic champion. Because I had gone over there and defied a man who changed the shape of the world, that didn't matter, I still had to sit in the back of the bus.'

The Chinese Problem

The island of Taiwan lies 100 miles from the coast of mainland China. In 1949, the republican General Chaing Kai-shek and his followers fled to Taiwan after defeat by Mao Tse-tung's communist army. Chaing Kai-shek claimed Taiwan to be a province of China, not a separate country. Right up to his death in 1975 he vowed that he would return to reunite the whole of China.

The People's Republic of China, as mainland China became known, withdrew from the Melbourne Olympics in 1956 because Taiwan was competing. Two years later they left the Olympic movement and also withdrew from most international sport. From then Taiwan was the sole representative of China in world sport competing as Taiwan but recognised under the title 'Republic of China'.

Since 1973-4, the People's Republic has had many contacts with world sport, competing in the Asian Games of 1974 in place of Taiwan. Gradually they have rejoined the Olympic sports federations, but only when Taiwan has been expelled.

When the International Weightlifting Federation voted to replace Taiwan with the People's Republic in 1974, an official in Taiwan commented: *'We were in the international federation in the 1950's at the same time as mainland China. We did not ask for their expulsion although we were members of the UN and they were not. Why should we suffer now? We have been good members, observed the rules, paid our dues. We have offered and received international competition from all countries without strings. The situation between us and the mainland is no different than between North and South Korea'.*

At the Olympic Games in Montreal, 1976, the Canadian government refused to allow Taiwan to compete as the 'Republic of China' and to use her own flag. This was in spite of the fact that the IOC had accepted Taiwan as a member country. The Canadian government only recognised the People's Republic of China and not Taiwan. Taiwan withdrew and its athletes went home.

The People's Republic of China and Taiwan took part in the 1984 Olympic Games in Los Angeles

In 1979 the People's Republic of China was readmitted by the IOC to join Taiwan in the Olympic movement. Taiwan was asked to submit a new anthem and flag. In 1984 the People's Republic of China and Taiwan under the title 'Chinese Taipei' took a full part in the Los Angeles Olympics.

Black Power at Mexico City and Munich

The use of slave labour in the southern states of the United States had helped the country to grow rich. Following the Civil War of 1861-5, slavery was abolished. Life for the black people in the southern states was still not easy. Only gradually were black people and other minority groups accepted into American society. Even today the situation is far from satisfactory in many parts of America.

It is against this background that the protests made by groups of black American athletes should be discussed.

Black power demonstration at the Mexico City Olympic Games in 1968

In Mexico, 1968, the 200m was won convincingly by Tommie Smith, a black American. John Carlos was beaten into third place by Peter Norman of Australia. When the two American athletes came out for the medal ceremony they each wore a black glove on one hand. They accepted their medals with good grace but, as their national anthem was played, they raised the gloved hand in a clenched fist salute and bowed their heads. Their protest was about black people in America being treated as second class citizens. Smith said afterwards, *'If I win I am an American, not a black American. But if I did something bad they would say a negro'*.

The 4 x 400m relay was won by a black American team and they too gave the black power salute after receiving their medals. Carlos, Smith and other black power militants were sent home.

A similar protest was seen in Munich in 1972 when Vince Mathews and Wayne Collett did not stand to attention during the playing of the national anthem at the victory ceremony. They had finished first and second in the 400m. They were also sent home.

For most sportsmen and sportswomen to receive a medal at an Olympic Games would be the highlight of their career. To use this special moment for a political demonstration shows how strongly the athletes felt about the position of black people in America. Smith said later, *'We are black and we are proud of being black. Black America will understand what we did tonight'*.

The Munich Massacre

The Munich Olympics of 1972 were a fine demonstration of technical brilliance. They are remembered more for the tragic killing of Israeli athletes and officials by Palestinian terrorists.

To understand how such an event could occur it is necessary to look at the political relationship between Israel and her Arab neighbours. In 1948 the state of Israel was born on land formerly called Palestine. The surrounding Arab countries refused to accept its existence and war broke out. In the years since, there have been a number of wars between Israel and her neighbours. The periods of peace have been full of tension. There have also been many attacks by terrorists against Israelis both inside and outside of Israel. In 1980 a peace treaty was signed between Israel and Egypt, and much land captured by Israel has been returned; but many problems remain.

The attack on the Israelis was made to gain widespread publicity for the Arab cause. They were also to be used as hostages for the release of terrorists held in Israel.

Although the German organisers had taken special security precautions, the terrorists were able to get into the Israeli rooms in the Olympic village. Two Israelis were killed at once and nine taken hostage. The Israeli government refused to talk to the terrorists. The German authorities agreed to fly the hostages and captors to an airfield. The terrorists, known as the Black September group, walked into a police trap.

Unfortunately things went wrong. All the Israelis were killed and three terrorists captured. In all eleven Israelis died, one athlete, two weight-lifters, two wrestlers, four coaches and two judges.

The dead and the remainder of the Israeli team were flown home. In Munich a day of mourning was called. A memorial service was held in the Olympic stadium the following morning. The IOC met to discuss the matter and the President, Avery Brundage, announced that the Games would go on. Many people thought that after such an outrage everyone should go home. The IOC said that they must continue in order to show the world that the Games could not be stopped by terrorism. Other reasons have been suggested for the Games continuing. For example, the years of preparation on the part of the competitors and the enormous cost of staging the Games. Nevertheless, some competitors quietly packed their bags and went home, their dreams shattered.

The Boycott of the Moscow Olympics

In 1974 the Nobel prize winner and dissident Alexander Solzhenitsyn was expelled from the Soviet Union and four other dissidents jailed. In that year Moscow was awarded the 1980 Olympic Games. From that moment, many groups and countries were unhappy about the Games going to Moscow because of the Soviet Union's record on human rights. There was, however, little evidence of discrimination in sport in the Soviet Union. In the past the Soviet Union had not been banned

because of its violation of human rights. In 1956, the Soviet Union took part in the Melbourne Olympics, having recently occupied Hungary and in the Mexico Olympics in 1968 also, having earlier marched into Czechoslovakia.

Dennis Follows, Chairman of the British Olympic Association, showed how the Olympic movement felt when he said, '*I am prepared to play against anybody at any time, because if I were to discriminate there would be three quarters of the world with whom I couldn't play*'.

The treatment of the dissidents was soon forgotten when Soviet troops invaded Afghanistan in 1979. The Soviet Union claimed that help had been requested by the Afghan Government, but the West was not impressed. The Soviet Union refused to withdraw its troops. A number of countries led by the USA, and including Canada, Japan, West Germany and others, announced a boycott of the games.

In Britain the Government made its position very clear. It did not want British sportsmen and sportswomen to take part in the Olympics. However, it was not willing to issue instructions or withdraw passports. Final decisions were to be left to the individual associations and the consciences of the individuals involved. Public opinion was divided and, although Britain was represented, some associations decided not to send teams. Some sportsmen and sportswomen decided not to compete.

Those who took part said that the invasion of Afghanistan was not a sporting matter. They thought that sportsmen and sportswomen should not be used as pawns in a political game, especially after spending so many years in preparation for their events. Those staying at home thought some principles were more important than sport.

In spite of the boycott, the Games did take place and were very successful in terms of organisation and competition. Some people claimed the true Olympic spirit was missing.

The Boycott of the Los Angeles Olympics

Following the boycott of Moscow in 1980, there was no great surprise when the Soviet Union and its allies withdrew from the Olympics in Los Angeles four years later. The official reasons given by the Soviet Union were the lack of security and the commercialisation of the Games.

The opening ceremony at the 1980 Olympic Games in Moscow

Prior to the Games, the media had focussed on what the lunatic fringe in California intended to do when the communist teams arrived. The USA promised tight security and reassured the Soviet Union about the safety of their team. The commercial approach to the Games by the Organizing Committee was in conflict with the socialist views of the Soviet Union. This was a position well-known to the organisers.

The Games were boycotted by the Soviet Union, Cuba and other communist countries of Eastern Europe, apart from Rumania. The Soviet Union waited until the last possible moment before withdrawing, having publicly complained about the problems as they saw them. It is thought that the loyalty of their friends, in such countries as East Germany, was strained almost to the limit by their decision.

After an opening ceremony more to do with Hollywood than Olympia, the Games went on to be a great success. There were no security problems and a huge financial profit was made.

The boycotting nations, as in 1980, allowed their officials to attend the many meetings of the international sports bodies held at the time of the Olympics. These bodies are very powerful in the world of sport. The absent nations did not want to be left out of the continuing struggle for power in sport.

Seoul 1988

At first sight the choice of Seoul for the 1988 Olympic Games seemed likely to bring further political problems. South Korea had no diplomatic links with communist countries and was practically in a state of war with North Korea.

Much credit for the forestalling of problems must go to the President of the IOC, Juan Samaranch. Shortly after the Los Angeles Games, the IOC made an important declaration. In effect it meant that, if a country boycotted the Games, their officials would also be excluded and not allowed to attend the meetings of the international bodies. Boycotting countries would lose much of their power in sport for the following four years. Since sports political power is important in international politics beyond sport, few countries would want the isolation a boycott would bring.

North Korea publically attacked South Korea for not allowing it to share in the staging of the Games. In the event only five other countries did not attend, the most prominent being Cuba. Nearer the Games, it was feared that student demonstrations would prove a problem. In fact there were no political problems and 161 countries, the highest number ever, participated. The Games were superbly organised and produced a considerable profit.

Germany Reunited

After the Second World War Germany was split in two. For the Olympic Games of 1956, 1960 and 1964 a combined team was selected to represent the whole of Germany. In 1968, at Mexico City, East and West Germany competed as two separate nations - East Germany as the German Democratic Republic and West Germany as the Federal Republic of Germany. The two Germanies were reunited in October 1990 and will compete in the 1992 Olympics in Barcelona as one nation again.

The sporting successes of the German Democratic Republic (GDR) were quite

East Germans in the 800m final at the World Championships in Rome, 1987

remarkable. In particular, its women dominated international athletics and swimming. It achieved success quite out of proportion to its population of 16 million people. Closely linked to the Soviet Union and other Eastern bloc countries, the government of the GDR claimed that its sporting success reflected the superiority of the communist system over the capitalist system of the Western nations.

The teams of the GDR had many advantages over other nations. The sports system was highly organised by the State. Each year many millions of pounds were given by the government to the organisation which governed sport. This money paid for centres for sporting excellence, centres for sports science and research and sports schools. Young children with sporting talent were spotted early and given the best possible help to become champions. This meant careful checking of progress by coaches and sports scientists. In 1989 the GDR had about 600 full-time athletic coaches compared with West Germany's 60 (population 57.5 m) and Great Britain's 9 (population 56 m)! Successful sportsmen and sportswomen had special privileges. They were able to train full-time as 'State' athletes and were given better housing, financial bonuses, travel abroad and a job for life.

The more sinister side of the system was the claim that widespread use of drugs was officially condoned. However, following the unification of Germany in 1990, the whole sports system of the GDR was disbanded. Although talks were held between the governing bodies of sport in the two Germanies, in practice the East Germans had to adapt to the system of sport in the West. It can be argued that there must have been some achievements in the GDR sport system that were worth saving. Nevertheless, the assumption was that the West German system was the best and that East German sport should be absorbed into it.

The famous Leipzig Sports Academy at the centre of the country's sports system was closed down. Many coaches left East Germany for other countries. Among those sports employees remaining, unemployment is high. In the past GDR sport concentrated on the elite. Today efforts are being made to ensure that 'Sport for All' is a reality. The new Germany could become a very powerful sporting nation if it can combine the wealth of West Germany and the sports knowledge and expertise of the GDR.

CHOOSING THE HOST CITY

In 1990, the IOC awarded the 1996 Summer Olympics to Atlanta in the USA. Five cities were in competition with Atlanta - Athens, Belgrade, Manchester, Melbourne and Toronto. Many people were disappointed that Athens was not chosen, for the first Olympics of the modern era had been held there a century earlier. However the committee was not swayed by sentiment but by the realities of organising a highly complicated event, costing vast sums of money. Atlanta marketed itself as a successful, efficient and attractive city. It convinced the IOC that it was willing to undertake the considerable financial investment necessary. It is likely the Games will be run in a business-like manner, with television and sponsorship deals generating vast sums of money.

It is estimated that the six candidates spent £52 million on their campaigns. Apart from promotional costs, there had been concern about the way cities had wined and dined members of the IOC. There is likely to be intense competition to host the Games in the year 2000. The IOC is now considering rules for the future to limit promotional spending and hospitality to members.

INTERNATIONAL COMPETITION

The Olympic movement and international sport in general aim to develop friendship and understanding between individuals and nations through sports competition. The events of recent years have emphasised that this is not a simple task. There are many different views about the way sport should be used. Politics now play an important part in world sport. The vital questions to be answered are:

Which countries, if any, should a nation refuse to compete against or take part with?

Should individual sportsmen and sportswomen be prevented from travelling anywhere in the world to take part in sport with whoever they wish?

Most countries of the world have decided that it would be wrong to compete against countries which openly discriminate against sportsmen or sportswomen on grounds of race. For this reason South Africa had been banned from world sport. However it is no secret that there is discrimination within many countries of the world against racial, religious or political groups. If it does happen at all it might be assumed that this discrimination is likely to occur in the sporting life of the country also.

Claims of discrimination in the USA have been made by black Americans and American Indians. In the Soviet Union broadly similar claims have been made by Jews and other religious and national groups. Both countries could reply that their laws forbid discrimination. Furthermore they could claim that their own internal affairs should not be the business of other nations. By competing against a country it does not mean that there is agreement with its political system. An investigation of world wide discrimination might leave few countries to compete together.

If all traces of apartheid were removed from sport there would be no reason for preventing South Africa from rejoining the Olympic movement. The political system is not a question to be considered by the IOC. However, some people would argue 'no normal sport with an abnormal society'.

The British Olympic Association supported the Moscow Olympics on the grounds that political considerations should not decide who we compete against and where competitions should take place. It might be argued that, had the world foreseen the future, taking part in the 1936 Olympics might have been unthinkable. When two countries are at war all sporting events cease, of course. There might be occasions when serious political situations, less than war, could provide good reasons for not competing with other nations. If, for example, the Olympic Games had been awarded to Iraq, with Saddam Hussein in power, would the world have attended?

The question of the right of individuals to pursue their own interests around the world in sport has caused problems for a number of countries and sports. British sportspeople are free to play and coach throughout the world. They are answerable only to their national and international associations.

Questions about who to play and not to play return eventually to the place of sport in the society of the nation concerned. State controlled sport is in a different position from that of sport controlled by organisations independent of government control. The freedom of the individual to travel and play sport is related to the view of human rights held by a country.

THE OLYMPICS AND THEIR PROBLEMS

Athens 1896

The first of the modern Olympic Games was held in Athens in 1896. There were political problems from the start. The Greek government was unable to finance the Games. They were only saved by a wealthy businessman. Thirteen nations took part, Australia, Austria, Britain, Bulgaria, Chile, Denmark, France, Germany, Hungary, Sweden, Switzerland, USA and Greece. Most competitors made their own way at their own expense! The programme included 9 sports and 43 events, one of which was the marathon, won by a Greek, Spyros Louis. All the events were held before enthusiastic crowds.

Paris 1900

After such an encouraging start, the Games of 1900 (Paris) and 1904 (St. Louis) were a great disappointment. They were both held at the same time as other events, the Paris Universal Exhibition and the World Fair in St. Louis. They lacked atmosphere, being merely side-shows to the main event.

St. Louis 1904

The marathon winner, Horz, was disqualified for taking a lift in a car. The eventual winner Hicks only completed the course with the help of injections and brandy!

London 1908

It was left to London (1908) to bring back pride to the Games. Proper sets of rules were drawn up for the Games. The metric system was introduced and women competed for the first time. There were complaints about national flags. When British judges declared that the British runner had been impeded by the Americans in the final of the 400 metres there was anger. The race had to be re-run, but his opponents withdrew and he jogged around for an empty victory. Arguments continued in the marathon when the Italian, Dorando Pietri, was disqualified for being given help after collapsing in the stadium.

Stockholm 1912

In Stockholm, 1912, Jim Thorpe an American Indian athlete, won the decathlon and the pentathlon. He was later disqualified for professionalism, having earlier played baseball for money. In 1983 he was declared an amateur and his medals presented to his family.

**World War I
1914-1918**

Antwerp 1920

The five ringed Olympic flag was first flown in 1920 in Antwerp, when 29 countries competed. None of the nations defeated in the First World War were allowed to compete. There were tragic gaps in the ranks of the athletes.

Paris 1924

There was a considerable increase in the number of countries taking part in the next Games in Paris in 1924 - 44 nations and 3 092 competitors. Austria, Hungary, Bulgaria and Turkey took part but Germany was still absent.

Amsterdam 1928

For the Games of 1928 (Amsterdam) and 1932 (Los Angeles) facilities and organisation continued to improve. In the period from 1920, the Games had developed in many ways.

Los Angeles 1932

The Winter Games had been established (1924), women had been included in athletics (1928) and records had tumbled all round.

Berlin 1936

The years of progress were almost destroyed by the 1936 Olympics in Berlin. The Nazi influence did not help the Olympic ideals of brotherhood and international understanding. Up until these Games political influences had been limited to relatively minor disputes. The use of the Games for Nazi propaganda was a new development.

London 1948

The 1948 Olympics in London were notable for the absence of two of the defeated nations, Germany and Japan, and one of the victors, the Soviet Union. To many people it was remarkable that the Games had survived the War and especially that they could be held in a blitzed city by a victorious but exhausted nation.

**World War II
1939 - 1945**

Helsinki 1952

In 1952 the Games at last came to Finland. Helsinki was the setting for one of the happiest occasions, with simplicity, friendship and sportsmanship in the true Olympic spirit.

Melbourne 1956

In Melbourne in 1956, political problems soon appeared. Australia's strict quarantine laws prevented the equestrian events from being staged. They were transferred to Sweden. Spain and Holland pulled out because of the Soviet Union's invasion of Hungary. The People's Republic of China withdrew because of the inclusion of Taiwan. Egypt and the Lebanon did not compete because of the fighting for the Suez Canal. In spite of these problems, the Games were successful. They brought together East and West German sportsmen and sportswomen in a combined Germany team.

Rome 1960

In contrast the 1960 Rome Olympics were free of political problems. They were spoilt by the death of a Danish cyclist who had been using drugs.

Tokyo 1964

The following games in Tokyo in 1964 were lavish and very expensive. They did not escape the influence of politics. In 1963, South Africa's invitation had been cancelled. Indonesia and North Korea were not allowed to compete because they had taken part in an international tournament considered unsatisfactory by the IOC.

Mexico City 1968

The threat of a boycott of the 1968 Games caused the IOC to withdraw South Africa's invitation for Mexico City. 'There will be those who will die' warned a respected athletics' coach, referring to the City's attitude. In fact nobody did die inside the stadium, but ten days before the Games opened, the army fired on a large demonstration in the city, leaving over 200 dead and many injured. The protest was against the use of government money for the Games when poverty was so widespread in the country. There were also demonstrations by black American athletes during the medal ceremonies.

Munich 1972

Although at the Munich Games of 1972 Rhodesia had a team of black and white sportsmen, there were charges of racial discrimination. They had complied with the requirements of the IOC. Despite this, a boycott was threatened just before the Games were due to start. The IOC met and withdrew Rhodesia's invitation. Avery Brundage, the retiring IOC President referred to this as naked political blackmail. These Games were dominated by the blatantly political and savage act that resulted in the deaths of Israeli athletes and officials.

Montreal 1976

The 1976 Games in Montreal suffered a wide variety of problems. The cost of the project was enormous and the deficit will be paid for by the city over very many years. Security precautions were massive and disliked by spectators and competitors alike. The Queen performed the opening ceremony and this angered many French Canadians. The boycott by the black African nations and the withdrawal of Taiwan continued the political influences. A distinguished Soviet Union modern pentathlete was convicted of cheating in the fencing. A number of competitors were banned for using anabolic steroids. Two Romanians and a 17 year old Soviet diver asked for political asylum in Canada.

Moscow 1980

The 1980 Olympics in Moscow were a controversial choice from the start because of the Soviet Union's record on human rights. However it was the invasion of Afghanistan that caused the boycott by many Western nations led by the USA.

Los Angeles 1984

There was worry that the choice of Los Angeles for the Summer Games in 1984 might give the Soviet Union a chance to repay the Americans. Therefore it was not entirely unexpected when the Soviet Union withdrew along with many Eastern European countries, Cuba and some others. The reasons given were that concern for the safety of their teams could not be guaranteed and that the organisers had violated the Olympic charter in many ways.

Seoul 1988

These Olympics were given to Seoul, although South Korea had no diplomatic links with communist countries. In the event the Games were very successful - no political disruptions, few absentee countries and expertly organised. Only Ben Johnson's disqualification for using drugs marred the event.

Barcelona 1992

IOC President Juan Samaranch hopes these Games in his own country will be the most successful ever. South Africa is set to return after an absence of 32 years. Germany will compete again as one nation. The organisers expect 15 000 competitors at 44 venues with an attendance of 400 000 and a television audience of 3.5 billion. The ever present terrorist threat remains, this time from the Basque separatists ETA.

SPORT AND INTERNATIONAL UNDERSTANDING

For Individuals

There is certainly considerable evidence that sportsmen and sportswomen get great personal enjoyment and pleasure from competing against individuals from other countries. This is especially true of individual activities, but is also true of team games. It would be reasonable to assume at this personal level, that contact between sportsmen and sportswomen of all nationalities can only be for the good and will bring greater understanding, if only in small ways.

For Teams

The identification of a number of players with different countries in a team competition in front of a large partisan crowd would seem to provide the ingredients for potential disaster in terms of friendship between nations! The players' individuality is hidden behind the team's mask. Their behaviour is often influenced by the expectations of their country and the reactions of the spectators. Only the great players are able to rise above this situation when sportsmanship and fairplay are swamped by the desire for success. Later, the competition over, individuals from both sides may make friendly contact in a social situation, if given the opportunity.

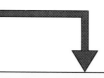

The torch bearer – the last of the runners bringing the Olympic flame from Greece, arriving at Wembley Stadium during the opening ceremony for the 1948 Olympic Games

For Nations

Nothing short of outright success in all aspects of sporting activity is likely to be acceptable to most nations today. Regardless of the level of competition, winning is usually regarded as the whole object of the exercise. The ideals of sport for its own sake, the joy of competition and the value of working hard and doing your best have no place in modern sport at international level. Many countries would seem to demand just winning from their sportsmen and sportswomen, who in their turn are cast aside as their success fades.

THINGS TO DO

1 On an outline map of the world, colour in all those countries which have held the summer and winter Olympic Games. Mark the host city and the date. Have the games been fairly distributed around the world? How would you decide on the next city?

2 Imagine you are representing your country in the finals of a world championship of your favourite sport. It is the morning of the competition. How do you feel? Are you thinking about what the papers will say? Can you think of failure? Explain your feelings about winning and losing.

3 Use the names of the countries below to complete the following sentences.

New Zealand, South Africa, Canada, Israel, Germany, USA, Soviet Union, Spain.

(i) Germany will again be represented by one team at the 1992 Olympics in

....

(ii) The athletes who demonstrated at Olympic victory ceremonies were in the team from ....

(iii) Ben Johnson of .... was disqualified for taking drugs.

(iv) The 1984 Olympic Games were boycotted by ....

(v) The policy of apartheid caused .... to be expelled from world sport.

(vi) In Munich, Palestinian terrorists killed officials and competitors from

....

(vii) The black African nations boycotted the Montreal Olympics because of the participation of ....

(viii) Jessie Owens upset Hitler at the 1936 Olympics held in ....

4 Find out all you can about apartheid and what it has meant in practice for people of different races in South Africa. Find out how the laws which have changed recently in South Africa will help to dismantle apartheid.

In pairs work out a conversation between a white office worker and a black factory worker. Get them to show how they feel about apartheid, how it has affected their everyday lives and their participation in sport. Let them explain their hopes for the future.

5 Write an article for a British sports magazine explaining why Germany once again has only one team for each sport. Write from the point of view of either an East or a West German. Explain the advantages and disadvantages as you now see them.

6 Talk to a person who remembers events before the Second World War. Ask what they remember about Hitler as he came to power in Germany. How did the people in Britain react? Did people think we should send a team to the Berlin Olympics in 1936?

7 Try to imagine you are an Israeli sportsman or sportswoman on your way home to Israel. You escaped from the hotel in Munich as the terrorists attacked. Describe your experience to a friend. Compare how you felt when you came to Munich with how you feel now.

8 'The 1980 Olympic Games should have been the last. They cause nothing but trouble these days. The Olympic spirit is dead.' What do you think of this point of view?

9 Imagine you are the mayor of a fictional city set in any country in the world. Prepare a speech to be given at the next general council meeting explaining why you believe your city should bid for the next Olympic Games. You will need to outline the procedure to be followed and show how you think you can persuade the IOC to vote for your city.

APPENDIX

ANALYSING DATA

To gain a full understanding of the results of the test scores which you obtained attempting the EUROFIT tests described in Chapter 4 you will need a basic knowledge of data collection, manipulation and interpretation.

You should gain the necessary understanding as a result of working through this appendix. The following list of scores was obtained by 15 year old boys and girls in a handgrip strength test.

Boys	44	47	36	34	32	41	39	40	33	34
Girls	34	24	32	25	25	24	27	29	30	23

From this data the following questions can be answered

- What is the average grip strength score for boys?
- What is the average grip strength score for girls?
- What was the best individual boy and individual girl grip strength score?
- Is there a wide difference in the grip strength scores of 15 year old boys?
- Is there a wide difference in the grip strength scores of 15 year old girls?
- What was the most frequently occurring score recorded for the grip strength of boys and girls?

Obtaining Answers from the Data

- The average or mean score may be obtained by the use of the following formula:

$$\text{Mean of boys' scores} = \frac{\text{Sum of scores}}{\text{Number of scores}} = \frac{380}{10} = 38$$

$$\text{Mean of girls' scores} = \frac{\text{Sum of scores}}{\text{Number of scores}} = \frac{273}{10} = 27.3$$

$$\text{Mean of all scores} = \frac{\text{Sum of scores}}{\text{Number of scores}} = \frac{653}{20} = 32.65$$

- If the data is rearranged into ascending order then a number of other facts will become obvious:

Boys		Girls	
32	39	23	27
33	40	24	29
34	41	24	30
34	44	25	32
36	47	25	34
Total group tested			
23	27	33	39
24	29	34	40
24	30	34	41
25	32	34	44
25	32	36	47

(i) The lowest score is:
32 (boys), 23 (girls) and 23 (total group).
(ii) The highest score is:
47 (boys), 34 (girls) and 47 (total group).
(iii) The range of the scores is:
boys = 15; girls = 11; total group = 24.
(iv) The most frequently occurring score (the mode) is:
34 (boys), 24 and 25 (girls) and 34 (total group).
(v) The point on the scale of measurement above which are exactly half the scores and below are the other half (the median) is:
boys = 37.5; girls = 26; total group = 32.5.
To calculate the median, add the middle two scores and divide by two.

• It is possible to classify the raw scores in the following way in order to see the results displayed graphically. The graphs shown indicate the scores of both the boys and girls.

(i) The range of the scores is divided into a number of class intervals. In this case class intervals of five are used.

(ii) The class intervals are marked off on the horizontal axis. The number of observations (frequencies) are drawn on the vertical axis. Both axes are labelled accordingly.

(iii) The number of raw scores within each class interval are added together and drawn either on a frequency histogram or a frequency polygon. A frequency polygon is formed by putting a dot on the centre of each class interval at the appropriate height; and then joining the dots.

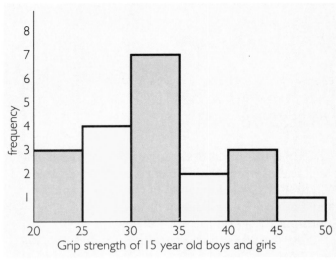

Frequency histogram

20–24	|||	3
25–29	||||	4
30–34	~~||||~~ ||	7
35–39	||	2
40–44	|||	3
45–50			1

Tally chart

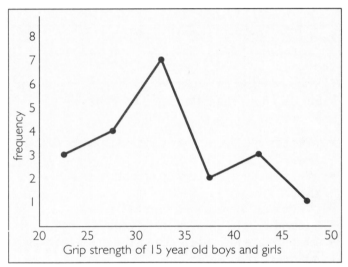

Frequency polygon

THINGS TO DO

1 Calculate the mean, median and mode for the girls' results and for the boys' and girls' combined.

2 Calculate the range of the scores for both the girls' results and for the boys' and girls' combined.

3 Construct a frequency histogram for the girls' test scores.

4 Construct a frequency polygon for the combined test scores.

5 Give reasons to explain the differences between the girls' and the boys' grip strength test scores.

6 Would you expect to get the same sort of differences if the persons tested were : a) 10 years old; b) 20 years old? Give reasons for your answer.

Summary

From the results of the analysis of the handgrip strength test scores the following conclusions about the boys results can be made.

• the average test score recorded was 38.
• the best individual result was 47.
• the poorest individual result was 32.
• the mid point of the test scores was 37.5 seconds.
• the most frequently occurring score was 34.

Eurofit Score Sheet

Name: _____   % Fat (body composition):

Age: _____   Sex (M or F): _____   Triceps _____ mm   Biceps _____ mm

Form or group: _____   Subscapular _____ mm

Height: _____ cm   Weight: _____ kg   Suprailiac _____ mm   Total _____ mm

EUROFIT TESTS	FITNESS COMPONENT	SCORE		
Flamingo balance	General balance	Number of attempts		
Plate tapping	Speed of limb movement	Test 1	Test 2	Better time in secs
Sit and reach	Flexibility	Test 1	Test 2	Better distance in cm
Standing broad jump	Muscular power	Test 1	Test 2	Better distance in cm
Hand grip	Muscular strength	Test 1	Test 2	Better score in kg
Sit-ups	Muscular endurance	No in 30 secs		
Bent arm hang	Arm and shoulder muscular strength	Time in tenths of sec		
50 m shuttle run	Sprint agility	Time needed to complete 5 cycles in secs		
Endurance shuttle run	Aerobic endurance	No of completed steps		

Eurofit Reference Scales

Eurofit variables for boys aged 12 years

Scale	Low score	Below average	Average	Above average	High score	Unit
Test						
St. broad jump	until inc. 151	152-154	155-168	169-175	from 176	cm
Bent arm hang	until inc. 10.3	10.4-15	15.1-21.6	21.7-30.7	from 30.8	0.1 sec
10 * 5 m run	from 20.8	20.0-20.7	19.4-19.9	18.7-19.3	until inc. 18.6	0.1 sec
Sit and reach	until inc.12	13-15	16-18	19-22	from 23	cm
Plate tapping	from 13.5	12.6-13.4	12.1-12.5	11.3-12.0	until inc. 11.2	0.1 sec
Sit-ups	until inc. 18	19-21	22-23	24-25	from 26	number in 30 sec
Body height	until inc. 152	153-156	157-160	161-165	from 166	cm
Body weight	until inc. 39	40-43	44-47	48-51	from 52	kg
Sum 4 skinfolds	until inc. 21	22-26	27-30	31-38	from 39	mm
20 m shuttle	until inc. 5.0	5.5-6.5	7.0-7.5	8.0-9.0	from 9.5	steps (paliers)
Handgrip (abs.)	until inc. 24	25-26	27-28	29-32	from 33	kg
Handgrip (rel.)	until inc. 54	55-59	60-63	64-69	from 70	kg/bdy w. (kg) * 100
Quetelet index	until inc. 16.2	16.3-17.3	17.4-18.2	18.3-19.7	from 19.8	bdy w. (kg)/ bdy h. (m)^2

Eurofit Reference Scales

Eurofit variables for girls aged 12 years

Scale	Low score	Below average	Average	Above average	High score	Unit
Test						
St. broad jump	until inc 139	140-149	150-157	158-165	from 166	cm
Bent arm hang	until inc.3.8	3.9-7.5	7.6-12.6	12.7-22.0	from 22.1	0.1 sec
10 • 5 m run	from 21.7	20.8-21.6	20.1-20.7	19.5-20.0	until inc.19.4	0.1 sec
Sit and reach	until inc.20	21-23	24-26	27-29	from 30	cm
Plate tapping	from 13.0	12.3-12.9	11.6-12.2	11.0-11.5	until inc.10.9	0.1 sec
Sit-ups	until inc.17	18-18	18-20	21-22	from 23	number in 30 sec
Body height	until inc.153	154-158	159-162	163-166	from 167	cm
Body weight	until inc.40	41-45	46-50	51-55	from 56	kg
Sum 4 skinfolds	until inc.26	27-34	35-42	43-51	from 52	mm
20 m shuttle	until inc.3.5	4.0-4.5	5.0-5.5	6.0-6.5	from 7.0	steps (paliers)
Handgrip (abs.)	until inc.21	22-24	25-26	27-30	from 31	kg
Handgrip (rel.)	until inc.45	46-52	53-57	58-63	from 64	kg/bdy w. (kg) * 100
Quetelet index	until inc.16.7	16.8-17.6	17.7-18.8	18.9-20.5	from 20.6	bdy w.(kg)/ bdy h. (m)^2

Eurofit Reference Scales

Eurofit variables for boys aged 13 years

Scale	Low score	Below average	Average	Above average	High score	Unit
Test						
St. broad jump	until inc. 152	153-162	163-172	173-184	from 185	cm
Bent arm hang	until inc. 8.6	8.7-15.2	15.3-22.0	22.1-31.3	from 31.4	0.1 sec
10 * 5 m run	from 20.7	19.9-20.6	19.3-19.8	18.6-19.2	until inc. 18.5	0.1 sec
Sit and reach	until inc. 11	12-15	16-19	20-22	from 23	cm
Plate tapping	from 13.1	12.3-13.0	11.5-12.2	10.8-11.4	until inc. 10.7	0.1 sec
Sit-ups	until inc. 18	19-21	22-23	24-25	from 26	number in 30 sec
Body height	until inc. 154	155-160	161-164	165-170	from 171	cm
Body weight	until inc. 42	43-46	47-50	51-56	from 57	kg
Sum 4 skinfolds	until inc. 21	22-25	26-31	32-42	from 43	mm
20 m shuttle	until inc. 5.5	6.0-6.5	7.0-7.5	8.0-8.5	from 9.0	steps (paliers)
Handgrip (abs.)	until inc. 25	26-28	29-31	32-36	from 37	kg
Handgrip (rel.)	until inc. 54	55-60	61-65	66-72	from 73	kg/bdy w. (kg)*100
Quetelet index	until inc. 16.6	16.7-17.7	178.8-18.7	18.8-20.1	from 20.2	bdy w.(kg)/ bdy h. (m)^2

Eurofit Reference Scales

Eurofit variables for girls aged 13 years

Scale	Low score	Below average	Average	Above average	High score	Unit
Test						
St. broad jump	until inc. 141	142-151	152-160	161-1,71	from 172	cm
Bent arm hang	until inc. 3.8	3.9-7.4	7.5-13.4	13.5-20.4	from 20.5	0.1 sec
10 * 5 m run	from 21.8	20.9-21.7	20.3-20.8	19.4-20.2	until inc. 19.3	0.1 sec
Sit and reach	until inc. 20	21-24	25-28	29-32	from 33	cm
Plate tapping	from 12.5	11.9-12.4	11.3-11.8	10.8-11.2	until inc. 10.7	0.1 sec
Sit-ups	until inc. 16	17-18	19-20	21-22	from 23	number in 30 sec
Body height	until inc. 156	157-160	161-164	165-168	from 169	cm
Body weight	until inc. 44	45-48	49-52	53-57	from 58	kg
Sum 4 skinfolds	until inc. 29	30-36	37-43	44-56	from 57	mm
20 m shuttle	until inc. 4.0	4.5-4.5	5.0-5.5	6.0-6.5	from 7.0	steps (paliers)
Handgrip (abs.)	until inc. 23	24-26	27-29	30-31	from 32	kg
Handgrip (rel.)	until inc. 47	48-52	53-57	58-62	from 63	kg/bdy w. (kg)*100
Quetelet index	until inc. 17.2	17.3-18.3	18.4-19.7	19.8-21.0	from 21.1	bdy w.(kg)/ bdy h.(m)^2

Eurofit Reference Scales

Eurofit variables for boys aged 14 years

Scale	Low score	Below average	Average	Above average	High score	Unit
Test						
St. broad jump	until inc. 157	158-170	171-181	182-194	from 195	cm
Bent arm hang	until inc. 10.5	10.6-17.6	17.7-25.4	25.5-38.5	from 38.6	0.1 sec
10 * 5 m run	from 20.4	19.6-20.3	19.0-19.5	18.2-18.9	until inc. 18.1	0.1 sec
Sit and reach	until inc. 11	12-17	18-21	22-26	from 27	cm
Plate tapping	from 12.4	11.7-12.3	11.0-11.6	10.2-10.9	until inc. 10.1	0.1 sec
Sit-ups	until inc. 19	20-21	22-23	24-25	from 26	number in 30 sec
Body height	until inc. 160	161-165	166-171	172-177	from 178	cm
Body weight	until inc. 46	47-52	53-57	58-63	from 64	kg
Sum 4 skinfolds	until inc. 21	22-25	26-29	30-40	from 41	mm
20 m shuttle	until inc. 6.0	6.5-7.0	7.5-8.0	8.5-9.0	from 9.5	steps (paliers)
Handgrip (abs.)	until inc. 29	30-33	34-38	39-44	from 45	kg
Handgrip (rel.)	until inc. 57	58-63	64-69	70-75	from 76	kg/bdy w. (kg)*100
Quetelet index	until inc. 17.2	17.3-18.4	18.5-19.6	19.7-21.0	from 21.1	bdy w.(kg)/ bdy h.(m)^2

Eurofit variables for girls aged 14 years

Scale	Low score	Below average	Average	Above average	High score	Unit
Test						
St. broad jump	until inc. 143	144-152	153-162	163-171	from 172	cm
Bent arm hang	until inc. 3.1	3.2-5.9	6.0-10.5	10.6-19.6	from 19.7	0.1 sec
10 * 5 m run	from 21.7	20.7-21.6	20.0-20.6	19.2-19.9	until inc. 19.1	0.1 sec
Sit and reach	until inc. 20	21-24	25-28	29-32	from 33	cm
Plate tapping	from 12.2	11.4-12.1	10.8-11.3	10.2-10.7	until inc. 10.1	0.1 sec
Sit-ups	until inc. 16	17-18	19-20	21-22	from 22	number in 30 sec
Body height	until inc. 161	162-164	165-168	169-171	from 172	cm
Body weight	until inc. 49	50-52	53-56	57-62	from 63	kg
Sum 4 skinfolds	until inc. 33	34-39	40-44	45-54	from 55	mm
20 m shuttle	until inc. 4.0	4.5-5.0	5.5-5.5	6.0-6.5	from 7.0	steps (paliers)
Handgrip (abs.)	until inc. 26	27-28	29-31	32-34	from 35	kg
Handgrip (rel.)	until inc. 47	48-52	53-57	58-63	from 64	kg/bdy w. (kg)*100
Quetelet index	until inc. 17.9	18.0-19.0	19.1-20.1	20.2-21.5	from 21.6	bdy w.(kg)/ bdy h.(m)^2

Eurofit variables for boys aged 15 years

Scale	Low score	Below average	Average	Above average	High score	Unit
Test						
St. broad jump	until inc. 169	170-182	183-193	194-206	from 207	cm
Bent arm hang	until inc. 15.3	15.4-25.3	25.4-35.3	35.4-46.6	from 46.7	0.1 sec
10 * 5 m run	from 19.9	19.0-19.8	18.2-18.9	17.7-18.1	until inc. 17.6	0.1 sec
Sit and reach	until inc. 12	13-18	19-23	24-27	from 38	cm
Plate tapping	from 11.9	11.2-11.8	10.3-11.1	9.6-10.2	until inc. 9.5	0.1 sec
Sit-ups	until inc. 20	21-22	23-24	25-26	from 27	number in 30 sec
Body height	until inc. 168	169-173	174-177	178-181	from 182	cm
Body weight	until inc. 53	54-58	59-62	63-69	from 70	kg
Sum 4 skinfolds	until inc. 21	22-24	25-27	28-35	from 36	mm
20 m shuttle	until inc. 6.5	7.0-7.5	8.0-9.0	9.5-9.5	from 10	steps (paliers)
Handgrip (abs.)	until inc. 34	35-41	42-45	46-51	from 52	kg
Handgrip (rel.)	until inc. 61	62-68	69-73	74-80	from 81	kg/bdy w. (kg)*100
Quetelet index	until inc. 18.0	18.1-19.2	19.3-20.2	20.3-21.8	from 21.9	bdy w.(kg)/ bdy h.(m)^2

Eurofit variables for girls aged 15 years

Eurofit Reference Scales

Scale	Low score	Below average	Average	Above average	High score	Unit
Test						
St. broad jump	until inc. 142	143-151	152-161	162-171	from 172	cm
Bent arm hang	until inc. 3.4	3.5-6.3	6.4-10.8	10.9-17.2	from 17.3	0.1 sec
10 * 5 m run	from 21.3	20.7-21.2	19.9-20.6	19.3-19.8	until inc. 19.2	0.1 sec
Sit and reach	until inc. 21	22-27	28-30	31-34	from 35	cm
Plate tapping	from 11.7	11..1-11.6	10.5-11.0	9.9-10.4	until inc. 9.8	0.1 sec
Sit-ups	until inc. 16	17-17	18-19	20-21	from 22	number in 30 sec
Body height	until inc. 161	162-165	166-169	170-173	from 174	cm
Body weight	until inc. 51	52-55	56-59	60-64	from 65	kg
Sum 4 skinfolds	until inc. 36	37-43	44-50	51-62	from 63	mm
20 m shuttle	until inc. 4.0	4.5-4.5	5.0-5.5	6.0-6.5	from 7.0	steps (paliers)
Handgrip (abs.)	until inc 27	28-30	31-33	34-37	from 38	kg
Handgrip (rel.)	until inc. 47	48-53	54-57	58-64	from 65	kg/bdy w. (kg)*100
Quetelet index	until inc. 19.0	19.1-20.0	20.1-21.2	21.3-22.4	from 22.5	bdy w.(kg)/ bdy h.(m)^2

Eurofit variables for boys aged 16 years

Eurofit Reference Scales

Scale	Low score	Below average	Average	Above average	High score	Unit
Test						
St. broad jump	until inc. 181	182-193	194-201	202-211	from 212	cm
Bent arm hang	until inc. 19.5	19.6-32.4	32.5-42.8	42.9-51.4	from 51.5	0.1 sec
10 * 5 m run	from 19.4	18.6-19.3	18.1-18.5	17.5-18.0	until inc. 17.4	0.1 sec
Sit and reach	until inc. 16	17-19	20-23	24-28	from 29	cm
Plate tapping	from 11.6	10.7-11.5	10.1-10.6	9.3-10.0	until inc. 9.2	0.1 sec
Sit-ups	until inc 20	21-22	23-24	25-26	from 27	number in 30 sec
Body height	until inc. 174	175-177	178-182	183-185	from 186	cm
Body weight	until inc. 57	58-62	63-66	67-72	from 73	kg
Sum 4 skinfolds	until inc. 19	20-22	23-26	27-32	from 33	mm
20 m shuttle	until inc. 7.5	8.0-8.0	8.5-9.0	9.5-10.0	from 10.5	steps (paliers)
Handgrip (abs.)	until inc. 42	43-47	48-51	52-56	from 57	kg
Handgrip (rel.)	until inc. 67	68-74	75-79	80-84	from 85	kg/bdy w. (kg)*100
Quetelet index	until inc. 18.3	18.4-19.5	19.6-20.2	20.3-21.6	from 21.7	bdy w.(kg)/ bdy h.(m)^2

Eurofit variables for girls aged 16 years

Scale	Low score	Below average	Average	Above average	High score	Unit
Test						
St. broad jump	until inc. 145	146-153	154-162	163-171	from 172	cm
Bent arm hang	until inc. 3.0	3.1-6.8	6.9-12.2	12.3-20.1	from 20.2	0.1 sec
10 * 5 m run	from 21.1	20.3-21.0	19.5-20.2	19.1-19.4	until inc. 19.0	0.1 sec
Sit and reach	until inc. 24	25-29	30-31	32-34	from 35	cm
Plate tapping	from 11.2	10.7-11.1	10.4-10.6	9.7-10.3	until inc. 9.6	0.1 sec
Sit-ups	until inc. 16	17-18	19-20	21-23	from 24	number in 30 sec
Body height	until inc. 162	163-166	167-168	169-171	from 172	cm
Body weight	until inc. 51	52-56	57-60	61-63	from 64	kg
Sum 4 skinfolds	until inc. 34	35-41	42-49	50-60	from 61	mm
20 m shuttle	until inc. 4.0	4.5-5.0	5.5-5.5	6.0-6.5	from 7.0	steps (paliers)
Handgrip (abs.)	until inc. 28	29-31	32-33	34-37	from 38	kg
Handgrip (rel.)	until inc. 48	49-55	56-59	60-63	from 64	kg/bdy w. (kg)*100
Quetelet index	until inc. 18.6	18.7-20.0	20.1-21.2	21.3-22.9	from 23.0	bdy w.(kg)/ bdy h.(m)^2

Acknowledgments

The authors and publishers wish to thank the following who have kindly given permission for the use of copyright material.

Controller of Her Majesty's Stationery Office for material from the General Household Survey 1987, p. 196

Football Trust for material from The Digest of Football Statistics 1990, p. 205

Health Education Authority for article on physical fitness, p. 193

International Olympic Committee for reproduction of Olympic Rule 26 and its bye-law, p. 156

Hugh McIlvanney/The Guardian for article 'Johnson plays Deputy', p. 104

RSL Sportscan for two tables on p. 182, table on p. 185, 3 tables on p. 186, table on p. 187

Sports Council for material from ' Sport in the Community - Into the Nineties', p. 197

The publishers have made every effort to trace the copyright holders, but where they have failed to do so they will be pleased to make the necessary arrangements at the first opportunity.

Fitness tape obtainable from sports specialists, e.g.
Davies the Sports People,
Ludlow Hill Road,
West Bridgeford, Notts. NG2 6HD

Photographs

Cover photographs & Frontispiece: Sporting Pictures;
A.D.T.: p. 49, 50, 161, 194;
Action Plus Photos: p. 56, 104, left, 108, 144, 206, 209, right, 236;
Richard Alasia: p. 181;
Allsport Photography: p. 104 right, 112;
Associated Press: p. 155 bottom right;
Associated Sports Photography: p. 153, 219, 220 left, 222;
Barnaby's Picture Library: p. 48;
British Amateur Wrestling Association/Robin Tomlinson: p. 113;
The British Museum: p. 137;
British Olympic Medical Centre/Dr Craig Sharp: p. 71, 72 (2);
British Ski Federation: p. 60;
British Triathlon Association: p. 57;
Channel Four Television: p. 189;
Dave Charman: p. 62 bottom right;
Gerry Cranham: p. 173, 211;
English Schools Swimming Association: p. 58 bottom left;
Mary Evans Picture Library: p. 139 left;
Golf Picture Library/Phil Sheldon: p. 149;
Sally and Richard Greenhill: p. 17, 18 (6), 25, 58 top left and right, 61 bottom left and right, 62 top and bottom left, 64, 65, 66, 67, 75, 77 right, 78 (2), 79, 80 (2), 81 (2), 82 (4), 135, 147 right, 166, 194 bottom;
The Independent/Michael Steele: p. 187;
Judo Photos Unlimited/David Finch: p. 92;

Lee Valley Park: p. 177;
Stephen J Line: p. 44 left;
Los Angeles Times: p. 233;
M.L.T.B.: p. 214;
The Mansell Collection: p. 139 right, 218;
Marylebone Cricket Club: p. 151;
Minet Group Services Ltd/Action Pictures: p. 183;
National Railway Museum: p. 44 right;
Orpington & Dartford Weightlifting Club/Geoff Whitlock: p. 14 top right;
Popperfoto: p. 141, 234;
Professional Sport: p. 111, 157, 235;
RYA/Tony Dallimore: p. 55;
Renault Cars: p. 209 left, 215;
Peter Robins: p. 226 bottom;
Chris Schwarz: p. 205;
Dave Shopland Sports Photography: p. 188;
John H Shore: p. 14 left, 63 bottom;
Sporting Pictures: p. 1, 85;
The Sports Council/Lisa Mackson: p. 163;
The Sports Council for Wales: p. 162;
Supersport/Eileen Langsley: p. 14 bottom right, 15, 16 left and right, 63 top, 118 middle and left, 129, 131, 147 top, 152, 153, 158, 165, 167, 211 left, 221, 231;
Andrew Varley: p. 100, 118 right, 210;
Whitbread Round The World Race: p. 182;
Mark Wohlwender: p. 201;
The Women's Sports Foundation: p. 54, 61 top (both Eileen Langsley), 226 top (Margot Klingberg).

Index

abrasions 86
actin 12
adenosine di-phosphate (ADP) 13,14,54
adenosine triphosphate (ATP) 13,14,54
administration 214,225
adrenalin 54
aerobic laboratory 71
aerobic/anaerobic 14,57,59
alcohol 51
alveoli 27
amateur sport 147-159,207,212
American football 136,188
amino acids 29,43
amphetamines 107-109
Amsterdam 239
anabolic steroids 109-110
anaerobic fitness 55,71-72
anaerobic threshold 58,71
anaerobic/aerobic 49
angina 25
animals and sport 215
antagonist muscles 16,61
anthropometric measures 81-83
anticipation 54
Antwerp 218,239
anxiety 111,112
aorta 21,22,24
apartheid 230,231,232
appendicular skeleton 7,8
appetite 48
Arnold, Dr. 141
arousal 133
arteries 24,60,86
Athens 237,238
athletics 141,152.212
Atlanta 237
autonomic nervous system 32
avulsion fractures 97
axial skeleton 6

balance 74,75
Barcelona 232,236,241
basal metabolic rate (BMR) 45
bent arm hang 79-80
benzodiazipanes 112
Bergman-Osterberg 217
Berlin 136,239
beta-blockers 112-113
black Americans 230,233,234
Blankers-Koen, Fanny 219
blisters 87
blood 26
blood doping 113
blood pressure 24,25,115
blood vessels 24,25
body fat 81-83
body mass index 46
bone – injuries 5,90-91
bones 4,5,90-91
boycotts 235,236
breathing 27,28
British Association of Sports Medicine (BASM) 102
British Olympic Association (BOA) 160,167,168

British Olympic Medical Association (BOMC) 70-73,168
bruising 88
Brundage, Avery 149,228
Budd, Zola 231

calorimetry 44
capillaries 24,26
carbohydrate loading 49
carbohydrates 37,38,42,43
carbon dioxide 24,44
careers in sport 209-216
cartilage 89-90,99
Central Council of Physical Recreation (CCPR) 143,160,161,164,165,184
central nervous system (CNS) 13,18
China, People's Republic of 230-233
cholesterol 25,39
cigarettes 115-116
cilia 115
circulatory system 20,54,58
class system 145,150,196,217
clothing in sport 50,100,203
coaching 213,225
COMA Report 45,47
Commaneci, Nadia 220
commercial enterprises 173,179
competition 48,153
competitors – elite 70-73
compulsory competitive tendering (CCT) 171,172
conditioned reflex 33
contraction – isokinetic 64-65
contraction –isotonic 16,64
contraction – isometric 16,65
coronary arteries 25,60
coronary heart disease 25
cramp 87-88
creatine phosphate 13,60,71
cricket 139,140,142,143,151,156
Crown Games 137-138
Cuba 229,236
cycling 201,218

d'Olivera, Basil 230
darts 189
de Klerk, President 232
deprived areas 250
diastolic blood pressure 25
Didrickson, "Babe" 219
diet 48,51
dietary fibre 42,47,51
digestion 29
disabled people 198,199
dislocation 89,90
diuretics 113
doping classes 106
drugs – definition 105
drugs – testing 106-107

Eastern Europe 229,236
eccentric action 16
economic impact of sport 202,203
ectomorphy 119,120
education 141,143

Education Acts 142,143
effector organs 30
electrolytes 51
eligibility code – IOC 156
Ellis, William Webb 141
employees' facilities 173
endocrine system 34
endomorphy 119-120
endurance – muscular 67-73
energy – food 44,45
energy – systems 57
entertainment, sport as 206
enzymes 29
epiglottis 27
equipment and sport 101,203
ergometer 72
Eurofit 73-83
Eurofit – reference scales 245-250
Eurofit – score sheet 245
Ever Thought of Sport? 199
exercise 48,53-56
expiration 27
extensors 16
exteroceptors 18,30,33
extravert 132-134
Eysenck 132

fast glycolytic fibres (fg) 15,54,56,58,68
fast oxidative fibres (fog) 15,54,56,58,68
fat 46,47,54
fatigue index 72
fatigue rate 72
fats 37,38,42,51
fatty acids 29
fibre typing 15
fibrinogen 26
first aid 85-103
fitness 53-69
fixators 16
flamingo balance 75-76
flexibility 61,62,77,95
flexors 16
fluids 50
Follows, Dennis 168,235
Football Association 141.151,205,221
fractures 91-92
fractures – stress 92,99
frequency polygon 224
fulcrum 17

gambling 139-140
Gatting, Mike 232
General Household Survey 1987 195,196
gentleman amateurs 150
German Democratic Republic (GDR) 236,237
glands 34
Gleneagles Agreement 231
glucose 14,43
glycerol 29
glycogen 43,48-49
golf 140,145,151,211,217
Governing Bodies 160,165,218

Griffiths Joyner, Florence 220
grip strength 78,243
ground staff 215

haemoglobin 26,60,123
hand grip 78,79
Harvey, Mary Glen 220
Health Education Council 143,193
heart 20-24,54
heart massage 94
heart rate – maximum 55
Helsinki 240
Henje, Sonja 219
heroin 109
Hitler, Adolf 136,230,232
hooliganism 204,205
horse racing 139,142,211
human growth hormone 111
human rights 230,235
hypnosis 25

ICE 86
industrial revolution 136
injuries – age related 96-98
injuries – chronic 88
injuries – distraction 87
injuries – overuse 99
Institute of Sports Sponsorship (ISS) 165,184
intensity 56
International Olympic Committee (IOC) 106,155, 156,160,166,218,230,237
International Sports Federation 156,160,166
International Women's Sports Federation (IWSF) 218
interoceptors 30,33
intestine – large 29
intestine – small 29,43
Into the 90's 197
introvert 132-134
invisible fats 38
isokinetic dynamometer 72
Israel 230,234,235

Jackman, Robin 231
Jockey Club 140
joints – types of 7-9
joule 44

kabaddi 188
kilocalories 44
kilojoules 44
King, Billie Jean 220
Korbut, Olga 220

lactic acid 13-14,54
Lee Valley Park 176-177
leisure 192-208
leisure centres 144
leisure industry 144,201
Lenglen, Suzanne 218,219
leverage 16-17
ligaments 90
limbs 7
liver 43
local authorities 170-172,203

local management of schools
  (LMS)   144,195
local sports council   160,175
London   217,219,239,241
Los Angeles 233,235,236,239,241
lungs   27,28

machines   215
macrominerals   39
magazines   204
marathon   95,138,193,200
market trends   181
massacre – Munich   234,235
maximum oxygen uptake   71
medical aspects of sport
                               85-103,215
Melbourne   228,233,235,240
menstrual cycle   120
mesomorphy   119-123
Mexico City 230,234,235,236,240
Milk in Action for Women   199
Millwall   205-206
minerals   37,39,41
mitochondria   13,60
mobility   61-62
Montreal   231,233
Moscow   230,235,238,240
motor end plate   12
mouth to mouth ventilation   93
Munich   230,234,235,240
muscle action   15,18
muscle biopsy   15
muscle injuries   87,88
muscle speed   15
muscle strength testing   72
muscles – cardiac   11
muscles – involuntary   11
muscles – torn   87
muscles – voluntary   11-13
myofybrils   12

narcotic analgesics   109
National Coaching Foundation
  (NCF)   166,213,225
National Curriculum   194-195
national identity   230
National Olympic
  Committee 156,167,168,232
National Playing Fields
  Association   143
National Sports Centres 162,168
Nazi Olympics   230,232,233
nerves – motor   30-31
nerves – sensory   3,33
nervous system   30-31
New Zealand   231
newspapers   204
nicotine   115-116
non-starch polysaccharides   42
nutrients   29,37,45,47

oesophagus   29
officials   125,214
Olympic Games
       139,142,149,155,156,167,
       217,218,228,231-241
Olympics, ancient   137-139,150
open sport   147,148,149,150
Osgood-Schlatter's disease   97
outdoor pursuit centres   213
overload   63,64

overweight   45,48
Owens, Jessie   124,230,232
oxygen   27,54,55
oxygen debt   14,55,59

Palmer report   148,158
pancreas   34,43
Paris   217,238,239
participation rates in sport
              149,161,195-198,233
passive stretching   62
patronage   139
peak power   72
pedestrianism   141
pelvic girdle   8
personality   132-134
physical activity level
  (PAL)   45
physical activity ratio
  (PAR)   45
physical education
144,194,195,212,217,221,224,225
physical recreation
              193,194,195,222,223
Pierre de Coubertin
              139,154,155,228
pituitary gland   30,34
plate tapping test   76-77
play   136
plyometrics   67-68
politics   228-242
polyunsaturated fats   38
posture   18
power   67
power testing   72-73
pre-load   67
Press, Tamara and Irena   219
prime movers   16
private clubs   173
prize fighters   140,142
professional sport
         147-159,206,209-212,215
progression   56,64
propaganda   230
proprioceptors   18,30
proteins   37,38,42,47
psychology   128-134
public schools   141,142
pulmonary artery   21
pyruvic acid   13

Quetelet index   245-250

railways   142
recreation management
                    213,225,226
reflex actions   33
Regional councils for sport and
  recreation   160,174,175
Regional Sports Councils 160,174
reporting sport   214,226
respiratory system   26,58
reversibility   56,64
RICE   86
Rollason, Helen   221
Romans   136,138
Rome   219,230,240
rugby league   145,151,210
rugby union   141,145,151
rules   97-100
running boom   200

salt   47,51
schools   136
Seoul
167,184,220,225,226,236,241
Sever's disease   97
sex and sporting success 120-124
sex discrimination   217,222
Sheldon   119
shuttle run (10*5m)   60,80,81
shuttle run (endurance) 60,74-75
sit and reach test   77
sit ups   79
skeleton   2,4-6
skill   96
skin fold measurement   81-82
skull   6
smoking   115-116
soccer   141,142,151,210
social change
  140,143,144,217,218,219,229
social drugs   114-116
social support   131
Solzhenitsen, Alexander   235
somatotyping   118-120
South Africa   230-232
Southern Council for Sport
  and Recreation   222
Soviet Union 229,230,235,236
specificity   63
speed   68
spinal cord   30,31,93
sponsorship 144,152,153,179-191
Sport for All   163,198
Sport for the Older Person   199
sport related economic
  activity   202,203
Sports Aid Foundation (SAF)
                              154,184
Sports Council
     160-164,172,196-198,223
Sports Council – campaigns
            143,163,198-200
sports journalism   214,226
sports medicine   101-102
sports scholarships   152,189
sports trade   214
sprains   89
St. Louis   217,238
staleness   99
standing broad jump   78
static stretching   62
steady state activity   59
stimulants   107-109
stitch   88
Stockholm   239
strength – dynamic   63
strength – explosive   63
strength – static   62-63
strength profiles   73
stress and sport   99,129
stretching – active   62
stretching – static   62
stroke volume   54
sugars   29,37
suppleness   61
sweat   50
synergists   16
synovial joints   9
systolic blood pressure   25

Taiwan   230,233
teaching   212
technology   144
television – Channel 4   188
television – sports coverage
                      144,185-189,204
tendon injury   88,89
tendonitis   89
tendons   16
tennis   151,154,212,218
testes   34
testosterone   106,110,123
The Next Ten Years   197
third world nations   229
thyroid   34
tobacco and sponsorship 184,185
Tokyo   230,240
traditional values   154
training   55-69
training – continuous   59
training – endurance   59-60
training – fartlek   59
training – interval   59
training – methods   57-70
training – pick up sprint   60
training – repetition   59
training – sprint   59
training – variable resistance 64
transport   142
triathlon   217
trust funds   152,212
twitch – fast and slow   68

unconsciousness   93

VO$_2$ max   60,71
veins   24,25
ventricles   21,22
vertebral column   6
violence   140,204,205
vitamins   37-38,40

water   37,42,50
weight training   65-68
What's Your Sport?   199
Whitehead, Linda   225
Why Sport?   128
Wingate test   72
women and sport   145,217-227
women's football   225
Women's League of Health
  and Beauty   219
Women's Sports Foundation
                              221,224
work   192,193

Young People and Sport   199